D1499563

Stephen Crane

An Annotated Bibliography of Secondary Scholarship

Stephen Crane

An Annotated Bibliography of Secondary Scholarship

Patrick K. Dooley

G.K. Hall & Co.
New York

Maxwell Macmillan Canada
Toronto

Maxwell Macmillan International
New York   Oxford   Singapore   Sydney

"Chronology," from *The Correspondence of Stephen Crane,* ed. Stanley Wertheim and Paul Sorrentino, pp. 21–26. Reprinted by permission of Columbia University Press.

G.K. Hall & Co.
An Imprint of Macmillan Publishing Company
866 Third Avenue
New York, NY 10022

Maxwell Macmillan Canada, Inc.
1200 Eglinton Avenue East
Suite 200
Don Mills, Ontario M3C 3N1

Macmillan Publishing Company is part of the Maxwell Communication Group of Companies.

Library of Congress Catalog Card Number: 91-38132

Printed in the United States of America

printing number
1   2   3   4   5   6   7   8   9   10

Library of Congress Cataloging-in-Publication Data

Dooley, Patrick K.
    Stephen Crane: an annotated bibliography of secondary scholarship
/ Patrick K. Dooley
    p.   cm.
    Includes bibliographical references and index.
    ISBN 0-8161-7265-X (alk. paper)
    1. Crane, Stephen, 1871-1900—Criticism and interpretation-
-Bibliography.   I. Title.
Z8198.2.D66   1992
[PS1449.C85]
813'.4—dc20   91-38132
                                                                                CIP

Dedicated to

Rev. Reginald Redlon, OFM
the late Dr. Boyd Litzinger
Dr. Stephen F. Brown

Contents

Foreword

In this annotated bibliography of secondary scholarship on Stephen Crane I have attempted to locate, annotate, and sort by category everything written in English on Crane and his works from 1901 to 1991. I will explain my decision to start with 1901 shortly. Let me begin by acknowledging that though I have made every effort (taxing the patience of a number of interlibrary loan librarians) to track down everything during this nearly 100-year period, I am sure some things have escaped me. I have no doubt, for instance, that I have missed a number of introductions to *The Red Badge of Courage*. Crane's classic has never gone out of print in the conventional hardback format and has had innumerable reprintings in textbooks, readers, anthologies, and drugstore paperbacks. Incidentally, I have not annotated dissertations on the grounds that the publishable ones are issued as monographs and the best portions of others appear as articles in scholarly journals. Excepting dissertations, then, I would appreciate being informed of any omissions (or errors).

Though much of my scholarly work in the past ten years has been in American studies and American literature, I am a philosopher by training and profession. My serious study of Crane began during a sabbatical leave at Duke University, January–August 1986, the eventual product being *The Pluralistic Philosophy of Stephen Crane* (see 2.5). While writing that book I decided I had better be aware of the influential and important literary criticism on Crane. Soon my reading of Crane secondary material took on a life of its own. For about a year my reading of Crane criticism was unsystematic. However, I found myself reduplicating and rereading articles I had already looked at, so I sorted out several boxes of material and prepared an alphabetical checklist. At that point a "completeness syndrome" took hold. My self-diagnosis of this scholarly malady was based on my notice of a telltale symptom—whenever I discovered a new article, even before reading it I found myself checking footnote references for additional new Crane items.

My literature search involved working through select bibliographies found in a number of monographs on Crane and collections of his works, the excellent bibliographical essays in *American Literary Scholarship* plus those by Pizer (14.16) and Wertheim (14.18) and the lists in *Thoth* and the *Stephen Crane Newsletter*. I then compared my checklist with the standard reference books and bibliographical indexes. In addition, since 1988, to adjust for the lag before articles and books make their way into reference books, I have regularly surveyed nearly forty general, American literature, and American studies journals. (Note: A list of these bibliographical indexes and journals can be found in Appendix 1.) Finally I compared my checklist with Robert Stallman's massive *Stephen Crane: A Critical Bibliography,* 1972 (14.3).

Since Stallman prepared his bibliography, the University of Virginia critical edition, *The Works of Stephen Crane,* 10 vols., 1969–1976 (12.2), edited by Fredson Bowers, and *The Correspondence of Stephen Crane,* 1988 (13.3), edited by Stanley Wertheim and Paul Sorrentino, have appeared. These two publications have supplanted four of the six sections of Stallman's bibliography. The Virginia edition completed and corrected three very lengthy sections: "Books and Contributions to Books," 1–65; "Miscellania and Curiosia," 61–66; and "Writings of Stephen Crane Arranged Alphabetically by Individual Titles," 153–233. *The Correspondence of Stephen Crane* displaced "Published Letters" (as well as *The Letters of Stephen Crane,* edited by Stallman and Gilkes (13.2)). Another of Stallman's sections, "Contemporary Reviews [he lists 437] and Parodies [he lists 18]," was remarkably complete. I have been able to find only twenty reviews Stallman had not identified. Moreover, eighteen of these twenty are reprinted in Richard Weatherford's invaluable research tool, *Stephen Crane: The Critical Heritage,* 1973 (2.17). I saw no reason to redo what Stallman and Weatherford had done so well. (Note: I have annotated many of the most important and most frequently reprinted early reviews plus all those appearing during 1901 and after. For those wanting to amend Stallman's list of contemporary reviews, see Appendix 2.)

The longest section of Stallman's bibliography, "Writings Biographical, Bibliographical and Critical about Stephen Crane," 237–623, covers 1888–1970 with a few items from 1971 and 1972. I find little fault with the items he has located (and sometimes annotated) from 1888 to 1900, including an impressive listing of fifty "Obituaries and Tributes." Also very ambitious was his discovery of numerous newspaper and magazine articles dealing with the "Lanthorn Club," "Philistines' Dinner in Honor of Stephen Crane," "Police Encounters" (especially the Dora Clark affair), "*Commodore,* Wreck of," and "Cuban War," as well as abundant newspaper comments, articles, and interviews sparked by Crane's *Red Badge* fame. The year after Crane's death, 1901, marked a clean break so that is where I began my attempt at a complete annotation of secondary scholarship on Stephen Crane.

The first two sections of my bibliography cover "Biography" and "General Criticism"; thereafter I have sorted items according to Crane's works. Naturally, *Red Badge* has attracted the most comment, followed by the Bowery Works, "The Open Boat," "The Blue Hotel," "The Bride Comes to Yellow Sky," and so on. I have cross-referenced articles dealing with particularly important, seminal, or controversial issues; additional articles located in other parts of the bibliography have been noted at the end of each section or subsection. Pieces dealing with Crane's life and career have been briefly noted and may require readers to refer to the Crane "Chronology." This helpful and accurate chronology is reprinted from *The Correspondence of Stephen Crane,* courtesy of Columbia University Press and Professors Wertheim and Sorrentino. My "Overview" comments at the beginning of each section are meant to highlight articles for students and beginning scholars; obviously, many other excellent articles could not be singled out.

Acknowledgments

A volume of this sort requires helpers and a computer equipped with bibliographical software. Most of my help came from one person—St. Bonaventure University's tireless, dedicated, and patient interlibrary loan librarian, Theresa Shaffer. Fully one third of the nearly 1,900 items found here were tracked down by her. Thank you, Theresa. A colleague in Bonaventure's English department, William Wehmeyer, read and made comments on many of my annotations as well as giving encouragement, advice, and help; so too Professor Louis Budd of Duke University.

My university has been very generous in its support: a computer loan, the purchase of nb *Citation* software plus travel grants for trips to the libraries of Cornell, Syracuse, Columbia, Virginia, and Duke Universities. Academic Vice-President John Watson, dean of the Graduate School Carol Diminie, dean of Arts and Science Richard Reilly, and Philosophy Department chairman Anthony Murphy enthusiastically supported my requests for St. Bonaventure University faculty development grants, which allowed me to spend two months each at Virginia and Duke during the summers of 1989 and 1991.

My thanks also to Lynn Fauss and Rick Cooper of nb *Citation,* Oberon Resources, who managed to recover nearly all of three floppy disks of annotations I somehow scrambled, and to Joe Kwiatkowski, Bonaventure's computer services guru.

Finally, this volume is dedicated to three former faculty members of St. Bonaventure University who urged me to pursue research and publication along with teaching. These three were my first university president, my first dean, and my first department chairman.

Chronology

1871   Stephen Crane born 1 November in Newark, New Jersey, fourteenth and last child of Jonathan Townley Crane, presiding elder of Methodist churches in the Newark district, and Mary Helen (Peck) Crane, daughter of a clergyman and niece of Methodist bishop Jesse T. Peck. Only eight of the thirteen Crane children who preceded Stephen were living at the time of his birth. His Revolutionary War namesake (1709–80) had been president of the Colonial Assemblies and delegate from New Jersey to the Continental Congress in Philadelphia. He returned home shortly before the Declaration of Independence was signed.

1874–80   Jonathan Townley Crane serves as minister of Methodist churches in Bloomington and then Paterson, New Jersey. Mrs. Crane active in the Women's Christian Temperance Union. Family moves in April 1878 to Port Jervis, New York, on the Delaware River, where father becomes pastor of the Drew Methodist Church, a post he holds until his death on 16 February 1880.

1883   Mother and younger children move to Asbury Park, a resort town on the New Jersey coast. Stephen's brother Townley operates a summer news reporting agency for the *New York Tribune*. Another brother, William Howe Crane, remains in Port Jervis, where he practices law and becomes a founding member of the Hartwood Club, an exclusive hunting and fishing preserve in nearby Sullivan County.

1884   Agnes Elizabeth, a sister who encouraged Stephen's first writings and was his closest companion, dies in May at the age of twenty-eight.

1885–87   Stephen attends Pennington Seminary (New Jersey), a Methodist boarding school where his father had been principal from 1849 to 1858.

1888   In January Crane enrolls in Claverack College and Hudson River Institute, a coeducational, semimilitary high school and junior college in Columbia County, New York. In summer months from 1888 through 1892 he assists Townley in gathering shore news at Asbury Park.

1890   Publishes first sketch, "Henry M. Stanley," in the February issue of the Claverack College *Vidette*. Is first lieutenant in the school's military regiment and adjutant to its commander, Colonel A. H. Flack. Writes the "Battalion Notes" column in the June issue of *Vidette*, in which he is gazetted captain. Leaves Claverack, having completed only two and a half years of the four-year curriculum and in the fall enters Lafayette College (Easton, Pennsylvania) as a mining engineering student. Joins Delta Upsilon fraternity. Withdraws from the college in the first month of the second semester, "without censure," according to minutes of the faculty.

1891   Transfers to Syracuse University in January. Plays catcher and shortstop on the varsity baseball team. Becomes Syracuse stringer for the *New York Tribune*. First short story, "The King's Favor," appears in the *University Herald* in May. Also publishes a literary hoax, "Great Bugs in Onondaga," in the 1 June *Tribune*. In August Crane meets Hamlin Garland, who was presenting a lecture series on American literature at Avon-by-the-Sea. Reports Garland's lecture on William Dean Howells in the 18 August issue of the *Tribune*. Becomes familiar with Garland's "veritism" and Howells's theories of literary realism. In mid-June Crane goes on a camping trip in Sullivan County, New York, near Port Jervis, with Syracuse Delta Upsilon fraternity brother, Frederic M. Lawrence, and two other friends, Louis E. Carr, Jr. and Louis C. Senger, Jr. This experience contributes to the background of his Sullivan County writings. Fails to return to college in the fall. Begins to explore the slums of lower Manhattan while living with his brother Edmund in Lake View, New Jersey. Mother dies on 7 December.

1892   A number of the Sullivan County tales and sketches appear in the *Tribune*. Also a New York City sketch, "The Broken-Down Van" (10 July), which anticipates *Maggie*. The *Tribune's* columns are closed to Crane shortly after his article, "Parades and Entertainments" (21 August), offends both the Junior Order of United American Mechanics and *Tribune* publisher Whitelaw Reid, Republican candidate for vice-president. In October Crane moves into the Pendennis Club, a rooming house at 1064 Avenue A in Manhattan inhabited by a group of medical students. Shares a room with Frederic M. Lawrence overlooking the East River and Blackwell's Island. Revises *Maggie*.

1893   *Maggie: A Girl of the Streets* privately printed in March under the pseudonym of Johnston Smith. Crane is introduced to Howells by Garland. Begins composition of *The Red Badge of Courage*, probably in late March or April. Shares a loft in the old Needham building on East 23rd Street, recently abandoned by the Art Students' League, with artist and illustator friends and lives in poverty in various New York City tenements.

1894   Writes social studies such as "An Experiment in Misery" and "In the Depths of a Coal Mine." Begins *George's Mother* in May and completes the novel in November. Takes some of his poems and the manuscript of *The Red Badge of Courage* to Garland in the spring. In August Crane camps with Lawrence, Carr, and Senger in Milford, Pike County, Pennsylvania. The *Pike County Puzzle*, largely written by Crane, is a burlesque account of this experience. Negotiates with the Boston publisher Copeland and Day over *The Black Riders*. Retrieves the manuscript of *The Red Badge* from S. S. McClure, who had held it from May until October, and sells it to the Bacheller, Johnson, and Bacheller newspaper syndicate. A truncated version of the war novel appears in the *Philadelphia Press,* the *New York Press,* and an undetermined number of other newspapers in December.

1895   Crane journeys to the West and Mexico as a feature writer for the Bacheller syndicate. Meets Willa Cather in the office of the *Nebraska State Journal* in February. His first Western sketch, "Nebraska's Bitter Fight for Life," describing drought and blizzard conditions in the state, is widely syndicated on Sunday, 24 February. Sends final revision of *The Red Badge* to D. Appleton and Company in early March. *The Black Riders* is published in May. Crane becomes a member of the Lantern Club on William Street in Manhattan, founded by a group of young journalists. Spends summer at the home of his brother

Edmund in Hartwood, New York, where he writes *The Third Violet*. Publication of *The Red Badge of Courage* in autumn projects Crane to fame in the United States and England.

1896   *George's Mother*, an expurgated version of *Maggie*, and *The Little Regiment* are published. *The Third Violet* is serialized by the McClure syndicate. Crane visits Washington in March to gather material for a political novel. Joins Authors Club. Becomes member of the Sons of the American Revolution in May. In September he becomes persona non grata with the New York City police by appearing in court to defend Dora Clark, a known prostitute who had falsely been arrested for soliciting while in his company on the night of 16 September. Leaves for Jacksonville, Florida, at the end of November on his way to report the Cuban insurrection for the Bacheller syndicate. Meets Cora Taylor at her "nightclub," the Hotel de Dream.

1897   The *Commodore*, carrying men and munitions to the Cuban rebels, sinks off the coast of Florida on the morning of 2 January. Crane and three others, the ship's captain, the steward, and an oiler, spend thirty hours on the sea in a ten-foot dinghy. Incident is the source for "Stephen Crane's Own Story" (*New York Press*, 7 January) and "The Open Boat." Crane goes to Greece to cover the Greco-Turkish War for the *New York Journal* and the *Westminster Gazette*. Cora, who accompanies him, sends back dispatches under the pseudonym Imogene Carter. *The Third Violet* published in May. Stephen and Cora settle in England at Ravensbrook, Oxted, Surrey, as Mr. and Mrs. Stephen Crane. In September they visit Ireland with Harold Frederic and Kate Lyon. Sidney Pawling, editor and partner in the firm of William Heinemann, Crane's English publisher, introduces him to Joseph Conrad in October. They become close friends. Also meets Ford Hueffer (later Ford Madox Ford). "The Monster," "Death and the Child," and "The Bride Comes to Yellow Sky" are written this autumn.

1898   "The Blue Hotel" is completed in the first week of February. The sinking of the *Maine* impels Crane to return to New York. He attempts to enlist in the United States Navy but fails the physical examination. *The Open Boat and Other Tales of Adventure* appears in April. Crane goes to Cuba as a correspondent for the *New York World*. Reports the landings at Guantánamo, the advance on Las Guásimas, and the Battle of San Juan Hill. When he is discharged from the *World* in July, he contracts with Hearst's *New York Journal* to cover the Puerto Rican campaign. After the Protocol of Peace is signed in August, he enters Havana and leads a semi-underground existence for three months, communicating infrequently with Cora and his family. Returns to New York at the end of December and sails for England on the 31st.

1899   In February the Cranes move to Brede Place, Sussex, rented by Cora from Moreton Frewen, whose wife, Clara, is a sister of Lady Randolph Churchill. They form friendships with Henry James, H. G. Wells, and Edward Garnett. Crane's second book of poems, *War Is Kind*, appears in May. Completes *Active Service*, which is published in October. Writes a series of stories about children set in the Whilomville (Port Jervis) setting of "The Monster" *The Monster and Other Stories* published by Harper in December. Finishes Cuban War stories and sketches of *Wounds in the Rain*. Increasingly forced into hackwork to repay enormous debts incurred through his and Cora's extravagance. Suffers tubercular hemorrhage at the conclusion of an elaborate three-day house party at Brede Place.

1900   Continues struggle to control debts and meet deadlines. *Whilomville Stories* and *Wounds in the Rain* published. Suffers new hemorrhages at the beginning of April. Travels to Germany's Black Forest in May, although little hope is held for his recovery. Dies on 5 June of tuberculosis in a sanitarium at Badenweiler. Body is returned to the United States for burial at Evergreen Cemetery in Elizabeth (now Hillside), New Jersey.

1901   *Great Battles of the World* appears. Researched and in part written by Kate Frederic.

1902   *Last Words*, an anthology compiled by Cora, published in England only. Contains a number of early pieces and eight new stories and sketches, two of which were completed by Cora.

1903   *The O'Ruddy* appears after delays caused by the reluctance of other writers to finish the novel, which was finally completed by Robert Barr, whom Crane had originally designated for the task.

Stephen Crane

An Annotated Bibliography of
Secondary Scholarship

1
Biography

Overview

There is considerable overlap between the material in the biography and general criticism sections. My rule of thumb was to put items that stressed Crane's life and personality in the biography section and those that stressed his works with general criticism. Still, the best and most important works in both categories have made significant contributions to each.

BOOKS. With regard to full-length biographies Beer (1.1), Berryman (1.2), Colvert (1.4), and Stallman (1.10) are essential. So too is Cazemajou (1.3), which is the best short introductory piece on Crane (and his works).

ARTICLES. Many of the items in this section are either brief reference book entries or personal remembrances. There are also several articles that summarize standard information on Crane; "Romantic Realist" (1.25) is a typical instance of a sound and informative introductory piece for the general reader. In addition to these sorts of items there are several dozen insightful general (and scholarly) articles on Crane's life and personality. At least ten deserve special attention; the five that are emphasized are especially valuable:

CONRAD 1.70
FOLLETT 1.90
Ford 1.93
FRENCH 1.94
Garland 1.98

Note: Hereafter in my overview comments, especially noteworthy and important articles are emphasized as are those listed above.

Gullason 1.108
Johnson 1.136
Sorrentino 1.199
Vosburg 1.211
Weinstein 1.214

Finally, with regard to information on Crane's life and personality, it is imperative to acknowledge how elusive he was (and continues to be); on this point consult Colvert (1.68) and Wertheim-Sorrentino (13.3).

Books

1.1   BEER, THOMAS. *Stephen Crane: A Study in American Letters*. New York: Knopf, 1923. 248. Though Wertheim and Sorrentino (*The Correspondence of Stephen Crane* [13.3]) have all but proved that Beer manufactured several "Crane" letters and that he fabricated a number of quips and even incidents in Crane's life, Beer's book remains a penetrating, provocative, and pregnant examination of Crane's life and works. If only for its impact on Crane scholarship this book remains essential. Beyond these historical points, however, Beer's reading is challenging and insightful. His comments on Crane's Western and Mexican stories are especially good.

      The status of Beer among current Crane scholars amounts to this: Read Beer, his book will help you a good deal, but be very careful when citing him—general references are acceptable but be wary of specific quotations.

1.2   BERRYMAN, JOHN. *Stephen Crane*. New York: William Sloane, 1950. xv+347. Beer's 1923 *Stephen Crane* (1.1) and Knopf's issue of *The Work of Stephen Crane* (12.5) revived interest in Crane. Stallman's *Stephen Crane: An Omnibus* (2.16) and Berryman's study raised scholarly attention to Crane several notches higher. Berryman's Freudian interpretation was from the beginning highly controversial; however, his analysis of all the major items in the Crane corpus is still worthy of attention.

      Of special note are first, his stress on the impact of Crane's western trip: It "was the happiest time perhaps he was to know" and it converted him to a self-reliant view of human nature. Second, Berryman's contention that one does not find in Crane plots but instead "maps of accidents" is pursued in Crane's prose and then extended to his first book of poems, *The Black Riders and Other Lines*. (Portions reprinted as "Crane's Art" in *Modern American Fiction:*

Essays in Criticism, ed. A. Walton Litz. New York: Oxford UP, 1963, 32–44.)

1.3 CAZEMAJOU, JEAN. *Stephen Crane.* Minneapolis: U of Minnesota P, 1969. 47. This abbreviated study (a volume in the *American Writer* series, "University of Minnesota Pamphlets on American Writers," later reprinted in vol. 1 of *American Writers: A Collection of Literary Biographies,* ed. Leonard Unger, New York: Scribner's, 1974) is clearly the best short introduction to Crane. Cazemajou sees Crane as a born moralist whose writings center on interests in "charity, fraternity, redemption and rescue." In remarkably few pages important details in his life are highlighted and all his major works are given insightful treatment. For comments on Cazemajou's full-length study (in French) see Elias (1.82).

1.4 COLVERT, JAMES B. *Stephen Crane.* New York: Harcourt Brace, 1984. 204. Though he modestly calls his book a "sketch of Crane's life," Colvert's study gives both beginning readers and Crane specialists not only an informative biography but also an even-handed assessment of the literary merit of Crane's work and an insightful interpretation of his literary creed.

Of note, though little analyzed by most commentators, Colvert provides illuminating details on Crane's early family as he explores the formative influence of Stevie's grandfathers, parents, and siblings. (Gullason is an exception here; he too has sought out family influences on Crane; see 1.108–1.115). Part of Harcourt's Album Biography series; contains a helpful chronology and an index plus forty-seven pictures.

1.5 FRANCHERE, RUTH. *Stephen Crane: The Story of an American Writer.* New York: Crowell, 1961. 216. A fictionalized biography written for young people. Franchere is unpretentious yet she often manages to capture some of the elusiveness of Crane's personality—for example, his ambiguity about his fame and notoriety. She suggests that whenever writer's block or self-doubt overtook him, Crane wrote to Nellie Crouse or Lily Brandon Monroe; hence those letters are especially revealing sources for insights into Crane.

1.6 LAWRENCE, FREDERIC M. *The Real Stephen Crane.* Ed. Joseph Katz. Newark, NJ: Newark Public Library, 1980. 27. A resurrected memoir inspired by Beer's *Stephen Crane* (1.1). Lawrence's manuscript was written about 1930 and brought into print by Katz. Lawrence was a close friend of Crane (he was "Pudge" in the Sullivan County sketches); his warm rapport with Crane is obvious in these pages.

Beyond biographical matters Lawrence took pains to point out Crane's ethical bent in his Bowery tales marked by his "keen and sympathetic, if detached vision."

Katz's Introduction (vi–xiii) provides details on the Crane-Lawrence friendship and rehearses standard biographical matters.

1.7   LINSON, CORWIN KNAPP. *My Stephen Crane*. Ed. Edwin Cady. Syracuse, NY: Syracuse UP, 1958. xiv+115. Cady edited Linson's impressionistic memoirs. Linson, a commercial artist, was sent by Bacheller with Crane to Scranton to provide illustrations for his landmark muckraking piece "In the Depths of the Coal Mine." Linson's account, including photographs, of this assignment and the composition of Crane's syndicated article is the center of gravity of Linson's reminiscences. Also valuable are his comments on Crane's style—"limpid veracity" and personality. "Stephen was a furious loafer, a furious worker, a furious smoker, and a furious arguer." Cady's Introduction (xi–xix) provides information on Linson's life and career, his friendship with Crane, and details on the editing that was necessary to make Linson's memoirs coherent and readable. Also see Stallman's review "Friendly Reminiscence," *New York Times Book Review,* 5 October 1958.

1.8   RAYMUND, THOMAS L. *Stephen Crane*. Newark, NJ: Carteret Book Club, 1923. 28. This "book" on Crane is actually a short essay—the address given by the ex-mayor of Newark at the dedication of the Crane memorial at the public library in Newark. Beyond standard biographical details Raymund stresses Crane's love of the active life; he admires Crane's compact style: "No word is wasted, we can skip no page."

1.9   ROBERTSON, MICHAEL. *Stephen Crane at Lafayette*. Easton, PA: Friends of the Skillman Library of Lafayette College, 1990. 10. A keepsake of an exhibition celebrating the Stephen Crane Centennial at Lafayette College. Robertson sorted out the details of Crane's freshman year (he was one of a class of ninety-three) including why, after one semester, he departed, having "managed to fail five out of seven classes." Also see Sloane (1.193).

1.10   STALLMAN, ROBERT W. *Stephen Crane: A Biography*. New York: George Braziller, 1968. xviii+664. Stallman set out to correct the fabrication and undocumented claims in Beer's biography of Crane and the Freudian excesses of Berryman. This very long and often overdetailed treatment shows Stallman's familiarity with Crane's life, output, and place in literary history. Stallman also uses the opportunity to bring into sharp focus his own view that the keys to reading Crane are religious symbolism, irony, and a flashing style. All of Crane's major works—novels, sketches, and tales along with his poetry and news reports—are examined.

While most reviewers and critics acknowledged the value of his reading of Crane, most did not think he bettered Beer and Berryman on matters of biographical fact. His book was widely reviewed. Joseph Katz's review (in *American Literature* 40 [1969]: 565–576) gave this assessment of its impact. "Books like this are never passively bad. This one will mislead readers by its bulk, its extravagant air of certitude, and the seeming plausibility of its elaborate apparatus. Equally unfortunate, its existence may block for some years the responsible biography needed now." Never at a loss to continue a good squabble, in his *Stephen Crane: A Critical Bibliography* (14.3: 551–571) Stallman lists nearly seventy reviews. These twenty pages, of course, include highlights of praise and Stallman's replies to every criticism. For those interested in pursuing the matter, see Daniel R. Buerger, "Book Review Consensus of *Stephen Crane: A Biography,* by R. W. Stallman," *American Literature Abstracts* 21 (1968): 335–337.

1.11   ZARA, LOUIS. *Dark Rider: A Novel Based on the Life of Stephen Crane.* Cleveland: World, 1961. 505. This fictionalized Crane is believable; the book is good on Crane as a boy, his lonely childhood, his fear and his multiple experiences with death in the family, and his ambiguity with the *Red Badge* fame.

Articles and Book Chapters

1.12   "The Author of *The Red Badge.*" *The Critic* ns 25 (1896): 163. A very early sketch of Crane that complains about his grammatical errors. A nice, good-sized photograph is included.

1.13   "Crane Biography." *Hackettstown Gazette* 22 August 1968. Information on Crane's father, who served as pastor of Trinity Methodist Church in 1867. See Stallman's *Stephen Crane: A Critical Bibliography* (14.3: 545).

1.14   "Crane, Stephen." *Columbia Encyclopedia.* 3rd ed. New York: Columbia UP, 1963. 509. Standard reference entry.

1.15   "Crane, Stephen." *Dictionary of American Authors.* Boston: Houghton Mifflin, 1901. 79. One-paragraph sketch.

1.16   "Crane, Stephen." *Webster's Biographical Dictionary*. Springfield, MA:
        G. & C. Merriam, 1966. 363. Standard one-paragraph entry.

1.17   ["CRANE, STEPHEN."] *Who Was Who in America*. Vol. 1. 1897–
        1942. Chicago: Marquis, 1943. 273. Stephen Crane was one of the
        them.

1.18   "Honor Crane, Famed Author." *Union-Gazette* (Port Jervis, NY) 6
        June 1962: 6. Crane's memorial at the Newark Public Library is
        described. See Stallman's *Stephen Crane: A Critical Bibliography* (14.3:
        464).

1.19   "Literary Notables Honor Stephen Crane's Memory." *Newark Star
        Eagle* 8 Nov. 1921: 4. One of several notices of the Newark
        Schoolman's Club placing a bronze tablet in honor of Crane at the
        Newark Public Library cited by Stallman, *Stephen Crane: A Critical
        Bibliography*, 304–305. Also noted by Stallman are articles in *Freeman*
        (7 December 1921), *Times Literary Supplement* (27 October 1921),
        and a rather lengthy comment by Theodore Dreiser, "A Letter About
        Stephen Crane," *Michigan Daily Sunday Magazine* (Ann Arbor, 27
        November 1921). Dreiser praises Crane as an innovator and he calls
        Red Badge "a fine picture of war."

1.20   *The Melange of the Class of '92*. Easton, PA: Lafayette College, 1892.
        The yearbook of Lafayette College. Crane is listed as a freshman (his
        home address is given as 170 E, Asbury Park, New Jersey) and a
        member of the Delta Upsilon Fraternity. Of interest is that a
        sophomore fraternity fellow is one Samuel K. Reifsnyder, no doubt
        the source of the name of the barber in *The Monster*.

1.21   "Misplaced Writer." *New Yorker* (7 Nov. 1936): 14. The actual burial
        place of Crane is Evergreen Cemetery in Hillside (not Elizabeth), New
        Jersey.

1.22   "Playlot to Rise at Birthplace of Stephen Crane." *New York Herald
        Tribune* 1 Jan. 1941: 20. Plans to demolish the old Crane home at 14
        Mulberry Place where Crane was born. The Stephen Crane Associa-
        tion had hoped to restore the building; they had to settle for a
        memorial plaque.

1.23   "[Portrait of Stephen Crane]." *Saturday Review of Literature* 32 (9 July
        1949): 9. A decent likeness.

1.24   "The Revival of Interest in Stephen Crane." *Current Opinion* 76 (Jan.
        1924): 39–40. Comments on renewed interest in Crane due to Beer's

Stephen Crane (1.1) and the efforts of the Stephen Crane Association of Newark, New Jersey. Also contains a photograph of Crane.

1.25 "Romantic Realist [Stephen Crane]." *MD Medical Newsmagazine* 12 (June 1968): 153–158. You need to go to a medical school library to find this article but it is worth it. The June 1968 issue of *MD* was devoted to "military medicine." The literature section featured Crane (the movie section covered the Russian film version of *War and Peace*). The article is a concise, accurate (except for the usual error that he died at 29) sketch of Crane's life plus nearly a dozen photographs. There are perceptive thematic comments—"as with almost all of Crane's fiction, the book [*Red Badge*] as an inquiry into the moral problems of conduct"—and on Crane's style the author comments, "He was an innovator in technique and forged a unique style; his ironic approach brilliantly pointed out the dichotomy between moral appearance and reality in society."

1.26 "Short, Hapless Life." *Newsweek* 30 (11 Dec. 1950: 97–98. A review of Berryman's *Stephen Crane* (1.2) complaining that "the lack of a consistent point of view" mars the book—an odd criticism in the face of the almost universal charge that Berryman's Freudianism dominated his observations.

1.27 "Some Prominent Members of Delta Upsilon." *Manual of Delta Upsilon*. 1958. 125. Crane is recognized by his old fraternity.

1.28 "Stephen Crane." *Concise Dictionary of American Biography*. New York: Scribner's, 1964. 198–99. Standard reference book sketch.

1.29 "Stephen Crane." *Library* (Newark) 1.9 (1923: 11. Brief sketch of Crane. See Stallman's *Stephen Crane: A Critical Bibliography* (14.3: 309).

1.30 "Stephen Crane Home Acquired." *Newark Evening News* 18 May 1924. The Stephen Crane Association acquired the Crane home to be preserved as a memorial. See Stallman's *Stephen Crane: A Critical Bibliography* (14.3: 312).

1.31 "Stephen Crane: A Wonderful Boy." *Literary Digest* 20 (1900): 750. An elaborate obituary with a photograph and several letters from and about Crane.

1.32 "Topics of the Week." *New York Times Book Review* 5 April 1914: 166. A full-volume rave about Garland's appreciation of Crane in the *Yale*

Review, "Stephen Crane as I Knew Him" (1.200). This article is important because it was a strong factor in the first Crane revival.

1.33   "Unconventional Son of a Parson, Crane Lived Hard and Died Young." *Life* 31 (10 Sep. 1957): 108. A sketch of Crane's life prompted by the John Huston filming of *The Red Badge of Courage:* Crane was the champion of "children, dogs and underdogs."

1.34   "The Work of Stephen Crane." *Book Buyer* 20 (1900): 433–34. Standard obituary, good picture, and brief comments on *Black Riders* and *Red Badge.*

1.35   "Young Man in a Hurry." *Time* 92 (30 Aug. 1968): 63–64. Review essay on Berryman's *Stephen Crane;* apt comments on Crane's "bold, uncluttered, staccato prose."

1.36   ALLEN, FREDERIC LEWIS. "The Agent and an Author: Stephen Crane." *Paul Revere Reynolds.* New York: Privately printed, 1944. 48–60. Reynolds was Crane's American agent (James B. Pinker was his English counterpart). Allen's chapter brings out details of the agent-author dealings; all Crane's letters to Reynolds were reprinted here. A good section on Reynolds's battle, on Crane's behalf, to save "B'Gawd" from being cut from "A Man and Some Others" by Richard Gilder of the *Century Magazine.*

1.37   BAASNER, PETER. "Stephen Crane and Joseph Conrad." *Kleine Beitrage Zur Amerikanischen Literaturgeschichte.* Ed. Hans Galinsky and Hans-Joachim Lang. Heidelberg: Carl Winter, 1961. 34–39. Conrad is the focus, Crane the add-on: Both see the world as a flatly indifferent arena in which salvation comes through human solidarity.

1.38   BACHELLER, IRVING. "The High-Brow Decade." *Coming Up the Road.* Indianapolis: Bobbs-Merrill, 1928. 267–316. The last chapter of Bacheller's memoirs briefly discusses the syndicated version of *Red Badge* and the $700 advance given to Crane to cover the war in Cuba—the money belt that Crane lost when the *Commodore* sank.

1.39   ———. "Genius." *From Stores of Memory.* New York: Farrar and Rinehart, 1933. 110–18. Bacheller takes credit for much of Crane's success with *Red Badge;* details on the literary luncheon society—the Lanthorne Club—which Bacheller founded and Crane joined.

1.40   BALCH, D. A. *Elbert Hubbard: Genius of Roycroft.* New York: Frederick A. Stokes, 1940. Passim. Scattered comments on Crane's dealings with Hubbard and *The Philistine.*

1.41 _____. "Fire Across the Sky." *Villager* 34 (Nov. 1961): 16–17, 33. The title refers to Crane's brief, meteoric rise. A standard biographical sketch with nothing surprising including typical errors: Crane died at 29 and that he leased Breed [sic] Place in England.

1.42 BARR, MARK. "Stephen Crane's Memorial." *New York Herald Tribune* 2 Jan. 1940, section 11: 9. Mention of the memorial of a playground on Crane's birthsite along with general comments on his life and work.

1.43 BARRETT, CLIFTON WALLER. "The Stephen Crane Society at Lafayette." *Antiquarian Bookman* 12 (1953): 83–85. Report of the founding of the society during the fall of 1953. Barrett is important for Crane scholars because his personal collection of manuscripts (and first editions) formed the bulk of the Crane papers at the University of Virginia, essential in the preparation of the critical edition. For more on this see Cahoon (12.3).

1.44 BEACH, JOSEPH WARREN. "Five Makers of American Fiction." *Yale Review* 40 (1951): 744–51. An essay on recent books about American naturalists and realists applauding Berryman's Freudian interpretation of Crane as "the most plausible and the subtlest application of the professional methods of analysis that is yet to be found in 'literary criticism.'"

1.45 BEER, THOMAS. ["On Stephen Crane."] *New York Evening Post* 17 Dec. 1921: 474. Remarks on Crane's life and writings; see Stallman's *Stephen Crane: A Critical Bibliography* (14.3: 305).

1.46 BERRYMAN, JOHN. "Preface to the Meridian Edition." *Stephen Crane*. Cleveland: World, 1962. ix–xii. Berryman asks if additional Crane materials, both textual and critical, made available in the dozen years between the first issue of *Stephen Crane* (see 1.2) and the paperback edition brought out by Meridian books require him to change his picture of Crane. Berryman's verdict: "I think: not substantially."

1.47 BORG, DOROTHY. "Newark Remembers Stephen Crane." *New York World* 8 Nov. 1925. A story on Newark's plans to honor Crane and details on his birthplace, 14 Mulberry Place.

1.48 BOYD, ERNEST. "Thomas Beer." *Portraits: Real and Imaginary*. New York: George H. Doran, 1924. 208–16. Comments on Beer's book on Crane (1.1); a remarkable anticipation of the Wertheim-Sorrentino view (13.3: 2–3, 661–92) that Beer fabricated key items in his biography. Boyd says that Beer's book displays "a personality which is stamped as clearly upon his life of Stephen Crane as if it were his own story."

1.49   BRADBURY, MALCOLM, and ARNOLD GOLDMAN. "Stephen Crane: Classic at the Crossroads." *Bulletin of the British Association of American Studies* 6 (1965): 42–49. Negative biographical sketch; depicts Crane as a hedging, egotistical, self-inflated pretender.

1.50   BRAGDON, CLAUDE. "The Purple Cow Period." *Merely Players*. New York: Knopf, 1905. 61–70. An account of the golden years of the little magazines; a few details on the testimonial banquet given in Crane's honor in December of 1895 by Elbert Hubbard and the Philistine Society in Buffalo, New York. The book was reissued in 1919 and often thereafter. This chapter was reprinted in *Bookman* 59 (1929): 475–78. The best information on Crane, Hubbard, and the Philistines is provided by White (1.222).

1.51   ———. *More Lives Than One*. New York: Knopf, 1938. Brief general comments on Crane (246–47) plus Bragdon's impressions of the Hubbard-Roycroft Society's dinner for Crane.

1.52   BRAUNSTEIN, SIMEON. "A Checklist of Writings by and about Stephen Crane in *The Fra*." *Stephen Crane Newsletter* 3.2 (1968): 8. *The Fra* was Hubbard's third journal (the others being *The Philistine* and *The Roycroft Quarterly*). Braunstein lists ten appearances by Crane between May 1909 and October 1916.

1.53   BROOKS, VAN WYCK. "From the Life of Stephen Crane." *Sketches in Criticism*. New York: Dutton, 1932. 156–58. A biographical note. Interesting comments on Crane's artistic and personal curiosity.

1.54   ———. *Howells: His Life and World*. New York: Dutton, 1959. 268–72 and passim. Passing comments on Howells's meetings with Crane and his opinion of his works, especially his sadness at the untimely deaths of Crane and Norris.

1.55   BROWN, CURTIS. "Some Old Press Men." *Contacts*. New York: Harper and Brothers, 1935. 254–80. Brown, the New York *Press* Sunday editor during Crane's early newspaper days, comments on the newspaper version of *Red Badge* and *George's Mother*. He visited the Cranes at Brede and attended Crane's wake.

1.56   CADY, EDWIN H. *The Realist at War: The Mature Years (1885–1920) of William Dean Howells*. Syracuse: Syracuse UP, 1958. Passim. Cady sorts out the "number of significant roles [Howells played] in Crane's development."

1.57 ———. "Stephen Crane." *Encyclopedia Britannica,* vol. 6. 1968. A reference-book sketch.

1.58 CAMBELL, CHARLES A. *Traditions of Hartwood.* Winter Park, FL: Orange. 1930. 31–34, 58–62, 125–48. Three sections of this small book are worthy of note. The first describes the founding of the Hartwood Club with William H. Crane as its first president. The second tells of the first clubhouse period. "It was during this period that Stephen Crane, author of 'The Red Badge of Courage,' was a frequent visitor here." Cambell asserts that "here he worked upon the book destined to give him a secure place among the great." Cambell later claims that the stranger walking along with and encouraging Fleming in chapter 12 of *Red Badge* retells an incident that happened to Crane "as he trudged through the mud of a country road" from Hartwood back to his brother William's house. (Sounds suspicious.) The third section of note is the chapter "Hunting and Fishing," which tells several hunting stories that could easily find their way into some of Crane's Sullivan County sketches.

1.59 CANTWELL, ROBERT. "Stephen Crane: Action and Adventure." *Famous American Men of Letters.* New York: Dodd, 1964. 135–45. A condensed, simplified, brief biography of Crane for young readers. Cantwell's expertise can be guessed from his contention that in "The Open Boat" Crane "went through seventy to eighty hours of exposure."

1.60 CARMICHAEL, OTTO. "Stephen Crane in Cuba: A Newly Discovered Biographical Sketch." *Prairie Schooner* 43 (1969): 200–203. Carmichael discovered an unsigned article in the Omaha *Daily Bee* (17 June 1900) by a fellow newscorrespondent in Cuba. Interesting for comments on Crane's bravery and how deliberately he composed his news dispatches.

1.61 CARRUTH, GORTON, et al. "Stephen Crane." *The Encyclopedia of American Facts and Dates* New York: Crowell, 1962. 364, 372, 380. Three events in Crane's life are found to have national significance: the publications of *Red Badge, Maggie* and "The Open Boat." The same entries appear in the 1972 edition of this book.

1.62 CARTER, EVERETT. *Howells and the Age of Realism.* Philadelphia: Lippincott, 1950. 231–33. Carter says of Howells's support for

Crane, "When *Maggie* was refused by publisher after publisher, it was Howells who found him one, and who wrote the essay which launched the young man on his literary career." Carter's first statement is an error; his second, if not wrong, is greatly exaggerated—Garland's review in the *Arena* was equally important.

1.63   CHAMBERLIN, RALPH. "Lafayette's Most Notorious Flunk-Out." *Lafayette Alumnus* Feb. 1961, 16–17, 27. Purporting to give a factual account of Crane at Lafayette Chamberlin is drawn to the bohemian, eccentric stereotypes of Crane's life. Standard details about *Maggie, Red Badge,* and Crane's transfer to Syracuse University. For reliable information on Crane at Lafayette see Robertson (1.10).

1.64   CHAMPNEY, FREEMAN. *Art & Glory: The Story of Elbert Hubbard.* New York: Crown, 1968. 68–69 and passim. Champney portrays Hubbard as an important Crane supporter and gives a few details on the Philistine dinner honoring him in December 1895.

1.65   CHANDLER, GEORGE F. "I Knew Stephen Crane at Syracuse." *Courier* 3 (1963): 12–13. A former classmate relates that Crane was "not popular but I liked him"; he said life was hard and college was a waste of time.

1.66   CHUBB, EDWIN WATTS. "Stephen Crane: A 'Wonderful Boy.'" *Stories of Authors, British and American.* New York: Macmillan, 1926. 361–63. A short snippet—some 100 authors are covered. The Crane section is mostly a stringing together of comments from several of his letters.

1.67   COBLENTZ, STANTON S. "Stephen Crane: Literary Meteor." *New York Times Book Review* 30 Dec. 1923: 8. A rave review of Beer's *Stephen Crane* (1.1), crediting it and Beer with the Crane revival. "This book should bring Crane back from the misty borderland that verges upon oblivion."

1.68   COLVERT, JAMES B. "Searching for Stephen Crane: The Schoberlin Collection." *Courier* 21 (1986): 5–34. In 1984 Syracuse University acquired the papers of Commander Melvin H. Schoberlin. From 1936 until the early 1950s Schoberlin struggled to complete a biography of Crane. "Flagon of Despair" was never published; after some 100,000 words Schoberlin thought himself only about two-thirds finished. Though Colvert's article discusses this unpublished manuscript, equally valuable are his comments about the mass of material Schoberlin collected and his account of the inventiveness and stamina of would-be biographer, Schoberlin.

1.69   CONRAD, JOSEPH. "Stephen Crane: A Note Without Dates." *London Mercury* 1 (1919): 192–93. A brief reminiscence not as long or as useful as his preface to Beer's *Stephen Crane* (1.1); still, his comments on Crane's eyes and his happiness when riding horses stand out. Also published in *Bookman* 20 (1920): 529–531.

1.70   ———. Introduction. *Stephen Crane: A Study in American Letters.* By Thomas Beer. New York: Knopf, 1923. 1–33. An essential article. Conrad's introduction added much to Beer's book. Conrad tells of his first meeting with Crane—a luncheon arranged by publisher Sidney Pawling. Pawling excused himself at 4:00 PM. Crane and Conrad left the restaurant to walk and talk of each other's work until 11:00 PM. Also details of Crane's deliberate writing pace and his cheerfully interrupting his own work to let his three dogs in and out of his study. See also Gullason (13.14).

1.71   CONRAD, MRS. JOSEPH (JESSE). "Recollections of Stephen Crane." *Bookman* 63 (1926): 134–37. Interesting details on the Conrad-Crane friendship. Not just Joseph and Crane are discussed but the two families. Poignant comments on Crane's love of horses, dogs, and the Conrad children.

1.72   CONWAY, JOHN D. "The Stephen Crane-Amy Leslie Affair: A Reconsideration." *Journal of Modern Literature* 7 (1979): 3–13. Five previously unpublished letters of Crane to Amy Leslie were the main reason for this article; all are reprinted in *The Correspondence of Stephen Crane* (13.3:#s 287, 288, 291, 292, 329). Conway examines the Crane-Leslie affair and concludes that Crane probably did not repay the money he borrowed and that "with money and women Crane was playing it fast and loose."

1.73   CRANE, MRS. GEORGE. (sister-in-law). "Stephen Crane's Boyhood." *New York World* 10 June 1900: E3. Boyhood reminiscences of Crane at Newark, Port Jervis, and Asbury Park. Mrs. Crane reports that Stevie was fond of all outdoor sports and everything pertaining to military affairs.

1.74   CRANE, HELEN R. "My Uncle, Stephen Crane." *American Mercury* 31 (1934): 24–29. Crane's niece Helen (daughter of William) was close to Stephen and Cora. She lived with them for about a year and a half at Sussex, and later she and Cora accompanied Crane's body to New York. Her matter of fact recollections respond to Beer's *Stephen Crane* (1.1) providing several interesting personal details on Crane as a youth: "His clothes reeked eternally of tobacco and garlic." Note: Stallman's *Stephen Crane: A Critical Bibliography* (14.3: 320) calls attention to an earlier brief memoir by Crane's niece, "In New Jersey," *Newark Star-Eagle* 7 July 1926: 10; 8 July 1926: 12.

1.75   DAHLBERG, EDWARD. "Stephen Crane: American Genius." *The Leafless American and Other Writings*. Ed. Harold Billings. New Paltz, NY: McPherson, 1986. 74–77. In an otherwise arrogant, uniformed, and error-filled note, Dahlberg managed two accurate observations: Crane had lots of energy and he died young. The misinformation in this essay was also contained in an earlier (1976) edition.

1.76   DALY, THOM. "Who's the Philistine?" *Philadelphia Evening Ledger* 27 July 1916: 10; 28 July 1916: 8. Important newspaper articles on Hubbard, *The Philistine,* and the dinner given in Crane's honor. Reprinted in *Stephen Crane: A Critical Bibliography* (14.3: 298–301).

1.77   DAVIS, RICHARD HARDING. "Madcap Genius Stephen." *New York Herald* 10 June 1900: E3. A splashy gossip piece with lots of drawings. Good comments on Crane's eyes: "restless, searching, eloquent and deeply blue."

1.78   DELL, FLOYD. "Stephen Crane and the Genius Myth." *Nation* 119 1924: 637–38. An attempt to counter the "lurid myths" and vicious rumors about Crane: He was a genius and he was unconventional, but Dell adds nothing new.

1.79   DIRLAM, H. KENNETH, and ERNEST E. SIMMONS. *Sinners, This Is East Aurora: The Story of Elbert Hubbard and the Roycroft Shops*. New York: Vantage. 1964. 24–29. Another description of the Philistine dinner for Crane.

1.80   EDWARDS, HERBERT. "Howells and the Controversy Over Realism in American Fiction." *American Literature* 3 (1931): 237–48. Stresses Howells's active interest in Crane.

1.81   EIDSON, JOHN O. "The Death Certificate of Stephen Crane." *Notes and Queries* 7 (1960): 149–50. Eidson translates (from the German) Crane's death certificate and he gives other details about his last days and death.

1.82   ELIAS, ROBERT H. "Stephen Crane: Encore." *Etudes Anglaises: Grande-Bretange, Etat-Unis* 24 (1971): 444–48. A helpful review of Jean Cazemajou's full-length study, *Stephen Crane (1871–1900): Ecrivain Journaliste* (Paris: Librairie Didier, 1969). This 578-page volume is not translated into English. Elias argues that Cazemajou's book is a comprehensive and fully documented study that "systematically separates the account of Crane's life from the close analysis of individual works." Though Elias finds flaws in all the major Crane studies (those of Stallman, Beer, and Berryman are briefly examined), he finds far fewer in Cazemajou's study, calling it a "significant contribution to the understanding of American literature."

1.83 FARLEKAS, CHRISTOPHER. "The Anatomy of a Memorial." *Stephen Crane: An Appreciation.* Ed. Christopher Farlekas. Port Jervis, NY: Colonial School and Camp, 1962. 2–3. An account of the establishment of a Crane memorial at the Colonial School and Camp by two teachers at that school, Glen Oldman and Chris Farlekas. Farlekas tells of Crane's Port Jervis days and of loneliness as a "pervading theme" in his works.

1.84 ———. "Stephen Crane of Port Jervis." *Views* 1.2 (1962): 203–4. *Views* is the official publication of the Orange County Community of Museums and Galleries. Farlekas reports a new oil painting of Crane and he recounts stories of a lynching incident Crane and his brother William had witnessed.

1.85 ———. "Stephen Crane of Port Jervis." *York State Tradition* 17.1 (1963): 11–14. A reprinting of a newspaper Sunday supplement about Crane's youth; the memorial bookshelves at the Port Jervis Free Library are also described.

1.86 ———. "Then and Now. Port Jervis Lynching: Part II." *Times Herald Record* (Middleton, NY) 5 May 1965: 48. Retells the story of Crane and his brother William trying to prevent the lynching of a Negro, Robert Lewis.

1.87 Federal Writers' Project. "Stephen Crane." *Stories of New Jersey: Its Significant Places, People and Activities.* New York: Barrows, 1938. A short biographical sketch containing a number of errors. A picture of the Crane bust at the Newark Public Library and a brief account of the Crane society are also included.

1.88 ———. "Stephen Crane." *New Jersey: A Guide to Its Present and Past.* New York: Viking, 1939. Passim. Crane is treated in several sections. Under "Fine Arts" he is cited as "perhaps the State's outstanding literary figure" and under "Newark" a detailed description of the Crane house at 14 Mulberry Place is given.

1.89 FERGUSON, JOHN DELANCEY, ed. *Men and Moments: A Book of Living Narratives.* New York: Cordon, 1938. Brief biographical remarks followed by a reprinting of "An Experiment in Misery."

1.90   FOLLETT, WILSON. "The Second Twenty-Eight Years: A Note on
       Stephen Crane, 1871–1900." *Bookman* 68 (1929): 532–37. One of
       the earliest (and best) general essays on Crane and his works. Useful
       observations on Crane's style and his use of types (instead of named
       characters). *The Monster* is singled out and attention given to Crane's
       sense of "the capricious power of public opinion."

1.91   FORD, FORD MADOX. " 'Stevie' " *New York Evening Post Literary
       Review* 12 July 1924: 881–82. An attempt to offset rumors of Crane
       as an eccentric rounder. Good comments on Crane's awareness of
       literary style, technique, and criticism.

1.92   ———. "Three Americans and A Pole." *Scribner's Magazine* 90
       (1931): 379–86. On W. H. Hudson, Henry James, Conrad, and
       Crane. Repeats his litany about Crane: his cowboy costume, his love of
       riding horses, and his tiny handwriting.

1.93   ———. "Stephen Crane." *American Mercury* 37 (1936): 36–45.
       Fond memories, mostly of interest to literary historians: life at Brede,
       his riding a large horse that made him look like "a frail eagle astride a
       gaunt elephant," and the hordes of parasitic guests. Reprinted in
       Portraits from Life (Boston: Houghton Mifflin, 1937) and *Mightier
       Than the Sword* (London: George Allen and Unwin, 1938).

1.94   FRENCH, MANSFIELD, J. "Stephen Crane, Ball Player." *Syracuse
       University Alumni News* 15.4 (1934): 3–4. The definitive essay on
       Crane as a ballplayer by a fellow teammate and classmate at Syracuse.
       (See also Jones, 1.137.)

1.95   GAINES, CHARLES K. "Rise to Fame of Stephen Crane." *Philadelphia
       Press* 15 Mar. 1896: 34. Gaines's (or some copy editor's) subtitle
       nicely summarizes the piece: "A sketch of a literary light who is
       winning unusual success in his early youth, his birth, education and
       characteristics." A nice picture of Crane by H. F. King.

1.96   GARLAND, HAMLIN. "Stephen Crane." *Booklover* 1 (1900): 6–9. A
       self-serving—"I recognized his genius and helped him all I could"—
       account of Garland's dealings with Crane.

1.97   ———. "Stephen Crane: A Soldier of Fortune." *The Saturday Evening
       Post* 173 (1900): 16–17. Garland's memoirs of Crane. Recounts
       standard tales: *Red Badge* manuscript in hock (pawned); when writing

poetry Crane simply drew off lines standing in rows in his head; and he was badly nourished and smoked continually.

1.98   ———. "Stephen Crane As I Knew Him." *Yale Review* 3 (1914): 494–506. The standard source for the standard stories on the starving Crane before his *Red Badge* fame. Partially reprinted, with a great photo of Crane, as "Crane as Hamlin Garland Knew Him," *Syracusan*, 1 December 1917, and in *Current Opinion* 56 (1914): 460. Also excerpted in "How Stephen Crane 'Drew Off' His Poems," *Current Opinion* 56 (1914): 460.

1.99   ———. "Stephen Crane." *Roadside Meetings*. New York: Macmillan, 1930. 189–206. Memoirs, self-serving in places, bitter in others, of Crane. By 1930 Garland's popularity had declined as Crane's waxed. Garland responded, in part, with aspersions, including charges of opium use, about Crane and his fondness for New York City lowlife. Reprinted with minor changes as "Crane the Bohemian" in *Bookman* 70 (1930): 523–28. Pizer (1.183) has sorted out the fact and fiction in the Garland-Crane relationship.

1.100   ———. "Stephen Crane." *Hamlin Garland's Diaries*. Ed. Donald Pizer. San Marino, CA: Huntington Library, 1968. 120–21. Diary entries on Garland's hearing of Crane's death—"he took little care of himself and I fear his death was due to his own habits of excessive smoking and I fear the use of opium"—and his 1922 opinion that "he made no advance over *The Red Badge*."

1.101   GILKES, LILLIAN. "No Hoax: A Reply to Mr. Stallman." *Studies in Short Fiction* 2 (1964): 77–83. Gilkes and Robert Stallman collaborated in publishing *The Letters of Stephen Crane* (13.2). Thereafter they had a falling out and spent several years feuding—in short, often nasty articles in various scholarly journals. This is round one of that feud and it concerns a minor detail about whether or not Crane went to Greece via Crete in 1897.

1.102   ———. "Some Omissions." *Saturday Review* 50 (31 Aug. 1968): 20. Round two of the Gilkes-Stallman feud (see Gilkes, 1.101, for the first scrap). "Some Omissions" lists several errors in Stallman's *Stephen Crane: A Biography* (1.10).

1.103   ———. "Corrections of R. W. Stallman's *Stephen Crane: A Biography*." *Stephen Crane Newsletter* 3.3 (1969): 6–7. More of the Stallman-Gilkes feud: "It is a painful [she is being coy] experience but an undeniable duty [she relished it] to list factual errors in the latest work of one so well-known for his pioneering efforts in Crane studies as R. W. Stallman. The following [she limits herself to a dozen] are some of the many errors. . . ."

1.104   ———. "Stephen Crane's Burial Place: Some Inconsequential Ghost Laying." *Serif* 7.2 (1970): 7–11. Crane is buried just where he is supposed to be at the Evergreen Cemetery, Hillside, New Jersey.

1.105   GRAY, CHARLESON. "The Splendid Years." *College Humor* Jan. 1931. According to Stallman's *Stephen Crane: A Critical Bibliography* (14.3: 334), this is a note on Crane's personal courage.

1.106   GULLASON, THOMAS A. "New Light on the Crane–Howells Relationship." *New England Quarterly* 30 (1957): 389–92. An early, interesting piece. Gullason argues that Howells never really appreciated Crane; for his part, Crane thought Howells a stuffed shirt.

1.107   ———. "Stephen Crane: Anti-Imperialist." *American Literature* 30 (1958): 237–41. Gullason holds that from his very early writings at Syracuse to his very last English newsletters Crane was an ardent anti-imperialist and a defiant humanitarian.

1.108   ———. "The Cranes at Pennington Seminary." *American Literature* 39 (1968): 530–41. Crane was a student at Pennington Seminary when his father was its principal. Gullason has sorted out the known facts about Crane and his father at the school where, Gullason argues, he "had an ideal opportunity to test his writing skills."

1.109   ———. "The Last Will and Testament of Mrs. Mary Helen Crane." *American Literature* 40 (1968): 232–34. Gullason's find brings these facts to light: Crane's mother's will gave him one fourth of her library, $300.00 a year for college, and one seventh of the Asbury Park home.

1.110   ———. "Stallman's Crane." *CEA Critic* 31.8 (1969): 8–9. A very critical notice of Stallman's *Stephen Crane* (1.10) and *Stephen Crane: Sullivan County Tales and Sketches* (9.10). Gullason notes in passing, "Mr. Stallman also resorts to his characteristic padding"; of course, Stallman will respond—see 1.200.

1.111   ———. "To the Readers of the *CEA Critic* and to Mr. Stallman." *CEA Critic* 32 (1970): 12–13. Gullason responds to Stallman's response to Gullason's response to Stallman (1.110 and 1.200). The editors of *CEA Critic* add, "We believe these two statements fairly conclude the Crane controversy in the *Critic*. May the issue rest in peace."

1.112 ———. "The Fiction of the Reverend Jonathan Townley Crane, D. D." *American Literature* 43 (1971): 263–73. Gullason discovered four pieces of fiction by Crane's father; Jonathan Townley Crane's animal fiction is nearly as poignant as his son's with regard to dogs and cats.

1.113 ———. "Stephen Crane's Sister: New Biographical Facts." *American Literature* 49 (1977): 234–38. Agnes Elizabeth Crane practically raised Crane and she was his first literary mentor. Because, he argues, biographical facts about her are important, Gullason works up a slim dossier on her.

1.114 ———. "A Cache of Short Stories by Stephen Crane's Family." *Studies in Short Fiction* 23 (1985): 71–106. Shows that his family's interest in stories influenced Crane's Sullivan County tales and *Third Violet*.

1.115 ———. "A Legacy for Stephen Crane: The Princeton Writings of the Reverend Jonathan Townley Crane." *Courier* 25 (1990): 55–79. Gullason makes brief comments on and reprints four essays and a poem that Crane's father wrote during his college days at Princeton (then the College of New Jersey). Gullason finds his long poem "The Battle of Waterloo" especially revealing.

1.116 GUNTZER, J. HENRY. "A Memorial to Stephen Crane." *Delta Upsilon Quarterly* 40 (1922): 36–38. Crane joined Delta Upsilon while at Lafayette. A fraternity brother recounts the constructing of the memorial to Crane at the Newark Public Library and gives a brief sketch of his life and works.

1.117 HAGEMANN, E. R. "The Death of Stephen Crane." *Proceedings of the New Jersey Historical Society* 77 (1959): 173–84. All the gritty details of Crane's last few months.

1.118 HAHN, EMILY. "Gaudy Aesthetes and Boy Socialists." *Romantic Rebels*. Boston: Houghton Mifflin, 1967. 93–118. Crane and Jack London are seen as antisocial romantic exiles who condemned American society.

1.119 HALL, CHARLOTTE H. "But Is He Relevant?" *Ridgewood Herald News* 4 Nov. 1971: 2, 21. Stallman reports *(Stephen Crane: A Critical Bibliography,* 14.3: 617) that this article was prompted by his loan to the Newark Library of his Crane materials to commemorate Crane's centennial. Hall laments the "rubble-strewn playground for neigh-borhood children" on the site of the Crane home at 14 Mulberry Place.

1.120 HALLAM, GEORGE. "Some New Stephen Crane Items." *Studies in Bibliography* 20 (1976): 263–66. An account of items belonging to Crane and Cora found in Jacksonville. Of most interest are Cora's copy of *Wounds in the Rain* and two of Crane's letters.

1.121 HART, JAMES D. "Crane, Stephen." *The Oxford Companion to American Literature.* New York: Oxford UP, 1983. 172–73. An updated sketch from the 1956 third edition and the 1965 fourth edition. All three are brief, reliable reference book entries on Crane and his works.

1.122 HEATH, MONROE. "Stephen Crane." *Authors.* Vol. 3 of *Great Americans at a Glance.* Redwood City, CA: Pacific Coast, 1962. 28. For grade school children: a drawing and a short biography of Crane.

1.123 HENDERSON, DION. "The Dark Splendor of Genius." *Milwaukee Journal* 1 Sept. 1961, Part 1: 12. A review essay of Louis Zara's fictional biography of Crane, *Dark Rider* (1.11).

1.124 HERZBERG, MAX. "Newark's Great Man of Letters." *Newarker* 1 (1 May 1936). A brief biographical sketch of Crane for a bulletin marking the 100th anniversary of the incorporation of Newark.

1.125 ———. "Stephen Crane—A Pioneer Novelist." *The World Review* 1 (1925): 74. A general essay trying to stir up interest in Crane.

1.126 HICKS, GRANVILLE. "A Gift for Disaster." *Saturday Review* 50 (10 Aug. 1968): 29–30. A critical, but fair, review essay of Stallman, *Stephen Crane* (1.10).

1.127 HILLIARD, JOHN NORTH. "Stephen Crane's Letters to a Friend about His Ambition, His Art, and His Views of Life." *New York Times* 14 July 1900: 466. A quasi-eulogy that pictures Crane as a quiet, unassuming, courageous gentleman. Also the first publication of Crane's letters to Hilliard; see *The Correspondence of Stephen Crane* (13.3: #s 78 and 197).

1.128 HIND, CHARLES LEWIS. "Stephen Crane." *Authors and I.* New York: John Lane, 1921. 70–74. A slight essay; memoirs of the Cranes at Brede Place.

1.129 HOFFMAN, DANIEL G. "Legends of Stephen Crane." *The Public Papers of a Bibliomaniac.* Mt. Vernon, NY: Golden Eagle. 120–121.

This article is cited in *Thoth* 13 (1973): 45. Several interlibrary loan librarians have been unable to locate it.

1.130　　──────. "Stephen Crane." *Reference Guide to American Literature*. Ed. D. L. Kirkpatrick. Chicago: St. James, 1978. 152–54. Standard reference book sketch. Hoffman stresses the importance of conflict in the prose and poetry of Crane.

1.131　　HOLLOWAY, JEAN. *Hamlin Garland: A Biography*. Austin: U of Texas P, 1960. Scattered comments on Garland's support for Crane during his starving days in New York City.

1.132　　HONAN, WILLIAM H., ed. *Greenwich Village Guide*. New York: Golden Eagle, 1950. 23. The guidebook points out that Crane lived in a boarding house at Number 61 on the south side of Washington Square. See Stallman's *Stephen Crane: A Critical Bibliography* (14.3: 378).

1.133　　HONIG, DONALD. "Stephen Crane: Boy Genius." *Caper* 12.1 (1966): 53, 60. Several interlibrary loan librarians tried without success to get this for me. Belatedly I looked in Stallman's *Stephen Crane: A Critical Bibliography* (13.4) and now I know why. The article is, Stallman says, "a sketch of Crane's life in *Caper,* a girlie magazine [520]."

1.134　　JOHNSON, ALLEN, and DUMAS MALONE, eds. *Dictionary of American Biography,* vol. 4. New York: Scribner's, 1930. 506–8. A typical reference-book sketch.

1.135　　JOHNSON, BRUCE. "Joseph Conrad and Crane's *The Red Badge of Courage.*" *Papers of the Michigan Academy of Science, Arts and Letters* 48 (1963): 649–55. Despite the idyllic relationship between Crane and Conrad, the latter bristled at the suggestion that *Red Badge* influenced *The Nigger of the "Narcissus."* Johnson finds Conrad to be peevish and often jealous.

1.136　　JOHNSON, WILLIS FLETCHER. "The Launching of Stephen Crane." *The Literary Digest International Book Review* 4 (1926): 288–90. Arguably the most informative and reliable of the many personal reminiscences triggered by Knopf's issue of *The Work of Stephen Crane* (12.5). Johnson, the day editor of the *New York Tribune,* tells of Crane's early newspaper apprenticeship, much of which Johnson supervised.

1.137　　JONES, CLAUDE E. "Stephen Crane at Syracuse." *American Literature* 7 (1935): 82–84. The known facts about Crane at Syracuse University; lots of baseball details. See also French (1.94).

1.138   JOSEPHSON, MATTHEW. "The Voyage of Stephen Crane." *Portrait of the Artist as American.* New York: Harcourt Brace, 1930. 232–64. A starving-artist-in-the-garret account of Crane, heavily dependent on Beer's *Stephen Crane* (1.1). Josephson stresses a fascination with death and the atmosphere of the expatriate American colony at Sussex.

1.139   KATZ, JOSEPH. "Some Light on the Stephen Crane–Amy Leslie Affair." *Mad River Review* 1 (1964): 43–62. Katz has sorted out the details of the romantic and financial entanglements of Crane with Leslie, late drama critic of the Chicago *Daily News.*

1.140   ———. "Stephen Crane's Birth Announcement." *Stephen Crane Newsletter* 1.4 (1967): 3. Katz reprints an entry from the Reverend Jonathan Townley Crane on the day of his son's birth.

1.141   ———. "Stephen Crane's Death Certificate." *Stephen Crane Newsletter* 1.4 (1967): 3–5. Katz offers a facsimile of "the certified photostat" owned by the Ohio State University Library.

1.142   ———. "Stephen Crane's Struggles." *Stephen Crane Newsletter* 1.3 (1967): 3–5. A journalist friend, Willis Brooks Hawkins, remembers the struggling days of Crane before *Red Badge.*

1.143   ———. "Stephen Crane at Claverack College and Hudson River Institute." *Stephen Crane Newsletter* 2.4 (1968): 1–5. Katz gleans information on Crane at Claverack from ten notes and bills from A. H. Flack to Mrs. Mary Helen Crane.

1.144   ———. "Stephen Crane Flinches." *Stephen Crane Newsletter* 3.1 (1968): 6. More memoirs by fellow journalist Willis Brooks Hawkins, this time about the Hubbard dinner.

1.145   ———. "Stephen Crane's Passport Applications, Parts I, II, III and IV." *Stephen Crane Newsletter* 3.1 (1968): 7–8; 3.2 (1968): 3–4; 3.4 (1968): 6–7; 4.1 (1969): 4–5. Photocopies of Crane's 1871, 1889, 1898, and 1900 applications.

1.146   ———. "How Elbert Hubbard Met Stephen Crane." *Stephen Crane Newsletter* 2.3 (1968): 8–12. Based on correspondence between Hubbard and Crane, Katz describes their meeting and subsequent relationship. Katz's account has recently been criticized by White (1.222).

1.147   ———. "Review [of Stallman's *Stephen Crane: A Biography*]." *American Literature* 40 (1969): 565–69. Katz concludes that unfortunately

Stallman's book (1.10) "may block for some years the responsible biography needed now."

1.148 _____. "Invited to the Philistine Banquet (Part I)." *Stephen Crane Newsletter* 4.4 (1970): 11–12. Apparently Katz planned to publish the invitation list for the Hubbard banquet. His list stops at "Brentano, Simon," and subsequent installments did not appear.

1.149 _____. "The Estate of Stephen Crane." *Studies in American Fiction* 10 (1982): 135–50. The last word on Crane's last will and testament; Katz sorts out the facts and figures and concludes that Crane's brother William performed his executor duties correctly.

1.150 _____. "Stephen Crane's Concept of Death." *Kentucky Review* 4.2 (1983): 49–55. Katz's conjectures that Crane's father's death (when Crane was eight) framed his concept of death: In Crane's fiction death is abrupt, without justice, and matter-of-fact. Several details about the Reverend Jonathan Townley Crane's accomplishments are provided.

1.151 KAUFFMAN, REGINALD WRIGHT. "The True Story of Stephen Crane." *Modern Culture* 12 (Oct. 1900): 143–45. An early effort to state correctly the events of Crane's life, especially the reception of the newspaper version of *Red Badge*.

1.152 KEET, ALFRED ERNEST. "'Stephen Crane: A New York Poet:' Who Through Starvation Achieved Success—But Too Late." *Bruno's Weekly* 11 (1916): 951–53. A brief, another starving-in-the-garret sketch of Crane. "He was a student at firsthand of the seamy side of life, an analyst of life's tragedies among the poor. His theme was the submerged tenth." This essay was also privately printed (50 copies) as *Stephen Crane: In Memoriam* in New York (no date given) and then reissued by the Folcroft Press (Folcroft, PA) in 1969.

1.153 KIRBY, DAVID. "The Measure of Man." *Times Literary Supplement* 4073 (24 Apr. 1981): 466. Crane is given passing comment.

1.154 KUNITZ, STANLEY J., and HOWARD HAYCRAFT. *American Authors, 1600–1900.* New York: Wilson, 1938. 188–90. Except for an error about Crane and Cora getting married, a competent sketch of Crane's life and a sound, if brief, commentary on his major works.

1.155 LINDER, LYLE D. "Applications from Social Sciences to Literary Biography: The Family World of Stephen Crane." *American Literary*

REALISM 7 (1974): 280–82. Linder argues that more study of Crane's family background and childhood is in order.

1.156   LINSON, CORWIN KNAPP. "Little Stories of 'Steve' Crane." *Saturday Evening Post* 117 (11 Apr. 1903): 20–21. Linson was one of Crane's closest friends. This abbreviated memoir contains numerous anecdotes of Crane's life and his struggles to break into print in the early days.

1.157   LITTLEDALE, CLARA. "Newark Discovers a Little Brick Shrine." *New York Herald* 15 Nov. 1925: 4. She describes the memorial plaque at Crane's birthplace, 14 Mulberry Place.

1.158   LYNN, KENNETH S. *William Dean Howells: An American Life*. New York: Harcourt Brace, 1970. 311–15. Standard stories of Howells's support (moral and critical) of Crane.

1.159   LYON, PETER. *Success Story: The Life and Times of S. S. McClure*. New York: Scribner's, 1963. Passim. Lyon, McClure's grandson, has written a volume of hagiography that must be read with skepticism, at least with regard to McClure's dealings with Crane. He kept the manuscript of *Red Badge* from January to November 1894 and was very tardy in paying for the stories his syndicate published. Lyon finds little fault in either of his grandfather's dealings with Crane.

1.160   MAGILL, FRANK N. "Stephen Crane, Biography." *Great Short Works of Stephen Crane*. Ed. James Colvert. New York: Harper and Row, 1968. 355–57. A brief sketch of Crane's life and works emphasizing naturalism and environmentalism in his thought.

1.161   MAJOR, STANLEY B. "No. 14 Mulberry Place." *The Polymnian* (of Newark Academy) 40 (1937): 4–7. A sketch of Crane's life, a drawing of him, and a picture of 14 Mulberry Place.

1.162   MARBLE, ANNIE RUSSELL. "Stephen Crane." *A Study of the Modern Novel*. New York: Appleton, 1928. 264–66. A short, unreliable biographical sketch followed by simplistic study-discussion questions on *Red Badge*.

1.163   MARSHALL, EDWARD. "Authors' Associations." *Manuscript* 1 (May 1901): 32–34. Recounts the early days of the "Lanthorne Club" with reminiscences of Howells and Irving Bacheller that mention Crane. See Stallman's *Stephen Crane: A Critical Bibliography* (14.3: 288).

1.164 MARTIN, THOMAS E. "Stephen Crane: Athlete and Author." *The Argot* (Syracuse University) 3.5 (1935): 1–2. Reminiscences of Crane at Syracuse including the usual comments on baseball and his visits to police court and the slums.

1.165 MATTHIESSEN, F. O. *Theodore Dreiser*. New York: William Sloane, 1951. Passim. Crane is treated in passing; interesting comments on Dreiser's publication of "A Mystery of Heroism" in his *Ev'ry Month*, though Dreiser seems never to "have had any feeling of close kinship with Crane's work."

1.166 MAURER, LEONARD. "[Letter About Crane's Birthplace]." *A Bookman's Weekly* 40 (1967): 652–53. A letter about Crane's birthplace in Newark and the deplorable conditions of the building on Mulberry Street.

1.167 MAURER, LEONARD, and SOL MALKIN. "[Stephen Crane's Birthplace]." *Antiquarian Bookman* 40.9 (1967): 652–53. An exchange of letters about Crane's birthplace to the effect that the house is long gone and the "Stephen Crane Playground" at 14 Mulberry Place is in a sad state.

1.168 MAYFIELD, JOHN S. "To Stephencraneites." *Courier* 5 (1965): 26. Mayfield calls to the attention of Crane scholars an article in the Syracuse student newspaper, the *Daily Orange* (12 November 1965), on Crane's student days.

1.169 ———. "S.C. at S. U." *Courier* 8 (1968): 8. Mayfield notes a half-dozen references to Crane in *The Onondagan,* the Syracuse University student annual for 1892.

1.170 MCBRIDE, HENRY. "Stephen Crane's Artist Friends." *Art News* 49 (1950): 46. Lively memoirs by an early friend of Crane, notable for anecdotes about unsold copies of *Maggie.*

1.171 MCCORMICK, LAWLOR. "If Stephen Crane Had Returned to Texas." *Bunker's Monthly* 1 (1928): 312–16. If Crane had gone to Texas (as a tuberculosis cure, according to Robert Barr) he could have recreated the inner experience of the men at the Alamo.

1.172 MENCKEN, H. L. "Stephen Crane." *A Menken Chrestomathy*. New York: Knopf, 1949. 496–97. A short section of this chapter discusses Crane in passing. Mencken celebrates "his eye for cold, glittering fact in an age of romantic illusion." Refashioned as "Sketches in Criticism" in *Literature in America,* ed. Philip Rahv, New York: Meridian, 1957, 303–4.

1.173 MORACE, ROBERT A. *"The Sketch's* 'Mr. Stephen Crane.'" *Studies in the Novel* 10 (1978): 154–55. Morace reprints an early English biographical sketch of Crane.

1.174 NEILSON, WILLIAM ALLEN, ed. "Stephen Crane." *Webster's Biographical Dictionary.* Springfield, MA: G. & C. Merriam, 1966. 363. A one-paragraph note.

1.175 NOXON, FRANK W. "The Real Stephen Crane." *Stepladder* 14 (1928): 4–9. A boyhood friend of Crane remembers his love of animals and his courage in war.

1.176 O'DONNELL, THOMAS F. "John B. Van Petten: Stephen Crane's History Teacher." *American Literature* 27 (1955): 196–202. Crane's history teacher at Claverack College as a chaplain of the 34th New York Volunteers had witnessed several large-scale battlefield panics providing Crane with the details he needed for *Red Badge.*

1.177 OLIVER, ARTHUR. "Jersey Memories—Stephen Crane." *Proceedings of the New Jersey Historical Society* 16 (1931): 454–63. Memoirs of a former newspaper apprentice with Crane; details of the firing of Crane and Townley following publication of "Parades and Entertainments" in the New York *Tribune,* 21 August 1892.

1.178 PAINE, RALPH D. "The Life and Art of Stephen Crane." *Bookman* 58 (1923): 470–71. A review essay on Beer's *Stephen Crane* (1.1); Paine is relieved that Crane has been rescued from gossip and rumor.

1.179 PATTEE, FRED LEWIS. "Shifting Currents in Fiction." *A History of American Literature Since 1970.* New York: Century, 1915. 397–98. Pattee dismisses Crane in a brief paragraph. Pattee holds that Crane was a "neurotic, intense" artist who "had no patience, no time for collecting materials."

1.180 PEASLEE, CLARENCE LOOMIS. "Stephen Crane's College Days." *The Monthly Illustrator and Home and Country* 13 (1896): 27–30. A fairly lengthy biographical sketch written just after the crest of Crane's *Red Badge* fame. Usual details about Crane at Syracuse plus a small photograph.

1.181 PECK, HARRY THURSTON. "Stephen Crane, Author of *The Black Riders, and Other Lines.*" *Bookman* 1 (1895): 229–30. Contemporary biographical sketch (along with a charcoal drawing) of Crane at the peak of his *Red Badge* fame. His command of the English language and his daring and terrible directness are singled out.

1.182 PHELPS, ROBERT, and PETER DEANE. "Related Events, Deaths: Stephen Crane." *The Literary Life: A Scrapbook Almanac of the*

Anglo-American Literary Scene from 1900 to 1950. New York: Farrar, Straus, 1968. 3–4. The authors begin their treatment of 1900 with a picture of Crane and comments about his "sudden departure."

1.183 PIZER, DONALD. "The Garland–Crane Relationship." *Huntington Library Quarterly* 24 (1960): 75–82. Though it is certain that Garland supported and influenced Crane, Garland's written comments on their relationship need to be sorted out and corrected. Pizer has done a masterful job of setting the record straight.

1.184 PRATT, LYNDON UPSON. "The Formal Education of Stephen Crane." *American Literature* 10 (1939): 460–71. A pioneering essay challenged the myth that Crane had little formal education. Pratt gives the details of Crane at Claverack and Lafayette Colleges and Syracuse University, concluding that Crane's "education may safely be called extensive." Pratt's assessment is an overstatement.

1.185 PRIAL, FRANK J. "Littered Lot His Memorial." *Newark Evening News* 5 June 1960. Short piece on the Crane homesite in Newark.

1.186 PUGH, EDWIN. "Stephen Crane." *Bookman* 74 (1924): 162–64. A review essay on Beer's *Stephen Crane* (1.1). Beyond Pugh's comments on Beer's book this piece is noteworthy. Pugh, a good friend of Crane's (seeing him frequently in England), provides interesting anecdotes; for example, he describes Crane's athletic prowess: "His hands were miracles of strength and cleverness. He could play hand-ball like a machine-gun." Also, this article contains a good picture of Crane.

1.187 RANDEL, WILLIAM PIERCE. "Crane, Stephen." *Collier's Encyclopedia.* Vol. 5. New York: Crowell-Collier, 1961. 616–17. Standard sketch.

1.188 RAY, MARTIN. "Joseph Conrad: His Letter to a Reviewer of *The Nigger.*" *Notes and Queries* 31 (1984): 505–6. A note about Conrad's defensiveness regarding his *The Nigger of the "Narcissus"* and Crane's *Red Badge.*

1.189 RICHARDS, ROBERT FULTON. "Crane, Stephen." *Concise Dictionary of American Literature.* New York: Philosophical Library, 1955. 34–35. A garden variety dictionary entry, complete with a telltale error: "Crane moved to England, and there *married* his loyal wife," Cora.

1.190 RICHTER, HEDDY A. "The Long Foreground of Corwin Knapp Linson's *My Stephen Crane.*" *Studies in the Novel* 10 (1978): 161–67. Richter discusses a series of letters from Linson to Hamlin Garland concerning the writing of *My Stephen Crane*. These letters remained unpublished until Edwin Cady edited and released Linson's memoirs in 1958.

1.191   SHLOSS, CAROL. "John Berryman on Stephen Crane: The Nature of Speculation in Biography." *Literature and Psychology* 13 (1972): 169–75. An essay on Berryman's *Stephen Crane* (1.2) that is critical of Berryman's Freudian conjectures.

1.192   SIDBURY, EDNA CRANE. "My Uncle, Stephen Crane, As I Knew Him." *The Literary Digest International Book Review* 4 (1926): 248–50. Fond, sugarcoated, warm reminiscences by the daughter of William Howe Crane, who finds some of Beer's portrait, *Stephen Crane* (1.1), especially that Crane swore and that he drank liquor, objectionable.

1.193   SLOANE, DAVID E. E. "Stephen Crane at Lafayette." *Resources for American Literary Studies* 2 (1972): 102–5. Reliable and detailed information on Crane's short stay at this engineering school. See also Robertson (1.10).

1.194   SMITH, ERNEST G. B. "Some Thoughts of Stephen Crane, '94." *The Lafayette Alumnus* 2.2 (1932): 6. Reminiscences of a classmate; tells the story of Crane's freshman hazing experiences. Compare with Robertson (1.10) and Sloane (1.193).

1.195   SMITH, M. ELLWOOD. "Stephen Crane, Ex-'94." *The Syracusan* 10 (1917): 2–7, 32. The tale of Crane's short stay at Syracuse and a few comments on his works. His poetry is especially noted and five of his poems are printed.

1.196   SOKOLOV, RAYMOND A. "Master of Realism." *Newsweek* 72 (12 Aug. 1968): 81–82. A review essay on Stallman's *Stephen Crane* (1.10) arguing that that Crane's sympathy with the poor was developed during his newspaper days.

1.197   SORRENTINO, PAUL. "Stephen and William Howe Crane: A Loan and Its Aftermath." *Resources for American Literature Study* 11 (1981): 101–8. From November 1898 to March 1899 Crane tried repeatedly to get a loan from his brother William. Sorrentino reprints and comments on four letters from Crane to William, which, he suggests, show an unreliable younger brother and a cautious, conservative senior sibling.

1.198   ——. "The Philistine Society's Banquet for Stephen Crane." *American Literary Realism* 15 (1982): 232–38. Sorrentino has marshaled all the known facts about the Philistine Society banquet that Elbert Hubbard arranged to toast Crane 19 December 1895. White's account (1.222) is even more complete.

1.199 ――――. "New Evidence on Stephen Crane at Syracuse." *Resources for the Study of American Literature* 15.2 (1985): 179–85. Sorrentino brings up to date what is known about Crane at Syracuse.

1.200 STALLMAN, ROBERT W. "Stallman's Crane." *CEA Critic* 32.9 (1970): 11–12. Stallman issues his rebuttal of the criticisms Gullason made in his *CEA Critic* (see 1.110) "nitpicking" review.

1.201 STANTON, THEODORE. "Stephen Crane and Frank Norris." *A Manual of American Literature.* Leipzig: Bernhard Tauchnitz, 1909. A predictable two-paragraph sketch on Crane and Norris in a reference book.

1.202 STARRETT, VINCENT. "Stephen Crane at Claverack." *Stephen Crane Newsletter* 2.1 (1976): 4. Memoirs about Crane at Claverack noting that he liked to sleep till the last possible moment in the morning.

1.203 STERN, MADELEINE B. "Stephen Crane and the Organ of Hope." *Markham Review* 6 (1977): 15–16. In 1900, Jessie Fowler in *Phrenological Journal* examined photographs of Crane and concluded that he had the right bumps on his head for a well-developed organ of hope.

1.204 STEVENS, WALLACE. *Letters of Wallace Stevens.* Ed. Holly Stevens. New York: Knopf, 1966. 41. A journal entry describing Stevens's impressions of Crane's funeral in New York City, 28 June 1900: It was badly conducted and poorly attended.

1.205 STRONKS, JAMES B. "Garland's Private View of Crane in 1898 (with a Postscript)." *American Literary Realism* 6 (1973): 249–50. Based on Garland's diary, Stronks argued that Crane's bohemianism put off the conventional and wholesome Garland.

1.206 TABER, HARRY P. "[Letter to Thomas Beer on Stephen Crane]." In Stallman's *Stephen Crane: A Critical Bibliography* (14.3: 310–12), a detailed letter by Taber on the Philistine Society banquet for Crane is reprinted. Though Stallman and others had put great stock in this letter, the full-length study by Bruce White (1.222) undercuts much of the substance of it.

1.207 ――――. "Letter to David Balch." *Stephen Crane: A Critical Bibliography* (13.4: 356–59). Stallman reproduces a letter to David Balch on the Hubbard dinner for Crane. Though Stallman regarded this letter as a critical landmark, recent scholarship (see especially White, 1.222) discounts this "witness."

1.208   THORP, CAROL, and CHRISTINE BAKER. "Stephen Crane at Syracuse." *Daily Orange* 12 Nov. 1968. The student newspaper at Syracuse deals with Crane's stay at Syracuse and the impact of his works.

1.209   TURNER, ARLIN. "Stephen Crane's Lifelong Experiment in Misery." *Virginia Quarterly Review* 44 (1968): 678–82. A review of Stallman's biography of Crane (1.10), which turns into reflections on Crane's personality—one of the best on that topic.

1.210   VAN DOREN, MARK. "Stephen Crane." *Nation* 16 Jan. 1924: 66. A rave review of Beer's *Stephen Crane* (1.1).

1.211   VOSBURG, R. G. "The Darkest Hour in the Life of Stephen Crane." *Criterion* 1 (1901): 26–27. Reliable memoirs about Crane by an artist-roommate in the Art Students' League building. The darkest hour was *Maggie*'s failure and waiting to find a publisher for *Red Badge*. Details about how (slowly and legibly) and when (between midnight and four or five o'clock) Crane did his writing. Reprinted in *Book Lover* 2 (1901): 338–39.

1.212   WARREN, DALE. "The Posthumous Fame of Stephen Crane." *Boston Transcript* 4 Sept. 1926. Photograph of a plaque of Crane's profile.

1.213   WASSERSTROM, WILLIAM. "Cagy John: Berryman as a Medicine Man." *Centennial Review* 12 (1968): 334–54. For those interested in Berryman's Freudian view of Crane, Wasserstrom gives us a Freudian view of Berryman.

1.214   WEINSTEIN, BERNARD. "Stephen Crane and New Jersey." *William Carlos Williams, Stephen Crane, Philip Freneau: Papers and Poems Celebrating New Jersey's Literary Heritage.* Ed. W. John Bauer. Trenton: New Jersey Historical Commission, 1989. 55–73. Weinstein traces Crane's New Jersey ancestors and makes brief comments on his early years and his education. Also to be found here are valuable analyses of Crane's newspaper articles on Asbury Park and Parkers, including his infamous dispatch on the Junior Order of the United American Mechanics parade.

1.215   WELLS, LESTER G. "Off the Press: By and about the Brothers." *Delta Upsilon Quarterly* 71.2 (1953): 89. Remarks on Stallman's *Stephen*

Crane: An Omnibus (2.16) plus a few details on Crane's association with the Syracuse University chapter of Delta Upsilon.

1.216 ———. "The Syracuse Days of Stephen Crane." *Syracuse* 10.2 (1959): 12–14, 40–42. The best single piece on Crane's brief stay at Syracuse University.

1.217 WERTHEIM, STANLEY. "Why Stephen Crane Left Claverack." *Stephen Crane Newsletter* 2.1 (1967): 5. Wertheim suggests that Crane went to Claverack to prepare for West Point but that he then left for Lafayette for a more practical curriculum—mine engineering.

1.218 ———. "Stephen Crane's Middle Name." *Stephen Crane Newsletter* 3.4 (1969): 2, 4. For a time while he was at Claverack, Crane gave himself the middle initial "T."

1.219 ———. "Stephen Crane Remembered." *Studies in American Fiction* 4 (1976): 45–64. Wertheim appraises and makes comments on four memoirs of Crane: by Nelson Green, Walter Parker, Mark Barr, and Cora Crane.

1.220 ———. "Stephen Crane in the Shadow of the Parthenon." *Columbia Library Columns* 32 (1983): 3–13. On Crane's dealings with his brother William Crane, especially on Crane's skating around whether or not he and Cora were married.

1.221 WHEELER, POST, and HALLIE ERMINE RIVES. "Rebels in Embryo; Sign O'Lanthorn." *Dome of Many-Coloured Glass*. New York: Doubleday, 1955. 19–22, 98–104. Interesting memoirs by one of Crane's early newspaper friends. Tells of Crane smoking and drinking at the age of ten (at a Temperance rally—Wheeler's mother and Crane's were temperance leaders) and gives information on the Lanthorn Club, a New York literary club they both belonged to.

1.222 WHITE, BRUCE A. "Stephen Crane and the 'Philistine.'" *Elbert Hubbard's "The Philistine: A Periodical of Protest": A Major American "Little Magazine."* Lanham, NY: UP of America, 1989. 52–87. A full-scale investigation of Hubbard, his relations with Crane being the central chapter of this monograph. White argues that Hubbard was an important booster for Crane and he examines the twenty-two items Hubbard published for Crane, concluding that the "Hubbard-Crane relationship was mutually beneficial." He sorts out the details of the Philistine testimonial dinner arguing that Crane was a rising but not well-known writer at that time; "the fact remains that Hubbard recognized Crane's originality [special attention is given to his poems], was supportive of his individuality, and intuited the importance of his work." A much more detailed account than Katz (1.146) or Sorrentino (1.198); calls into question the accounts of Taber (2.206) and Balch (1.40).

1.223   WICKHAM, HARVEY. "Stephen Crane at College." *American Mercury* 7 (1926): 291–97. Memoirs of a Claverack classmate about Crane's college days there.

1.224   WILLIAMS, HERBERT P. "Mr. Crane as Literary Artist." *Illustrated American* 20 (1896): 126. A very early interview with Crane; notes on his fascination with color, his impressionism, and his workplace, "an enormous room at the top of a house in the heart of the city, in the shopping district."

1.225   WILSON, EDMUND. "A Vortex of the Nineties: Stephen Crane." *New Republic* 37 (2 Jan. 1924): 109–14. A rave review of Beer's *Stephen Crane* (1.1) crediting Beer with rescuing Crane from vicious gossip. Reprinted in *The Shores of Light: A Literary Chronicle of the Twenties and Thirties*. New York: Farrar, Straus, 1952. 109–14.

1.226   WOLFE, T. F. *Literary Rambles at Home and Abroad.* Philadelphia: Lippincott, 1901. 46. Describes Crane's birthplace. See Stallman's *Stephen Crane: A Critical Bibliography* (14.3: 289).

1.227   WOOLLCOTT, ALEXANDER. "Stephen Crane." *Enchanted Isles.* New York: Putnam, 1924. 130–35. A brief, favorable notice of Beer's *Stephen Crane* (1.1).

Also on Crane's life and personality see the following:

2.1–2.19	9.64
2.34	9.66
2.38	9.68
2.49	9.69
2.98	9.71–9.74
2.112	9.76
2.124	9.86
2.187	9.97
2.188	9.100
2.204	13.3

2
General Criticism

Overview

BOOKS. Nineteen full-length studies are annotated in this section. They fall into two categories: thematic examinations and monographs pursuing a single thesis. In the former category the volumes by Bergon (2.3), Cady (2.4), Dooley (2.5), Halliburton (2.9), and Stallman (2.16) deserve special mention; in the latter, the studies by Holton (2.10), LaFrance (1.13), Nagel (2.14), and Solomon (2.15) merit recognition. Cady's book (2.4) is the best place to start.

ARTICLES. From the beginning Crane was considered a naturalist even though, early on, it was clear that some of his works did not conform to such interpretation. In the nearly 100 intervening years tremendous scholarly effort has been expended in claims that Crane was a prototypical realist, a doctrinaire naturalist, the first true impressionist, or a thoroughgoing ironist, and, finally, that Crane was so idiosyncratic than his works resist categorization. Across that broad spectrum the following essays are noteworthy:

BEER 2.38	Levenson 2.133
Colvert 2.63	Schneider 2.173
Conder 2.64	Stallman 2.186
Edwards 2.75	Stein 2.193
GREENFIELD 2.86	VAN DOREN 2.204
JOHNSON 2.112	WELLS 2.210
Katz 2.117	Westbrook 2.215
LaFrance 2.129	

All fifteen are excellent; five are especially concise and worth special attention.

Books

2.1   AHNEBRINK, LARS. *The Beginnings of Naturalism in American Fiction.*
       Uppsala: American Institute of the University of Uppsala, 1950. 505.
       Ahnebrink's book is subtitled "A Study of the Works of Hamlin
       Garland, Stephen Crane, and Frank Norris with Special Reference to
       Some European Influences." He sees the following European influ-
       ences on or "sources" for Crane: *Red Badge*—Tolstoy's *Sebastapol* and
       Zola's *La Debacle; Maggie*—Zola's *L'Assommoir; George's Mother,*
       Turgenev's *Fathers and Sons;* and *The Monster*—Ibsen's *The Enemy of
       the People.* As scholars gradually abandoned the assumption that Crane
       was a naturalist and as more American influences on Crane were
       identified, a general endorsement of Ahnebrink's thesis softened.
       Though somewhat dated, this volume is still valuable and worthy of
       study, especially the sections on Garland and Norris. Reprinted in
       1961 by Russell and Russell (New York).

2.2   BASSAN, MAURICE, ed. *Stephen Crane: A Collection of Critical Essays.*
       Englewood Cliffs, NJ: Prentice-Hall, 1967. 184. Representative criti-
       cism: two sketches on Crane's life, six general discussions on his whole
       corpus, as well as ten commentaries on individual works. (All these
       essays are reprints and are treated elsewhere in this bibliography.) With
       regard to his short introduction (1–11), Bassan speculates that despite
       himself Crane was, to the end, a preacher's kid (PK), who valued the
       "romantic" ideals "of the truth of 'primitive' Christianity, of the
       nobility of military behavior, of the excellence of the sportsman's
       code, of the high purpose of art." See Cady (2.4) for more on Crane as
       a PK.

2.3   BERGON, FRANK. *Stephen Crane's Artistry.* New York: Columbia UP,
       1975. xi+174. A thorough and helpful examination of all Crane's
       important works from the point of view of his style. In particular
       Bergon analyzes the techniques Crane uses to disorient the reader so
       that common ways of seeing things are called into question. In place
       of ordinary experiences Bergon finds Crane seeking elusive, strange,
       demonic, even hallucinatory perceptions.

2.4   CADY, EDWIN H. *Stephen Crane.* New Haven, CT: College and
       University Press, 1962. 186. This short book, slightly revised in 1980
       and reissued by Twayne, is found in virtually every library. A suave and
       reliable introduction to Crane's life and work. Though he describes
       Crane as "an uncrystallized experimenter" and "a youthful pluralist"
       most of Cady's observations can be related to his contention that
       Crane was a PK—a preacher's kid. Cady's volume is also valuable for

the insight he gives his readers into America's intellectual climate during the 1890s.

With regard to the 1980 version of this volume, Cady's new introductory chapter describes his view of the impact of Crane scholarship over the past twenty years as he decries the nastiness of some of the feuds and the ongoing controversy over various editions of *Maggie* and *Red Badge*. He also acknowledges the futility of putting Crane into conventional literary categories and the growing awareness of the complexity and elusiveness of Crane's character. On this last point Cady presents a retouched photo of Crane and then the rather different original. Beyond this new chapter, however, Cady's revisions of the 1962 version are very minor, generally the deletion or addition of a paragraph, a sentence, or a clause.

2.5 DOOLEY, PATRICK K. *The Pluralistic Philosophy of Stephen Crane.* Urbana: U of Illinois P, 1992. An exposition and analysis of Crane's philosophy from a consideration of his entire oeuvre. This volume examines Crane's thought with close attention to his fundamental metaphysical and epistemological positions as well as his ethics, social philosophy, and humanism.

The full range of Crane's output has been examined. Of particular interest are metaphysical and epistemological analyses of several middle works—"An Episode of War," "The Clan of No-Name," for instance. *The Monster* is the focus of the ethics chapter, and Crane's poetry is treated at length in the final chapter, "Philosopher-Poet."

2.6 FRIED, MICHAEL. *Realism, Writing, Disfiguration: On Thomas Eakins and Stephen Crane.* Chicago: Chicago UP, 1987. xvi+215. Fried's earlier jumbo-length essay, "Realism, Writing, and Disfiguration in Thomas Eakins's *Gross Clinic,* with a Postscript on Stephen Crane's Upturned Faces" (*Representations* 9 [1985]: 33–104), was expanded into a book. In both versions the material on Crane *is* a postscript.

Fried's controversial thesis: Whenever an upturned face occurs in Crane's works (which is quite often) Crane is thematizing the act of writing. Beyond his questionable thesis, many Crane scholars have been put off by Fried's convoluted and supercharged prose. The final straw, however, is the contention that Crane's fascination with words that have the letters "sc" in them—for several pages these letters are put in boldface for us—proves Crane's obsession with the physical act of writing. This volume created a great stir and much heat, but it has not added much to our understanding of Crane. For a full-scale negative critique see James Nagel's review in *American Literature* 60 (1988): 479–81 and Carney (2.59); for a positive reaction see Janet Malcolm (2.136).

2.7   GIBSON, DONALD B. *The Fiction of Stephen Crane*. Carbondale:
       Southern Illinois UP, 1968. xviii+169. Though Gibson's monograph
       is now somewhat dated it was a breakthrough volume. Gibson treats
       all of Crane's major works, examining each to test the extent of its
       espousal of naturalistic determinism. Gibson holds that Crane had no
       central vision but that he responded to the concerns of late nineteenth-
       century America: Darwinism, environmentalism, and the closing of
       the frontier. Gibson concludes: "'The Open Boat' being the
       highpoint in his brief career . . . [he is] our greatest minor author."

2.8   GULLASON, THOMAS A., ed. *Stephen Crane's Career: Perspectives and
       Evaluations*. New York: New York UP, 1972. xi+532. Gullason's
       Introductions (1–5, 9, 53–56, 159–60, 219–20, 281–84, 311–14,
       407–9) offer general information on Crane's family heritage (bio-
       graphical and literary), the sources of his art, and comments on
       representative criticism from Crane's contemporaries, the middle
       years (1920–1950), and late-breaking (1960–1970) reaction.
       Gullason then reprints many of the best secondary pieces on Crane's
       life and works.
             Gullason's volume also contains a special article, "Stephen
       Crane's Short Stories: The True Road" (470–85), which offers general
       comments on the critical reaction to Crane's noted short stories. He
       observes that Crane's "characters do not develop; they simply react";
       he adds that Crane has an "amazing feeling for particulars" and that
       the children he portrays are mysterious to their parents.

2.9   HALLIBURTON, DAVID. *The Color of the Sky: A Study of Stephen
       Crane*. Cambridge: Cambridge UP, 1989. 358. A long, close-grained
       analysis of all (even *The O'Ruddy* and *The Third Violet* are discussed)
       of Crane's longer works as well as a great many of his shorter tales and
       sketches. (Only a half-dozen journalistic dispatches are treated.)
             No single expository thesis is advanced; instead, Halliburton uses
       "not only the many insights provided by previous students of Crane,
       but [also] ideas from intellectual and social history, philology, lexicog-
       raphy, stylistics, and philosophical discourse." The chapters on
       George's Mother and Crane's poetry are especially helpful. Several
       painstaking examinations of Crane's language, syntax, and rhythm are
       offered. For instance, the famous openings of *Red Badge* ("The cold
       passed reluctantly from the earth . . .") and of "The Open Boat"
       ("No one knew the color of the sky") are treated in great depth.

2.10   HOLTON, MILNE. *Cylinder of Vision: The Fiction and Journalistic
       Writing of Stephen Crane*. Baton Rouge: Louisiana State UP, 1972.
       xi+353. A detailed and sophisticated examination of Crane's explora-
       tion of "differences between human apprehension of reality and
       reality itself." It is Crane's wrestling with the difficulties that observers

(as well as participants) have in apprehending the world that interests Holton as he treats all of Crane's major works as well as his best short stories. Holton concludes that for Crane reality is probably indecipherable and, as a consequence, Crane flirted with "an ethic of the absurd."

2.11   KATZ, JOSEPH, ed. *Stephen Crane in Transition: Centenary Essays*. De Kalb: Northern Illinois UP, 1972. xii+247. Katz's volume was very important in Crane scholarship. In his introduction (xi–xii) Katz explains that the title of the collection was carefully chosen: "Now, however, it seem that Stephen Crane is at last in transition from a legendary figure to comprehensible author." Also mentioned is that the essays in Katz's collection look at all of Crane's work; *Red Badge* is important, but so too are several other works. All the articles in this volume are annotated elsewhere in this bibliography.

2.12   KNAPP, BETTINA L. *Stephen Crane*. New York: Ungar, 1987. ix+198. A general account of Crane and his works. Knapp's study relies heavily on Stallman's *Stephen Crane* (1.10) and *Stephen Crane: Letters* (13.2) and several dozen pieces of shorter secondary literature. No clear theme or focus is evident; Knapp surveys Crane's most important works with innocuous broad-stroke comments. There is, however, one interesting claim: As *The O'Ruddy* would make a good adventure movie it deserves a more sympathetic reading.

2.13   LAFRANCE, MARSTON. *A Reading of Stephen Crane*. Oxford: Clarendon, 1971. x+272. A careful, insightful, full-length study of Crane's ironic point of view. LaFrance is keen on explicating how Crane understood the relationships between the external world and our experience, and between the world of facts and the ethical imperatives we respond to. LaFrance concludes that the world of human experience functions at considerable distance from the amoral world of physical facts and mechanical events. Second, since the world of our experience depends on our "weak mental machinery" humans never totally overcome the illusions and partial values resulting from the human perspective. LaFrance examines all Crane's major works in light of his theses; though his readings are not all or equally compelling, they are interesting and worth consideration and reflection.

LaFrance's study is akin to Milne Holton, *Cylinder of Vision* (2.10), who stresses Crane's exploration of the impact of each individual's position and perspective on the world each experiences.

2.14   NAGEL, JAMES. *Stephen Crane and Literary Impressionism*. University Park: Penn State UP, 1980. x+190. A landmark book on Crane. Early categorizations of Crane as a doctrinaire realist and/or naturalist were never satisfactory. Though Crane scholars attempted to move away from those labels, they had no clear alternative tag. For many, Nagel's contention that impressionism is the key to Crane's work filled that void.

Nagel begins with a discussion of impressionistic art, from which, he proposes, "the characters in impressionistic fiction are constantly in a state of having to interpret the world around them and to distinguish the 'real' from their own views of it." It is not just the limited and perspectival situation of human experiencers but also the opaqueness of reality that Nagel finds at the core of Crane's works: Both "the ineluctable flux in human perceptions of even the most stable object [and also that] reality is a matter of perception, it is unstable, everchanging, elusive, inscrutable." The central sections of Nagel's study are an examination of all Crane's major works, best short stories, and tales in light of impressionism. Nagel's thesis has not been universally adopted but it has caused Crane scholars to reread Crane and to rethink their own positions.

2.15   SOLOMON, ERIC. *Stephen Crane: From Parody to Realism.* Cambridge, MA: Harvard UP, 1966. 301. Solomon's thesis is provoking, often illuminating, but by the end, forced. He proposes that "far from being a reporter, or a war novelist, or an uneducated genius, Stephen Crane, I contend, was that most conscious of literary artificers, a parodist." When Solomon casts about for nineteenth-century genres that might have been Crane's targets he finds several: *Maggie* is a parody of melodramatic slum treatises, *Red Badge* debunks romantic war novels, *George's Mother* turns Horatio Alger's success stories upside down, *The Monster* satirizes small-town innocence and safety, and his Western tales are dime novels "writ small." Though Solomon's focus on parody provides insights into some of Crane's works, it ill fits, even misfits, others. Meanwhile the theme of the movement of parody to realism gets lost in the shuffle. See Frohock (3.67) for a critical review of Solomon's monograph.

2.16   STALLMAN, ROBERT W., ed. *Stephen Crane: An Omnibus.* New York: Knopf, 1952. xlv+703. Stallman's large volume reprints the best of Crane's works: novels, tales, short stories, poems, and letters. Interspersed are historical, textual, and thematic comments (3–20, 175–224, 373–78, 415–20, 479–85, 533–37, 565–75, 581–86). The common denominator of Stallman's critical remarks is the contention that religious symbolism (see 3.215) is the key to Crane. The *Omnibus* introductions and notes were reprinted in a shortened paperback version, *Stephen Crane: Stories and Tales* (Knopf [Vantage], 1955), that also contained "for the first time portions of the earliest known manuscript of *The Red Badge of Courage* and [the] first American publication of the final handwritten manuscript." With reference to the latter, Stallman initiated the, by now, perennial questions: Which version of *Red Badge* has superior literary merit and/or which version did Crane really intend?

2.17   WEATHERFORD, RICHARD M. *Stephen Crane: The Critical Heritage*. London: Routledge, 1973. xviii+343. This volume is essential for understanding the contemporary critical reception that Crane "enjoyed." Virtually all the significant reviews of all Crane's works are reprinted. Weatherford's Introduction (1–34) convincingly establishes that until nearly 1950 critical reaction focused on Crane's personality rather than his works. Above all, Weatherford's general survey of literary criticism from 1893 to 1926 is worth the price of the book.

2.18   WOLFORD, CHESTER A. *Stephen Crane: A Study of the Short Fiction*. Boston: Twayne, 1989. xv+154. A general survey of Crane's short works aimed at nihilistic, skeptical Crane: "The predominant theme of Crane's fiction is the conflict between chaos and order, that of humanity's puny efforts to survive, to shore up fragments of order against a universe ruled by an indifferent, inexorable chaos." Beyond excerpts of some of Crane's most telling letters and his selection of noted literary criticism, Wolford's book is a good resource for comments on little-analyzed stories such as "The Reluctant Voyagers," "Opium's Varied Dreams," "Moonlight in the Snow," "The Wise Men," and "A Mystery of Heroism."

2.19   _____. *The Anger of Stephen Crane: Fiction and the Epic Tradition*. Lincoln: U of Nebraska P, 1983. xvi+169. An examination of "formalism in Crane—his use of myth, epic and literary tradition in general." Wolford argues that Crane's best works are epic and his lesser ones fall short because they lack "the universalizing qualities" that come from classic myths.

     Wolford's chapters on *Red Badge* and Crane's western stories are his most convincing. The view that Crane's best works are epic is shared by Barbara Howard Meldrum, who reprinted Wolford's chapter "Classic Myth Versus Realism in Crane's 'The Bride Comes to Yellow Sky'" in her *Under the Sun: Myth and Realism in Western American Literature*, Troy, NY: Whitson, 1985.

Articles and Book Chapters

2.20   "Badge of Courage." *Times Literary Supplement* 8 June 1951: 356. Review essay on Berryman's *Stephen Crane* (1.2); complains about excessive Freudianism.

2.21   "English Views of Stephen Crane." *Literary Digest* 21 (1900): 12. A selection of typical reviews of the "late Mr. Stephen Crane" stressing his study of characters under "special moments of stress and emotion."

2.22   "Man in Search of a Hero." *Time* 25 Dec. 1950: 58–59. A review of Berryman's Stephen Crane (1.2), which argues that Crane liberated American fiction "from the cocoon of euphemism and sentimentality."

2.23   "The Revival of Interest in Stephen Crane." *Current Opinion* 76 (Jan. 1924): 39–40. An assessment of the impact of Beer's biography (1.1) that stresses Crane's honesty and literary integrity. Also includes a small photograph.

2.24   "Stephen Crane." *Encyclopedia Americana*. 1952. Vol. 8: 155. A one-paragraph biography.

2.25   "Stephen Crane." *Encyclopedia Americana*. 1964. Vol. 8: 155. Standard reference-book sketch; contains the error that *Maggie* was first published in 1892, not 1893.

2.26   "Stephen Crane." *Encyclopedia Americana*. 1990. Vol. 8: 150–51. A two-column sketch; interesting comments on Crane's "uncompromising realism [which is] often more impressionistic than photographic." Mistakenly states that Crane and Cora "were married."

2.27   "Stephen Crane." *Encyclopedia Britannica*. 1970. Vol. 7: 366. A one-paragraph note.

2.28   "Stephen Crane." *Poole's Index to Periodical Literature,* Supplements, 1882–1906. Vol. 4: 138; vol. 5: 141. Numerous one-line citations dealing with Crane and his works. For those who wish to pursue the matter see *Cumulative Author Index for Poole's Index to Periodical Literature.* Ed. C. Edward Wall. Ann Arbor: Pierian, 1971: 100.

2.29   AARON, DANIEL. "Stephen Crane." *Hudson Review* 4 (1951): 471–73. A review essay on Berryman's *Stephen Crane* (1.2). Aaron compliments Berryman on his grasp of Crane's "sense of what the surface betrays." Several interesting comments on Crane's impressionism.

2.30   ADAMS, JAMES DONALD. "Winds for the Sail." *The Shape of Books to Come.* New York: Viking, 1944. 44–53. A surmise on the influence of Zola's naturalism on Crane; brief comments on *Maggie* and *Red Badge.*

2.31 AHNEBRINK, LARS. "Toward Naturalism in American Fiction." *Moderna Sprak* 53 (1959): 365–72. A summary version of Ahnebrink's contention that Crane (Norris, and Garland) are strict, pessimistic determinists. See 2.1 for the full development of his thesis.

2.32 ALLEN, WALTER. "Bret Harte, Bierce, Frank Norris, Garland, Crane, O. Henry." *The Short Story in English.* Oxford: Clarendon, 1981. 51–60. A broad-brush sketch; "The Bride Comes to Yellow Sky" and "The Open Boat" receive a passing mention.

2.33 APPLEJOY, PETRONIUS. "Stephen Crane Is News in 1940." *Catholic World* 151 (1940): 586–94. A fond, reverent tribute to Crane, especially his skill with indirect moral comment as opposed to other naturalists' less effective, preachy moralizing.

2.34 BARNEY, E. C. "Stephen Crane." *Overland Monthly* 90 (1932): 309. A belated tribute to Crane as a realist of life's horrible side.

2.35 BAUER, W. JOHN. Introduction. *William Carlos Williams, Stephen Crane, Philip Freneau: Papers and Poems Celebrating New Jersey's Literary Heritage.* Ed. W. John Bauer. Trenton: New Jersey Historical Commission, 1989. 51–54. Bauer describes "New Jersey's second Literary Heritage Conference, 'The Worlds of Stephen Crane,' that took place on November 1, 1980, at the New Jersey Historical Society and the Public Library in Newark and included an afternoon visit to Evergreen Cemetery, Hillside, where the author is buried. The following pages present the scholarly papers and commemorative poems written for the occasion." (These papers and poems are annotated elsewhere in this bibliography.) Of special note, in Bauer's piece, is information on all the film adaptations of Crane's works: "The Blue Hotel," "Three Miraculous Soldiers," "The Upturned Face," *The Monster,* and *The Red Badge of Courage,"* plus a radio broadcast version of "The Open Boat" and an opera version of "The Bride Comes to Yellow Sky."

2.36 BATES, H. E. "Stephen Crane: A Neglected Genius." *Bookman* 81 (1931): 10–11. An early attempt to revive Crane that bemoans Crane's decline, not in America, but in England. Although Bates celebrates Crane's "economy" of material he finds that Crane fell prey to the danger of mixing reporting with fiction. A nice photo is included.

2.37 BEAVER, HAROLD. "With Desperate Resolution." *Times Literary Supplement* 20–26 January 1989: 55–56. An essay review of *The Correspondence of Stephen Crane* (13.3). Beaver objects to the editors' decision to move the suspected Beer letters to an appendix—for these apocryphal letters "echo the humour and imagery of Crane's authentic fiction." Beaver's essay ends with a good sketch of Crane's last years in England.

2.38   BEER, THOMAS. "Fire Feathers." *Saturday Review of Literature* 2 (1925): 425–27. An essay on the Follett edition of *The Work of Stephen Crane.* One of the best short, general introductions to Crane and his work. Stunning comments on Crane's deliberate intelligence, his discipline and intense restraint, and his cool detachment. Unlike almost no one else Beer recognized the great value of "War Memories," calling it "the last rally of his astonishing talent." Note: The *Saturday Review of Books'* high opinion of Beer's piece was underscored by reprinting it as "The Works of Stephen Crane" in *Designed for Reading: An Anthology Drawn from "The Saturday Review of Literature, 1924–1934,"* ed. Henry Seidel Canby (New York: Macmillan, 1934), 253–262.

2.39   ———. *The Mauve Decade: American Life at the End of the Nineteenth-Century.* New York: Knopf, 1926. Passim. A breezy, ancedotal history with passing comments on Crane and *Maggie* and his Western sketches.

2.40   BELASCO, DAVID. "The Genius of Stephen Crane." *Metropolitan Magazine* 12 (1900): 666. The tragedy of his premature death. Interesting comments about his tense dramatic prose, suggesting that *Maggie* or *Red Badge* could be transcribed readily into plays.

2.41   BENDER, BERT. "Hanging Stephen Crane in the Impressionist Museum." *Journal of Aesthetics and Art Criticism* 35 (1976): 47–55. An expanded treatment of the suggestion by H. G. Wells that Crane is an impressionist. Some interesting comments on Crane's use of color to evoke moods.

2.42   BENET, WILLIAM ROSE. "Crane, Stephen [Townley]." *The Readers Encyclopedia.* Ed. William Benet. New York: Crowell, 1965. 232–33. A typical reference book sketch.

2.43   BENFEY, CHRISTOPHER. "The Courage of Stephen Crane." *New York Review of Books* 16 March 1989: 31–34. An essay in response to the issue of *Stephen Crane: Prose and Poetry* (12.11) and *The Correspondence of Stephen Crane* (13.3). Comments on Crane's penchant for crisis situations that required courage and produced comradeship; calls attention to the value of his newspaper sketches.

2.44 BERTHOFF, WARNER. *The Ferment of Realism: American Literature, 1884–1919.* New York: Free Press, 1965. 227–235 and passim. The volume is a general survey of some twenty authors. Berthoff's style and helpfulness can be estimated by his cryptic summary of Crane: "the best of it [Crane's work] must be granted that minimal integrity of voice and registered perception the securing of which in the general slackness of the 90's, was bound to be a precedent of genuine value."

2.45 BLANKENSHIP, RUSSELL. "Naturalism: Stephen Crane." *American Literature as an Expression of the National Mind.* Ed. Russell Blankenship. New York: Holt, 1931. 521–27. Typical survey treatment: Crane was our pioneer naturalist and in *Red Badge* "American naturalism has its first triumph." Though a revised edition of Blankenship's volume was released in 1949, the Crane section remained the same.

2.46 BLODGETT, HAROLD. "Stephen Crane." *Chambers Encyclopedia.* 1966. Vol. 4: 212. Typical three-paragraph sketch except for comments that stress Crane's "able studies of men before danger."

2.47 BLOOM, HAROLD. Introduction. *Stephen Crane: Modern Critical Views.* Ed. Harold Bloom. New York: Chelsea House, 1987. 1–6. A quick-dash introduction to a reprinting of eight articles and/or book chapters representative of modern criticism of Crane. (All these pieces are described elsewhere in this bibliography.) Bloom cites Crane's irony, his originality, and his debt to Kipling. Bloom uses the identical six-page introduction for his *Stephen Crane's "The Red Badge of Courage": Modern Critical Interpretations* (3.18).

2.48 BRADBURY, MALCOLM. "Art and Reality in Stephen Crane." *Journal of American Studies (UK)* 2 (1968): 117–20. Broad-stroke comments on Crane's "worldview" wondering whether he believes in an objective reality.

2.49 BRADLEY, SCULLEY, et al. "Stephen Crane." *The American Tradition in Literature. Vol. 2.* New York: Norton, 1967. 816–18. A general essay focused on Crane as "the herald of the twentieth-century revolution in literature. . . . he made a clean break with the past in his selection of material, his craftsmanship, and his point of view." The editors also reprint several poems, "The Open Boat," and "The Bride Comes to Yellow Sky."

2.50 BROOKS, VAN WYCK. "New York: East Side." *The Confident Years.* New York: Dutton, 1952. 129–41. A section of a survey chapter. Nothing remarkable except comments to the effect that Crane's technique leaves most of the deductions and the inferences to the reader.

2.51   BRUCCOLI, MATTHEW J. "Review of Stallman's *Stephen Crane.*" *Stephen Crane Newsletter* 3.2 (1968): 9–10. A nasty review consisting of a list of some two dozen errors. I have included this review to give some indication of the bad blood between Stallman and other Crane scholars. See Stallman's "That Crane, That Albatross around My Neck: A Self-Interview" (2.190) for his side of the feud.

2.52   BUDD, LOUIS J. "Objectivity and Low Seriousness in American Naturalism." *Prospects* 1 (1975): 41–61. A long, thoughtful examination of naturalism's (especially Norris's) "ideals of fully disciplined objectivity and respect for any level of subject." With regard to Crane, "though determined to set down man's feckless vacuity, precocious Stephen Crane had quickly moved to add vibrancy through an arresting style."

2.53   _____. "Review of Stallman's *Stephen Crane.*" *Modern Fiction Studies* 4 (1968): 490–92. Included as a sample of an even-handed review of Stallman's *Stephen Crane* (1.10) which bypassed "the feud." Explains how Crane's complex character—his posturing versus his talk of honesty—must be carefully assessed.

2.54   BURKE, W. J., and W. D. HOWE. "Stephen Crane." *American Authors and Books: 1640–Present.* New York: Crown, 1962. 165. A one-paragraph entry on Crane's dates and main works.

2.55   CADY, EDWIN H. *The Light of Common Day: Realism in American Fiction.* Bloomington: Indiana UP, 1971. Passim. A well-regarded volume aimed at a definition of "realism." Scattered comments on Crane's realism and its difference from that of other realists, especially Howells. With regard to *Maggie,* Cady contends that "moral rather than physical violence lies at the heart of the book."

2.56   CAIRNS, WILLIAM B. "Recent Years: Stephen Crane." *A History of American Literature.* New York: Oxford UP, 1912. 473–74. Crane is treated as a minor figure of whom Cairns reports "his reputation has faded and it is doubtful that it will be revived." Some things have definitely changed since World War I! (Note: They had not changed by the 1930 revised edition of Cairns's volume.)

2.57   CALLAHAN, ROBERT. "Moral Rearmament as Mobilized Counterfantasy." *West Coast Review* 7 (1972): 53–59. I have included this item because it appears on several Crane checklists. The piece is actually a contentious and confused review of Marston LaFrance's *A Reading of Stephen Crane* (2.13). Little on moral rearmament or Crane will be found here.

2.58 CARGILL, OSCAR. "American Naturalism." *Intellectual America: Ideas on the March*. New York: Macmillan, 1941. 82–89. A brief section on Crane in an outdated discussion that worries about naturalism versus realism tags. *Maggie* is "smartly written . . . undisguised naturalism." "Open Boat" and "Blue Hotel" are singled out for praise.

2.59 CARNEY, RAYMOND. "Crane and Eakins." *Partisan Review* 55 (1988): 464–73. A review essay on Fried's *Realism, Writing, Disfiguration: On Thomas Eakins and Stephen Crane* (2.6). A harsh criticism of Fried's study: his fixation with the bizarre, his stress on melodrama, and his argumentativeness. "In this linguistic hothouse, everything is extraordinary and bizarre. Nothing is in the midrange of human experience."

2.60 CHELIFER [ROBERT HUGHES]. "The Rise of Stephen Crane." *Godey's Magazine* Sept. 1897: 317–19. An early review of *Maggie, Black Riders, George's Mother,* and *Red Badge*. Contains insightful and perceptive remarks plus some humorous handwringing about Crane's flagrant and desecrating false grammar.

2.61 COLVERT, JAMES B. "The Origins of Stephen Crane's Literary Creed." *University of Texas Studies in English* 34 (1955): 179–88. This is the first contribution of one of the most distinguished of Crane scholars. He argues that it is not the case that Crane had no literary apprenticeship or that he modeled himself after Zola and Tolstoy. Instead Colvert argues that Crane read, at an extremely impressionable age, Kipling's "The Light That Failed" and thereafter adopted a literary creed that included the value of direct personal experience, absolute honesty, and stress on colors. For the contrary view of Crane's literary education see Levenson (2.133).

2.62 _____. "Structure and Theme in Stephen Crane's Fiction." *Modern Fiction Studies* 5 (1959): 199–208. The thesis that Crane's technique involves a contrasting of two perspectives, those of actor and spectator, is convincingly posed. Further, Colvert argues that Crane's heroes move from vanity and self-conceit as actors to distance and competence as spectators. *Red Badge* and "The Open Boat" are paradigms of this technique but Colvert shows its application to other works, too.

2.63 ———. "Stephen Crane." *American Realists and Naturalists*. Vol. 12 of *Dictionary of Literary Biography*. Ed. Donald Pizer and Earl N. Harbert. Detroit: Gale Research, 1982. 100–124. A long introductory sketch that ably combines biography and literary analysis. Colvert argues that a "radical sense of man's alienation in a problematic universe" is the central theme in all of Crane's works. Several pictures as well as manuscript samples are included.

2.64 CONDER, JOHN J. "Stephen Crane and the Necessary Fiction." *Naturalism in American Fiction: The Classic Phase*. Lexington: UP of Kentucky, 1984. 22–68. Conder refuses to give up the contention that Crane is a naturalist. After a general discussion of the concept of literary naturalism, his monograph takes up Crane, Norris, Dreiser, Dos Passos, Steinbeck, and Faulkner. In the Crane chapter Condor argues for strict and often a dark Hobbesian pessimism in "The Blue Hotel," *Maggie,* and *Red Badge*. While he has an easier time with these three works, he has to struggle very hard to sustain his thesis with regard to "The Open Boat."

2.65 CONN, PETER. "An Age of Literary Enterprise." *Literature in America: An Illustrated History*. Cambridge: Cambridge UP, 1989. 231–94. A survey chapter on late nineteenth-century American literature. The section on Crane (285–89) depicts him as a Darwinian naturalist "fascinated with randomness and determinism."

2.66 COWLEY, MALCOLM. "Naturalism in American Literature." *Evolutionary Thought in America*. Ed. Stow Persons. New York: George Braziller, 1950. 300–333. Cowley describes naturalism as an effort by younger writers to break free of the tyranny of the old guard "genteel realism" with its stress on the sunny side of life. Mostly on Norris and Dreiser with a small section on irony in Crane. An earlier version appeared as " 'Not Me': A Natural History of American Naturalism," *Kenyon Review* 9 (1947): 414–435. Also reprinted by George Becker in his influential *Documents of Modern Literary Realism* (Princeton, NJ: Princeton UP, 1963).

2.67 CRAVEN, THOMAS. "Stephen Crane." *The Freeman* 8 (1924): 475–77. Craven's excuse for this piece was to review Beer's *Stephen Crane* (1.1). Craven quickly dispenses with his reviewer duties (Beer is given a rave); in addition, however, Craven's observations on Crane are excellent, worthy of note on their own. Of "The Open Boat" Craven writes that "we discover the inherent futility of the grande programme, and are made to understand how proud and impotent a thing is the talking mammal." Craven's comments on other aspects of Crane are equally striking.

2.68 CURTIN, WILLIAM M. *The World and the Parish: Willa Cather's Articles and Reviews, 1893–1902. Vol. 2.* Lincoln: U of Nebraska P, 1970, 585–587, 700–705. Excerpts from and brief comments on Cather's reviews and essays. Though Crane and his works are frequently mentioned by Cather, her only sustained examination is the famous account of her meeting with Crane in Lincoln during his Western trip. See Cather (6.9) and Woodress (6.30).

2.69 DELBANCO, ANDREW. "The Disenchanted Eye." *New Republic* 199.2 (1988): 33–36. An essay on recent Crane scholarship. Delbanco argues for a solipsistic, nihilistic Crane. Great comments on the descriptive austerity of Crane's astringent prose.

2.70 DENNY, NEVILLE. "Imagination and Experience in Stephen Crane." *English Studies in Africa* 9 (1966): 28–42. A good introductory survey with a stress on the moral tone of Crane's works. Denny argues that a central theme in Crane is the quest of moral maturity by way of a pattern of disruption, recognition, and regeneration.

2.71 DICKERSON, LYNN C. "Stephen Crane and the Dispossessed Character." *A Festschrift for Professor Marguerite Roberts.* Ed. Freida Elaine Penninger. Richmond, VA: U of Richmond P, 1976. 188–204. An implausible and extreme view of Crane: "he never doubted . . . that life is hell and that people are damned." She finds that Crane had contempt for his characters and that he himself was reluctant to recognize human values in his fiction. Not worth the bother of tracking down this hard-to-find *festschrift*.

2.72 DICKEY, JAMES. "Stephen Crane." *Stephen Crane in Transition: Centenary Essays.* Ed. Joseph Katz. De Kalb: Northern Illinois UP, 1972. vii. A short pungent paragraph on Crane's "slant of vision."

2.73 EARLY, JAMES, et al. "Stephen Crane: Introduction." *Adventure in American Literature.* New York: Harcourt, Brace 1986. 391–92. Standard introduction to textbook reprintings, *Red Badge* and poetry selections; stresses Crane's interest in heroism.

2.74 EDELSTEIN, ARTHUR. Introduction. *Three Novels by Stephen Crane: Maggie, George's Mother, The Red Badge of Courage.* Greenwich, CT: Fawcett, 1970. A general treatment of Crane's life, works, and brief comments on the three novels here reprinted. See Stallman, *Stephen Crane: A Critical Bibliography* (14.3: 606).

2.75 EDWARDS, FOREST CAROL. "Decorum: Its Genesis and Function in Stephen Crane." *Texas Quarterly* 18 (1975): 131–43. A thoughtful, meaty analysis arriving at a Frank Sinatraesque "I-did-it-my-way" Crane. Thesis: "Whether the product of a flawed personality, of the spiritual deprivation of the era, or of both, the conflict which was Crane's and his endless quest for a viable adjustment, were distinctly social in nature." Edwards argues that Crane made his own code of decorum to organize his life and to bring order to chaos. This piece engages the views of important Crane critics, responding directly to Johnson (2.112).

2.76   FARLEKAS, CHRISTOPHER. "Port Marks Stephen Crane Day." *Times Herald Record* (Middletown, NY) 5 July 1964: np. An article on Port Jervis's celebration of New Jersey's literary genius.

2.77   FRIED, MICHAEL. "'Almayer's Face': On Impressionism in Conrad, Crane and Norris." *Critical Inquiry* 17 (1990): 193–236. Conrad is the focus here, Norris briefly treated, and Crane looked at in passing. With regard to Crane, Fried is content to quote himself (from *Realism, Writing, Disfiguration: On Thomas Eakins and Stephen Crane* [2.6]) to restate his view of thematized writing in Crane.

2.78   GARNETT, EDWARD. "Some Remarks on American and English Fiction." *Atlantic Monthly* 114 (1914): 747–56. A general essay on the state of American and English fiction including comments about Crane's "grudging, inadequate" recognition by Europeans.

2.79   _____. "A Gossip on Criticism." *Atlantic Monthly* 117 (1916): 174–85. American culture and its fiction are infected with commercialism, best-sellerism, and the view that all must come out right in the end. Garnett sees Crane as a clear countercase.

2.80   _____. "Stephen Crane and His Work." *Friday Nights*. New York: Knopf, 1922. 201–17. A survey of the state of Crane in 1922 when Crane's sun had clearly set. Also a reprinting of Garnett's famous 1898 piece "Mr. Stephen Crane: An Appreciation," *Academy* 55 (1898): 483–84, followed by comments on Crane's use of irony and his selectivity in matters of details; "as Goethe has pointed out, the artist has a license to ignore actualities."

2.81   GEISMAR, MAXWELL. "Naturalism Yesterday and Today." *College English* 15 (1954): 195–200. An interesting glimpse into the fifties. Geismar hopes that McCarthyism will not stifle young authors; naturalism is alive and well having persisted beyond Dreiser, Norris, and Crane.

2.82 GIBSON, WILLIAM M. Introduction. *New England: Indian Summer.* By Van Wyck Brooks. New York: Dutton, 1951. vii–viii. Gibson's remarks refer to Brooks's scattered comments on Crane.

2.83 ———. Introduction and Postscript to the Third Edition. *"The Red Badge of Courage" and Selected Prose and Poetry by Stephen Crane.* New York: Holt, Rinehart, 1968. v–xxiii. A general biographical and thematic sketch. Gibson sees many naturalistic elements in Crane; he finds him "preoccupied with the manner in which men die" and that he wrote "prose-poetry." First edition, 1950, and second edition, 1956, lack the "Postscript." Note the *Red Badge* version presented in this volume plugs the omitted passages (see 3.294) into the 1895 Appleton version.

2.84 GILKES, LILLIAN. "Stephen Crane and the Biographical Fallacy: The Cora Influence." *Modern Fiction Studies* 16 (1970): 441–61. Thesis: Crane's later works are the by-product of "the tensions introduced in his life by the unsanctified relationship with Cora." Gilkes cites the trouble that Potter's marriage causes in "The Bride Comes to Yellow Sky," the theme of rejection in *The Monster,* and the several "matrimonial dilemmas" in *Active Service.*

2.85 GOHDES, CLARENCE. "The Facts of Life *VERSUS* Pleasant Reading." *The Literature of the American People: Historical and Critical Survey.* Ed. Arthur Hobson Quinn. New York: Appleton-Century-Crofts, 1951. 737–62. Crane is treated in a short section (754–60) of Gohdes's chapter. He finds Crane preoccupied with the environment; *Maggie* and *Red Badge* are mentioned in this connection.

2.86 GREENFIELD, STANLEY B. "The Unmistakable Stephen Crane." *PMLA* 73 (1958): 562–72. Among the very best general essays on Crane. Starting with *Red Badge,* Greenfield finds that Crane's "religious phrasing . . . unfortunately predisposes the reader toward an interpretation of spiritual redemption." To the contrary, Greenfield argues for a humanistic, melioristic Crane who finds limited meaning and human solidarity in the face of an indifferent world. That is, "The Open Boat" and "The Blue Hotel" express the central vision of Crane. Humans are neither doomed nor guaranteed salvation; modest achievements in both knowledge and actions are all we can expect.

2.87 GULLASON, THOMAS A. "Stephen Crane: In Nature's Bosom." *American Literary Naturalism: A Reassessment.* Ed. Yoshinobu Hakutani and Lewis Fried. Heidelberg: Carl Winter, 1975. 37–56. Gullason argues that Crane was a literary naturalist. His case is relatively simple with *Maggie,* more difficult with *George's Mother* and *Red Badge,* and implausible with reference to "The Open Boat" and other Crane stories.

2.88 ———. "The Permanence of Stephen Crane." *Studies in the Novel* 10 (1978): 86–95. An extremely glowing tribute to Crane; Gullason cites his boldness without romanticism, his precocity, and his humanism.

2.89 ———. "The Short Story: Revision and Renewal." *Studies in Short Fiction* 19 (1982): 221–30. Gullason emphasizes "story" and downplays "short" to argue that writers like Hemingway, Steinbeck, Falkner, and Crane have used the short story medium because it "approximates the reality and truth of everyday life and everyday experiences." "The Open Boat" is discussed in this connection.

2.90 ———. "What Makes a 'Great' Short Story Great." *Studies in Short Fiction* 26 (1989): 267–77. Crane's contributions to the canon of "great" short stories are discussed. Also Gullason proposes that "An Illusion in Red and White" ought to be "placed in the company of his [Crane's] great short stories."

2.91 HAGEMANN, E. R. "Crane's 'Real' War in His Short Stories." *American Quarterly* 8 (1956): 356–67. An ex-marine marveling at how well Crane understood war, especially "the lure of violence." Brief comments are made about more than a dozen of Crane's stories.

2.92 ———. "Stephen Crane Faces the Storms of *Life*." *Journal of Popular Culture* 2 (1968): 347–60. Hagemann examines parodies of *Red Badge* as well as other humorous treatments of Crane. Hagemann holds that "a humor magazine . . . is one of the best sources for determining an author's contemporary reputation." Crane was highly thought of; hence, he was routinely roasted.

2.93 HALBERSTAM, DAVID. "Introduction; About Stephen Crane." *Stephen Crane: Great Stories of Heroism and Adventure.* Ed. David Halberstam. New York: Platt and Munk, 1967. v–x, 494–502. A brief, breezy, informal introduction followed by a reprinting of *Red Badge* and eleven other stories followed by a shallow biographical sketch that contains several (minor) errors.

2.94 HASTINGS, WILLIAM T. "Literature Since 1870." *Syllabus of American Literature.* Chicago: U of Chicago P, 1923. 60–77. Crane is cited for his "brutal realism . . . without pruriency" and his attack on religion in his poetry, and *Maggie* is singled out as a pioneer city novel.

2.95   HATCHER, HARLAN. "America Catches Step." *Creating the Modern American Novel.* Murray Hill, NY: Farrar and Rinehart, 1935. 12–20. Crane's objective approach, impressionism, and choice of materials contributed to the rise of American Naturalism.

2.96   HAYS, PETER. "Joseph Conrad and Stephen Crane." *Etudes Anglaises* 31 (1978): 26–37. A sketchy and derivative piece on Crane's influence on Conrad and the symbolism and impressionism in each's works.

2.97   HEINEY, DONALD, and LENTHIEL H. DOWNES. "Stephen Crane." *Recent American Literature to 1930.* Woodbury, NY: Barron's Educational Series, 1973. 57–65. A typical study-guide treatment: a biographical sketch, comments on Crane's major works with predictable remarks on *Red Badge* and *Maggie.*

2.98   HELM, JOHANNES. "In Memory of Stephen Crane." *The American-German Review* 26 (1959): 16–17, 36. An interesting historical sketch of efforts to gain readership of Crane. Valuable comments on Crane's international reputation.

2.99   HERZBERG, MAX J. "Stephen Crane (1871–1899)." *New York Times Book Review* 15 March 1925: 10. A letter nominating Crane to the Hall of Fame Committee of New York University. Some twenty other authors and Crane critics are listed as endorsing Herzberg's nomination.

2.100   ———. "Stephen Crane." *Encyclopedia Britannica.* 1929. Vol. 6: 634. Typical short sketch; notes that "his epigrammatic tang in *Black Riders* and *War Is Kind* has rarely been equaled."

2.101   ———, ed. *This Is America.* New York: Pocket Books, 1951. 104–6. Patriotic comments with Crane cited as America's noted contributor to war fiction; a part of chapter 12 of *Red Badge* is reprinted.

2.102   HICKS, GRANVILLE. "Struggle and Fight." *The Great Tradition: An Interpretation of American Literature Since the Civil War.* New York: Macmillan, 1935. 146–63. Crane is treated at the conclusion of this chapter (159–163). Hicks portrays a nihilistic Crane: a bitter, disillusioned young man with "no clear purpose."

2.103   ———. "The Short Story Was His Medium." *Saturday Review* 50 (22 July 1967): 31–32. A brief essay review on *The Complete Short Stories and Sketches of Stephen Crane* (12.8). Hicks's title aptly describes his thesis. Interesting comments that while Crane's late novels fell considerably below his standards, his late short stories were better than ever.

2.104 [HIGGINSON, THOMAS WENTWORTH.] ["Stephen Crane."] *Philistine* 19 (Apr. 1904): 172. Brief comments on Crane and *Red Badge*.

2.105 HONCE, CHARLES. "Farewell to Stephen Crane." *Mark Twain's Associated Press Speech*. Mt. Vernon, VA: Privately printed, 1940. 120–21. This is probably worthwhile; I have not seen it. The University of Illinois has it in their rare book collection; their directory catalogue says only 100 copies were printed. Stallman, *Stephen Crane: A Critical Bibliography* (14.3: 256) also cites it.

2.106 HOOK, ANDREW. "Stephen Crane." *American Literature in Context, III*. London: Methuen, 1983. 129–42. A brief general chapter contending that Crane's worldview is so deterministic that "man's survival or non-survival is a purely random matter." Hook's views are interesting but with so little evidence and such limited argumentation his contentions amount to interesting assertions.

2.107 HOWELLS, WILLIAM DEAN. ["Appreciation of Stephen Crane."] *Delta Upsilon Quarterly* 1 March 1901. Howells's tribute to Crane; see Stallman, *Stephen Crane: A Critical Bibliography* (14.3: 289).

2.108 HUBBARD, ELBERT. ["Crane and Howells."] *Philistine* 17 (Aug. 1903): 88–89. Hubbard said that Crane said to him, speaking of Howells, "I hate the rogue—he is too dam [sic] successful."

2.109 ———. ["Crane, Keats, Chopin, and Chatterton."] *Philistine* 20 (Apr. 1905): 141–42. Hubbard's comments on the short lives of these four geniuses.

2.110 ———. "The Open Road." *Fra* 3.2 (1909): 30. Hubbard asserts, "It was Ambrose Bierce who taught Stevie Crane how to write. Ambrose does not know that—I tell him now, as Stevie told me." Highly unlikely; Hubbard got carried away in his tribute to Bierce as "the modern High Priest of the Divine Art of Fooling."

2.111 ITABASHI, YOSHIE. "'To Be a Man'—A Study in Fear and Courage in Stephen Crane's Stories." *Tsuda Review* 10 (1965): 1–48. An ambitious effort to study a pervasive thematic in Crane. Thesis: Crane's "obsession" to explain true heroism moved him from naturalism to humanism. Itabashi's remarks cover virtually all of Crane from *Maggie* to "Death and the Child."

2.112 JOHNSON, GEORGE W. "Stephen Crane's Metaphor of Decorum." *PMLA* 78 (1963): 250–56. One of the best short general examinations of Crane's personality and his works. Johnson argues that the keys to Crane were his rejection of "the 'nonsense' of civilizations, traditional rituals and the 'furniture' of conventional dress [which he] could not abide." With society's ordinary structures called into question, Crane's lifelong quest was to find other meanings and rules to structure human experience.

2.113 JOHNSON, GLEN M. "Stephen Crane." *American Short-Story Writers, 1880–1910.* Vol. 78 of *Dictionary of Literary Biography.* Ed. Bobby Ellen Kimbel. Detroit: Gale Research, 1989. 117–35. A very sound introduction to Crane's works and a good treatment of his best short stories. After his treatment of themes and techniques, Johnson concludes, "his [short] stories are a chief accomplishment in American Literature"; his place in the American canon is secure.

2.114 KATZ, JOSEPH. "Elbert Hubbard's Watermark." *Stephen Crane Newsletter* 4.3 (1970): 8–10. Not especially relevant to Crane scholarship other than the fact that it gave Katz an opening: "It is a small point, but R. W. Stallman is all wrong about Elbert Hubbard's writing paper." Stallman, however, ignored the barb.

2.115 ———. "Theodore Dreiser and Stephen Crane: Studies in a Literary Relationship." *Stephen Crane in Transition: Centenary Essays.* Ed. Joseph Katz. De Kalb: Northern Illinois UP, 1972. 174–204. A long, detailed examination. Katz's analysis of the styles of each and his treatment of Dreiser's "Curious Shifts of the Poor" as an inferior version of Crane's "The Men in the Storm" are worthy of study.

2.116 ———. "Stephen Crane." *Colliers Encyclopedia.* 1973. Vol. 7: 418–20. A useful and reliable brief summary of Crane's life, works, and outlook. Katz argues, "Crane projected a vision of a badly organized world in which man has to reject traditions and guide himself by the lessons of his own experience if he is to ensure some measure of meaning to his life." The plots of *Red Badge* and *Maggie* are given attention.

2.117 ———. "Stephen Crane: The Humanist in the Making." *William Carlos Williams, Stephen Crane, Philip Freneau: Papers and Poems Celebrating New Jersey's Literary Heritage.* Ed. W. John Bauer. Trenton: New Jersey Historical Commission, 1989. 75–85. Katz examines Crane's humanism, which he describes as "his extraordinary ability to empathize with people quite unlike himself." Katz traces Crane's growth in overcoming prejudice (both his own and his society's) from his early sketch "Greed Rampant" to his Western travel piece "Mexican Lower Classes."

2.118   KAZIN, ALFRED. *On Native Grounds: An Interpretation of Modern American Prose Literature.* New York: Harcourt Brace, 1942. Passim. A sketchy treatment (67–72) of Crane as a naturalist: "the ferocious pessimism of naturalism suited his temperament exactly."

2.119   ———. "A Century of American Realism: John A. Garranty Interviews Alfred Kazin." *American Heritage* 21.4 (1970): 12–15, 86–90. An interesting general discussion on the rise of realism in America. Crane is cited as an ideal good reporter-novelist; "he observed everything with a cold, clear eye. That shocked readers, too; he was able to write about things with merciless detachment."

2.120   ———. "The Youth: Stephen Crane." *An American Procession.* New York: Knopf, 1984. 256–74. A helpful, quotable, sprightly summary of all of Crane. Crane delighted in the conscious "distortion" of the external scene. War fascinated him because it released energy, "demonstrated the unpredictable and crazy-seeming correlation of the human animal to extreme situations."

2.121   KEATING, L. CLARK. "Francis Viele-Griffin and America." *Symposium* 14 (1960): 274–81. Keating argues that because of the influence of Viele-Griffin, "the American who became the leader of the French symbolists" and who with Davray translated *Red Badge* into French, Crane has been neglected by the French. "The pity of it was that their flat, uninspired version of *The Red Badge of Courage* was responsible for such reputation as Stephen Crane acquired in France."

2.122   KIBLER, JAMES E. "The Library of Stephen and Cora Crane." *Proof* 1 (1977): 199–246. Kibler has cataloged more than 200 books that belonged to Stephen and Cora Crane. There are a great many religious books, by his ancestors as well as other authors, and a good number of works by contemporary artists. From this catalog, Kibler avers, Crane scholars can gauge Crane's exposure to standard authors and estimate matters of influence.

2.123   KIRK, CLARA MARBURG, and RUDOLF KIRK, eds. *William Dean Howells: Representative Selections, with Introduction, Bibliography and*

Notes. New York: American Book Company, 1950. cxxxvii, 385–386. Notes on Howells's support of Crane with representative selections of his comments on Crane's works.

2.124　KIRSCHKE, JAMES J. "The Art of Stephen Crane." *Modern Age* 18 (1974): 105–9. A general essay on Crane's importance. Comments on Crane's energy, vitality, sports ability, and his anticipation of modern prose, both style and content.

2.125　KNAPP, DANIEL. "Son of Thunder: Stephen Crane and the Fourth Evangelist." *Nineteenth-Century Fiction* 24 (1969): 253–91. A very long and convoluted examination of religious influence and themes in Crane's works. Thesis: Crane's basic structure and responses are religious, his stories are "morality plays," and his narrative models are from the New Testament, especially the evangelist John.

2.126　KNIGHT, GRANT C. *The Critical Period in American Literature.* Chapel Hill: U of North Carolina P, 1951. Passim. A generally competent survey without controversy or surprise. Crane is portrayed as "a blazer of trails"; a good sense of the 1890s is conveyed.

2.127　KRONEGGER, M. E. "Impressionistic Literature and Narrative Theory: Stephen Crane." *Review* 2 (1982): 129–34. A full-scale review essay on Nagel's *Stephen Crane and Literary Impressionism* (2.14). Kronegger is very impressed with the Nagel book.

2.128　KUDO, KOZO. "Stephen Crane's Psychologism." *Yamagata Daigaku Eigo Eibungaku Kenkyu* 11 (Feb. 1966): 27–60. Promising, but I have not been able to locate it; cited by Stallman, *Stephen Crane: A Critical Bibliography* (14.3: 522).

2.129　LAFRANCE, MARSTON. "Stephen Crane in Our Time." *The Chief Glory of Every People: Essays on Classic American Writers.* Ed. Matthew J. Bruccoli. Carbondale: Southern Illinois UP, 1973. 27–51. Crane's timelessness comes from his use of irony and his insistence on a moral duty to seek the truth. In the latter, Crane explored experiencers' "point of view" and depicted with lucidity and honesty the limited range that individuals are actually able to perceive.

2.130　LANG, MARTIN. *Character Analysis Through Color.* Westport, CT: Crimson Press, 1940. A rare book (only 75 were printed) that makes very brief comments on Crane's use of color.

2.131　LEARY, LEWIS. "Too Brilliant to Last." *Sewanee Review* 77 (1964): 294–300. A review essay on Stallman's *Stephen Crane* (1.10). Leary's piece is notable for two reasons: it is one of the few complimentary reviews of Stallman's book and he examines if and why the quality of Crane's work tailed off badly at the end.

2.132 LEAVER, FLORENCE. "Isolation in the Work of Stephen Crane." *South Atlantic Quarterly* 61 (1962): 521–32. Dated: Crane anticipated David Reisman's *The Lonely Crowd* and he worried about fear, which suggests that he anticipated the isolation of twentieth-century America.

2.133 LEVENSON, J. C. "Stephen Crane." *Major American Writers.* 2 vols. Ed. Perry Miller. New York: Harcourt, 1962. Vol. 2: 383–97. A thickly textured, sophisticated general essay that stresses Crane's lack of historical, cultural, and literary resources—"an innocent in a fallen world." (See Colvert [2.61] for the contrary view.) Levenson explores Crane's mastery of episodes (rather than plots) in which he transfers his feelings to a story to tell his readers how events affected him.

2.134 LITTELL, ROBERT. "Notes on Stephen Crane." *New Republic* 54 (1928): 391–92. A perceptive review essay on the issue of *The Work of Stephen Crane* (12.5). Though Littell believes Crane belongs in an American Literature Hall of Fame (along with only eleven other authors), he is bothered by the uneven quality of Crane's work. He calls Crane a painter rather than a narrator, who was better with imagination than observation. His writings are marked by irony because Crane found that "the right things of this world are on the losing side."

2.135 LOGGINS, VERNON. "Stephen Crane." *I Hear America: Literature in the United States Since 1900.* New York: Crowell, 1937. 23–31. A short, witty chapter on Crane. Usual biographical details and sketch of his major works. "He was the master of the plotless short story—the brief narrative with significance."

2.136 MALCOLM, JANET. "The Purloined Critic." *New Yorker* 5 Oct. 1987: 121–26. A review essay, generally favorable, on Michael Fried's controversial *Realism, Writing, Disfiguration: On Thomas Eakins and Stephen Crane* (2.6). For an equally detailed, highly critical examination see James Nagel's review in *American Literature* 60 (1988): 479–81.

2.137 MARTIN, JAY. "Stephen Crane." *Harvests of Change: American Literature, 1865–1914.* Englewood Cliffs, NJ: Prentice-Hall, 1967. 55–70. A brief, general, survey treatment of Crane.

2.138 MAURICE, ARTHUR BARTLETT. "Old Bookman Days." *Bookman* 66 (Sept. 1927): 20–26. An old *Bookman* editor's memoirs contain one paragraph on Crane's coming to the offices to check on some of his poems to be printed in *Bookman*. "He was a strange and moody creature."

2.139 MAXWELL, DESMOND. "Appendix B: Stephen Crane." *American Fiction: The Intellectual Background*. New York: Columbia UP, 1963. 294–99. Maxwell sees Crane as stretching and then abandoning naturalism; *George's Mother* and *Maggie* are examined.

2.140 MAYHALL, JANE. "Stephen Crane to the Rescue." *New York Review of Books* 10 Aug. 1972: 29–30. A long, thoughtful review of the first six volumes of the Virginia edition: stresses Crane's episodic style and his attention to underdogs and fallen women.

2.141 McCARTNEY, GEORGE. "The Only Impressionist." *National Review* 40.18 (1988): 54–56. A review essay on *Correspondence of Stephen Crane* (13.3) and *Stephen Crane: Prose and Poetry* (12.11). McCartney sees a nihilistic and atheistic Crane.

2.142 MENCKEN, H. L. "Stephen Crane." *The Dial* 2 (1924): 73–74. A very positive review of Beer's *Stephen Crane* (1.1), plus the view that "Conrad's dull introduction damages what is otherwise an exhilarating and extraordinary book." The latter view is not widely shared.

2.143 MITCHELL, EDWIN VALENTINE. *The Art of Authorship*. New York: Loring and Mussey, 1935. 69–70. Mitchell notes that Crane kept a notebook and that he has seen it.

2.144 MONTEIRO, GEORGE. "A Capsule Assessment of Stephen Crane by Hamlin Garland." *Stephen Crane Newsletter* 3.1 (1968): 2. Another ambivalent opinion by Garland on Crane: "His marked individuality is probably his undoing."

2.145 ———. "Stephen Crane and the Antinomies of Christian Charity." *Centennial Review* 16 (1972): 91–104. Because of his Methodist background Crane did not fully commit himself to naturalism and determinism. In light of this residual religious influence, Monteiro explores Crane's attitude toward social injustice.

2.146 ———. "*The Illustrated American* and Stephen Crane's Contemporary Reputation." *Serif* 6 (1969): 49–54. A statement of Crane's reputation among his contemporaries is gleaned from "important weeklies of the nineties."

2.147 MOORE, HARRY T. Preface. *The Fiction of Stephen Crane by Donald B. Gibson.* Carbondale: Southern Illinois UP, 1968. v–vii. Comments on Gibson's Crane monograph (2.7). Moore cites Gibson's attention to the beginnings of several of Crane's works.

2.148 MORGAN, H. WAYNE. "Stephen Crane: The Ironic Hero." *Writers in Transition: Seven Americans.* New York: Hill and Wang, 1963. 1–22. Morgan's chapter on Crane is a competent, standard sort of general essay. He emphasizes Crane's attention to heroic resistance to oppressive environments *(Maggie)* and his use of irony to deflate *(Red Badge).*

2.149 MORRIS, LLOYD R. "The Discourse of the Elders." *Outlook* 119 (14 Sept. 1921): 67–68. A general essay on the literary canon in 1921. Interesting because, in the opinion of Morris, Crane was grouped with other minor figures in "the local color school." He comments that Beer's biography and Follett's edition had much inertia to overcome!

2.150 ———. "The Skepticism of the Young: A Gospel of Doubt." *Post-scripts to Yesterday: America, The Last Fifty Years.* New York: Random House, 1947. 107–10. Crane receives brief treatment in a section of a chapter on writers of the 1890s. Crane is noted for his attention to misery in society in the face of the official sunny view of American life.

2.151 MORRIS, WRIGHT. "Stephen Crane." *Earthly Delights, Unearthly Adornments: American Writers as Image-Makers.* New York: Harper and Row, 1978. 51–57. A short general piece stresses that Crane's irony was so natural he stayed free of cynicism.

2.152 MULLER, HERBERT J. "Naturalism in America." *Modern Fiction: A Study of Values.* New York: Funk and Wagnalls, 1937. 199–201. Crane's contributions to naturalism were plunging it into muddy waters *(Maggie)* and treating it impressionistically *(Red Badge).*

2.153 NAGEL, JAMES. "Stephen Crane: Nine Recent Books." *Studies in American Fiction* 1 (1973): 232–40. A review essay on the state of Crane scholarship in nine books published between 1970 and 1972 with pithy comments on each book and author.

2.154 NETTELS, ELSA. "Conrad and Stephen Crane." *Conradiana* 10 (1978): 267–83. An interesting discussion of biographical parallels and shared artistic tenets, especially both artists' belief in a pluralism of perspectives and the unknowableness of an absolute Truth. *Nigger of the "Narcissus"* and *Red Badge* are compared in some detail.

2.155   NOEL, EDGAR E. "Stephen Crane: A Realist Who Painted with Words." *Kyushu American Literature* 12 (1970): 20–31. A sketchy and superficial lecture for audiences unaware of Crane: Readers with any knowledge of Crane will find this piece faulty and/or obvious.

2.156   NYE, RUSSEL B. "Stephen Crane as Social Critic." *The Monthly Critic* 11 (1940): 48–54. A dated socialist organ argues that Crane was a prototypical social reformist: Though humans are powerless against nature, we can resist social forces, a thesis that finds little support in the works of Crane.

2.157   O'BRIEN, EDWARD J. "Turn of the Century: [Stephen Crane]." *The Advance of the American Short Story*. Rev. ed. New York: Dodd, Mead, 1931. 176–82. A journeyman note on Crane with brief attention to his most celebrated short stories.

2.158   OVERTON, GRANT. "Stephen Crane." *Cargoes for Crusoes*. New York: Appleton, 1924. 242. Brief notes on Crane's place in American literature. Overton holds that Crane belongs with Poe, Hawthorne, Whitman, and Melville in an American literature hall of fame.

2.159   ———. *An Hour of the American Novel*. Philadelphia: Lippincott, 1929. 71–76. A brief treatment of Crane's use of color.

2.160   PARRINGTON, VERNON LOUIS. "Naturalism in American Fiction." *The Beginnings of Critical Realism in America. Main Currents in American Thought*. New York: Harcourt, Brace 1930. 323–29. Crane is discussed in passing: *Maggie* cited as the first example of naturalism in America and *Red Badge* singled out for its treatment of crowd psychology and blind chance.

2.161   PATTEE, FRED LEWIS. "Stephen Crane." *The New American Literature, 1890–1930*. New York: Century, 1930. 64–72. In a short chapter in Pattee's book Crane is judged critically. In addition, Pattee argues that Crane's work and his impact are overvalued by his supporters. Pattee singles out his style and "his desire . . . to make his reader see as he sees." The extent of Pattee's bias is obvious in a letter to Alfred A. Knopf (19 December 1939—see Stallman's *Stephen Crane: A Critical Biography,* 14.3: 353) declining to do a selection of Crane's short stories for Knopf. "As I define the short story, Crane was not a short story writer at all."

2.162   PEDEN, WILLIAM. "Stephen Crane." *Encyclopedia Americana*. 1990. 8: 150–151. A two-column sketch; interesting comments on Crane's "uncompromising realism [which is] often more impressionistic than photographic." Mistakenly states that Crane and Cora were "married" in 1898.

2.163   PIZER, DONALD. "Romantic Individualism in Garland, Norris and Crane." *American Quarterly* 10 (1958): 463–75. Crane is an add-on to this article, which holds that these three authors embraced the American belief in individuals' ability to grasp truth so an artist has a responsibility to be faithful to his own experiences.

2.164   PLEKHANOV, GEORGE V. *Art and Society.* New York: Critic's Group, 1936. Passim. Crane is cited in connection with Plekhanov's comments on the French realists.

2.165   PRITCHETT, V. S. "Books in General: Robert Stallman's *Stephen Crane: An Omnibus.*" *New Statesman and Nation* 48 (10 July 1954): 46–47. Pritchett rehearses Crane's self-destructive lifestyle and stresses his moral quest for authenticity. He then quarrels with Stallman's penchant for seeing religious symbolism everywhere in Crane's works. "Crane is a personality, an impressionist who catches the incredulous solitary in other human beings."

2.166   QUINN, ARTHUR HOBSON. "The Journalists." *American Fiction.* New York: Appleton-Century-Crofts, 1936. 532–38. Crane gets part of a chapter on journalists who were also novelists. Virtually all Crane's important stories and tales are briefly commented upon.

2.167   RAHV, PHILIP. "Fiction and the Criticism of Fiction." *Kenyon Review* 18 (1956): 276–99. A sound general essay on literary criticism decrying three biases—symbolism, allegory, and mythic patterning —that debilitate. With reference to the first, Robert Stallman and his fixation with religious symbols is cited as the worst offender. Reprinted in *The Myth and the Powerhouse,* New York, 1965: 33–60. See Stallman (3.216) for a response.

2.168   RICHIE, DONALD. "Eight American Writers: III. Stephen Crane." *The Study of Current English* (Tokoyo) 10 Oct. 1955: 33–41. This article is in several bibliographies, including Stallman, *Stephen Crane: A Critical Bibliography* (14.3: 408) but several interlibrary loan librarians have been unable to locate it for me.

2.169   ROSENFELD, ISAAC. "Stephen Crane as a Symbolist." *Kenyon Review* 15 (1953): 311–14. A review essay on Stallman's *Stephen Crane, An Omnibus* (2.16) critical of his exaggerated stress on symbolism in Crane.

2.170 ROTH, RUSSELL. "A Tree in Winter: The Short Fiction of Stephen Crane." *New Mexico Quarterly* 23 (1952): 188–96. A general survey of Crane's short stories with reference to his ability to give the reader "a chain of shrewdly selected, perfectly realized places and things (not 'persons,' in the humanist sense) in Crane, the persons are also 'things.'"

2.171 SADLER, ELVA ELIZABETH. "Stephen Crane, 1871–1900: Forerunner of the Modern Literary Movement." *English Teaching Forum* 8 (Jan.-Feb. 1970): 11–15. This too is cited in several bibliographies (including Stallman, *Stephen Crane: A Critical Bibliography,* 14.3: 610) but I have been unable to take a look at it.

2.172 SCHNEIDER, ROBERT W. "Stephen Crane and the Drama of Transition." *American Studies* 2 (1960): 1–16. A broad survey of Crane's works (his poetry is given prominence) arguing that despite naturalistic, pessimistic, and deterministic strains in his works, Crane believed in freedom and individual responsibility. For Crane, though success is not often the outcome, "the important thing is the attempt."

2.173 ———. "Stephen Crane: The Promethean Protest." *Five Novelists of the Progressive Era.* New York: Columbia UP, 1965. 60–111. A useful essay locating Crane in his cultural setting. Following a long section on the characteristics of the progressive era (especially the gospel of wealth and social optimism), Schneider argues that Crane is skeptical of these ideals. Instead, Crane's heroes are Promethean because struggle and perseverance, rather than victory and reward, animate his protagonists.

2.174 SCHNITZER, DEBORAH. "'Ocular Realism': The Impressionist Effects of an 'Innocent Eye.'" *The Pictorial in Modernist Fiction from Stephen Crane to Ernest Hemingway.* Ann Arbor: U of Michigan P, 1988. 7–62. After an elaborate discussion of impressionism, which Schnitzer defines as 'fidelity to the perceptual experience," she briefly (29–35) examines Crane's stress on episodes and how his prose uses focus and blur as impressionistic techniques.

2.175 SHARMA, D. R. "The Naturalistic and the Esthetic in Stephen Crane." *Punjab University Research Bulletin* 3 (1972): 75–84. Beginning with dogmas on naturalism, "social and biological determinism and the ultimate defeat of human endeavor," Sharma looks at *Maggie, Red Badge,* and "The Blue Hotel."

2.176 SHIMADA, TARO. "The Aesthetics of Fin-de-Siecle—The Case of Stephen Crane." *The Emergence of Modern America.* Ed. Nagayo

Homma. Tokyo: Tokyo UP, 1988. 27–43. In his naturalism, impressionism, and determinism Crane demonstrates that he shared with his turn-of-the-century fellows a hightened awareness of human limitations. *Red Badge* and other of Crane's shorter works are examined.

2.177   SHROEDER, JOHN W. "Stephen Crane Embattled." *University of Kansas City Review* 17 (1950): 119–29. Driven by his assumption that Crane is a naturalist, Shroeder struggles to find determinism in every Crane work he examines, even those that are clearly nondeterministic.

2.178   SIMPSON, CLAUDE. "Stephen Crane." *Masters of American Literature: Shorter Version.* Ed. Leon Edel, et al. Boston: Houghton Mifflin, 1959. 1096–101. A standard introductory general essay on Crane's life and works; interesting comments on his fidelity to lived experience and biblical rhythms in his poetry.

2.179   SMITH, ALLAN GARDNER. "Stephen Crane, Impressionism and William James." *Revue Francaise D'Etudes Americaines* 8 (1983): 237–48. Smith argues (contra Nagel, 2.14) that Crane's connection with French impressionistic painters is tenuous and he suggests instead that William James's discussion of selective attention in *Principles of Psychology* is a more likely American source for Crane's epistemology.

2.180   SOLOMON, ERIC. "Stephen Crane: An Autobiography." *Studies in the Novel* 10 (1978): 96–102. A breezy, interesting reminiscence about a lifetime of scholarly work on Crane.

2.181   SOLOMON, M. "Stephen Crane: A Critical Study." *Masses & Mainstream* 9: 1 & 2 (1956): 25–47, 31–42. A sketchy survey of Crane and his works stressing the presence of a humanistic ethic in both. Though Solomon correctly notes that "The Open Boat" gives the best account of Crane's "ethic of loyalty and brotherhood," he is not careful about details: "It is a narrative (based on fact) of four men drifting in a life-boat *for many days.*"

2.182   SPILLER, ROBERT E. "Great Stylist." *Saturday Review* 34 (27 Jan. 1951): 11. A lukewarm review of Berryman's *Stephen Crane* (1.2).

2.183   _____. "A Problem in Dynamics: Adams, Norris, Robinson [and Crane]." *The Cycle of American Literature: An Essay in Historical Criticism.* New York: Macmillan, 1955. 143–61. Though Crane is only mentioned in passing (two paragraphs) as a deterministic nihilist,

Spiller states that "there is no finer short novel in English than *The Red Badge of Courage* (1895) or short story than "The Open Boat" or "The Blue Hotel." First edition appeared in 1953 with multiple reissues thereafter.

2.184 ———. "Toward Naturalism in Fiction [Stephen Crane]." *Literary History of the United States.* Ed. Robert E. Spiller, et al. 4th ed., rev. New York: Macmillan, 1974. 1020–26. A short but reliable discussion of Crane and his works, stressing the influence of Garland in what is termed Crane's "impressionistic veritism." Comments on Crane's interest in life at moments of crisis.

2.185 STAHL, J. D. "Stephen Crane: A Revaluation, Virginia Tech Conference, 1989." *Dictionary of Literary Biography Yearbook, 1989.* Detroit: Gale Research, 1990. 165–69. A summary of the nearly two dozen papers presented at "the conference 'Stephen Crane: A Revaluation,' organized by Paul Sorrentino and held at Virginia Polytechnic Institute and State University on 28–30 September 1989, [that] offered new insights and interpretations of Stephen Crane's life, as well as his poetry, fiction and journalism."

2.186 STALLMAN, ROBERT W. "Stephen Crane: A Reevaluation." *Critiques and Essays on Modern Fiction: 1920–1951.* Ed. John Aldridge. New York: Ronald, 1952. 244–69. A superb general essay on Crane and his works. Belongs on the top ten list. The center of gravity of this seminal essay is Stallman's contention that "The Open Boat" "is the perfect fusion of the impressionism of *Maggie* and the symbolism of *The Red Badge of Courage.* The two main technical movements in modern American fiction—realism and symbolism—have their beginnings here in these early achievements of Stephen Crane." Irony and other elements of Crane's style are discussed too. Stallman's ability to stir up controversy can be gauged by his offhand comment concerning "the off-key tone of the appended section," which set off round after round of debate about the final section of "The Blue Hotel."

2.187 ———. "Crane's Short Stories." *The Houses That James Built.* East Lansing: Michigan State UP, 1961. 103–10. A general discussion of Crane's short stories, which Stallman argues, support his view that the keys to Crane are symbol, paradox, and irony. Special attention is given to "An Episode of War," "The Upturned Face," "The Blue Hotel," and "A Mystery of Heroism."

2.188 ———. "Stephen Crane." *The Reader's Encyclopedia of American Literature.* Ed. Max J. Herzberg. New York: Crowell, 1962. 219–23. A lengthy (by reference book standards) and informative essay on

Crane's life, works, and impact. Stress is laid on his unique style and his anticipation of twentieth-century topics and techniques. This is the best of the encyclopedia articles on Crane.

2.189   ———. "Inflated by Facts." *Saturday Review* 50 (31 Aug. 1968): 20. An aggressive response to a review by Granville Hicks of Stallman's *Stephen Crane: A Biography* (1.10) in *Saturday Review*. Hicks called Stallman's biography "inflated"; Stallman rebuts that if it is inflated it is by facts.

2.190   ———. "That Crane, That Albatross around My Neck: A Self-Interview by R. W. Stallman." *Journal of Modern Literature* 7 (1979): 147–69. Though his tone is both whining and arrogant, and though all the old battles are given full postmortems, this is a fascinating look at the career of a dogged and strong-handed Crane scholar who was, indeed, the major force in the Crane renaissance. See Bruccoli (2.51) for the sort of article to which Stallman is responding.

2.191   ———. "Stephen Crane." *The New Encyclopedia Britannica.* 1986. Vol. 3: 711–12. Rather lengthy treatment of Crane's life and work. Attention is given to Crane's being a "voracious reader of all 19th-century English writers, Shakespeare, Plutarch's *Lifes of Noble Grecians and Romans,* and the classics of Greece and Rome." Stallman also states, "A great stylist, Crane was a master of the contradictory effect." A very good short bibliography is added.

2.192   STARRETT, VINCENT. "Stephen Crane." *Chicago Tribune Books Today* 4 June 1967: 15. The state of Crane scholarship in 1967; see Stallman, *Stephen Crane: A Critical Bibliography* (14.3: 542).

2.193   STEIN, WILLIAM BYSSHE. "Stephen Crane's *Homo Absurdus.*" *Bucknell Review* 8 (1959): 168–88. Stein proposes that Crane's works "record the anxiety, the frustration, the despair, the irrationality, and the absurdity of existence," and then he traces existentialist themes in virtually all of Crane's longer works and noted short stories.

2.194   STEVENSON, JOHN W. "The Literary Reputation of Stephen Crane." *South Atlantic Quarterly* 51 (1952): 286–300. Stevenson traces Crane's reputation from *Red Badge* through World War II. Nothing fresh or striking except for Stevenson's belief that Crane dogmatically adhered to naturalism.

2.195   STIRLING, NORA. "Stephen Crane." *Who Wrote the Classics?* New York: John Day, 1968, vol. 2:279–315. A general introduction for younger readers. Contains the usual biographical and thematic points.

2.196 STONE, EDWARD. *Voices of Despair: Four Motifs in American Literature.* Athens: Ohio UP, 1966. Passim. One of the four motifs is animalism, and Stone notes Crane's tendency to liken humans to various animals.

2.197 TANNER, TONY. "Stephen Crane's Long Dream of War." *London Magazine* 8.9 (1968): 5–19. Crane's central metaphor is that life is war: in cities (*Maggie* and *George's Mother*), with nature ("The Open Boat"), and literally (*Red Badge*.)

2.198 ――――. "Stephen Crane." *Scenes of Nature, Signs of Men.* Cambridge: Cambridge UP, 1987. 133–47. A slightly revised and expanded version of Tanner's 1968 piece; see (2.197) for annotation.

2.199 TAYLOR, WALTER FULLER. "The Naturalistic Revolt: Crane, Norris, and London." *A History of American Letters.* New York: American Book, 1936. 309–12. A typical short sketch: Crane as pioneer naturalist.

2.200 ――――. *The Economic Novel in America.* New York: Farrar, Straus, 1942. Passim. Passing references to Crane as a naturalistic novelist.

2.201 THORNE, J. O. "Stephen Crane." *Chamber's Biographical Dictionary.* New York: St. Martin's Press, 1962. 327. Standard brief biographical sketch and comment on *Red Badge*.

2.202 THORP, WILLARD. *American Writing in the Twentieth Century.* Cambridge, MA: Harvard UP, 1960. Passim. Passing comments on Crane as a naturalist à la Zola.

2.203 TSUNEMATSU, MASAO. "Toward Men in Society—A Study of Stephen Crane." *Shimane Daigaku Bunrigaku-bu Kiyo* Jinbunkagaku Hen 1 (Dec. 1967): 78–89. Cited in Stallman, *Stephen Crane: A Critical Bibliography* (14.3: 544). I have not seen it; I believe it is in Japanese.

2.204 VAN DOREN, CARL. "Stephen Crane." *American Mercury* 1 (1924): 11–14. Arguably the best short essay on Crane, his works, his style, and the moral purpose of his art. With reference to the last, Van Doren argues that Crane taught "later novelists to lift their stories, out of the low plane of domestic sentimentalism, with its emphasis on petty virtues and vices, to the plane of the classics, with their emphasis on the major vices of meanness and cruelty and the major virtues of justice and magnanimity."

2.205 ———. "Emergence of Naturalism." *The American Novel, 1780–1939.* New York: Macmillan, 1940. 225–44. Crane's section of this chapter is brief (228–33) with comments on Crane's intensity and immediacy in *Maggie, Red Badge,* and his Western tales.

2.206 ———. Introduction and Notes. *Stephen Crane: Twenty Stories.* New York: Knopf, 1940. v–xvii, 501–7. Van Doren selected the best of Crane's short work, and in his introduction he makes predictable and routine comments about them. He concludes that Crane's accomplishments were noteworthy because of artistic excellence, not to mention his new style.

2.207 VAN DOREN, CARL, and MARK VAN DOREN. "Prose Fiction: Stephen Crane." *American and British Literature Since 1890.* New York: Century, 1925. 44–48. Brief comments on Crane's honest pictures of real life and his "spare, pungent, intense" style.

2.208 VOSS, ARTHUR. "The Short Story in Transition: Stephen Crane, Jack London, Edith Wharton, Willa Cather and Theodore Dreiser." *The American Short Story: A Critical Survey.* Norman: U of Oklahoma P, 1973. 158–82. Given the length of this chapter and the fact that Crane must share space with Jack London, Edith Wharton, Willa Cather, and Theodore Dreiser, it is not surprising that nothing worth noting can be found here.

2.209 WEALE, EMMA JANE. "Stephen Crane—Man of Letters." *Union-Gazette* (Port Jervis) 8 June 1962: 4. "The Stephen Crane Memorial Program, held in the public library of Port Jervis on June 5, was the first official recognition of Crane by the city." (See Stallman's *Stephen Crane: A Critical Bibliography,* 14.3: 476.)

2.210 WELLS, H. G. "Stephen Crane from an English Standpoint." *North American Review* 171 (1900): 233–42. An early outstanding personal and critical tribute to Crane: *Red Badge* started a new school of literature, "The Open Boat" is "the crown of all his work," and in his opinion *Maggie* and *George's Mother* had not been given their due in England. Reprinted in Weatherford, *The Critical Heritage,* 2.17: #267.

2.211 WERTHEIM, STANLEY. "Stephen Crane and the Wrath of Jehova." *Literary Review* 7 (1963–1964): 499–508. Wertheim argues that subsequent to his rejection of his parents' religion, Crane continued to search for absolutes. Finding none, "themes of futility, self-deception and isolation . . . permeate his writings."

2.212 _____. "The Fiction of Stephen Crane." *Literature and Psychology* 10 (1969): 125–29. A review essay of Gibson's use of depth psychology in his *The Fiction of Stephen Crane* (2.7). Wertheim argues that Gibson's "exclusive concern with the development of consciousness" skews his estimate of both the best and the weakest of Crane's works.

2.213 _____. "[Dissertations On] Stephen Crane." *American Literary Realism* 8 (1975): 227–41. Wertheim surveys Ph.D. dissertations from 1943 to 1975; an interesting record of who wrote on what and where and under whom.

2.214 WEST, RAY B. "Stephen Crane: Author in Transition." *American Literature* 34 (1962): 215–28. A general essay considering Crane's depiction of the human world (civilized by ceremonies) and nature (sunny, blizzardy, or indifferent). Reprinted in *The Writer in the Room,* East Lansing: Michigan State UP, 1968.

2.215 WESTBROOK, MAX. "Stephen Crane: The Pattern of Affirmation." *Nineteenth-Century Fiction* 14 (1959): 219–29. Westbrook argues (convincingly) that Crane's works do not fit the pattern of naturalism: His orientation is neither pessimistic nor optimistic but affirmative, the indifferent world is a preliminary, not a final setting for human actions, and finally, heroes abound in Crane's works, ranging from Billie the oiler in "The Open Boat" to Dr. Trescott in *The Monster.*

2.216 _____. "Stephen Crane and the Personal Universe." *Modern Fiction Studies* 8 (1962): 351–60. A survey of the tenacity of critics in the fifties who struggled to keep Crane in the naturalist camp despite his apparently humanistic values. Westbrook offers the path of least resistance: Consider Crane a humanist who affirms the value of personal responsibility, the significance of human actions, and the reward of brotherhood.

2.217 _____. "Fiction and Belief." *Canadian Review of American Studies* 2 (1972): 63–67. A favorable notice of *A Reading of Stephen Crane* (2.13), agreeing with LaFrance's bootstrap morality: "Man is the sole proprietor of morality" with a complete separation between physical fact and ethical value.

2.218 WINTERICH, JOHN T. "Stephen Crane: Lost and Found." *Saturday Review* 34 (3 Feb. 1951): 21, 43. An account of the Crane revival in the 1950s: The biographies by Beer and Berryman, John Huston's movie version of *Red Badge,* and the reissue of the manuscript versions of *Red Badge.*

2.219 WYNDHAM, GUY, ed. *George Wyndham: Letters.* Edinburgh: T. and H. Constable, 1915. References to Wyndham's review of *Red Badge* (see 3.258) and to a letter dictated by Wyndham regarding Crane's request for a visa to cover the Boer War (see *The Correspondence of Stephen Crane,* #566).

2.220 YOSHIDA, HIROSHIGE. "A Note on Stephen Crane's Use of Colloquial and Slangy Words and Idioms." *Kansai Daigaku Anglica* 4.3 (1961): 59–71. The longer version of 4.181; see also Slotkin's reply (4.173).

2.221 ZIFF, LARZER. "The Other Lost Generation: The Strange Story of a Literary Eclipse." *Saturday Review* 48 (20 Mar. 1965): 15–18. The cultural setting of the 1890s; compare with Beer's *The Mauve Decade* (2.39).

2.222 _____. "Outstripping the Event: Stephen Crane." *The American 1890's: Life and Times of a Lost Generation.* New York: Viking, 1969. 185–205. General essay on Crane and the 1890s stressing Crane's gift for teasing the expectations of the reader and his conscious challenge of established values.

3

The Red Badge of Courage

Overview

This American classic has inspired a minor industry of critical response. Virtually everything written on Crane mentions *Red Badge* in one way or another, in varying depth and detail. Textual controversies have added, especially recently, heat and some light to this literature. Accordingly, this section of the bibliography is divided into subsections: general criticism and textual controversies.

TEXTUAL CONTROVERSIES. It is widely known that a shortened, serialized version of *Red Badge* was published by a number of newspaper syndicates on 3–8 December 1894 (see Katz, 3.265), and the full-length book version was published by Appleton in October 1895. The appearance of an even longer version of *Red Badge* has sparked a tremendous amount of high-intensity and heated scholarly exchange. The manuscript of *Red Badge* was preserved (see Bowers's facsimile 3.261). Study of this manuscript has revealed numerous alterations that Crane himself made; some of these editorial changes, it is argued, were inspired and/or forced by Hamlin Garland and Appleton editor Ripley Hitchock. In addition, an early draft version of *Red Badge* has further preserved a number of canceled passages, for instance, seven consecutive paragraphs of chapter 15 and, most controversial of all, bits and pieces plus several whole paragraphs of chapter 24, the final chapter. In 1951 the London Folio Society (see Winterich 3.295) published a version of *Red Badge* that interspersed Crane's canceled and draft passages into the text. Since then Binder (plus Parker and a few others) has insisted that this expanded version of *Red Badge* restores Crane's intentions with regard to his best seller. However, most Crane scholars accept the 1895 Appleton version—the version Crane himself prepared and proofread and the version that introduced young genius Crane to millions of readers.

The Folio Society version (a similar expanded version was also published by Norton), then, significantly alters the *Red Badge* text. As a result, differences of tone and eventually matters of interpretation are at stake. Of most significance, the Folio Society version removes much of the ambiguity from the ending of Crane's novel. Readers have long wondered how much irony ought to be factored into the statement, four paragraphs from the end of the novel, that Fleming "had become a man." The passages that the Folio Society version adds make the ending highly ironic, leaving readers with a deluded, egotistical Fleming who has learned nothing and changed little from three days of war.

The best short essay on the textual controversy is DOMERASKI (3.275). For the full account of the dispute see, on behalf of the longer version, Binder (3.267 and 3.270), Mailloux (3.279), and Parker (3.285); on behalf of the traditional 1895 Appleton edition, see Bowers (3.271), Colvert (3.273), and Pizer (3.289).

The Virginia critical edition of *Red Badge* has caused controversy, too. Bowers did not insert the canceled and draft passages but he altered the Appleton edition—for example, by regularizing the dialect; see Bower's defense of his edition (3.262) and Parker's critique (3.283–287). The textual debate has been so divisive (and distracting) that Levenson's *Stephen Crane: Prose and Poetry* (12.11), which reprinted virtually all of the Virginia edition, sidestepped it, using the 1895 Appleton edition. (Levenson also selected the 1893 *Maggie;* more of this in the next section.)

LITERARY CRITICISM. There is an extensive and impressive body of literary comment on *Red Badge*. One way of calling attention to the most influential scholarship is to sort articles by issues. The following are representative examples; the emphasized items should be looked at first:

Is the interpretive key to *Red Badge* religious symbolism, Darwinism, or common sense?

> Cox 3.39
>
> FRYCKSTEDT 3.69
>
> Kent 3.121
>
> LaFRANCE 3.128
>
> LEVENSON 3.137
>
> Marcus 3.149
>
> Satterfield 3.201
>
> Shulman 3.209
>
> STALLMAN 3.215
>
> Tuttleton 3.232

Does Fleming achieve a measure of maturity or does he remain a deluded young man?

FRENCH 3.64
GIBSON 3.72
Hart 3.88
Hoffman 3.100
Kapoor 3.112
Klotz 3.124
MCDERMOTT 3.158
RECHNITZ 3.192
Solomon 3.212

Was *Red Badge* inspired by Greek classics, the Bible, Zola, or Tolstoy?

ANDERSON 3.10
Dunn 3.49
DUSENBURY 3.50
Gibson 3.72

Were Fleming's battlefield heroics manifestations of courage or panic-fear?

BEAVER 3.16
Brooke-Rose 3.25
Conder 3.37
FRASER 3.62
KRAUTH 3.126
Miller 3.160
PIZER 3.181
Vanderbilt and Weiss 3.236
WEISS 3.248

Beyond these issues the annotations that follow describe clusters of articles on historical details, on Crane's varying narrative perspectives, and on his stylistic techniques (especially his use of color). Also, there has been much inventive and interesting source hunting, especially on "the red badge," on "The red sun was pasted in the sky like a wafer" (ch. 9), and the "hot plowshares" (ch. 24) images.

A final caveat is important. Each of the full-length studies recommended above in the Biography and General Criticism sections has devoted considerable space to *Red Badge* and should not be ignored in any study of this American classic.

LITERARY CRITICISM

Book

3.1   GIBSON, DONALD B. *"The Red Badge of Courage": Redefining the Hero.* Boston: Twayne, 1988. xii+111. A monograph on *Red Badge* that explores the tensions between the traditional initiation story in which Fleming matures and the persistent, undercutting comments to the effect that Fleming is deluded and more egotistical at the story's end. Gibson's thesis is that Crane intended both readings: "Throughout the text Henry appears more or less sympathetic, more or less deserving of blame or censure. This modulation of the reader's response is carefully and intentionally managed, largely through irony—and, as well, through editing of irony when the negative or positive response elicited toward Henry seems too great or too little." Since Gibson stresses the value of ambiguity and ambivalence in *Red Badge,* he rejects the Binder-Parker "expanded" version that leaves Fleming clearly deluded at the end.

Articles, Book Chapters, and Study-Guide Pamphlets

3.2   "A Boy and a Battle." *Life* 31 (10 Sept. 1951): 102–8. Descriptions, pictures, and cartoons (by Bill Mauldin, who also acted in the film) of the filming of *Red Badge.*

3.3   "A Green Private Under Fire." *New York Times* 18 Oct. 1895: 3. Discusses contemporary reaction to *Red Badge,* especially the authenticity of Crane's picture of combat and his deromanticizing of war. Reprinted in Pizer (3.184).

3.4   "[John Huston's Film Version of *The Red Badge of Courage*]." *Loew's Incorporated: Report of Annual Meeting.* 1952. 5, 13. The news that though the Huston film version of *Red Badge* was named one of the best pictures of the year, it did not make any money for the studio.

3.5   "Redeeming the 'Red Badge.'" *Bookman* 35 (1912): 235–36. An early version of the story of the *Red Badge* manuscript in pawn with the typist, who refused to give it back until paid the $15 owed for typing. See Garland (1.97) for more on this incident.

3.6   "Stephen Crane and *The Red Badge of Courage.*" *New York Times Book Review* 30 September 1945: 4. Brief comments on Crane and *Red Badge.*

3.7 AARON, DANIEL. "Stephen Crane and Harold Frederic." *The Unwritten War: American Writers and the Civil War.* New York: Knopf, 1973. 210–25. This chapter compares Frederic's and Crane's handling of the Civil War. Aaron sees Frederic as anti–Civil War but Crane as antiwar generally. That is, for Crane, war strips men of their freedom and autonomy; they survive by becoming more animalistic and machinelike—amounting to "a picture of war that resembles a religious revival in hell."

3.8 AGRAWAL, D. C. "Vision and Form in *The Red Badge of Courage.*" *Banasthali Patrika* 11 (July 1968): 86–90. This article is cited in several bibliographies, for instance, *PMLA International Bibliography* 1968: 889. Unfortunately, I have not been able to locate a copy of it.

3.9 ALBRECHT, ROBERT C. "Content and Style in *The Red Badge of Courage.*" *College English* 27 (1966): 487–92. A helpful and convincing essay. Thesis: Crane wrote at a time when confidence in any absolutes was crumbling so he lays out several versions of "reality." He concludes that though Fleming has matured he has not achieved manhood and he has not come to any final answers—not because his character is deficient but because reality, including his "real" self, is ongoing and changing.

3.10 ANDERSON, WARREN D. "Homer and Stephen Crane." *Nineteenth-Century Fiction* 19 (1964): 77–86. Anderson seeks out the obvious references, mostly in *Red Badge,* to Homer and the classics.

3.11 ANDREWS, LARRY. "The Realistic View of the Civil War as Seen in *The Red Badge of Courage* and *Miss Ravenel's Conversion.*" *Missouri English Bulletin* 24 (1969): 1–6. Cited in *Annual Bibliography of English Language and Literature* 1969: 381 (but not in Stallman's *Stephen Crane: A Critical Bibliograhy* or the *PMLA International Bibliography.* I have not been able to examine it.

3.12 BACHE, WILLIAM B. "*The Red Badge of Courage* and 'The Short Happy Life of Francis Macomber.'" *Western Humanities Review* 15 (1961): 83–84. Crane's alleged influence on Hemingway.

3.13 BAKER, RAY STANNARD. "The New Journalism." *The American Chronicle.* New York: Scribner's, 1945. 98–101. Baker was a McClure syndicate editor; one short paragraph describes Crane, basking in his *Red Badge* fame, visiting the syndicate offices: "He was often in our office. I recall finding him one day sitting on top of my desk with his knees drawn up to his chin and his long arms clasping his legs—a pale, slim, tired-looking young fellow, full of half cynical, half pessimistic talk, but always interesting."

3.14   BANKS, NANCY HUSTON. "The Novels of Two Journalists." *Bookman* 2 (1895): 217–20. An early perceptive review of *Red Badge*. Unlike Edward Townsend, who wrote the novel *A Daughter of the Tenements*, Crane does not write like a journalist: his "short, sharp sentences hurled without sequence give one the feeling of being pelted from different angles by hail—hail that is hot." (Reprinted in Weatherford, *A Critical Heritage*, 2.17: #32).

3.15   BASTEIN, FRIEDEL H. "A Note on the Contemporary German Reception of Stephen Crane's *The Red Badge of Courage*." *American Literary Realism* 12 (1979): 151–54. The title is self-explanatory. The Germans thought *Red Badge* was gory and reminiscent of Zola. Of interest: *Red Badge* was not brought to the German public in a German translation until the 1950s.

3.16   BEAVER, HAROLD. "Stephen Crane: The Hero as Victim." *Yearbook of English Studies* 12 (1982): 186–93. Contrary to real heroes' "cool deliberation," Crane's heroes, Fleming *par excellence,* display "the passionate heroism of . . . pseudo-heroes." Beaver's point is broader than the familiar observation that Fleming's courage (and his coward- ice) are animalistic and reflexive. Beaver writes of the difficulties Crane faced in examining "the quandary of heroism in an unheroic age."

3.17   BERRYMAN, JOHN. "Stephen Crane: *The Red Badge of Courage.*" *The American Novel from James Fenimore Cooper to William Faulkner.* Ed. Wallace Stegner. New York: Basic Books, 1965. 86–96. Berryman's chapter sketches Crane and *Red Badge* and comments on Crane's style, his empathy yet his coolness and distance, and his intense selectivity. Cautions readers about the irony of the concluding chapter.

3.18   BLOOM, HAROLD. Introduction. *Stephen Crane's "The Red Badge of Courage": Modern Critical Interpretation.* Ed. Harold Bloom. New York: Chelsea House, 1987. 1–6. A quick-dash introduction to a reprinting of eight articles and/or book chapters representative of modern criticism on *Red Badge*. Bloom cites Crane's irony, his originality, and his debt to Kipling. Bloom used the identical six-page introduction to his *Stephen Crane: Modern Critical Views* (2.47).

3.19   BRADBURY, MALCOLM. Introduction. *"The Red Badge of Courage" by Stephen Crane.* London: Dent, 1983. v–xiii. Typical paperback introduction. *Red Badge* was the first modern war novel; there are two

Cranes in the novel: the impressionist of imagination and the naturalist of experience.

3.20   BRADLEY, SCULLEY, et al. Introduction. *"The Red Badge of Courage":
An Annotated Text, Backgrounds and Sources, Essays in Criticism.* Ed.
Bradley Sculley. New York: Norton, 1962. vii–ix. A general sketch of
Crane and his works; with regard to *Red Badge* Bradley discusses
impressionism and veritism. "He sought 'truth,' he said, apparently
meaning to represent emotional actuality or being, at the expense of
depiction if necessary."

3.21   BRADNICK, JEAN A. Foreword. *The Red Badge of Courage,* Limited
Edition of West Virginia Pulp and Paper Co., (Christmas 1968). A
Thoth bibliography 11 (1970): 29 says it is available in the Mayfield
Library of Syracuse University. I contacted the Syracuse George Arents
Research Library; they are still trying to locate and send me a copy of
this note.

3.22   BRERETON, FREDERIC. Introduction. *"The Red Badge of Courage" by
Stephen Crane.* London: Collins, 1939. vii–xi. A reissue to honor the
war dead: Crane's understanding of war will help those suffering the
futility and disillusionment from World War II.

3.23   BRESLIN, PAUL. "Courage and Convention: *The Red Badge of
Courage.*" *Yale Review* 66 (1976): 209–22. *Red Badge* is a study in
Fleming's practical adjustment to "generic" war. That is, "Crane is
among a handful of writers to ignore the ideology of either side."

3.24   BRODY, E. C. "Tolstoy and Crane's *The Red Badge of Courage.*"
Studia Slavica Hungaricae 24 (1978): 39–54. Despite talk of "the
jolting dreams of Henry Fielding (sic)" this analysis, worthy of note,
will be useful in classroom situations. Brody is "certain that Tolstoy
greatly influenced Crane" and he shows detailed parallel treatments of
battles, nature, sky, confusion, contempt of officers, and so on.

3.25   BROOKE-ROSE, CHRISTINE. "Ill Logics of Irony." *New Essays on
"The Red Badge of Courage."* Ed. Lee Clark Mitchell. Cambridge:
Cambridge UP, 1986. 129–46. A contemporary analysis of *Red
Badge* but the upshot is familiar: Crane's book is about fear; in his
novel cowardice and courage are opposite ways of dealing with it. She
suggests that Fleming's most shameful deed is not abandoning the
tattered man but blackmailing Wilson.

3.26   BROOKS, VAN WYCK. " 'Makers and Finders.' " *The Writer in America.* New York: Dutton, 1953. 32–62. Passing mention (37–38) about
the early reputation of *Red Badge* as "sensational trash."

3.27   BURHANS, CLINTON S. "Judging Henry Judging: Point of View in
        The Red Badge of Courage." *Ball State University Forum* 15.2 (1974):
        38–48. Which standard is appropriate to judge Fleming: his, Crane's
        objective narrator, or the reader's common sense? Burhans concludes
        that, at the novel's end, Fleming is still a deluded adolescent.

3.28   ——. "Twin Lights on Henry Fleming: Structural Parallels in *The
        Red Badge of Courage.*" *American Quarterly* 30 (1974): 149–59.
        Useful as a class handout; helpful discussions on the structure of *Red
        Badge* and the "complex and brilliant irony of his [Crane's] point of
        view."

3.29   CARLSON, ERIC W. "Crane's *The Red Badge of Courage.*" *Explicator*
        16 (1958): Item 34. Another note on the source and meaning of the
        red wafer reference at the end of chapter 9. Carlson argues that Crane
        was referring to the red disk of wax used to seal a document. Compare
        with Osborne (3.176).

3.30   CARRUTHERS, SHARON. "'Old Soldiers Never Die': A Note on Col.
        John L. Burleigh." *Studies in the Novel* 10 (1978): 158–60. An
        elaborate note: Many veterans were so impressed with the verisimili-
        tude of *Red Badge* they were sure Crane had been in combat. Col.
        Burleigh represents the last word on this response: He declared in an
        article in *The Roycroft Quarterly,* "I was with Crane at Antietam!" See
        also Pratt (3.185).

3.31   CAZEMAJOU, JEAN. "*The Red Badge of Courage:* The 'Religion of
        Peace' and the War Archetype." *Stephen Crane in Transition: Centenary
        Essays.* Ed. Joseph Katz. Dekalb: Northern Illinois UP, 1972. 54–65.
        Short piece: Crane was not a nihilist; the irony in *Red Badge* sought to
        deflate the splendor and crusade of war and hence served a "deeply-felt
        sense of justice."

3.32   ——. "Mediators and Mediation in Rudolfo Anyaya's Trilogy: *Bless
        Me, Ultima, Heart of Aztlan* and *Tortuga.*" *European Perspectives on
        Hispanic Literature of the United States.* Ed. Genevieve Fabre. Hous-
        ton: Arte Publico, 1988. 55–65. Cazemajou sees the influence of
        Crane on Anaya's *Heart of Aztlan.* He finds that the phrase, "the sun
        hung like a gold medallion in the blue sky," has "a Cranean ring to
        it."

3.33   CHASE, RICHARD. Introduction. *"The Red Badge of Courage" by
        Stephen Crane.* Cambridge, MA: Riverside, 1960. x–xix. A typical
        short introduction with predictable comments: Crane was a naturalist

who sought to discuss the meaning of life by examining the behavior and emotions of an individual in the midst of violence. Reprinted as the introduction in *The Red Badge of Courage,* edited by Chase (Cambridge, MA: Riverside, 1960).

3.34   CHUNG, YOUN-SON. "The Concept of Fear: Psychoanalysis and *The Red Badge of Courage.*" *English Language and Literature* 33 (1987): 43–54. Nothing particularly original here. Chung's piece is basically a roundup of other psychological analyses of *Red Badge.* Thesis: Fear and courage are both essentially brute, unconscious reactions.

3.35   CLARK, ROBERT LUTHER. "Stephen Crane and *The Red Badge of Courage.*" *Stephen Crane: An Appreciation.* Ed. Christopher Farlekas. Port Jervis, NY: Colonial School and Camp, 1962. 4–7. An interesting short essay. Thesis: The impact of *Red Badge* was strong because it was at once traditional, a "romance novel . . . [describing] a young man's initiation," and new, treating "the impact of a single consciousness in which the actual and the imaginary intermingle and conflict."

3.36   COLVERT, JAMES B. "*The Red Badge of Courage* and a Review of Zola's *La Debacle.*" *Modern Language Notes* 71 (1956): 98–100. Though many literary historians have speculated that Zola's *La Debacle* was the source of *Red Badge,* it is very unlikely that Crane read the Frenchman's naturalistic war novel. Colvert makes a convincing case that it is more plausible that Crane read a review of *La Debacle* in the 10 July 1892 New York *Tribune,* and he shows that Crane's novel resembles the descriptions in several important particulars.

3.37   CONDER, JOHN J. "*The Red Badge of Courage:* Form and Function." *Modern American Fiction: Form and Function.* Ed. Thomas Daniel Young. Baton Rouge: Louisiana State UP, 1989. 28–38. A restatement of his 1984 monograph on American naturalism (2.64). Conder argues that because the characters in *Red Badge* are not individuals but types, conditions, not consciousness control actions: "Conditions create Henry's fear and shame . . . conditions create his illusions . . . induce his [partly false] education." This, of course, is too black and white. Also, since Henry's consciousness filters his awareness of the conditions, a conscious, at least partly autonomous, self must be present.

3.38   CONRAD, JOSEPH. "His War Book: A Preface to Stephen Crane's 'The Red Badge of Courage.'" *Last Essays.* New York: Doubleday, 1926. 119–24. Conrad speaks to the observation by several English critics that there were remarkable similarities between *Red Badge* and *The*

Nigger of the "Narcissus." Conrad responded with compliments on Crane's "monodrama" masterpiece: its modernity, its concern with primitive emotions and elemental truth, and its profundity. Also appearing in the London Heinemann edition of 1925 and later expanded into his preface for Beer's *Stephen Crane* (1.70).

3.39   COX, JAMES TRAMMELL. "The Imagery of 'The Red Badge of Courage.'" *Modern Fiction Studies* 5 (1959): 209–19. Cox casts Crane as a Darwinian and *Red Badge* as a story of the struggle for survival in a hostile universe. Much attention is paid to color symbolism.

3.40   CREWS, FREDERIC C. "Introduction and Annotations." *"The Red Badge of Courage" by Stephen Crane*. Indianapolis: Bobbs-Merrill, 1964. vii–xxiii. An unsatisfactory introduction. The biographical sections are not current and contain errors; for example, Crews states that Crane *bought* Brede Place. The sections on *Red Badge* waffle continuously on Crane's point of view as author, leading Crews to claim both that Fleming grows, acquiring new poise and competence, and also that Henry merely trades his "childish tantrums" for "manly self-deception."

3.41   DECKLE, BERNARD. "Stephen Crane: *The Red Badge of Courage*." *Profiles of Modern American Authors*. Tokyo: Charles E. Tuttle, 1969. 19–14. A superficial introductory piece written for Japanese audiences.

3.42   DELBANCO, ANDREW. "The American Stephen Crane: The Context of *The Red Badge of Courage*." *New Essays on "The Red Badge of Courage*." Ed. Lee Clark Mitchell. Cambridge: Cambridge UP, 1986. 49–76. A sophisticated examination tracing, as a theme, Crane's sensitivity to missed social obligations and, as a strategy, Crane's pursuit of actualities. War is the best setting for both tasks for it is "an experience that obliterates all inherited points of moral and even perceptual reference." Among the best of very recent analyses of *Red Badge*.

3.43   DETWEILER, ROBERT. "Christ and the Christ Figure in American Fiction." *The Christian Scholar* 47 (1964): 111–24. Preachy theology that betrays its 1960s date. With regard to Crane there is a predictable paragraph on Jim Conklin as Jesus Christ in *Red Badge*.

3.44   DEVOTO, BERNARD. "Fiction Fights the Civil War." *Saturday Review* 17 (18 Dec. 1937): 3–4, 15–16. Reflections on the current popularity of *Gone with the Wind; Red Badge* is not really about the Civil War but about an individual in battle.

3.45 DIETZ, RUDOLPH F. "Crane's *The Red Badge of Courage.*" *Explicator* 42 (1984): 37–38. A neat and important note. Many Crane commentators, among them several respected ones, talk of Fleming's "running like a rabbit." Dietz notes that Crane said this of another soldier; Fleming runs "like a chicken" after others have begun to run. The upshot is that with more attention to the text a less cowardly Fleming emerges.

3.46 ———. "Crainway and Son: Ralph Ellison's *Invisible Man* as Seen through the Perspective of Twain, Crane, and Hemingway." *Delta* 18 (1984): 25–46. This article is really on Ellison; Crane is mentioned in passing. Thesis: A *Red Badge* wound-image is an important symbol for both authors.

3.47 DILLINGHAM, WILLIAM B. "Insensibility in *The Red Badge of Courage.*" *College English* 25 (1963): 194–98. A heavy-handed and grossly overstated thesis: Henry does not grow in *Red Badge;* indeed he regresses, for he reverts to animal-like courage to become a "hero."

3.48 DIXSON, ROBERT J. *The Red Badge of Courage.* New York: Regents, 1954. A simplified and modified version of *Red Badge* (a vocabulary range of 2,600 words) along with study exercises.

3.49 DUNN, N. E. "The Common Man's *Iliad.*" *Comparative Literature Studies* 21 (1984): 270–81. A thoughtful, strongly argued piece concluding that Fleming remains deluded at the end of the *Red Badge.* Thesis: *Red Badge* is an old tale, based on *The Iliad;* "Crane intended to establish and to maintain consistently a correlation between his story and that of the epic poem." The parallels that Dunn has teased out would be a useful classroom handout.

3.50 DUSENBERY, ROBERT. "The Homeric Mood in 'The Red Badge of Courage.'" *Pacific Coast Philology* 3 (1968): 31–37. One of the first statements of similarities between *Red Badge* and *The Iliad.* Conclusion: "Crane's realism is more Homeric than late nineteenth-century naturalistic realism."

3.51 EBY, CECIL D. "The Source of Crane's Metaphor, 'Red Badge of Courage.'" *American Literature* 32 (1960): 204–7. More source hunting; Eby proposes the patch worn by Gen. Philip Kearny's New Jersey "red badge" division. Reprinted as "General Philip Kearny's

'Red Badge of Courage' in *The Red Badge of Courage,* eds. Sculley Bradley, et al. (3.263). See also Kearny (3.120).

3.52   ———. "Stephen Crane's 'Fierce Red Wafer.' " *English Language Notes* 1 (1963): 128–30. Ever since Stallman suggested in 1951 (3.215) that Crane's line "The red sun was pasted in the sky like a wafer" was a religious symbol referring to a communion wafer, Crane critics have gone around and around. Eby argues that there is nothing symbolic involved; rather, the whole matter has only to do with Crane's fondness for the words "fierce" and "red."

3.53   EGRI, PETER. "The Genetic and Generic Aspect of Stephen Crane's *The Red Badge of Courage.*" *Acta Litteraria Academiae Scientiarum Hungaricae* 22 (1980): 333–48. Of interest for its Marxian analysis of Crane (he "found an inspired idiom and a prophetic pattern which have been paving the way for the modern American novel in the age of alienation") and for its description of the Crane industry in eastern Europe.

3.54   ELLISON, RALPH. Introduction. *"The Red Badge of Courage" and Four Great Stories of Stephen Crane.* New York: Dell, 1960. 7–24. *Not* just another paperback introduction. This distinguished American novelist shows how Crane's moral seriousness ("the playboy author was engaged in the most desperate moral struggle") permeates *Red Badge,* "The Open Boat," "The Bride Comes to Yellow Sky," *The Monster,* and "The Blue Hotel." Reprinted as "Stephen Crane and the Mainstream of American Fiction," *Shadow and Act* (New York: Random House, 1964): 74–78.

3.55   EMPEY, ARTHUR GUY. Introduction. *The Red Badge of Courage.* New York, 1917. Cited by Stallman, *Stephen Crane: A Critical Bibliography:* 302. Interlibrary loan librarians were not able to find a copy; apparently it is rare, as it does not show up in the OCLC data bank.

3.56   EVANS, DAVID L. "Henry's Hell: The Night Journey in *The Red Badge of Courage.*" *Utah Academy Proceeding* 44 (1967): 159–66. An overblown examination of the mystical overtones, "specifically, the archetypical pattern of the Night Journey," in *Red Badge.* Evans concludes that despite Fleming's symbolic death and rebirth he achieved neither permanent change nor significant growth.

3.57   FADIMAN, CLIFTON. Afterword. *The Red Badge of Courage* by Stephen Crane. New York: Macmillan, 1967. 203–5. Very brief comments on *Red Badge* to the effect that Crane's story "might be [about] any war, any very young man."

3.58   FARBER, MANNY. "Film [*The Red Badge of Courage*]." *Nation* 173 (1951): 409–10. A highly critical review of John Huston's film version of *Red Badge*.

3.59   FEIDELSON, CHARLES. "Three Views of the Human Person: *The Scarlet Letter, Walden,* and *The Red Badge of Courage.*" *Reports and Speeches of the Sixth Yale Conference on the Teaching of English* 8 and 9 April 1960: 47–52. Better on Thoreau, outstanding on Hawthorne. On Crane, Feidelson argues that failing to get direction from society (the officers), nature, or his comrades, Fleming must construct his own self. Useful as a class handout.

3.60   FELDMAN, ABRAHAM. "Crane's Title from Shakespeare?" *American Notes and Queries* 8 (1950): 185–86. Offers the phrase "murder's crimson badge" found in *Henry VI: Part II* (Act III), as the source.

3.61   FLEISHMAN, AVROM. "The Landscape of Hysteria in *The Secret Agent.*" *Conrad Revisited: Essays for the Eighties.* Ed. Ross C. Murfin. Tuscaloosa: U of Alabama P, 1985. 89–105. Comments on the influence of *Red Badge* and *Maggie* on Conrad.

3.62   FRASER, JOHN. "Crime and Forgiveness: 'The Red Badge' in Time of War." *Criticism* 9 (1967): 243–56. A perceptive and illuminating investigation of *Red Badge* as a study in the ability of morality to cover both ordinary and exceptional situations. Fraser argues that though early in the novel Fleming's psyche disintegrates from battlefield stress and "ethical over-intensities," by the end he recovers his moral bearings and so he matures.

3.63   FREE, WILLIAM JOSEPH. "Smoke Imagery in *The Red Badge of Courage.*" *CLA Journal* 7 (1963): 148–52. A naturalistic Crane: Smoke in *Red Badge* symbolizes a chaotic, inhuman, meaningless war that blinds humans who are already directionless and lost.

3.64   FRENCH, WARREN. "Stephen Crane: Moment of Myth." *Prairie Schooner* 55 (1981): 155–67. A thoughtful and interesting thesis: Fleming's maturation is practical. French proposes a pragmatic Henry who "has learned to make the world work for him." French extends his case to Crane's other tale of Fleming, "The Veteran," which shows "that the same individual might be both shrewd and unexploitative enough to rise above the victimizing power of institutions, while remaining a functioning and even respected member of his hometown society."

3.65   FRIEDMAN, NORMAN. "Criticism and the Novel: Hardy, Heming-
        way, Crane, Woolf, Conrad." *Antioch Review* 18 (1958): 343–70. The
        section of Friedman's essay on Crane (356–361) argues that Fleming
        changes not from cowardice to heroism or from irresponsibility to
        maturity but from ignorance to knowledge in "his conception of
        himself in relation to war as experience."

3.66   FRIEDRICH, OTTO. "The Passion of Death in Ambrose Bierce." *Zero*
        2 (1956): 72–94. The article deals with Bierce with a few comments
        on how his treatment of combat differs from Crane's *Red Badge*.

3.67   FROHOCK, W. M. *The Red Badge* and the Limits of Parody." *Southern
        Review* 6 (1970): 137–48. Frohock argues that while Solomon's
        (2.15) thesis that the key to Crane is parody goes a long way, such is
        not the case with *Red Badge*. In that great novel, "Crane's genius
        shows itself fully as much in his knowing when *not* to parody and
        when to leave stereotypes and clichés intact"; both the techniques
        are employed with great skill, avoiding both melodrama and senti-
        mentality.

3.68   _____. "American Realism and the Elegiac Sensibility: Stephen Crane
        and Frank Norris." *Geschichte Und Fiktion: Amerikanische Prosa Im 19.
        Jahrhundert*. Ed. Alfred Weber and Grandel Harmut. Gottingen:
        Vanderhoeck and Ruprecht, 1972. 216–37. A carefully argued,
        convincing case is made that Crane was well aware of and made good
        use of contemporary literary patterns. In particular, in *Red Badge*
        Crane effectively uses (without sentimentality or triteness) the theme
        of a country boy leaving a pleasant landscape to be initiated into
        manhood by the rigors of war.

3.69   FRYCKSTEDT, OLAF W. "Henry Fleming's Tuppenny Fury: Cosmic
        Pessimism in Stephen Crane's *The Red Badge of Courage*." *Studia
        Neophilologia* 33 (1961): 265–81. Thesis: Crane's worldview of
        "naturalistic pessimism" is especially clear in the excised portions of
        the *Red Badge* manuscript wherein Fleming's thoughts of revolt
        against the universe are concentrated. Fryckstedt concludes that the
        shorter (that is, standard Appleton version) presents the possibility of
        relief in an absurd world, whereas the longer, Binder version (3.260)
        has an unrelieved atmosphere of despair.

3.70   FULWILER, TOBY. "The Death of the Handsome Sailor: A Study of
        Billy Budd and *The Red Badge of Courage*." *Arizona Quarterly* 26
        (1970): 101–12. Fulwiler's premise is very suspicious: While
        Melville's prose must be carefully and repeatedly studied with several
        close readings, "Crane's style, on the other hand, is lucid, simple, and

quickly apprehensible on one reading." Knowing this, if you are still tempted to read Fulwiler's piece you will find that while *Billy Budd* and *Red Badge* were written within four years of each other, Melville's novel exhibits nineteenth-century romanticism, while Crane's antici- pates twentieth-century existentialism.

3.71   GALE, ROBERT L. *Barrons's Simplified Approach to "The Red Badge of Courage" by Stephen Crane.* Woodbury, NY: Barrons Educational Series, 1966. xiv+110. A surprise: The biographical sketch is sound and reliable, the cultural chronology is interesting, and *Red Badge* is helpfully analyzed as an initiation story. The chapter-by-chapter summaries will be useful in composing classroom handouts. Under- graduate students relying on this guide will be better prepared than many in a class.

3.72   GIBSON, DONALD B. "Crane's *The Red Badge of Courage.*" *Explicator* 24 (1966): Item 49. Gibson points out Homeric and other classical myths in *Red Badge*.

3.73   GLASSER, WILLIAM. "The Red Badge of Courage." *Americana Austraica* 4 (1978): 24–39. A conventional reading of *Red Badge* as an initiation story: Though Henry grows, even at the end "he never becomes aware of the larger, ironic perspective of himself offered by the narrator."

3.74   GOETHALS, THOMAS. Introduction. *The Red Badge of Courage.* New York: Collier Books, 1962. 7–12. Brief biographical sketch followed by a discussion that *Red Badge* is a romance novel because it deals with "the impact upon a single consciousness in which the actual and the imaginary intermingle and conflict."

3.75   GOLLIN, RITA K. "'Little Souls Who Thirst for Fight' in *The Red Badge of Courage.*" *Arizona Quarterly* 30 (1974): 111–18. Gollin holds that "Crane's war novel is clearly an antiwar novel," for his interest is not in combat but in the pointless quarrels of the men, their "petty pugnaciousness and . . . intrinsically quarrelsome nature."

3.76   GORDON, CAROLINE. *How to Read a Novel.* New York: Viking, 1957. 91–93. Gordon mistakenly asserts that Crane said the inspiration for the battle scenes of *Red Badge* came from Stendahl's *The Charterhouse of Parma.*

3.77   GOTTSCHALK, HANS. *"Maggie", "The Red Badge of Courage": Selected Short Stories, Representative Poems—A Study Guide.* Bound Brook, NJ: Shelly, 1963. 120. Gottschalk gives the standard biographical sketch of Crane along with study-guide information on *Maggie, Red Badge,* and a half-dozen poems and short stories. Beware of the "information" in this book. For instance, apparently Gottschalk is unsure whether the story about *Red Badge* being in hock at the typewriter refers to the person who types or the machine, so he combines both possibilities: "Early in 1894 Crane had to borrow $30 from Garland to get back his typewriter which he had given as security for the cost of having *The Red Badge of Courage* typed."

3.78   GRENNAN, JOSEPH E. *Monarch Notes: Stephen Crane's "The Red Badge of Courage."* New York: Simon and Schuster, 1965. 80. Typical Monarch study guide. Detailed chapter-by-chapter summaries, with comments on Crane's thematic and stylistic innovations, brief character analysis, sample term paper questions, and a survey of influential criticism, especially in the 1940s, 1950s, and 1960s. All in all, Grennan provides solid information.

3.79   GULLASON, THOMAS A. "New Sources for Stephen Crane's War Motif." *Modern Language Notes* 72 (1957): 572–75. Gullason's brief, pioneering study looks at the books of Crane's father, Jonathan Crane, concluding that "there was more than enough in the father's books to inspire his son's war theme."

3.80   GWYNN, FREDERICK. Editorial Note. *College English* 16 (1955): 427. Gwynn scoffs at Stallman's (3.215) identification of Jim Conklin with Jesus Christ.

3.81   HABEGGER, ALFRED. "Fighting Words: The Talk of Men at War in *The Red Badge.*" *Critical Essays on Stephen Crane's The Red Badge of Courage.* Ed. Donald Pizer. Boston: G. K. Hall, 1990. 229–38. An examination of the speech of the soldiers in *Red Badge.* Habegger concluded that the soldiers' general inexpressiveness in speech is highlighted in Fleming after he is "wounded": His "red badge of courage marks his inability thenceforth to speak the truth about himself and the war. *The Red Badge* tells the story of an irreparable moral injury." Habegger also has several interesting observations on speech in "The Open Boat."

3.82   HACKETT, ALICE PAYNE. "1896." *60 Years of Best Sellers.* New York: Bowker, 1956. 96. *Red Badge* was the eighth-placed seller in 1896. Incidentally, Crane's friend (some years later) Harold Frederic's *The Damnation of Theron Ware* was fifth.

3.83   HACKETT, FRANCIS. "Another War." *New Republic* 11 (1917): 250–51. The perennial nature of *Red Badge* will help Americans to understand the nature of war—in this case World War I.

3.84   HAFER, CAROL B. "The Red Badge of Absurdity: Irony in *The Red Badge of Courage.*" *CLA Journal* 14 (1971): 440–43. Hafer goes one step beyond those critics who see the ending of the *Red Badge* as totally ironic; she sees instead an absurd ending.

3.85   HAGEMANN, E. R. "Stephen Crane and *The Argonaut:* 1895–1901." *Stephen Crane Newsletter* 5.1 (1970): 8–11. A list of some 43 advertisements, articles, news items, reviews, and an obituary Hagemann found in the noted San Francisco weekly.

3.86   HAIGHT, GORDON S. Introduction. *Miss Ravennel's Conversion.* New York: Rinehart, 1955. v–xix. Haight argues that Crane read the popular Civil War novel by John William De Forest but that he turned De Forest's masterful realism into "a somewhat decadent impressionism."

3.87   HALLADAY, JEAN R. *Sartor Resartus* Revisited: Carlylean Echoes in Crane's *The Red Badge of Courage.*" *Nineteenth Century Prose* 16 (1988–89): 23–33. Halladay holds that "Henry Fleming's ordeal and eventual triumph in the *Red Badge* may well be a kind of subconscious reenactment of the ordeal and triumph of Diogenes Teufelsdrockh in that central section [the 'Everlasting No'—Everlasting Yea' chapters] in that central portion of *Sartor Resartus.* Of course, anything is possible. It does not even have to be subconscious influence either, for as Halladay herself admits, "Perhaps it is a matter of simple coincidence." On this point also see O'Donnell (3.173).

3.88   HART, JOHN E. *"The Red Badge of Courage* as Myth and Symbol." *University of Kansas City Review* 19 (1953): 249–56. An early, pioneering *Red Badge* piece. Hart concludes that Fleming is reborn when he identifies with the group. Also treated are demon and serpent images, plus the tattered soldier, the tall soldier, and the loud soldier as symbolic types.

3.89   HARTWICK, HARRY. "The Red Badge of Courage." *The Foreground of American Fiction.* New York: American Book Company, 1934. 21–44. A short chapter in a survey treatment of American literature. Hartwick sees in all of Crane's works, especially in *Red Badge,* a nihilistic naturalism. Interesting comments on Crane's "impressionism . . . [as] sensory kodaking."

3.90   HASSAN, IHAB. "'The Dialectic of Initiation'". *Radical Innocence: Studies in the Contemporary American Novel.* Princeton, NJ: Princeton UP, 1961. 25–58. *Red Badge* is briefly (42–43) discussed in terms of Fleming's partial initiation.

3.91   HAYES, KEVIN J. "How Stephen Crane Shaped Henry Fleming."
        Studies in the Novel 22 (1990): 296–307. A close examination of the
        changes Crane made between the draft and the final manuscript of *Red
        Badge:* "Crane's revisions to the first part of the manuscript make
        Fleming's behavior more consistent, anticipate his conduct in battle,
        and consequently undermine any possible growth." His last conten-
        tion aligns Hayes with Binder-Parker's insistence on a clear and
        unambiguous ending of *Red Badge.*

3.92   HEMINGWAY, ERNEST. Introduction; Note. *Men At War.* New
        York: Bramhill, 1942. xvii, 120. Crane's sources were his imagina-
        tion, conversations with veterans, and Matthew Brady's great photo-
        graphs. "Creating his story out of this material he wrote that great
        boy's dream of war that was to be truer to how war is than any war
        the boy who wrote it would ever live to see. It is one of the finest
        books of our literature and I included it entire [121–210] because it
        is all as much of one piece as a great poem is." Hemingway speaks
        of trying and then abandoning his attempt to cut sections of it.
        "The Crane book . . . could not be cut at all. I am sure he cut it all
        himself as he wrote it to the exact measure of the poem it is." A
        similar, much abbreviated comment about Brady's photographs and
        Red Badge is contained in *A Moveable Feast* (New York: Scribner's,
        1964): 133.

3.93   HENDERSON, HARRY B. "Bellamy, Cable, James, Adams, Crane:
        Towards *The Red Badge of Courage.*" *Versions of the Past: The Historical
        Imagination in American Fiction.* New York: Oxford UP, 1974.
        198–231. Crane is treated in the final section of a chapter on several
        American authors. *Red Badge* is considered as an examination of
        heroism in a naturalistic world.

3.94   HERGESHEIMER, JOSEPH. Introduction. *The Red Badge of Courage
        and "The Veteran."* Vol. 1 of *The Works of Stephen Crane.* Ed. Wilson
        Follett. New York: Knopf, 1925. ix–xvii. Hergesheimer recalls how
        Red Badge seemed to him at his first reading at the age of fifteen. He
        also argues that *Red Badge* changed all subsequent war novels, and he
        stresses   the   impact   of   Crane's   "directness   and   candor."
        Hergesheimer's piece is reprinted in *Fifty Years,* ed. Clifton Fadiman
        (New York: Knopf, 1965), 769–771), a retrospective volume of the
        best of Knopf from 1915 to 1965.

3.95   HERZBERG, MAX J. Introduction. *"The Red Badge of Courage" by
        Stephen Crane.* New York: Modern Library, 1925. v–xli. A lengthy
        attempt to get the Crane revival in high gear. Beer's *Stephen Crane*

(1.1) is highly touted and the Newark Crane Society praised (Herzberg was its president for several years). Also of much value are Herzberg's comments about Crane's life, reminiscences by college friends and literary acquaintances, and an insightful discussion of Crane themes, especially how "his keen mind instantly caught the absurd, bizarre, or ridiculous aspect of any incident." Reprinted in 1954 in a paperback edition. Note: A shortened version (v–xx) of this Introduction was included in the 1926 Appleton reissue of *Red Badge*.

3.96   _____. Introduction. *The Red Badge of Courage*. New York: Pocket Books, 1954. i–xxiv. See entry 3.95.

3.97   _____. Introduction. *"The Red Badge of Courage" and Other Stories by Stephen Crane*. New York: Dodd, Mead, 1957. v–vii. A minisketch with comments on Crane's "genius for vivid phrasing."

3.98   _____. Afterword. *"The Red Badge of Courage" by Stephen Crane*. New York: Pocket Books, 1963. 167–70. A brief note, mostly longish quotes from Crane letters and Beer's *Stephen Crane* (1.1).

3.99   HITCHCOCK, RIPLEY. Introduction. *The Red Badge of Courage*. New York: Appleton, 1900 and 1917. This could be significant or just a perfunctory piece; in either case, I have not been able to see it. Cited by Stallman, *Stephen Crane: A Critical Bibliography:* 14.3: 303.

3.100   HOFFMAN, DANIEL G. Introduction. *"The Red Badge of Courage" and Other Stories by Stephen Crane*. New York: Harper, 1959. vii–xxix. Written when attributing naturalism to Crane was beginning to be questioned, Hoffman's essay is a fence straddler: Crane's worldview is naturalistic though his characters have the responsibility of their own destinies in a world that is indifferent to them. Major themes and literary sources for *Red Badge* are discussed.

3.101   HOFFMAN, MICHAEL J. *"The Red Badge of Courage:* Between Realism and Naturalism." *The Subversive Vision: American Romanticism in Literature*. New York: Kennikat, 1972. 130–39. A simplistic thesis and jargon-laden piece: Though Crane is "visually deterministic" he is not a naturalist in the full sense. Hoffman portrays Fleming as a "semicomic Everyman" whom Crane reduces to namelessness at novel's end.

3.102   HOUGH, ROBERT L. "Crane's Henry Fleming." *Forum* (Houston) 3.9 (1961): 41–42. A potentially valuable contribution undermined by the lack of argument and textual support. Hough wonders about Fleming's inconsistent speech: Even though Fleming's observations are exceptional his descriptions are "banal and commonplace." See also on this point Ross (3.196) and Schmitz (3.202).

3.103   HOWELLS, WILLIAM DEAN. "Editor's Easy Chair." *Harper's Magazine* 130 (1915): 796–99. Howells rebuts Garnett's assertion that the British responded positively to *Red Badge* before we Americans did.

3.104   HUBBELL, JAY B. *Who Are the Major American Writers?* Durham, NC: Duke UP, 1972. 289–291, 301–303. A study of the changing literary canon; Hubbell shows two pollings: one in 1926 and another in 1948 showing Crane and *Red Badge* on the squad but not on the all-star starting lineup in either case.

3.105   HUNGERFORD, HAROLD R. "'That Was Chancellorsville': The Factual Framework for *The Red Badge of Courage*." *American Literature* 34 (1963): 520–31. Crane's novel does not identify the scene of Fleming's battlefield initiation; Hungerford convincingly establishes that it was, as long suspected, Chancellorsville.

3.106   HUSNI, KHALIL. "Crane's *The Red Badge of Courage*." *Explicator* 39 (1981): 16–18. Asserts that Fleming has not matured by the end of *Red Badge*.

3.107   IRSFELD, JOHN H. "Art and History: *The Red Badge of Courage*." *American Notes and Queries,* Supplement 1 (1978): 297–300. A superficial piece to the effect that Crane had done his homework: He was good at military jargon, he understood the camaraderie of soldiers, and his casualty figures were realistic.

3.108   JONES, WINIFRED W. Preface. *Stephen Crane's "The Red Badge of Courage."* Englewood Cliffs, NJ: Prentice-Hall, 1962. v–viii. A brief introduction to a modified version of *Red Badge* simplified for students of English as a second language.

3.109   JUDD, KIRBY E. "Suggestions for Reading and Discussion." *The Red Badge of Courage* by Stephen Crane. Boston: Houghton Mifflin, 1964. 123–137. A student guide with study questions, chapter summaries, and term-paper ideas.

3.110   KAPLAN, AMY. "The Spectacle of War in Crane's Revision of History." *New Essays on "The Red Badge of Courage."* Ed. Lee Clark Mitchell. Cambridge: Cambridge UP, 1986. 77–108. A dense, deconstructionist exploration of the theme of *Red Badge* as a critique of late nineteenth-century militarization. Kaplan supports her reading by arguing that *Red Badge* is a parody of a heroic account of the Civil War. For a much earlier full-length examination of parody in the works of Crane, see Eric Solomon (2.15).

3.111 KAPLAN, HAROLD. "Vitalism and Redemptive Violence." *Power and Order: Henry Adams and the Naturalistic Tradition in American Fiction.* Chicago: U of Chicago P, 1981. 115–30. Only six pages (121–127) of this chapter deal with Crane, who Kaplan says "developed a poetry of violence." Only to the extent that *Red Badge* is a naturalistic work are Kaplan's observations helpful.

3.112 KAPOOR, KAPIL. "Desertion in the Fields: A Note on the Interpretation of *The Red Badge of Courage.*" *Journal of the School of Languages* 7 (1980): 65–69. A very brief but interesting piece: Fleming's desertion of the tattered man in the field is the crucial event in *Red Badge.*

3.113 KATZ, JOSEPH. Introduction. *"The Red Badge of Courage" by Stephen Crane: A Facsimile Reproduction of the New York Press Appearance of December 9, 1894.* Gainesville, FL: Scholars' Facsimiles and Reprints, 1967. 9–42. Katz explains the events surrounding the abbreviated version of *Red Badge* along with details of its syndication. Katz also supplies information on pictures, cartoons, and installment divisions. See also Katz (3.265).

3.114 ———. "An Editor's Recollection of *The Red Badge of Courage.*" *Stephen Crane Newsletter* 2.3 (1968): 3–6. Wright Patterson, editor of the newspaper version of *Red Badge,* gives a detailed account of the event; unfortunately, reports Katz, Patterson's account "is mainly untrue."

3.115 ———. "The Red Badge of Courage Contract." *Stephen Crane Newsletter* 2.4 (1968): 5–10. Katz reprints the contract and wonders why Crane's attorney brother, William, did not save him from such "disadvantageous terms."

3.116 ———. Introduction. *The Red Badge of Courage.* Columbus, OH: Charles Merrill, 1969. v–xiii. A simplified introduction pitched toward high school readers. The *Red Badge* version reprinted here is a fascimile of the 1895 Appleton edition; see 3.266.

3.117 ———. "The Red Badge of Courage: A Preliminary History of the Appleton Printings." *Stephen Crane Newsletter* 4.3 (1970): 5–7. Katz lists and makes comments on various printings and editions, sixty-five in all from 1895 to 1941.

3.118   _____. *The Red Badge of Courage* from 1911—1923." *Stephen Crane Newsletter* 5.1 (1970): 1–2. Katz argues that Crane's work died with him: In twenty-two and a half years only 4,755 copies were sold, with royalties paid of only $623.97, a mere $31 per year.

3.119   KAZIN, ALFRED. Introduction. *"The Red Badge of Courage" by Stephen Crane.* New York: Bantam, 1983. vii–xviii. A general essay for the beginning reader. Standard themes are laid out; comments that Crane's detached yet driving style is the perfect vehicle for his depiction of Fleming's "mechanical courage."

3.120   KEARNY, THOMAS. *General Philip Kearny: Battle Soldier of Five Wars.* New York: Putnam's, 1937. 267–268. Kearny alleges that the red patch worn by General Kearny's troops (initially in the battle at Seven Pines) inspired the title of Crane's novel. He comments: "Crane born in Newark, while resident in Asbury Park before he became famous visited 'Kearny Castle.' When his fame was achieved he again visited General Kearny and told the General the symbolic meaning hidden under the title of his famous book."

3.121   KENT, THOMAS L. "Epistemological Uncertainty in *The Red Badge of Courage.*" *Modern Fiction Studies* 27 (1982): 621–28. Kent examines the techniques Crane uses to impress upon his readers the difficulties that stand in the way of a true apprehension of reality. Therefore, for example, "no single meaning given to the [hotly disputed] wafer simile [at the end of chapter 9] is finally correct."

3.122   _____. "The Epistemological Text: *The Red Badge of Courage,* 'The Open Boat' and 'The Blue Hotel.'" *Interpretation and Genre.* Lewisburg, PA: Bucknell UP, 1986. 124–42. A strident, somewhat repetitive expansion of Kent's two earlier articles on epistemology in Crane (3.121 and 5.52). Once again a skeptical, nihilistic Crane emerges, this time with a deconstructionist bonus to the effect that the meaning of the text is that there is no meaning.

3.123   KLOTZ, MARVIN. "Crane's 'The Red Badge of Courage.'" *Notes and Queries* 6 (1959): 68–69. Klotz's source-hunting found a nineteenth-century book that explored heroism *(The Coward* by Henry Morford) and another that uses type names instead of proper names (also by Morford, *Red-Tape and Pigeon-Hole Generals).*

3.124   _____. "Romance or Realism?: Plot, Theme and Character in *The Red Badge of Courage.*" *College Language Association Journal* 6 (1962): 98–106. Klotz wonders whether Fleming's "self-congratulatory musings at the end of the novel" make him a kinsman to the swashbuckling romantic heroes. He concludes that Fleming is an ordinary (young) man whose moral deficiency (notably abandoning the tattered man) is on a par with that of the soldiers with whom he serves. Therefore, Crane has realistically depicted ordinary soldiers' experience of war.

3.125   KNIGHT, GRANT C. "Frank Norris and Stephen Crane." *The Novel in English.* New York: Richard R. Smith, 1931. 298–305. A brief essay on Crane's career, especially the impact of *Red Badge:* "a bombshell" on both sides of the Atlantic.

3.126   KRAUTH, LELAND. "Heroes and Heroics: Stephen Crane's Moral Imperative." *South Dakota Review* 11 (1973): 86–93. A provocative but helpful thesis: Crane fumbled the ending of *Red Badge* because of an inability to combine soldierly conventional heroism and humanly compassionate aid. Krauth also points out the tensions between altruistic morality and egoistic heroism.

3.127   LABOR, EARLE. "Crane and Hemingway: Anatomy of Trauma." *Renascence* 11 (1959): 189–96. Thesis: Both authors, seeking the meaning of suffering, turned to heroes to find order in chaos.

3.128   LAFRANCE, MARSTON. "Stephen Crane's Private Fleming: His Various Battles." *Patterns of Commitment in American Literature.* Ed. Marston LaFrance. Toronto: U of Toronto P, 1967. 113–33. LaFrance rejects both symbolism and naturalism as categories, offering instead a common-sense reading of *Red Badge.* Fleming is a young man, and as he changes (and matures) he attempts to be personally honest "in fulfilling the commitments such a perception demands of the individual." Conclusion: Though Fleming has not yet achieved manhood he "has undergone considerable readjustment."

3.129   _____. "Crane, Zola, and the Hot Ploughshares." *English Language Notes* 7 (1970): 285–87. Source-hunting; LaFrance argues that "hot plowshares" (in the last chapter of *Red Badge*) did not come from Zola (as suggested by Edward Stone [3.223]) but from a poem by Shelley.

3.130   LAROCCA, CHARLES. "Stephen Crane's Inspiration." *American Heritage* 42.3 (1991): 108–9. Crane's sources for the *Red Badge* were the 124th New York State Volunteers, the red patch worn by the men of the 1st Division, III Corps, of the Union Army of the Potomac under General Philip Kearny, and the battle of Chancellorsville.

3.131   LASS, ABRAHAM H. *"The Red Badge of Courage." A Student's Guide to 50 American Novels.* New York: Washington Square, 1968. 72–76. A study guide for high schoolers.

3.132   LAVERS, NORMAN. "Order in *The Red Badge of Courage.*" *University of Kansas City Review* 32 (1966): 287–95. Lavers argues for a Freudian-Oedipal reading of *Red Badge (George's Mother* and "The Open Boat," too): The pattern is that of separation from the mother in order to achieve full development as an individual. Lavers expands this "pattern" into six distinct steps.

3.133   LEE, A. ROBERT. "Inside the Moving Box: Stephen Crane's *The Red Badge of Courage.*" *Atlantis* 5.1–2 (1983): 97–110. A shortened, earlier version of the next entry (3.134).

3.134   ———. "Stephen Crane's *The Red Badge of Courage:* The Novella as 'Moving Box.'" *The Modern American Novella.* Ed. A. Robert Lee. London: Vision, 1989. 30–47. A fresh reading of *Red Badge.* Lee examines Crane's use of moving boxes to describe Henry and his comrades and, on a second level, how "the text itself . . . can be equally thought 'a moving box,' a means of enclosing the reader for a calculated amount of time in its own claustrophobia and pressure."

3.135   LEEB, DAVID, ed. *The Red Badge of Courage.* Philadelphia: Educational Research Associates, 1966. This study-guide pamphlet is several cuts above the average. Stallman, *Stephen Crane: A Critical Bibliography* discusses it at some length (14.3: 523–24).

3.136   LETTIS, RICHARD, ROBERT F. McDONNELL, and WILLIAM E. NORRIS, eds. *Stephen Crane's "The Red Badge of Courage": Text and Criticism.* New York: Harcourt Brace, 1960. Reprints *Red Badge* along with a selection of contemporary reaction and several subsequent critical studies. All of the latter have been abstracted elsewhere in this bibliography.

3.137   LEVENSON, J.C. Introduction. *The Red Badge of Courage. The Works of Stephen Crane.* Ed. Fredson Bowers. Charlottesville: UP of Virginia, 1975. xiii–xcii. A major essay on *Red Badge,* essential for anyone who wants to sort out literary, historical, and political influences on this classic of everyman and war. Levenson examines the discarded drafts of the manuscript, concluding that Crane was responding to his own artistic reasons in his revisions. What emerges, concludes Levenson, is a tale of a boy becoming not a hero but a man; a story of initiation and growth tempered by a "residual egotism which makes the ending ambiguous."

3.138 LINNEMAN, WILLIAM R. "Satires of American Realism, 1880–1900." *American Literature* 34 (1962): 80–93. Linneman shows how humor magazines mocked authors, mostly Howells and James, by parodying their styles. Though Crane was parodied, Linneman argues, they meant to compliment *Red Badge* with takeoffs like "The sun hung like a custard pie in a burnt blanket."

3.139 LIVELY, ROBERT A. *Fiction Fights the Civil War.* Chapel Hill: U of North Carolina P, 1957. Passim. *Red Badge* is treated briefly: Fleming's "Homeric illusions" versus the real thing (136–137) and the fine line between "irrational courage and irrational cowardice" (152–155).

3.140 LOFTUS, MARGARET F. "Two Soldiers: A Comparative Study of Stephen Crane's *The Red Badge of Courage* and Tayama Katai's *One Soldier." Studies in American Literature* 9 (1971): 67–79. A comparison of how two cultures treat war in a naturalistic manner.

3.141 LORCH, THOMAS M. "The Cyclical Structure of *The Red Badge of Courage." College Language Association Journal* 10 (1967): 229–38. A useful teaching tool on the structure of *Red Badge;* among other things Lorch argues that Crane's classic goes in a large circle: Crane's ending is ironic and Fleming is back to where he started, a naïve farm boy.

3.142 LYBYER, J. M. *Red Badge of Courage Notes.* Lincoln, NE: Cliff's Notes, 1964. 71. Lybyer gives chapter summaries and brief commentaries on the characters in the novel and on Crane's techniques.

3.143 LYNN, KENNETH S. Introduction. *The Red Badge of Courage.* By Stephen Crane. Boston: Houghton Mifflin, 1964. A brief biographical sketch and general comments on *Red Badge,* stressing Fleming's initiation and maturation.

3.144 LYNSKEY, WINFRED. "Crane's *The Red Badge of Courage." Explicator* 8 (1949): Item 18. Lynskey argues that Crane's naturalism commits him to an ethic in which "rewards and punishment fall by chance upon the just and the unjust." This is an interesting assertion but more argumentation is needed.

3.145 MALE, ROY. "Stephen Crane: 1871–1900, An Introduction." *American Literary Masters.* 2 vols. Ed. Charles R. Anderson. Vol. 2. New

York: Holt, 1965. 215–226. A general introduction to *Red Badge* published as part of this two-volume set. Male stresses Crane's depiction of the disparities between mood and objective reality.

3.146   MANGUM, A. BRYANT. "The Latter Days of Henry Fleming." *AN&Q* 13 (1975): 136–38. A short, source-hunting note: The "hot plowshares" phrase in the final chapter of *Red Badge* is from Isaiah 2:4.

3.147   ———. "Crane's *Red Badge* and Zola." *American Literary Realism* 9 (1976): 279–80. Source-hunting: Crane "probably" read Zola's *La Debacle* in translation. On this point compare Stone (3.223).

3.148   MARCH, JOHN L. *"The Red Badge* Revisited." *Exercise Exchange* 13 (Nov. 1965): 17–18. A high-school classroom exercise stressing the songs Henry Fleming sang and marched to.

3.149   MARCUS, MORDECAI. "The Unity of *The Red Badge of Courage." Stephen Crane's "The Red Badge of Courage": Text and Criticism.* Ed. Richard Lettis. New York: Harcourt, Brace, 1960. 189–95. Marcus explains that *Red Badge* is unified by Crane's use of irony and animal imagery.

3.150   MARCUS, MORDECAI, and ERIN MARCUS. "Animal Imagery in *The Red Badge of Courage." Modern Language Notes* 74 (1959): 108–11. Animal imagery in *Red Badge* underscores Crane's naturalism.

3.151   MARIN-MADRAZO, PILAR. "The Meaning of Henry Fleming's Initiation in the Complete *The Red Badge of Courage." Revista Canaria de estudios ingleses* 12 (1986): 75–87. If one accepts the Binder "complete" version of *Red Badge,* Fleming emerges as a romantic rebel in a naturalistic world, who saves his egotistical sense of self-importance by entering the amoral zone: Public deeds, not private events are what count.

3.152   MARLOWE, JEAN G. "Crane's Wafer Image: Reference to an Artillery Primer?" *American Literature* 43 (1972): 645–47. Crane's often-discussed image of the red sun "pasted in the sky like a wafer" refers to "an explosive primer used in Civil War artillery."

3.153   MARTIN, JAY. *"The Red Badge of Courage:* The Education of Henry Fleming." *Twelfth Yale Conference on the Teaching of English.* New Haven: Yale University Office of Teacher Training, 1966. 75–85. An ambitious and persuasive account of the six stages of consciousness that mark Henry's initiation and maturation. Also brief comments on "The Veteran" as the last stage of Henry's growth.

3.154   MAULDIN, WILLIAM. "A Buddy's Tribute to Audie Murphy." *Life* 70.22 (1971): 77. Audie Murphy played Fleming in the Huston film version of *Red Badge;* Mauldin had a part in the movie. He here talks about the filming of the movie and Murphy as genuine Medal of Honor Award recipient.

3.155   MAYNARD, REID. "Red as a Leitmotiv in *The Red Badge of Courage.*" *Arizona Quarterly* 30 (1974): 135–41. Maynard argues that red is thematically significant as a leitmotif in *Red Badge;* compare with Wogan (3.255).

3.156   McCAFFREY, JOHN, W. C. ROGERS, and LYMAN BRYSON. "Stephen Crane: *The Red Badge of Courage.*" *Invitation to Learning English and American Novels.* Ed. George D. Crothers. New York: Basic Books, 1953. 272–81. A transcript of a brief and superficial conversation about reading *Red Badge;* reissued in 1966.

3.157   McCOLLY, WILLIAM. "Teaching *The Red Badge of Courage.*" *English Journal* 50 (1961): 534–38. A patronizing discussion of obvious themes in *Red Badge.*

3.158   McDERMOTT, JOHN J. "Symbolism and Psychological Realism in *The Red Badge of Courage.*" *Nineteenth-Century Fiction* 23 (1968): 324–31. Thesis: Crane portrayed in Fleming "a complicated, only partially rational, psychological change." McDermott provides an interesting comparison of the hidden psychic wounds of Fleming and Dimmesdale in *The Scarlet Letter.* Compare with Newberry (3.168).

3.159   McILVAINE, ROBERT. "Henry Fleming Wrestles with an Angel." *Pennsylvania English* 12 (1985): 21–27. A repackaging of other secondary scholarship asserting that there are interesting parallels between Jacob (Genesis 32:11) and Fleming.

3.160   MILLER, WAYNE CHARLES. "A New Kind of War Demands a New Kind of Treatment: The Civil War and the Birth of American Realism." *An Armed America, Its Face in Fiction: A History of the American Military Novel.* New York: New York UP, 1970. 58–91. Crane is given a strong treatment in a lengthy section (70–81) of this chapter. Miller argues that heroism in modern war is "absurd" and "accidental" and that *Red Badge* thoroughly debunks the conception of traditional heroism.

3.161   MITCHELL, LEE CLARK. "The Spectacle of Courage in Crane's *The Red Badge of Courage.*" *Determined Fictions: American Literary Naturalism.* New York: Columbia UP, 1989. 96–116. Mitchell attempts to get a serious reading of naturalists who have been ignored, he argues, because they do not measure up to "high culture" and because their styles are said to be repetitious. Mitchell's thesis is that naturalists have depicted impoverished, diffuse selves unable to understand themselves and marshal the sort of will and determination to lead responsible lives. In his chapter on *Red Badge* he argues that Fleming, in addition to an underdeveloped self, has to meet the added complexity of his immersion in the chaos of war.

3.162   MOOREHEAD, A. H., et al. "Stephen Crane." *100 Great Novels.* New York: Signet, 1966. 145–149. A biographical note on Crane along with a four-page plot summary of *Red Badge.*

3.163   MORACE, ROBERT A. "A 'New' Review of *The Red Badge of Courage.*" *American Literary Realism* 8 (1975): 163–65. A previously unnoticed review of *Red Badge* in a West Coast publication; though "new," Morace admits it is full of misjudgments.

3.164   MULCAIRE, TERRY. "Progressive Views of War in *The Red Badge of Courage* and *The Principles of Scientific Management.*" *American Quarterly* 43 (1991): 46–72. Mulcaire explores parallels between Crane's use of machine metaphors in *Red Badge* and Taylor's treatise on standardized, efficient industrial production. He argues that "the *Red Badge* virtually catalogs the concerns of industrial reformers, picturing the Civil War both as the historical source of the problems those reformers addressed and as the genesis of the martial, industrial solution."

3.165   MYERS, FRANKLIN G. *Barnes and Noble Book Notes: Stephen Crane's "The Red Badge of Courage."* New York: Barnes and Noble, 1966. 90. Myers offers a standard student guide complete with multiple-choice questions (and answers) plus a brief biographical sketch. He also provides a short discussion of literary influences, chapter-by-chapter summaries (nearly as long as Crane's work), a sample of typical critical comment, and a two-page bibliography.

3.166   NASH, OGDEN. "Little and Better." *Book Dial.* Autumn 1925. A brief note on *Red Badge.* See Stallman, *Stephen Crane: A Critical Bibliography* (14.3: 318).

3.167   NELSON, CARL. "The Ironic Allusive Texture of *Lord Jim:* Coleridge, Crane, Milton, and Melville." *Conradiana* 4 (1972): 47–59. Crane is an afterthought here—one small paragraph (53–54) to the effect that *Red Badge* helped Conrad deal with romantic self-deception.

3.168 NEWBERRY, FREDERIC. *"The Red Badge of Courage* and *The Scarlet Letter."* Arizona Quarterly 38 (1982): 101–15. Predictable: In both novels nature is probed for signs; both Fleming and Dimmesdale suffer from secret sins. Compare with McDermott (3.158).

3.169 NICHOLS, PRESCOTT S. *"The Red Badge of Courage:* What is Fleming Fleeing?" *Literature and History* 12 (1986): 97–102. Nichols tabulates: Fleming flees war, bullets, the dead, the wounded, danger, peace, and himself.

3.170 NOSE, TOSHI. "On Stephen Crane's *The Red Badge of Courage. Okayama Daigaku Kyoyo-bu Kiyo* 2 (1966): 12–36. See Stallman, *Stephen Crane: A Critical Bibliography* (14.3: 525). It is probably in Japanese; I have not seen this item.

3.171 O'BRIEN, MATTHEW C. " 'The Sweet Teaching of the Heavens': The Significance of the Sun in Civil War Literature." *Helios: From Myth to Solar Energy.* Ed. M. E. Grenander. Albany, NY: SUNY, 1978. 411–20. Crane and *Red Badge* mentioned in passing.

3.172 O'DONNELL, THOMAS F. "Charles Dudley Warner on *The Red Badge of Courage."* American Literature 25 (1953): 363–65. O'Donnell reprints and comments on a late-nineteenth-century reaction to *Red Badge.*

3.173 ———. "DeForest, Van Patten, and Stephen Crane." *American Literature* 27 (1956): 578–80. O'Donnell argues contra Haight (3.86) that Crane's familiarity with battle scenes came from his Claverack history teacher Van Patten instead of the 1867 novel *Miss Ravenel's Conversion from Secession to Loyalty* by John W. DeForest.

3.174 OKADA, RYOICHI. "Another Source of Crane's Metaphor, 'The Red Badge of Courage.' " *American Notes and Queries* 14 (1976): 73–74. Source-hunting: "Red Badge" was taken from Cooper's *The Last of the Mohicans.*

3.175 OSBORN, NEAL J. "William Ellery Channing and *The Red Badge of Courage."* Bulletin of the New York Public Library 69 (1965): 182–96. After he decries today's distaste for source-hunting, Osborn argues that "so far as theme and thematic strategies are concerned *The Red Badge* would make an almost perfect 'exemplum' of Channing's 1816 sermon, 'War.' "

3.176 OSBORN, SCOTT C. "Stephen Crane's Imagery: 'Pasted Like a Wafer.'" *American Literature* 23 (1951): 362. Many of Crane's symbols come from Kipling's *The Light That Failed*"; Osborn also holds that the wafer image comes from "a red wafer of wax used to seal an envelope." Compare with Carlson (3.29).

3.177 OVERTON, GRANT. *Portrait of a Publisher.* New York: Appleton, 1925. 76–77. Overton's short biography of William W. Appleton and the house of Appleton notes the publication of *Red Badge* as the significant event of 1894. Overton calls *Red Badge* "one of the fiction classics of the Appleton list." Also included is a nice photograph of Crane.

3.178 _____. "Do You Remember?" *Mentor* 17 (1929): 45, 62. Overton provides a good photograph of Crane and states the plot line of *Red Badge*.

3.179 PEASE, DONALD. "Fear, Rage, and Mistrials of Representation in *The Red Badge of Courage.*" *American Realism: New Essays.* Ed. Eric J. Sundquist. Baltimore: John Hopkins UP, 1982. 155–75. A convoluted and often dense treatment arguing that *Red Badge* treats war purged of ideology, history, and political context so that battles and soldiers are presented in a contextless-pure contingency.

3.180 PELLETIER, GASTON. "*Red Badge* Revisited." *English Journal* 57 (1968): 24–25, 99. Highly critical of *Red Badge:* because of his supercharged prose, "Crane's story became a carnival riot, overwhelming with its color, smoke clouds, and clamor."

3.181 PIZER, DONALD. "Late Nineteenth-Century American Naturalism." *Realism and Naturalism in Nineteenth-Century American Literature.* Carbondale: Southern Illinois UP, 1966. 11–32. Pizer stresses the naturalistic elements in *Red Badge* with reference to Crane's depiction of "courage . . . not as a conscious striving for an ideal mode of behavior but a temporary delirium derived from animal fury and social pride or fear." This article originally appeared in the *Bucknell Review* 13 (1965): 1–18.

3.182 _____. "A Primer of Fictional Aesthetics." *College English* 30 (1969): 572–80. Pizer gives broad-stroke characterizations of four schools of fictional aesthetics (point of view, symbolism, myth, and style), and he shows how *Red Badge* can support all four interpretations.

3.183 _____. "Nineteenth-Century American Naturalism: An Approach Through Form." *Forum* 19 (1976): 43–46. Pizer sees "naturalist" as a

significant category in understanding American fiction and he suggests that symbols such as Fleming's wound ironically undercut the
normal, common-sense, humanistic view of humans in control of
their lives.

3.184   _____. Introduction. *Critical Essays on Stephen Crane's "The Red
Badge of Courage."* Boston: G. K. Hall, 1990. 1–11. A brief biographical sketch of Crane, a history of critical and popular reaction to *Red
Badge,* and comments on the articles Pizer has selected to illustrate
important thematic and textual discussions. (All of these articles are
treated elsewhere in this bibliography.)

3.185   PRATT, LYNDON UPSON. "A Possible Source of *The Red Badge of
Courage." American Literature* 11 (1939): 1–10. Crane's history
professor at Claverack was General John Bullock Van Patten whose
regiment was forced into flight at the Battle of Antietam. Pratt admits
that *Red Badge* retells Chancellorsville though "Antietam may well
have provided at least two additional elements: the ideal of Henry's
panic and flight, and the heroism of the wounded color-bearer." See
also Carruthers (3.30).

3.186   PRICE, LAWRENCE M. *The Reception of U. S. Literature in Germany.*
Chapel Hill: U of North Carolina P, 1966. Passim. *Red Badge* is briefly
mentioned.

3.187   PRITCHETT, V. S. "Books in General: *The Red Badge of Courage.*"
New Statesman and Nation 24 (1942): 95. A little noted but excellent
essay on *Red Badge.* Of special note are Pritchett's comments on
Crane's attention to individual soldiers' views of the "mass mind" of
the army.

3.188   _____. Introduction. *"The Red Badge of Courage" and Other Stories.*
London: Oxford UP, 1960. vii–xii. General introductory comments:
Red Badge is a poetic fable and Crane's style employs random irony.
Reprinted as "V. S. Pritchett on Stephen Crane" by Gullason in
Stephen Crane's Career (2.8: 151–55).

3.189   _____. "Two Writers and Modern War." *The Living Novel.* New York:
Reynal and Hitchcock, 1946. 167–78. Crane and Whitman
deromanticized combat by an "unrhetorical attitude toward war."

3.190   RANDALL, DAVID A., and JOHN T. WINTERICH. "One Hundred
Good Novels: Crane, Stephen: *The Red Badge of Courage." Publishers'
Weekly* 136 (1939): 1625–26. Randall describes the first edition of
Red Badge and Winterich explains that Crane's success with *Red*

Badge brought him war correspondent assignments. However, his imagination was better than experience, for *Active Service* is a hackney coach alongside the flaming chariot of *The Red Badge of Courage*.

3.191   RATHBUN, JOHN W. "Structure and Meaning in *The Red Badge of Courage*." *Ball State University Forum* 10 (1969): 8–16. Rathbun examines *Red Badge*'s structure in light of four action "blocks": Fleming as introspective, untried soldier; Fleming's flight; battle and "Wilson's newly won maturity;" and Wilson and Fleming's heroism. A useful classroom teaching aid.

3.192   RECHNITZ, ROBERT M. "Depersonalization and the Dream in *The Red Badge of Courage*." *Studies in the Novel* 6 (1974): 76–87. A thought-provoking and convincing case is made that while the ending of *Red Badge* ("He was a man") is ironic, Crane gives us a young man who has undergone considerable alteration. If not a man, he has been forced, by the depersonalization of combat, to come to grips with a partially new self.

3.193   REED, JARED. *A Selection from "The Red Badge of Courage," [Crane's] Poetry and the Story, 'The Veteran.'* New York: Folkways Records. 1961. Recorded readings by Reed.

3.194   REYNOLDS, KIRK M. "*The Red Badge of Courage*: Private Henry's Mind as Sole Point of View." *South Atlantic Quarterly* 52 (1987): 59–69. Thesis: If irony is dismissed and the reader adopts Fleming's point of view, Fleming becomes a man. Of course, Crane is famous for irony, Fleming is not always in touch with reality, and Reynolds knows both of these things. Nonetheless, this article gives a nice summary of the range of readings about irony and Fleming's appreciation of reality.

3.195   ROSCH, WILLIAM. Introduction. *The Red Badge of Courage*. Evanston, IL: Harper, 1964. Standard information on Crane's life and works with general comments on *Red Badge*.

3.196   ROSS, DONALD, JR. "Who's Talking? How Characters Become Narrators in Fiction." *Modern Language Notes* 91 (1976): 1222–42. A half-dozen novels are discussed with relation to Ross's question. He briefly takes up (1228–42) Crane's strategies in dealing with "the great distance between a lyrical and learned narrative and the country boy it depicts." See also Hough (3.102) and Schmitz (3.202).

3.197   ROSS, LILLIAN. "Picture." *Reporting*. New York: Simon and Schuster, 1964. 223–442. A very long, but ever interesting and even exciting account of John Huston's filming of *The Red Badge of Courage* for Metro-Goldwyn-Mayer in the early fifties. Beyond the film star-director-studio executive battles we are treated to Huston's struggles to portray on film a story that so heavily depends on the inner thoughts and perceptions of the main protagonist. Huston's sense of "the ironically thin line between cowardice and heroism" is fully explored. Note: Ross's piece was originally a series of articles, "Onwards and Upwards through the Arts," published in the 24 May, 31 May, 7 June, 14 June, 21 June 1952 issues of the *New Yorker*.

3.198   RUTHERFORD, ANDREW. "Realism and the Heroic: Some Reflections on War Novels." *Yearbook of English Studies* 12 (1982): 194–207. *Red Badge* is briefly discussed with reference to Rutherford's thesis: Realistic treatments are necessary to capture the reality of war and to state the moral value of heroic conduct.

3.199   SADLER, FRANK. "Crane's 'Fleming': Appellation for Coward or Hero." *American Literature* 48 (1976): 372–76. A note on the derivation of Fleming from "Fleme," which can mean either to flee or to put to flight, thus covering Fleming both as coward and as hero.

3.200   SAFRANEK, WILLIAM. "Crane's *The Red Badge of Courage*." *Explicator* 26 (1967): Item 21. Safranek sketches how the transformation of the "loud soldier," Wilson, anticipates and parallels Fleming.

3.201   SATTERFIELD, BEN. "From Romance to Reality: The Accomplishment of Private Fleming." *CLA Journal* 24 (1980–81): 451–64. A Christian symbolism interpretation of *Red Badge:* In the chapel scene Henry, after confronting his animal nature (and death), sets out to become a man. Satterfield argues that Fleming grows from romanticism to reality by way of his moral choice to return to battle.

3.202   SCHMITZ, NEIL. "Stephen Crane and the Colloquial Self." *Midwest Quarterly* 13 (1972): 437–51. Schmitz explores the contrast between Fleming's slang and the narrators' elevated diction and he proposes that while Fleming appears to grow from a rude farm boy to a reflective, poetic young man, at the end "Fleming stumbles out of his ordeal a supple neurotic, busily revising his delusions." See also Hough (3.102) and Ross (3.196).

3.203   SCHNEIDER, MICHAEL. "Monomyth Structure in *The Red Badge of Courage*." *American Literary Realism* 20 (1987): 45–55. Schneider sees *Red Badge* as a "quest-romance" that works through "the three

stages of the monomyth adventure—departure, initiation, and return." Though Fleming's improvement is too abrupt at the novel's
end, Schneider finds real growth has occurred.

3.204 SCRIBA, JAY. "His 'Pot Boiler' Became a Classic." *Milwaukee Journal*
14 Aug. 1968: 20. Comments on the success of *Red Badge* along with
a photograph of Crane.

3.205 SELTZER, MARK. "Statistical Persons." *Diacritics* 17 (1987): 82–98.
A reading of *Red Badge* (as well as several other Crane short novels and
tales) as social criticism of late nineteenth-century progressive indus-
trialization and systematization. Seltzer's thesis is a dense obfuscation
of Crane's well-known attention to types: "[His] stories are populated
if not peopled by statistical persons: by the figure of the gambler and
the prostitute and also by that emphatically embodied and paradoxi-
cally particularized 'type' that is, at once, the intended product and
the apparently accidental by-product of war—the wounded soldier or
casualty."

3.206 SEWALL, R. B. "Crane's *The Red Badge of Courage.*" *Explicator* 3
(1945): Item 55. An early comment about the unsatisfactory ending
of *Red Badge,* especially Henry's rationalization.

3.207 SHARMA, D. R. "War and the Individual Man in *The Red Badge of
Courage.*" *Literary Criterion* 9 (1970): 56–64. A bland, unoriginal
middle-of-the-road reading of *Red Badge:* As Fleming undergoes war
he matures.

3.208 SHAW, MARY NEFF. "Henry Fleming's Heroics in *The Red Badge of
Courage:* A Satiric Search for a 'Kinder, Gentler' Heroism." *Studies in
the Novel* 22 (1990): 418–28. A useful approach in which Shaw
examines *Red Badge,* especially the ambiguous ending, in light of a
"kinder, gentler" heroism she identifies as one of Crane's personal
values that she finds in the canon of his war fiction. Stressing Crane's
use of satire she concludes that Crane's novel "attacks the romanticized notion of heroism . . . [and] allows the reader to identify Henry
Fleming as an unreliable character who is finally a pawn and exemplar
of the traditional notion of heroism."

3.209 SHULMAN, ROBERT. "*The Red Badge* and Social Violence: Crane's
Myth of His America." *Canadian Review of American Studies* 12
(1981): 1–19. Thesis: Crane wrote *Red Badge* at an especially violent
time in American society (and during a period of deep economic
depression); Fleming's growth in *Red Badge* explored the possibility
of regeneration through violence.

3.210   SILVA, FRED. "Uncivil Battles and Civil Wars." *The Classic American Novels and the Movies.* Ed. Gerald Peary and Rogers Shatzkin. New York: Frederick Ungar, 1977. 114–23. An account of John Huston's difficulties in filming *Red Badge* and the cuts made by MGM brass. See also Lillian Ross's "Picture" (3.197) for much more detail on the same points.

3.211   SOLOMON, ERIC. "Another Analog for *The Red Badge of Courage.*" *Nineteenth-Century Fiction* 13 (1958): 63–67. Solomon finds that while other works resemble *Red Badge,* "none provides quite so exciting a plot [as] Joseph Kirkland's *The Captain of Company K.*"

3.212   _____. "The Structure of *The Red Badge of Courage.*" *Modern Fiction Studies* 5 (1959): 220–34. Solomon argues that though war can be "brutally deterministic," Henry manages to take responsibility for his life. Further, he argues that "the standards by which Henry's development is measured are those of group loyalty rather than fear and courage." Five soldiers come into contact with Fleming in his passage from apprenticeship to mastery; see Stone (3.222) for a sixth.

3.213   _____. "Stephen Crane, English Critics, and American Reviewers." *Notes and Queries* 12 (1965): 62–64. A brief comparison of American and English critical response to *Red Badge,* with special emphasis on Crane's countrymen who panned it and foreigners who praised it.

3.214   _____. "Yet Another Source for *The Red Badge of Courage.*" *English Language Notes* 2 (1965): 215–17. Solomon adds to his own list of sources. Beyond Kirkland's *The Captain of Company K* (see 3.211) Solomon here suggests that an article by Horace Porter, "The Philosophy of Courage," in *Century Magazine* 36, (1888), which sharply separates physical and moral courage, influenced Crane's treatment of the same in *Red Badge.*

3.215   STALLMAN, ROBERT W. Introduction. *"The Red Badge of Courage" by Stephen Crane.* New York: Modern Library, 1951. v–xxxiii. A challenging and seminal essay. Stallman proposes Christian symbolism as the interpretive key to *Red Badge:* themes of redemption through loss of self, Jim Conklin as Jesus Christ, and "The red sun was pasted in the sky like a wafer" as a sacramental communion wafer. Portions reprinted as the Introduction to Stallman's *Stephen Crane: Stories and Tales* (12.12).

3.216   _____. "Fiction and Its Critics: A Reply to Mr. Rahv." *Kenyon Review* 19 (1957): 290–99. Rahv (2.167) objected to the communion iwafer symbolism on grounds of a sharp distinction between prose and poetry. Stallman responds by arguing for a gray area between the two, where Crane's symbolic prose-poetry belongs and where his wafer image is very fitting.

3.217   _____. "Notes Toward an Analysis of *The Red Badge of Courage.*" *[Teacher's Manual to Accompany] Adventures in American Literature.* Ed. James Early and Robert Freier. New York: Harcourt, Brace, 1968. Stallman's study and discussion notes.

3.218   _____. "The Scholar's Net: Literary Sources." *College English* 17 (1955): 20–27. Stallman's contentiousness makes its debut. He begins his attempt to refute all who disagreed (some did so with much derision and hooting) with his communion wafer interpretation of "The red sun was pasted in the sky like a wafer." In this piece he takes on Osborn's (3.176) suggestion of a wax seal, an unnamed critic [Edmund Wilson] (3.254) in the *New Yorker,* and a letter by Frederick Gwynn (3.80).

3.219   STEVENSON, JAMES A. "Kubrick and Crane in *Full Metal Jacket.*" *Humanist* 48.2 (1988): 43–44. Film director Kubrick shares Crane's "grand sense of the ironic"; both see abundant incongruities and absurdities.

3.220   _____. "Beyond Stephen Crane: *Full Metal Jacket.*" *Literature/Film Quarterly* 16 (1988): 238–342. Stevenson points out parallels in Kubrick's film and Crane's *Red Badge:* Both depict loss of individuality in combat, though Kubrick goes beyond Crane in terms of loss and brutality.

3.221   STONE, EDWARD. "The Many Suns of *The Red Badge of Courage.*" *American Literature* 29 (1957): 322–26. An excellent classroom aid. Thesis: Crane uses the various appearances of the sun to guide the reader's interpretation of various themes and incidents in the novel.

3.222   _____. "Introducing Private Smithers." *Georgia Review* 16 (1962): 442–45. Solomon (3.212) argues that in his passage from apprenticeship to mastery Fleming comes into contact with five soldiers. Stone suggests a sixth, Private Smithers, who himself did not change but remained, from beginning to end, competent and reliable.

3.223   _____. "Crane and Zola." *English Language Notes* 1 (1963): 46–47. Argues the influence of Zola's *L'Assommoir* on *Red Badge:* "The macabre description of Tom Conklin's death can be traced back to the death scene of Zola's alcoholic tinsmith Coupeau." See also Mangum (3.147).

3.224 ———. *The Battle and the Books: Some Aspects of Henry James*. Athens: Ohio UP, 1964. 150 and passim. Brief comments on interpretations of religious symbols in *Red Badge*.

3.325 STONE, ROBERT. Introduction. *The Red Badge of Courage* by Stephen Crane. New York: Vintage/Library of America. xi–xvii. Despite Crane's overall sense of the "earth as battleground" and life as war, Stone argues that *Red Badge* celebrates "life as pilgrim's progress, as moral journey."

3.226 STOWELL, ROBERT. "Stephen Crane's Use of Colour in *The Red Badge of Courage*." *Literary Criterion* 9 (1970): 36–39. Stowell's tabulation of the colors Crane used is useful; the rest is not.

3.227 SWANN, CHARLES. "Stephen Crane and a Problem of Interpretation." *Literature and History* 7 (1981): 91–123. A discussion for those who have the stamina to weather a long, dense deconstructionist treatise. Swann sees difficulty in interpreting *Red Badge* since "modernist texts are *notoriously* self-consciously parodic, and *The Red Badge* is, in this sense at least, an exemplary modernist text." Does Fleming mature? Probably not, according to Swann, who sees chaos and nihilism in Crane's general worldview.

3.228 TAMKE, ALEXANDER R. "The Principal Source of Stephen Crane's *Red Badge of Courage*." *Essays in Honor of Esmond Linworth Marilla*. Ed. Thomas Austin Kirby and William John Olive. Baton Rouge: Louisiana State UP, 1970. 299–311. Tamke convincingly argues that Crane's sources were historical accounts of the battle of Chancellorsville, Kirkland's *The Captain of Company K* and, last but not least, his imagination.

3.229 TARG, WILLIAM. Introduction. *Stephen Crane's "The Red Badge of Courage."* Cleveland: Fine Editions Press, 1951. v–xii. A sketchy summary of *Red Badge* plus long quotations (without documentation) from standard critical pieces. The real value of this volume is its illustrations (made from wood engravings) of drawings by Winslow Homer

3.230 THOMAS, DONALD. "[Biblical Parallelism in *The Red Badge of Courage*."] *Stephen Crane: A Collection of Critical Essays*. Ed. Maurice Bassan. Englewood Cliffs, NJ: Prentice-Hall, 1967. 137–40. Brief comments on biblical allusions in *Red Badge*.

3.231 ———. "Crane's *The Red Badge of Courage*." *Explicator* 27 (1969): Item 77. A minor, useful point for classroom discussion: When the soldiers walk around the body of the dead soldier (in chap. 3), they ask themselves what is "the answer to the Question?"

3.232   TUTTLETON, JAMES W. "The Imagery of *The Red Badge of Courage.*" *Modern Fiction Studies* 8 (1963): 410–15. Symbolism in *Red Badge,* especially on the religious half-light in the chapel scene.

3.233   VAN DOREN, CARL. Introduction. *Stephen Crane, "Red Badge of Courage."* New York: Heritage Press, 1944. vii–xiii. Stallman's *Stephen Crane: A Critical Bibliography* (14.3: 364) states that this edition is "a simple-minded version of a very complicated novel for simple-minded readers, appropriately printed in large type." I could not agree more or say it any better.

3.234   VAN DOREN, MARK. "First Glance." *Nation* 121 (1925): 735. A review essay on the Follett edition, *Work of Stephen Crane* (12.5), including comments on the elusiveness of the qualities that make *Red Badge* the important book it is.

3.235   VAN METER, JAN R. "Sex and War in *The Red Badge of Courage:* Cultural Themes and Literary Criticism." *Genre* 7 (1974): 71–90. Van Meter's title will get reader's attention; his article will lose it.

3.236   VANDERBILT, KERMIT, and DANIEL WEISS. "From Rifleman to Flagbearer: Henry Fleming's Separate Peace in *The Red Badge of Courage.*" *Modern Fiction Studies* 11 (1966): 371–80. Thesis: Fleming conquers fear, ironically, by becoming a noncombatant, a flag-bearing auxiliary who cannot fire back when fired upon.

3.237   VEDRO, STEPHEN S. "Biographical Note and Introduction. *The Red Badge of Courage.* New York, 1964. v–xiv. A young readers' edition with large print and an introduction suitable for them.

3.238   VICKERY, OLGA W. "The Inferno of the Moderns." *The Shaken Realist: Essays in Modern Literature in Honor of Frederick J. Hoffman.* Ed. Melvin J. Friedman and John B. Vickery. Baton Rouge: Louisiana State UP, 1970. 147–64. Vickery uses Dante's *Inferno* to explicate *Red Badge.* Crane's "concept of an endless war, as well as specific scenes, are reminiscent of Dante," and she sees Jim Conklin as a scapegoat, Christ figure. Both her claims are vague enough to be admitted (Crane is one of fifteen modern American writers she examines), though little interpretive gain is forthcoming.

3.239   VIDAN, IVO. "*The Red Badge of Courage:* A Study in Bad Faith." *Studica Romanica et Anglica Zagrebiensis* 33–36 (1972–1973): 93–112. As the title indicates, Vidan is highly critical of Henry. He sees in

Red Badge no integrity, no moral growth, only bad faith. He sees Henry's desertion as "his desolidarity with his fellow-soldiers." See Dunn (3.49) and Schmitz (3.202) who also see no need to excuse Henry on account of his youth.

3.240 VON ABELE, RUDOLPH, and WALTER HAVIGHURST. "Symbolism and the Student." *College English* 16 (1955): 424–34, 461. Though the authors insist that students need to be taught to see symbolism in literature, they find Stallman's religious interpretation (3.215) of the wafer image unwarranted.

3.241 WALCUTT, CHARLES CHILD. *"The Red Badge of Courage* as Literary Naturalism" *Arizona Review* 1 (1950): 371–373. A review essay of Ahnebrink's *The Beginnings of Naturalism in American Fiction* (2.1).

3.242 WARNER, DEANE M. "Huck and Holden." *CEA Critic* 27 (1965): 4a–4b. *Red Badge* briefly discussed as an example of an initiation story.

3.243 WASSERSTROM, WILLIAM. "Hydraulics and Heroics: William James and Stephen Crane." *Prospects* 4 (1979): 215–35. James and Crane (along with many other nineteenth-century Americans) were intrigued by what James called "hidden energies" in men. Wasserstrom explores how war pumps reserves from a hidden psychic reservoir. According to Wasserstrom, Crane overdid, however, for Henry's reaction to combat is a reckless abandon, that is "rabid," though only temporarily so. Reprinted in Wasserstrom's *The Ironies of Progress: Henry Adams and the American Dream,* Carbondale: Southern Illinois UP, 1984: 77–99.

3.244 WEATHERFORD, RICHARD M. "Stephen Crane and O. Henry: A Correction." *American Literature* 44 (1973): 666. Weatherford located a parody of *Red Badge,* "The Blue Blotch of Cowardice," by O. Henry. See Stallman's *Stephen Crane: A Critical Bibliography* (13.4: 151–152) for a list of other contemporary parodies of Crane.

3.245 WEBSTER, H. T. "Wilbur F. Hinman's *Corporal Si Klegg* and Stephen Crane's *The Red Badge of Courage." American Literature* 11 (1939): 285–93. Webster argues that "unless chance violates probability" Crane drew extensively from Hinman's novel about an ordinary soldier's battle initiation.

3.246 WEEKS, ROBERT P. "The Power of the Tacit in Crane and Hemingway." *Modern Fiction Studies* 8 (1962): 415–18. Similarities (and differences) between Crane and Hemingway—*Red Badge* and *For Whom the Bell Tolls* are used as illustrations.

3.247 WEISBURGER, BERNARD. "The Red Badge of Courage." *Twelve Original Essays on Great American Novels*. Ed. Charles Shapiro. Detroit: Wayne State UP, 1958. 96–123. A sound, if garden variety, essay on *Red Badge* that stresses the "interior action" of the novel and the general view that war is incomprehensible.

3.248 WEISS, DANIEL. "The Red Badge of Courage." *Psychoanalytic Review* 52 (1965): 176–96, 460–84. The first, best and most complete psychoanalytic examination of *Red Badge* focusing on the psychology of fear. The concluding sections are on Crane's Western stories, especially "The Blue Hotel" as a counterinstance of the normal condition wherein a sane and normal mind makes possible freedom and personal responsibility. Reprinted in *The Critic Agonistes: Psychology, Myth and the Art of Fiction,* edited by Eric Solomon and Stephen Arkin, Seattle: U of Washington P, 1985, 57–107.

3.249 WERNER, W. L. "Stephen Crane and *The Red Badge of Courage.*" *New York Times Book Review* 30 Sept. 1945: 4. On the fiftieth anniversary of the publication of *Red Badge* Werner briefly summarizes its writing, publishing history, and impact.

3.250 WERTHEIM, STANLEY. *"The Red Badge of Courage,* and Personal Narratives of the Civil War." *American Literary Realism* 6 (1973): 61–65. Source-hunting: There are thematic and situational parallels to *Red Badge* in many autobiographical narratives of Civil War soldiers.

3.251 WHYTE, FREDERIC. *William Heinemann: A Memoir*. London: J. Cape, 1928. 146, 170. Comments on Crane by his English publisher.

3.252 WILLIAMS, G. L. "Henry Fleming and the 'Cheery Voiced Stranger.'" *Stephen Crane Newsletter* 4.2 (1969): 4–7. Williams discusses the mature, confident, and reliable "cherry-voiced" stranger as a foil to the doubtful and insecure Fleming.

3.253 WILMERDING, JOHN. *Winslow Homer*. New York: Praeger, 1972. Passim. Passing comments (45) on Crane, Winslow Homer, and Matthew Brady on war as a machine that grinds up soldiers.

3.254 WILSON, EDMUND. "Review." *New Yorker* 29 (2 May 1953): 124. In his review of Stallman's *Stephen Crane: An Omnibus* (2.16) Wilson objects to the communion wafer symboism on the ground that Crane was a Methodist, not a Catholic. For Stallman's reply, see (3.218).

3.255 WOGAN, CLAUDIA, C. "Crane's Use of Color in *The Red Badge of Courage.*" *Modern Fiction Studies* 6 (1960): 168–72. A tabulation and statistical analysis of Crane's use of color. For instance, forty-two percent of his use of colors occurs in the first and last eighths of the book.

3.256 WOODRESS, JAMES. *"The Red Badge of Courage." Reference Guide to American Literature.* Ed. D. L. Kirkpatrick. Chicago: St. James P, 1978. 677–78. Reference-guide piece with plot summary and a few comments on Crane's style and his focus on a psychological study of fear.

3.257 WRIGHT, MOORHEAD. "The Existential Adventurer and War: Three Case Studies from American Fiction." *American Thinking about Peace and War: New Essays on American Thought and Attitudes.* Ed. Ken Booth and Moorhead Wright. New York: Barnes and Noble, 1978. 101–10. A sketchy essay on Crane, Hemingway, and Vonnegut. His brief Crane section stresses "a predominant fallible and self-deceptive" Fleming and *Red Badge* as a deflation of myths of courage and heroism in war.

3.258 WYNDHAM, GEORGE. "A Remarkable Book." *New Review* 14 (Jan. 1896): 30–40. An outstanding early review of *Red Badge;* "he stages the drama of war, so to speak, within the mind of one man, and then admits you as to a theater." Reprinted as "An Appreciation," the introduction to *Pictures of War,* a selection of Crane works published in London, 1898. Also in *Critical Heritage,* 2.17: #36.

3.259 ZAMBRAMO, ANA LAURA. "The Role of Nature in *The Red Badge of Courage.*" *Arizona Quarterly* 30 (1974): 164–66. An interesting thesis lacking argument or documentation: Nature is an indifferent participant in the novel because Fleming interprets it as such.

See also on literary criticism of *Red Badge.*

1.38	9.14
1.55	9.19
1.58	9.60
1.151	9.62
1.176	9.95
2.1 to 2.19	10.22
2.64	10.25
2.87	10.63
2.101	10.89
2.176	11.18

2.186	11.32
2.194	11.40
2.197	11.45
4.109	12.10

TEXTUAL CONTROVERSIES

Books

3.260   BINDER, HENRY, ed. *The Red Badge of Courage: An Episode of the CivilWar.* New York: Norton, 1982.ix, 173. This is the "infamous" Binder version of *Red Badge.* Binder inserted the excised manuscript sections along with a complete chapter. Whether such a procedure was in keeping with Crane's intentions and whether this "expanded" version is artistically superior have been roundly and hotly debated. Binder also includes in this volume an "expanded" version of his defense of his editing strategies. *"The Red Badge of Courage* Nobody Knows." See below (3.267) for more on this essay.

3.261   BOWERS, FREDSON. *Stephen Crane, "The Red Badge of Courage": A Facsimile Edition of the Manuscript.* 2 vols. Washington,DC: NCR/Microcard Editions, 1972. ix+123,263. A photographic facsimile of the manuscript of *Red Badge* including discarded sections and fragments of antecedent drafts. Though the facsimile reduces Crane's beautiful handwriting "to four-fifths its regular size" it is still very legible and a wonderful experience to read. See (3.271) for Bowers's textual and general introduction.

3.262   _____. *The Red Badge of Courage. The Works of Stephen Crane,* Vol. 2. Ed. Fredson Bowers. Charlottesville: UP of Virginia, 1975. scii+424. Bowers's critical edition of *Red Badge* rejects the canceled passages and the discarded chapter that Binder added to his edition. See Bowers's "The Text: History and Analysis" (183–252) for an *exhaustive* discussion of the manuscript, including discarded chapters, and an account of Bowers's theory of the order and rationale involved in Crane's revisions. Especially interesting are the "corrections" made by Crane and by Hamlin Garland. See above (3.137) for Levenson's excellent general introduction.

3.263   BRADLEY, SCULLEY, et al. *"The Red Badge of Courage;* The Manuscript: Unpublished Passages." *"The Red Badge of Courage"* by Stephen

Crane: An Annotated Text, Backgrounds and Sources, Essays in Criticism. New York: Norton, 1962. 5–11, 113–117. A reprinting from "the first American edition" plus expunged passages. Note: Not included is the chapter Crane deleted (added to *Red Badge* in the Binder edition). Also the Bradley et al. reprint of some three dozen pieces of criticism (all described elsewhere in this bibliography).

3.264   FOLLETT, WILSON, ed. *The Red Badge of Courage [and "The Veteran": The Works of Stephen Crane,* Vol. 1. New York: Knopf, 1926. xviii+209. A reprinting of the first 1895 Appleton edition. See 3.94 for Hergesheimer's introduction.

3.265   KATZ, JOSEPH. *"The Red Badge of Courage" by Stephen Crane: A Facsimile Reproduction of the New York "Press" Appearance of December 9, 1894.* 117. Gainesville, FL: Scholars' Facsimiles and Reprints, 1967. Katz has photocopied the actual newspaper pages, which are interesting for a while, but the pages are so blurred reading becomes a chore. Still, the newspaper illustrations and the headings give the modern reader a sense of the excitement and flavor Crane's contemporaries felt in reading the abbreviated version of this great American classic. Note: Some six months before Katz's volume appeared Gullason printed in conventional format the newspaper version of *Red Badge* in his *The Complete Novels of Stephen Crane* (12.9).

3.266   ———. *The Red Badge of Courage.* Columbus OH: Charles Merrill. A fascimile of the first impression, first printing (1895 Appleton) text. See 3.116 for Katz's introduction.

Articles and Book Chapters

3.267   BINDER, HENRY, "The *Red Badge of Couarge* Nobody Knows." *Studies in the Novel* 10 (1978): 9–47. This article is the full-blown defense of Binder's contention that sections that Crane deleted from *Red Badge* should be put back into the text. Thesis: "The heavy-handed cutting that went into the preparation of *Red Badge* for Appleton publication concerned itself only with the removal of certain pieces of the story, not at all with recasting what remained into intelligible form." The upshot of Binder's text is to make the final chapter of *Red Badge* fully ironic, with the result that Fleming experiences no growth from the three days of combat.

3.268   ———. "Unwinding the Riddle of Four Pages Missing from *The Red Badge of Courage* Manuscript." *Papers of the Bibliographical Society of*

America 72 (1978):100–6. Textual niceties with a lecture for Gregian copy-text editors: Fredson Bowers (general editor of the University of Virginia critical edition of Crane) was aware of these pages but did not include them in the Virginia text. Binder sees himself as rectifying. Bowers's error with his Norton edition of *Red Badge* (3.260).

3.269   ————. "Donald Pizer, Ripley Hitchcock, and *The Red Badge of Courage*." *Studies in the Novel* 11 (1979): 216–23. Of interest to those who enjoy the point–counterpoint of the *Red Badge* text controversy. Binder produced a version of *Red Badge* that integrated into the text deletions that Crane himself made before the manuscript was submitted to Appleton. Binder here reiterates his preference for the expanded, "new" version of this American classic.

3.270   ————. "*The Red Badge of Courage* Nobody Knows: Expanded Version." *"The Red Badge of Courage" by Stephen Crane.* Ed. Henry Binder. New York: Norton, 1982. 111–58. Binder vigorously defends with some new and several old arguments that recast version of *Red Badge* he has presented. He reiterates that *Red Badge* was an ironic story changed by Ripley Hitchcock, editor at Appleton. Matters of both text editing and literary criticism are at stake; Binder's view is clearly the minority opinion on both matters.

3.271   BOWERS, FREDSON. Foreword and Introduction. *Stephen Crane, "The Red Badge of Courage": A Facsimile Edition of the Manuscript.* Washington DC: NCR/Microcard Editions, 1973. ix–xi, 1–54. Bowers's volume offers "a photographic facsimile of the manuscript" of *Red Badge*. Included also are discarded leaves of the original and fragments of the antecedent draft. Bowers's long, interesting introduction examines evidence from Crane's letters and friends about the writing of this famous novel, and he draws conclusions concerning the order of revisions and the reasons for certain of Crane's changes.

3.272   ————. "Regularization and Normalization in Modern Critical Texts." *Studies in Bibliography* 42 (1989): 79–102. Besides editing the University of Virginia critical edition of Crane, Bowers was also textual editor for the Harvard edition of William James and the Ohio State edition of Hawthorne. Using examples from each author Bowers explains the principles that were used to regularize and normalize both editions. His Crane examples deal with Crane's punctuation idiosyncracies and inconsistencies in dialogue spoken by Wilson and Conklin (they vacillate between heavy dialect and normal correct speech) in *Red Badge*. (See on this point Hough [3.102], Ross [3.196], and Schmitz [3.202]. Bowers's article is also noteworthy for footnote

23: a rapid-burst, no-nonsense recitation of eight reasons to reject the "expanded" Binder version of *Red Badge*.

3.273 COLVERT, JAMES B. "Crane, Hitchcock, and the Binder Edition of *The Red Badge of Courage*." *Critical Essays on Stephen Crane's "The Red Badge of Courage*." Ed. Donald Pizer. Boston: G. K. Hall, 1990. 238–63. A full examination of the Binder-Parker case for the expanded version of *Red Badge*. Colvert convincingly argues that their case lacks documentary evidence, is based on "unwarranted conjectures" about Riply Hitchcock as an "exceptionally censorious editor," and requires Crane to have been "a humble and powerless author." Above all, Colvert, going beyond Pizer (3.287), establishes that the Parker-Binder insistence on an unambiguous ending drastically weakens the irony and ambivalence that are fundamental to the great American novel published by Appleton in 1894. See also Binder (3.270).

3.274 COVICI, PASCAL. Introduction. *"The Red Badge of Courage" by Stephen Crane*. New York: Viking, 1974. 7–34. An ambitious and valuable treatment of grand themes in *Red Badge* as well as a good summary of the textual controversies stirred up by the Binder expanded version printed by Norton. Covici sketches three possible reading of Fleming and *Red Badge:* as studies of fear, of initiation, or of ego-deflation.

3.275 DOMERASKI, REGINA. "A Note on the Text." *"The Red Badge of Courage" by Stephen Crane*. New York: Bantam, 1983. 133–35. Domeraski succinctly argues that there is no call to add, after the fact, the sections Crane discarded before he presented the final draft to Appleton. In addition to the obvious points that Crane himself proofread the Appleton text and never attempted to revise the original Appleton text during his own lifetime, she holds that the longer (Binder) version is inferior as literature. "Restoring Crane's deleted manuscript passages to the text may lead to stimulating scholarly debate—but, perhaps, at the expense of the terse and more poetic pace Crane himself insured as he prepared the 1895 Appleton edition of his novel for publication."

3.276 HORSFORD, HOWARD C. "He Was a Man." *New Essays on "The Red Badge of Courage*." Ed. Lee Clark Mitchell. Cambridge: Cambridge UP, 1986. 109–27. A detailed exploration of the persistent ambiguities surrounding the conclusion of *Red Badge*. Crane says of Fleming at the very end, 'He was a man"; however, readers have long worried over how much irony ought to be factored into a reading of this phrase. Horsford concludes that "no single statement expressing his [Fleming's] state of mind is ever really final." Further, an appeal to either the traditional or to Binder's version of the text will not avoid the problem, for "either version of the novel authenticates a reader's skepticism regarding Fleming's concluding self-satisfaction."

3.277 HOWARTH, WILLIAM L. *"The Red Badge of Courage* Manuscript: New Evidence for a Critical Edition" *Studies in Bibliograhy* 18 (1965): 229–47. This piece is for the Crane scholar concerned with the nitty gritty of text. Howarth attempts to reconstruct Crane's composition of *Red Badge* by comparing physical details of the five kinds of paper he used in the second (longer) draft. He concludes that a text better than the Appleton book version is possible but even then the ambiguities surrounding Fleming's maturation would remain in this "improved" version.

3.278 KATZ, JOSEPH. "Practical Editions: Stephen Crane's *The Red Badge of Courage.*" *Proof* 2 (1972): 301–19. Katz examines and condemns most of the paperback editions of *Red Badge* used in classrooms. He gives a table of some fifteen version–the least of objectionable edition was published by Bobbs-Merrill and the worst by Fawcett.

3.279 MAILLOUX, STEVEN. *"The Red Badge of Courage* and Interpretative Conventions: Critical Response to a Maimed Text." *Studies in the Novel* 10 (1978): 48–63. A clearly polemical piece in support of the Binder "complete" version: Given that version, Crane's ending is fully ironic and Fleming remains deluded. For those interested in this textual controversy, Mailloux surveys the range of opinions.

3.280 ———. "Literary History and Reception Study." *Interpretive Conventions: The Reader in the Study of American Fictions.* Ithaca, NY: Cornell UP, 1982. 159–91. A full-blown defense of the "complete" Binder versin of *Red Badge:* basically a restatement of Mailloux's 1978 piece (3.279) on the same point.

3.281 MITCHELL, LEE CLARK. Introduction. *New Essays on "The Red Badge of Courage."* Cambridge: Cambridge UP, 1986. 1–23. A general discussion of *Red Badge,* Crane, and the essays that Mitchell has selected for this volume. (All these essays are treated elsewhere in this bibliograhy.) Mitchell gives attention to the textual controversy surrounding *Red Badge,* early reviews, whether Fleming is a hero, and whether he matures.

3.282 MITGANG, HERBERT. " 'Red Badge' Is Due Out As Crane Wrote It." *New York Times* 2 Apr. 1982: Sections A1 and C30. An interview with

Harry Binder, who asserts the point made in the title of the article and that the new text is both an improved and a different novel.

3.283   PARKER, HERSHEL. "Review of Recent Editions of *The Red Badge of Courage.*" *Nineteenth-Century Fiction* 30 (1976): 558–62. Parker assesses Fredson Bowers's editorial work on *Red Badge;* he is not pleased and says so with a dozens of sarcastic quips, for instance, "He rigorously regularizes accidentals . . . even to the point of sticking a prissy apostrophe into every 'aint' that Crane wrote."

3.284   _____. "Aesthetic Implications of Authorial Excisions: Examples from Nathaniel Hawthorne, Mark Twain, and Stephen Crane." *Editing Nineteenth-Century Fiction*. Ed. Jane Millgate. New York: Garland, 1978. 99–119. Parker quarrels with modern textual editing principles such as "last is best" and "deletions always improve." In the case of Crane, Parker argues for the 1893 *Maggie* and Binder's expanded version of *Red Badge*.

3.285   _____. "The 'New Scholarship': Textual Evidence and Its Implications for Criticism, Literary Theory, and Aesthetics." *Studies in American Fiction* 9 (1981): 181–97. A fesity and defensive account of Parker's side in the *Maggie* and *Red Badge* textual controversies. Basically a reptition of the views expressed in his 1978 piece (3.284).

3.286   _____. "*The Red Badge of Courage:* The Private History of a Campaign That Succeeded?" *Flawed Texts and Verbal Icons: Literary Authority in American Fiction*. Evanston, IL: Northwestern UP, 1984. 147–79. A personal narrative of Parker's part in the struggles to get the Binder "expanded" version of *Red Badge* as the accepted text. Contains several detailed critiques of Bowers's Virginia edition of *Red Badge*.

3.287   _____. "Getting Used to the 'Original' Form of *The Red Badge of Courage.*" *New Essays on "The Red Badge of Courage."* Ed. Lee Clark Mitchell. Cambridge: Cambridge UP, 1986. 25–47. Parker attempts to reconstruct Crane's mental state when he wrote and struggled to bring to press his *Red Badge* manuscript. Armed with these "findings" Parker alleges that Crane was susceptible particularly to the editorial pressures Ripley Hitchcock and Appleton applied in getting Crane to cut his manuscript. It is these cuts that Binder and Parker insist ought to be reinserted into the *Red Badge* text.

3.288   PIZER, DONALD. Introduction. *Stephen Crane's "The Red Badge of Courage": An Authoriative Text, Backgrounds, and Sources Criticism*. Ed. Sculley Bradley, et al. New York: Norton, 1976. vii–viii. This volume presents the 1895 Appleton edition of *Red Badge* and, in appendixes, Crane's "uncanceled but unpublished manuscript passages." Pizer's brief comments also introduce the selections of secondary scholarship included in this volume. (All these articles are found elsewhere in this bibiography.)

3.289   _____. "'*The Red Badge of Courage* Nobody Knows': A Brief Rejoinder." *Studies in American Fiction* 11 (1979): 77–81. Pizer offers a convincing rebuttal of Binder's position for an "expanded" version of *Red Badge:* there is no evidence that Appleton editor Hitchcock forced Crane to revise and there is no need to assume that a clear and consistent novel is better than an ambivalent and ambiguous one.

3.290   _____. "Self-Censorship and Textual Editing." *Textual Criticism and Literary Interpretation.* Ed. Jerome J. McGann. Chicago: U of Chicago P, 1985. 144–61. A good general discussion of modern textual scholarship and its ability to handle self-censorship by authors. *Red Badge* serves as an example of the published version's (Appleton, 1895) being better than Crane's manuscript version.

3.291   _____. "*The Red Badge of Courage:* Text, Theme, and Form." *South Atlantic Quarterly* 84 (1985): 302–13. A restatement of the Binder-Pizer debate over which version of *Red Badge* is better and which reflects Crane's final intention. Pizer examines in great detail the first paragraphs to argue that though *Red Badge* is an initiation story, Crane was able to capture realistically the "permanent ambiguity" that fills every stage of human growth.

3.292   STALLMAN, ROBERT W. "'The Red Badge of Courage': A Collation of Two Pages of Manuscript Expunged from Chapter XII." *Papers of the Bibliographical Society of America* 49 (1955): 273–77. Stallman reprints for comparison, the draft version of several sections of chapter 12 of *Red Badge.*

3.293   _____. Introduction. *Stephen Crane: Stories and Tales.* New York: Vantage, 1955. vii–xxxii. A shortened version of Stallman's Introduction to his 1951 Random House *The Red Badge of Courage* (see 2.215). In addition, the notes for the volume are taken from his *Stephen Crane: An Omnibus* (see 2.16). Also, this volume contains "for the first time portions of the earliest known manuscript of *The Red Badge of Courage* and presents the first American publication of the final handwritten manuscript." With reference to the latter, Stallman initiated the by now perennial questions: Which version of *Red Badge* has superior literary meit and/or which version did Crane really intend?

3.294   _____. Introduction and Notes. *"The Red Badge of Courage" and Selected Stories*. New York: New American Library, 1960. vii–x, 206–224. Stallman describes and reprints five new manuscript pages of *Red Badge* and gives a brief history of the manuscript.

3.295   WINTERICH, JOHN T. Introduction and A Note on this edition. *The Red Badge of Courage*. London: Folio Society, 1951. 5–19, 21–25. Winterich's Introduction gives British readers historical and social background on the Civil War. With regard to *Red Badge* he comments on the lasting value of Crane's story and makes interesting comments on Crane's terseness—"there is a lean economy in the telling of the tale that struck a taut new note in writing—Crane at times may have abused words, but he never wasted them"—and his skill at dialect. The Note on the Text explains the canceled manuscript passages he has integrated into the regular text.

3.296   _____. "'The Red Badge of Courage.'" *Times Literary Supplement* 2579 (6 July 1951): 421. Short piece on the printing of the manuscript versions of *Red Badge* with comments on Crane's troubles with spelling and punctuation; "he seemed to carry his commas in a kind of salt-cellar whereof the top kept plugging up or flying off."

See for more on textual issues and *Red Badge:*

3.39
3.91
9.40
12.9
12.32
12.42
12.43
13.31

4

Bowery Works

Overview

MAGGIE. As noted above, *Maggie* has had its share of textural controversy, though the situation is not nearly as complicated as with *Red Badge.* Crane could not find a regular publisher for his first Bowery novel so he paid a medical publishing firm, which issued it under the pen name of Johnston Smith in 1893—see Katz 4.3 and Pizer 4.4 for publishing details and facsimiles of that edition. The 1893 *Maggie* was a flat sales failure—see Weatherford (2.17). After *Red Badge* rose to the top of the best-seller lists Appleton published an expurgated version of *Maggie* in 1896. When Bowers did the Virginia edition of *Maggie* (4.2) he produced an eclectic version combining the 1893 and 1896 versions—a version that Bowers argues (see 4.12) restored the deletions that Appleton editor Hitchcock forced Crane to make. Bowers's Virginia edition has not been widely accepted. The current scholarly consensus is that both the 1893 and 1896 versions are worthy of independent study, though the most commonly used text is the 1893 version emended of its typographical errors. Such a version of *Maggie,* for instance, appears in Levenson's *Stephen Crane: Prose of Poetry* (12.11). Indeed, several studies have argued the priority of the 1893 version, especially the importance of the paragraph concerning the gross, fat man in chapter 17: see Bruccoli (4.17), Katz (4.63), Salemi (4.95), and STALLMAN (4.103).

The best general essay on *Maggie* is by COLVERT (4.22). More specific articles on *Maggie* have assessed the factors that caused her demise. BAUM (4.9), CADY (4.19), FITELSON (4.29) HAPKE (4.49), and HOWELLS (4.57) have argued that the Bowery environment crushed her; Graff (4.38), HOLTON (4.52), Krause (4.68), OLIVERO (4.86), PIZER (4.92), and Walcutt (4.112) have contended that she was doomed by illusions, including an inappropriate middle-class morality.

A second important area of *Maggie* scholarship has dealt with the sources of and the inspirations for Crane's novel: Zola and the French naturalists, argue AHNEBRINK (2.1) and Fryckstdt (4.136); American literature, especially the slum sociology of Jacob Riis, insist CUNLIFFE (4.23), Fine (4.28), and Gullason (4.42).

GEORGE'S MOTHER. This novel has been relatively ignored. Some attention has focused on Crane's skillful contrast of George's escape to the barroom and his mother's refuge in the mission chapel; see Brennan (4.122) and Jackson (4.126). Recently the fine book by GIAMO (4.125), which devoted several sections to *George's Mother,* will perhaps prompt more examination of Crane's second Bowery work.

NEW YORK CITY SKETCHES. Stallman and Hagemann were instrumental in discovering and publishing a great many previously unknown newspaper sketches by Crane; see 4.137 and 4.174. Concerning general essays on Crane's New York City sketches, the article by TRATCHENBERG (4.176) is essential. A few individual sketches have received scholary attention.

"An Experiment in Misery" and "An Experiment in Luxury":

BASSAN 4.140–4.142
Bonner 4.143
Johnson 4.154
NAGLE 4.170
Slotkin 4.173

"An Ominous Baby":

Hall 4.151

"In the Depths of a Coal Mine":

KATZ 4.157

Also annotated in this section are several pieces on the Dora Clark affair and Crane's run-in with the New York City police; the article by GALLAGHER (4.150) is very good; see also Stallman and Hagemann (4.174).

MAGGIE

Books

4.1 BASSAN, MAURICE, ed. *Stephen Crane's "Maggie": Text and Context.* Belmont, CA: Wadsworth, 1966. xvi+191 Bassan reprints the 1893 version of *Maggie* plus essays and comments described elsewhere in this bibliography. See 4.8 for Bassan's introduction to this volume. (Note: Joseph Katz, 4.3, also issued a facsimile reproduction of the 1893 *Maggie* in 1966.)

4.2   BOWERS, FREDSON. *[Maggie]: Bowery Tales. The Works of Stephen Crane*, Vol. 1. Ed. Fredson Bowers. Charlottesville: UP of Virginia, 1969. xcviii+178. Bowers's *Maggie* is a hybrid text combining elements fro the 1893 and 1896 editions. See Bowers's textual introduction (4.12) for his account of his eclectic edition of *Maggie*: also see 4.23 for Colvert's general introduction.

4.3   KATZ, JOSEPH, ed. *Maggie: A Girl of the Streets (A Story of New York)*. Gainesville, FL: Scholars' Facsimiles and Reprints, 1966. xxiv+163. A facsimile reproduction of the 1893 version of *Maggie* along with introductory comments and brief notes. See 4.6 for Katz's introduction. Bassan (4.1) also reproduced the 1893 *Maggie* in 1966.

4.4   PIZER, DONALD. *"Maggie, A Girl of the Streets" by Stephen Crane*. San Francisco: Chandler, 1968. xxxiv+163. Pizer has published a facsimile of the 1893, first edition of *Maggie*. See 4.93 for Pizer's introduction.

Articles and Book Chapters

4.5   AARON, DANIEL. "Howells' 'Maggie.'" *New England Quarterly* 38 (1965): 85–90. One of the vignettes in Howells's *Suburban Sketches* depicts the suicide by drowning of an Irish girl. Aaron compares his handling of this incident with Crane's.

4.6   ANGOFF, CHARLES. "A Fiction without Women." *American Mercury* 33 (1934): 375–78. Angoff argues, unconvincingly, that *Maggie* is not about Maggie, but is a study of the streets of New York.

4.7   BASSAN, MAURICE. "Crane, Townsend, and Realism of a Good Kind." *Papers of the New Jersey Historica Society* 82 (1964): 128–35. Crane's realism is compared with the melodramatic "realism of a good kind" practiced by, among others, Edward Townsend in his stories about tough kids from the slums who overcome all odds.

4.8   _____. Introduction *Stephen Crane's "Maggie": Text and Context*. Belont, CA: Wadsworth, 1966. ix–xvi. Bassan aims to have *Maggie* appreciated on its own artistic merits instead of having it see as an example of naturalism or as a parallel to European period novels. He also gives a brief description of the four drafts and the two published versions of Crane's first novel. The 1893 version of *Maggie* is reprinted, followed by a dozen short contemporary accounts of life in the slums and excerpts from some two dozen critical perspectives on the novel. All of the latter are treated elsewhere in this bibliography.

4.9   BAUM, ROSALIE MURPHY. "Alcoholism and Family Abuse in *Maggie* and *The Bluest Eye.*" *Mosiac* 19 (1986): 91–105. Thesis: Crane's *Maggie* (and Toni Morrison's 1970 book *The Bluest Eye*) accords with the view of alcoholism advanced by social and behavioral scientists, especially the view that alcohol is more the result than the cause of intolerable family situations.

4.10   BEGIEBING, ROBERT J. "Stephen Crane's *Maggie* and the Death of the Self." *American Imago* 34 (1977): 50–71. An elaborate discussion of the reasons for Maggie's downfall. Thesis: Maggie faces the chaos of the city in terms of her fantasies about Pete, which complicate and eventually cause her destruction.

4.11   BLACKMUR, R. P. "Introduction." *American Short Novels.* Ed. R. P. Blackmur. New York: Crowell, 1960. 8–9. Describes *Maggie* as a burlesque allegory of reality. Reprinted in Bassan's *"Maggie": Text and Context* (4.1: –144–46).

4.12   BOWERS, FREDSON. "Textual Introduction [To *Maggie*]." *Bowery Tales. The Works of Stephen Crane,* Vol 1. Ed. Fredson Bowers. Charlottesville: UP of Virginia, 1969. liii–xcviii. Bower's *Maggie* is a hybrid text combining elements from the 1893 and 1896 editions. He explains that he attempted to capture the 1896 revised version except for those revisions that were imposed by Appleton editor Ripley Hitchcock. Bowers argues that he has arrived at a text that represents the last chance Crane had to improve upon his story: "A synthesis of the two editions [will] create a form of the text that will represent his final artistic intentions divorced from censorship alterations." Though Bowers's hybrid version has not been generally adopted (even Levenson's *Stephan Crane: Prose and Poetry,* 12.11, which reprints nearly everything of significance from the Virginia edition, declines to use Bowers's *Maggie*), still, Bowers's comments on the text of *Maggie* are most valuable. Especially noteworthy are his detailed comments on the paragraph in chapter 17, "the huge fat man in torn and greasy garments," and his contention that "the fat man is the obverse of the stout clergyman whose rejectin of Maggie at the end of the preceding chapter had led to her 'damnation' as a prostitute." For more on the objections to the hybrid text see the review by Donald Pizer, "The

Virginia Edition of *Bowery Tales* and *Tales of Whilomville,*" *Modern Philology* 68 (1970): 212–14.

4.13 BRADBURY, MALCOLM. "Romance and Reality in *Maggie.*" *Journal of American Studies* (UK) 3 (1969): 111–21. Sociologically based examination of *Maggie* treating urban conditions in America in the 1890s. *Maggie* is a romance with a realistic basis.

4.14 BRENNAN, JOSEPH X. "Ironic and Symbolic Structure in Crane's *Maggie.*" *Nineteenth-Century Fiction* 16 (1962): 303–15. A "formal analysis" of *Maggie.* Insightful comments on the self-righteousness of all the characters in the novel and the city dwellers' human indifference to human suffering.

4.15 BROOKS, VAN WYCK. Introduction. *Two Novels by Stephen Crane: "Maggie, A Girl of the Streets" and "George's Mother."* Greenwich, CT: Fawcett, 1960. 5–8. Extremely brief; one striking line: "He left the reader to invest with sentiment the facts that he related barely and boldly."

4.16 BRUCCOLI, MATTHEW J. "An Unrecorded Review of *Maggie.*" *Stephen Crane Newsletter* 1.1 (1966): 4. Bruccoli reprints most of a short notice in the *Yale Courant* 33.3 (1986): 81. The reviewer, Sidney R. Kennedy, finds *Maggie* a disappointment after *Red Badge.*

4.17 ———. "Maggie's Last Night." *Stephen Crane Newsletter* 2.1 (1967): 10. A short two-paragraph note in which Bruccoli suggests that there are two time-schemes in chapter 17 of *Maggie:* "a literal account of one night; and symbolic compression of Maggie's remaining nights as she becomes progressively more degraded over a period of years."

4.18 BRUCCOLI, MATTHEW, and JOSEPH KATZ. "A Third Printing of *Maggie* (1896)." *Stephen Crane Newsletter* 1.1 (1966): 2–3. Details on a third impression of the Appleton *Maggie* of 1896.

4.19 CADY, EDWIN H. "Stephen Crane's *Maggie, A Girl of the Streets.*" *Landmarks of American Writing.* Ed. Hennig Cohen. New York: Basic Books, 1969. 172–81. A general essay showing that Crane, last of the nineteenth-century novelists, was the first of the moderns in writing *Maggie.* He discusses the novel in ecological terms—"the total relationship of an organism to its condition—" as he explains Maggie's downfall in chapter 17.

4.20 CARGILL, OSCAR. "The Social Revolt." *The Social Revolt: American Literature from 1888 to 1914.* New York: Macmillan, 1933. 1–18.

Cargill argues that though Crane was sensitive to social injustice, he shied away from preaching and social crusades. Cargill makes brief comments on *Maggie* and he reprints selections from *War Is Kind, Black Riders,* "The Price of the Harness," and chapter 5 of *Maggie* containing her initial meeting with Pete: "Maggie thought he must be a very elegant and graceful bartender."

4.21 CHAMBERLAIN, JOHN. *Farewell to Reform.* Gloucester, MA: Peter Smith, 1958. 177 and passim. A revised edition (New York, 1912) of a monograph on "the rise, life and decay of the progressive mind in America," offering the standard view that though Crane was very sensitive to social injustice, he was no crusader.

4.22 COLBERT, JAMES B. Introduction [*Maggie*]. *Bowery Works: [Maggie]. The Works of Stephen Crane,* Vol. 1. Ed. Fredson Bowers. Charlottesville: UP of Virginia, 1969. xxxiii–lii. Arguably *the* best article on *Maggie.* Colvert contends that *Maggie* "initiated modern American writing." Colvert describes biographical and literary influences on Crane's writing and revising of *Maggie,* concluding that the 1896 version "relieved some of the exuberant overwriting and graceless phrasing that marred the earlier edition." In either edition, readers will find that Crane's art, "the almost perfect detachment, the brilliant impressionism, the critical power of its irony," elevate a hackneyed plot to the level of "a minor classic."

4.23 CUNLIFFE, MARCUS. "Stephen Crane and the American Background of *Maggie.*" *American Quarterly* 7 (1955): 31–44. An early, convincing, and eventually very influential examination of American influences (as opposed to those of Zola or Tolstoy) on *Maggie;* especially impressive are the parallels Cunliffe finds between Crane's first novel and the newspaper-syndicated sermons of the Reverend T. DeWitt Talmage. Treatises by prominent muckrakers are also examined.

4.24 DEW, MARJORIE. "Realistic Innocence: Cady's Footnote to a Definition of American Literary Realism." *American Literary Realism* 5 (1972): 487–89. Dew objects to Cady's contention (in *The Light of Common Day: Realism in American Fiction,* 2.55) that realistic fiction understates evil. Crane's *Maggie* is one of her counterexamples.

4.25 DICKASON, DAVID H. "Benjamin Orange Flower, Patron of the Realists." *American Literature* 14 (1942): 148–56. Flower's *Arena* was a popular and influential reform journal in the late 1890s. Flower was aware of the heavy tone of his journal and he sought truthful fiction to lighten things up. Flower's support of Crane was a favorable review of *Maggie* (by Hamlin Garland) followed by the printing of his sketches "The Ominous Baby" and "Men in the Storm."

4.16   FALK, ROBERT P. "The Literary Criticism of the Genteel Decades, 1870–1900." *The Development of American Literary Criticism.* Ed. Floyd Stovall. New Haven, CT: College and University Press, 1964. 114–47. One paragraph on the shock caused by *Maggie.*

4.27   FIEDLER, LESLIE A. *Love and Death in the American Novel.* New York: Stein and Day, 1966. 247–48. Fiedler cites *Maggie* as an important contribution in deromanticizing love.

4.28   FINE, DAVID M. "Abraham Cahan, Stephen Crane, and the Romantic Tenement Tale of the Nineties." *American Studies* 14 (1974): 95–107. Before *Maggie,* romantic tales of slum life were prevalent in American fiction—the rich are devious and the poor honest. *Maggie* and *George's Mother* obviously challenged that and other stereotypes.

4.29   FITELSON, DAVID. "Stephen Crane's *Maggie* and Darwinism." *American Quarterly* 16 (1964): 182–94. Useful as an articulation of the old view of a rigorous, Darwinian determinism in *Maggie.* That is, those in the Bowery have no choice because their environment reduces them to animals in the survival of the fittest.

4.30   FORD, PHILIP H. "Illusion and Reality in Crane's *Maggie.*" *Arizona Quarterly* 25 (1969): 293–303. Ford's interesting, if unconvincing, reading counters typical environmental accounts of *Maggie;* his thesis is that Maggie's self-induced illusions (like those of the Swede in "The Blue Hotel") caused her downfall.

4.31   FOX, AUSTIN McC. Introduction. *"Maggie" and Other Stories by Stephen Crane.* New York: Washington Square, 1960. v–xviii. A typical general introductory essay on Crane, *Maggie,* and the other works that Fox has collected. Though none of the works is treated at any length, Fox argues that Crane was not a social crusader but a writer concerned with "the moral and psychological aspects of a situation."

4.32   FRIERSON, WILLIAM C., and HERBERT EDWARDS. "Impact of French Naturalism on American Critical Opinion, 1877–1892." *PMLA* 63 (1948): 1007–16. A detailed examination of the critical (and popular) climate that greeted *Maggie* in 1893.

4.33   FURST, LILLIAN R. "Stephen Crane's *Maggie* and *Papa Hamlet* by Arno Holtz and Johannes Schlaf." *Actes Du VIIe Congres de L'Association Internationale de Litterature Comparee.* Ed. Milan V.

Dimic and Juan Ferrate. Stuttgart: Bieber, 1979. 165–68. While Furst explicitly denies any influence, she sees strong thematic and stylistic parallels between *Maggie* and the 1891 "experimental sketch" by Holtz and Schlaf.

4.34 GATES, ROBERT A. "The Polarized City: Edith Wharton's *House of Mirth* and Stephen Crane's *Maggie." The New York Vision: Interpretations of New York City in the American Novel.* Lanham, MD: UP of America, 1987. 29–61. The superpoor in Crane's *Maggie* are compared with the super-rich in *House of Mirth.* Gates's treatment of Crane is confined to analyses of Crane by Cady and Stallman; his limited research is indicated by his apparent ignorance of the publication history of *Maggie.*

4.35 GELFANT, BLANCHE. *The American City Novel.* Norman: U of Oklahoma P, 1954. Passim. *Maggie* is cited as a precursor to later, more serious slum fiction.

4.36 GEMME, FRANCIS R. Introduction. *Maggie and Other Stories.* New York: 1968. Stallman cites it in *Stephen Crane: A Critical Bibliography* 14.3: 547, but I have not seen it.

4.37 GIBSON, WILLIAM M., and GEORGE ARMS, eds. *A Bibliography of William Dean Howells.* New York: New York Public Library, 1948. 120–23. A section of Howells's "Life and Letters" column for *Harpers' Weekly* noting his own reviews of *Maggie, Red Badge,* and *Black Riders.*

4.38 GRAFF, AIDA FARRAG. "Metaphor and Metonymy: The Two Worlds of Crane's *Maggie." English Studies in Canada* 8 (1983): 422–36. An elaborate and complex analysis of the two worlds of Maggie: the Bowery and Maggie's illusions about the Bowery. In addition, Graff makes the interesting observation that though all the other characters have a place (Pete, the saloon; Mrs. Johnson, the house; Jimmie, the street corner), Maggie has none.

4.39 GRAHAM, D. B. "Dreiser's Maggie." *American Literary Realism* 7 (1974): 169–70. An influence note: Dreiser alludes to Crane's *Maggie* at the end of chapter 4 of *Sister Carrie.*

4.40 GRAU, SHIRLEY ANN. Introduction. *"Maggie: A Girl of the Streets" by Stephen Crane.* Norwalk, CT: Heritage, 1974. 5–11. A sketchy essay contending that Crane was obsessed "with the ugly, the harsh and the unfortunate" and that he "implicitly believed that truth lies nearer the unpleasant than the pleasant."

4.41 GREEN, CAROL HURD. "Stephen Crane and the Fallen Women." *American Novelists Revisited: Essays in Feminist Criticism.* Ed. Fritz Fleischmann. Boston: G. K. Hall, 1982. 225–42. Cady (2.4), among others, observed that Crane did not convincingly describe women in his works; Green's thesis is much more condemnatory: Crane's works are misogynic. She alleges that "there are no creative women in Crane. . . . [all of them were] the troublemakers, noisy, disloyal, and destructive," and then she turns to *Active Service, Maggie, The Monster,* and several poems for confirmation.

4.42 GULLASON, THOMAS A. "The Sources of Stephen Crane's *Maggie.*" *Philological Quarterly* 38 (1959): 497–502. Following Cunliffe (4.23), Gullason argues for American influences on *Maggie:* his father's anti-alcohol treatises and Jacob Riis's slum tract *How the Other Half Lives.*

4.43 ———. "Thematic Patterns in Stephen Crane's Early Novels." *Nineteenth-Century Fiction* 16 (1961): 59–67. Thesis: The central characters of Crane's early novels—Maggie, Fleming, and George— are autobiographical, depicting Crane's struggles with ideals versus reality, mother dominance, and fear.

4.44 ———. "The First Known Review of Stephen Crane's 1893 *Maggie.*" *English Language Notes* 5 (1968): 300–302. This review in the Port Jervis (New York) *Union* is important. It is not too surprising that a small, hometown paper recognized the accomplishment of a former resident; what is remarkable is that this review is more perceptive than many later big-city notices of *Maggie.*

4.45 ———. "The Prophetic City in Stephen Crane's 1893 *Maggie.*" *Modern Fiction Studies* 24 (1978): 129–37. Gullason argues that the shock of the city turned Crane from comedy (the tall tales of his Sullivan County sketches) to tragedy and that the key to Crane's first novel is the "scapegoat as heroine."

4.46 ———. "Tragedy and Melodrama in Stephen Crane's *Maggie.*" *Stephen Crane's "Maggie: A Girl of the Streets."* Ed. Thomas A. Gullason. New York: Norton, 1979. 245–53. A useful, short, insightful essay on *Maggie.* Gullason sees in *Maggie* parody, satire, and melodrama and he argues that with her limited alternatives Maggie does as well as could be expected.

4.47 HAPKE, LAURA. "Maggie's Sisters: Nineteenth-Century Literary Images of the American Streetwalker." *Journal of American Culture* 5

(1982): 29–35. Compared with other nineteenth-century treatments of prostitutes *Maggie* shines. Still, despite Crane's clear grasp of environmental influences, Hapke wonders how any woman dwelling in that society could be so innocent and so naive.

4.48 _____. "The Alternate Fallen Women in *Maggie: A Girl of the Streets.*" *Markham Review* 12 (1983): 41–43. An interesting comparison of the other prostitute in *Maggie,* self-confident, prosperous Nell, with the timid, stunted Maggie.

4.49 _____. "Stephen Crane and the Deserted Street Girl." *Girls Who Went Wrong: Prostitutes in American Fiction, 1885–1917.* Bowling Green, KY: Bowling Green U Popular P, 1989. 45–67. An important and convincing analysis of Crane's exploration of "lower-depth experience"—see also Giamo (4.125) on this point. The thesis of Hapke's chapter on Crane deals with what she terms Crane's "contradictory attitudes toward prostitution. . . . [H]e is alternately interested and repelled" by the unchaste woman. Hapke argues that Crane neither condemned nor absolved Maggie. For Maggie, unlike the confident and successful Nell, "is too reduced and passive to be a sexual aggressor, i.e., a 'real prostitute.'" It is the Bowery's crushing environment that victimizes her. "What *is* clear is Crane's message: the woman bereft of male protection will end up in the hell of prostitution. . . . To defend her prostitution as a response to desertion, Crane minimizes Maggie's hired sexuality . . . in her robotic soliciting [she] acts out a trancelike response to the trauma of abandonment."

4.50 HARRISON, STANLEY R. "Stephen Crane and Death: A Moment between Two Romanticisms." *Markham Review* 2 (1971): 117–20. Thesis: Crane's *Maggie* and *George's Mother* illustrate the Turner thesis: With the American frontier closed in 1890, Crane's naturalism was "a flight in reverse, both inward and backward" toward the evil, bestial slum. Harrison attempts to support his reading by appealing to Crane's use of the color red and his many jungle references.

4.51 HAZLITT, HENRY. Introduction. *"Maggie" Together with "George's Mother" and 'The Blue Hotel.'* New York: Knopf, 1931. vii–xi. A brief introduction; interesting comments on the characters in Crane's Bowery works as "less individuals than types."

4.52 HOLTON, MILNE. "'The Sparrow's Fall and the Sparrow's Eye': Crane's *Maggie.*" *Studia Neophilologia* 41 (1969): 115–29. A convincing, ambitious examination of *Maggie,* casting it as an anti-

Darwinistic, antinaturalistic study. Holton argues that Crane's first novel examines a failure of understanding; "if we are to assert that central to Crane's concern is the representation of Maggie's and Jimmie's illusions, then it is the causes of those illusions which are being set forth in the first half of the book, their consequences in the second."

4.53   HONCE, CHARLES. "Johnston Smith." *Authors in False-face: Diverse Details on Anonymity and Pseudonymity in Literature.* Mt. Vernon, VA: Golden Eagle, 1939. 7–8. A brief discussion of Crane as "Johnston Smith" in the 1893 *Maggie.*

4.54   HOWARD, JUNE. *Form and History in American Literary Naturalism.* Chapel Hill: U of North Carolina P, 1985. Passim. Though her theoretical vocabulary uses the current (and complex) jargon, naturalism remains largely unchanged as a concept. *Maggie,* assumed to be naturalistic, is given attention along with several of Norris's novels.

4.55   HOWARD, LEON. "Review of the Virginia Edition of *The Works of Stephen Crane,* Volumes I and VII." *Nineteenth-Century Fiction* 25 (1970): 232–35. Howard objects (many others were soon to follow) that the Bowers edition of *Maggie,* which follows neither of the texts Crane saw published in 1893 and 1896, is a new hybrid creation. Now, twenty years later, the Virginia edition of *Maggie* is generally ignored and Crane scholars use either the 1893 or the 1896 version, clearly identifying the text they prefer.

4.56   HOWELLS, WILLIAM DEAN. "Frank Norris." *North American Review* 175 (1902): 769–78. Howells makes extended comparisons between Norris's *McTeague* and Crane's *Maggie.*

4.57   ——. "An Appreciation." *Major Conflicts: "George's Mother," 'The Blue Hotel,' "Maggie." The Work of Stephen Crane,* vol. 10. Ed. Wilson Follett. New York: Knopf, 1926. 135–36. A reprint of a section of Howells's review of *Maggie* (New York *World* 26 July 1896, 18; see *The Critical Heritage* 2.17:#8). This excerpt is important for several reasons, among them warm endorsement by Howells and his influential comment that *Maggie* has "that quality of fatal necessity which dominates Greek tragedy."

4.58   HUSSMAN, LAWRENCE E. "The Fate of the Fallen Women in *Maggie* and *Sister Carrie.*" *The Image of the Prostitute in Modern Literature.* Ed. Pierre Horne and Mary Beth Pringle. New York: Frederic Ungar, 1984. 91–100. Hussman is bothered because neither Crane nor

Dreiser wrote the sort of book Hussman wanted: "a realistic presentation of the prostitute's plight." He asserts that neither book was revolutionary; neither Crane nor Dreiser challenged sexual stereotypes; neither of them managed to avoid "indulging his [own] moral prejudices."

4.59   IVES, C. B. "Symmetrical Design in Four of Stephen Crane's Stories." *Ball State University Forum* 10 (1969): 17–26. Ives finds in *Maggie, George's Mother, Red Badge,* and *The Monster* a careful structure of balance and symmetry. Ives provides much more detail than is necessary; however, his piece would be useful as a class assignment.

4.60   JACKSON, JOHN A. "The Map of Society: America in the 1890's." *Journal of American Studies* 3 (1969): 103–10. Jackson treats *Maggie* as sociology. Crane was writing fiction but he deromanticized the city. From a moral point of view Jackson finds Crane holding not an absolute standard but a standard realistic given the environment of the Bowery.

4.61   JORDAN, PHILIP D. Introduction. *"Maggie: A Girl of the Streets" by Stephen Crane.* Lexington: UP of Kentucky, 1970. v–xi. Discusses *Maggie* as sociology: "an outstanding novel of social protest" and Crane as a crusading reformer.

4.62   KAHN, SHALOM J. "Stephen Crane and Whitman: A Possible Source for *Maggie." Walt Whitman Review* 7 (1961): 71–77. The title is accurate. These are, at best, possible influences; much is made of affinities that Kahn himself suggests may be "a mere coincidence."

4.63   KATZ, JOSEPH. "The *Maggie* Nobody Knows." *Modern Fiction Studies* 12 (1966): 200–12. Katz convincingly argues that the differences between the 1893 and the 1896 *Maggie* are substantial. Katz shows that beyond bowdlerizing the first version to please Appleton editor Ripley Hitchcock, Crane, in his revisions, "was to temper the brutality and to subdue the coarseness of the original."

4.64   ———. *"Maggie: A Girl of the Streets* (1893): A Census (Parts I, II, III)." *Stephen Crane Newsletter* 2.2 (1967): 7–9; 3.1 (1968): 6; 3.3 (1969): 10–11. Katz describes twenty-three located copies of the 1893 *Maggie.*

4.65   ———. Introduction. *"Maggie, A Girl of the Street" by Stephen Crane.* Delmar, NY: Scholars' Facsimiles and Reprints, 1978. v–xxiii. This volume is a facsimile reproduction of the first (1893) edition of

Maggie; Katz's comments deal with the changes Crane made for the 1896 version.

4.66   KNIGHT, GRANT C. "The Literature of Realism: Stephen Crane." *American Literature and Culture.* 1932. 395–400. Crane is quickly covered in a small section of a chapter on realism. Of note, Knight sees moral passion beneath the cold objectivity of *Maggie* and he observes that readers of "The Blue Hotel" are surprised that the Swede whips Johnnie in the fistfight in the snow.

4.67   KRAMER, MAURICE. "Crane's *Maggie: A Girl of the Streets.*" *Explicator* 22 (1964): Item 49. Crane as an ironist who combines in *Maggie* themes in clear tension: war and religion, realism and melodrama, toughness and delicacy, hypocrisy and honesty.

4.68   KRAUSE, SYDNEY J. "The Surrealism of Crane's Naturalism in *Maggie.*" *American Literary Realism* 16 (1983): 253–61. Krause argues that *Maggie* is much more than simple melodrama or undisguised naturalism. "When pushed to deformity, [Crane's art] acquires an aspect of surrealism." Krause explains how, in Maggie's dreams and nightmares, people turn into things and vice versa; Krause deals with the bizarre monk metaphor in chapter 19: "In a room a woman sat at a table eating like a fat monk in a picture."

4.69   KUSPIT, DONALD B. "Charles Dana Gibson's Girl." *Jahrbuch fur Amerikastudien* 7 (1962): 183–87. Kuspit attacks Gibson's image of ideal feminity. Further, he argues that Crane's *Maggie* depicted reality while Maggie's illusory dreams entertained appearances for she dreamed of being a Gibson girl!

4.70   LAFRANCE, MARSTON. "A Few Facts about Stephen Crane and 'Holland.'" *American Literature* 37 (1965): 195–202. LaFrance discovered the identity of "Holland," who revived Crane's morale in the dark days when *Maggie* failed to attract attention and buyers.

4.71   ———. "*George's Mother* and the Other Half of *Maggie.*" *Stephen Crane in Transition: Centenary Essays.* Ed. Joseph Katz. De Kalb: Northern Illinois UP, 1972. 35–53. LaFrance finds "no evidence of philosophical determinism" in Crane's Bowery works. Instead, he argues that Crane explored the moral inertia that Maggie, Pete, and George failed to overcome: The destroyer of lives in the slums "is a moral failure which is entirely a failure of the will." Unfortunately, LaFrance's bootstrap ethic flies in the face of philosophic proponents of free will (from Aristotle on down) who insist that necessary conditions of free actions are intelligence, education, good habits, and a humane environment. So, while Bowery persons might be free, in theory, their freedom is severely restricted.

4.72 LAINOFF, SEYMOUR. "Jimmie in Crane's *Maggie.*" *Iowa English Yearbooks* 10 (1965): 53–54. A mininote laying out the four stages of Jimmie's collapse.

4.73 LENEHAN, WILLIAM T. "The Failure of Naturalistic Techniques in Stephen Crane's *Maggie.*" *Stephen Crane's "Maggie": Text and Context.* Ed. Maurice Bassan. Belmont, CA: Wadsworth, 1966. 166–73. Lenehan's article is marred by rigid assumptions: Crane is a naturalist and moral values are absolute. For Lenehan, *Maggie* is the story of a youth who fails to adjust to her society whereas Jimmie and Nell, unworried about respectability, prosper. However, in the process, Lenehan's theme of "the failure of naturalistic techniques" falls by the wayside.

4.74 MACMILLAN, DUANE J. "*Sister Carrie,* 'Chapter IV': Theodore Dreiser's 'Tip-of-the-Hat' to Stephen Crane." *Dreiser Newsletter* 10 (1979): 1–7. MacMillan is convinced that in the chapter in question, Dreiser "deliberately contrived an almost perfect paradigm of the style consistently exemplified by Crane's serious fiction." Beyond that he also lays out broad parallels between Maggie and Sister Carrie.

4.75 MAGILL, FRANK N. "Stephen Crane." *Cyclopedia of World Authors.* New York: Harper and Row, 1958. 255–57. A longish reference book sketch with dates, names, and titles stressing *Maggie:* "In it Crane had discovered the slum as literary material; thus naturalism entered American letters."

4.76 MCILVAINE, ROBERT. "Crane's *Maggie:* A Source for *The Hairy Ape.*" *Eugene O'Neil Newsletter* 2 (1979): 8–9. "Some of the style and substance of *The Hairy Ape* was probably derived from *Maggie.*"

4.77 MINKS, TAMARA S. "Maggie Johnson: An American Eve in a Fallen Eden." *Recovering Literature* 16 (1988): 23–35. This one goes downhill after the title. Sloppy and shallow scholarship to belabor the obvious. It is bad enough to refer to James Nagel as James Nagal; Minks's use of a Cliff-note type reference book (*Recent American Fiction,* Barron's Educational Series) is worse; unfortunately, she gets the author of that volume wrong, too—his name is Donald Heiney, not Donald Heiny, and his coauthor, Lentheil H. Downs, ought to be acknowledged.

4.78   MITCHELL, LEE CLARK. "Naturalism and the Language of Determinism." *Columbia Literary History of the United States.* Ed. Emory Elliott. New York: Columbia UP, 1988. 525–45. Mitchell begins with an elegant and clear characterization of naturalism: "Individuals no longer appeared as morally independent actors in a Christian universe; rather like filings aligned by magnets, they succumbed to the logics of heredity and environment." While some realists straddled the fence and others were "hybrid practitioners," most realist authors, Mitchell argues, embraced the dire and dark upshot of a world without choice. Crane, he finds, is the most bleakly nihilistic of the group, which includes London, Norris, and Dreiser. While his thesis fits *Maggie* and perhaps *Red Badge,* he stretches to render both "The Open Boat" and "The Blue Hotel" deterministic. He can do so only by appealing to irony to undercut the limited success won by joint effort in the former and Crane's indictment of complicity in the latter.

4.79   MONTEIRO, GEORGE. "Bernard Berenson's Notes on Stephen Crane." *Stephen Crane Newsletter* 2.3 (1968): 1–2. The impact of the realism of *Maggie* upon a noted first-time reader of Crane.

4.80   ———. "Paul Limperly's *Maggie* (1893), and a New Stephen Crane Letter." *Stephen Crane Newsletter* 3.3 (1969): 7–9. The letter is an inscription in *Maggie* (see *Correspondence of Stephen Crane,* 13.3: #273); more interesting are prices paid for 1893 *Maggies.* Limperly's *Maggie* is also described in Paul Limperly, *Among My Books* (Cleveland, 1929): 44 and in his *The Library of the late Paul Limperly, Lakewood, Ohio* (New York, 1940): 38–39.

4.81   ———. "Amy Leslie on Stephen Crane's *Maggie.*" *Journal of Modern Literature* 9 (1981): 147–48. Monteiro reprints Amy Leslie's (one-time actress, theater critic for the *Chicago Daily News,* and Crane's girlfriend) short notice on *Maggie.*

4.82   MORRIS, LLOYD. *Incredible New York: High Life and Low Life of the Last Hundred Years.* New York: Random House, 1951. 179–80. Standard tales about Crane's difficulty finding a publisher for the 1893 *Maggie.*

4.83   NOBEL, DAVID W. "The Naturalists: Norris, Crane, Dreiser." *The Eternal Adam and the New World Garden: The Central Myth in the American Novel Since 1930.* New York: George Braziller, 1968. 115–23. A brief (one section of a short chapter), thesis-ridden treatment: Crane did not believe in the New Adam Myth—his interest was in the city as hell, rather than the city on the hill.

4.84 NYREN, DOROTHY, ed. "Crane, Stephen." *A Library of Literary Criticism: Modern American Literature.* New York: Frederick Ungar, 1960. 120–24. Short excerpts from selected critical essays on *Maggie* (and also on Crane's life and *Red Badge*.)

4.85 OLIVER, LAWRENCE J. "Brander Matthews' Re-visioning of Crane's Maggie." *American Literature* 60 (1988): 645–58. Crane seeking support for *Maggie* sent a copy to Matthews, influential critic and professor of drama at Columbia University in 1893. Matthews's response was roundabout—a romanticized retelling of the story "Before the Light of Day" in which Maggie and her husband heroically conquer the slums with hard work and love for each other.

4.86 OLIVIERO, TONI H. "'People as They Seem to Me': Determinism and Morality as Literary Devices in Three Novels of Stephen Crane." *Seminares* 2 (1976): 167–81. A convincing and philosophically sophisticated case is made that though Crane rejected naturalistic determinism he well understood that free will is severely limited in oppressive environments (*Maggie* and *George's Mother*) and in situations of stress (*Red Badge*).

4.87 OVERMEYER, JANET. "The Structure of Crane's *Maggie*." *University of Kansas City Review* 29 (1962): 71–72. Though Overmeyer claims that her objective is to state the relation of structure to theme in *Maggie,* neither the former nor the latter is made clear enough to test her contentions.

4.88 PARKER, HERSHEL, and BRIAN HIGGINS. "Maggie's 'Last Night': Authorial Design and Editorial Patching." *Studies in the Novel* 10 (1978): 64–75. An argument for the 1893 version of *Maggie*. Both the 1896 version and Bowers's attempts to generate a single version combining both texts (his eclectic text appears in the Virginia edition) are rejected on the ground that censoring chapter 17, especially excising the gross, fat man, removes the motivation that led to Maggie's suicide. For more on this last point see Salemi (4.95).

4.89 PETRY, ALICE HALL. *"Gin Lane* in the Bowery: Crane's *Maggie* and William Hogarth." *American Literature* 56 (1984): 417–26. Thesis: Because of association with artists Crane must have known of Hogarth's engraving *Gin Lane,* which Petry alleges influenced Crane's *Maggie*.

4.90 PHILLIPS, JAYNE ANNE. Introduction. *"Maggie, A Girl of the Streets" and Other Short Fiction by Stephen Crane.* New York: Bantam,

1986. vii–xv. A lengthy general introduction stressing family influences, Crane's interest in life under stress and extreme conditions, his use of types, and his graphic and accurate depiction of the Bowery. (The original 1893 *Maggie* is printed in Phillips's volume.)

4.91   PHILLIPS, WILLIAM. Introduction. *Great American Short Novels.* New York: Dial, 1950. vii–xiv. Phillips reprints a half-dozen short novels, including *Maggie.* Several paragraphs deal with *Maggie,* noting especially Crane's discipline and spareness in style.

4.92   PIZER, DONALD. "Stephen Crane's *Maggie* and American Naturalism." *Criticism* 7 (1965): 168–75. A seminal essay that convincingly shows that Maggie is doomed by a middle-class moral code that was inappropriate to her environment.

4.93   ———. Introduction and A Note on the Text. *"Maggie, A Girl of the Streets" by Stephen Crane.* San Francisco: Chandler, 1968. vii–xxxiv. Pizer has published a facsimile of the 1893, first edition of *Maggie.* His introduction provides details about when and where Crane wrote his first novel; thematic and stylistic considerations are also given some space.

4.94   PONCET, ANDRÉ. "Functional Jeffersonianism in the Naturalistic Novel." *All Men Are Created Equal: Ideologies, Rêves et Réalities.* Ed. Jean-Pierre Martin. Aix-en-Provence: U of Provence, 1983. 137–46. An examination of the place of American naturalism against the backdrop of the Jeffersonian ideals of democracy, freedom, and equality: *Maggie* is discussed in passing.

4.95   SALEMI, JOSEPH S. "Down a Steep Place into the Sea: Suicide in Stephen Crane's *Maggie.*" *American Notes and Queries* ns 1.2 (1988): 58–61. The penultimate paragraph of *Maggie* (omitted in the 1896 edition) describes "a huge fat man in torn and greasy garments." Salemi argues that this paragraph is essential, as it gives explicit motivation for Maggie's suicide. For more on this last point see Parker (4.88).

4.96   SANSOM, WILLIAM. Introduction. *"Maggie: A Girl of the Streets" by Stephen Crane.* Ed. Herbert Van Thal. London: Cassell, 1966. vii–xiv. A good short introduction emphasizing how Crane told a familiar Victorian story without cliches or maudlin notes.

4.97   SEYERSTED, PER. "The American Girl from Howells to Chopin." *Arbeiten aus Anglistik und Amerikanistik* 13.2 (1988): 183–92.

Maggie's failed attempt to develop a will and life of her own is briefly noted.

4.98 SEYMOUR-SMITH, MARTIN. *Fallen Women.* London: Nelson, 1969. 182–85. *Maggie* is briefly discussed as an early depiction of prostitution. Unlike many other authors of these tomes, "Crane is a natural historian of absolute integrity."

4.99 SIMONEAUX, KATHERINE G. "Color Imagery in Crane's *Maggie: A Girl of the Streets.*" *CLA Journal* 18 (1974): 91–100. A carbon-copy iteration (this was before the days of photocopy) of her color imagery piece on *George's Mother,* (see 4.130). This time 113 (instead of 139) instances are used to prove Crane's deterministic "ideology."

4.100 SMITH, HERBERT F. *Richard Watson Gilder.* New York: Twayne, 1970. Smith repeats the story that Gilder found *Maggie* "cruel," to which Crane supposedly responded, "You mean the story is too honest?"

4.101 SNELL, GEORGE. "Naturalism Nascent: Crane and Norris." *The Shapers of American Fiction, 1798–1947.* New York: Cooper Square, 1947. 223–49. Crane as a naturalist; *Maggie* and *Red Badge* are very briefly discussed.

4.102 STALLMAN, ROBERT W. "Stephen Crane's Primrose Path." *New Republic* 113 (19 Sept. 1955): 17–18. Stallman surveys the history of the reception of *Maggie,* contending that his style and the ironic viewpoint from which Crane designs his "forthright moral and social intent" make the crucial difference, a difference that saves *Maggie* from the dustbin of outdated sociological novels.

4.103 ———. "Stephen Crane's Revision of *Maggie: A Girl of the Streets.*" *American Literature* 26 (1955): 528–36. Another Stallman first: He reveals the minor revisions Crane made before Appleton republished *Maggie* in 1896 plus the deletion of the crucial last paragraph of chapter 17 concerning "a huge fat man in torn and greasy garments."

4.104 ———. "Crane's *Maggie:* A Reassessment." *Modern Fiction Studies* 5 (1959): 251–59. An expansion of Stallman's "Stephen Crane's Primrose Path" (4.102). Interesting comments on "Crane's *Maggie* as a Bowery version of Flaubert's *Madame Bovary.* Reprinted by Bassan (4.1: 139–44).

4.105 ———. "Crane's *Maggie* in Review." *The Houses That James Built.* East Lansing: Michigan State UP, 1961. 63–72. A useful, if self-serving piece. Stallman selects contemporary reviews of *Maggie* that "substantiate my [Stallman's] reading of *Maggie:* 'Innocence thwarted and betrayed by environment.'"

4.106   STEIN, WILLIAM BYSSHE. "New Testament Inversions in Crane's *Maggie.*" *Modern Language Notes* 73 (1958): 268–72. Even though Crane rebelled against Methodism he retained "an aggressive moral impatience with the scientific naturalism" of his day. Stein, *pace* Stallman (4.102), sees biblical patterns and symbols in *Maggie.*

4.107   TANSELLE, G. THOMAS. "Note 282: Samuel Roth's *Love Secrets,* 1927.*" *Book Collector* 15 (1966): 486–87. Tanselle discovered in a single issue of *Love Secrets* a complete, pirated version of *Maggie.*

4.108   ———. "Problems and Accomplishments in the Editing of the Novel." *Studies in the Novel* 7 (1975): 323–60. Beer quoted Crane as saying that Tolstoy "goes on and on like Texas"; so too this discussion of the theory and problems of producing critical editions. Also discussed is the eclectic Bowers text of *Maggie;* Tanselle argues for maintaining the integrity of both the 1893 and the 1896 versions of *Maggie.*

4.109   TAYLOR, GORDON O. "The Laws of Life: Stephen Crane." *The Passages of Thought: Psychological Representation in the American Novel, 1870–1900.* New York: Oxford UP, 1969. 110–35. Helpful psychological analyses of *Maggie* and *Red Badge:* Maggie is too naive and/or stupid for self-conscious reflection, so morality is not an issue for her; for Fleming, both cowardice and courage are biochemical processes.

4.110   TRAIL, H. D. "The New Fiction." *The New Fiction and Essays on Literary Subjects.* London: Hurst and Blackett, 1897. 1–26. An important contemporary reaction to *Maggie,* arguing that Crane has painted a "worst case scenario" of slum life.

4.111   TUTTLETON, JAMES W. "Two Books by Stephen Crane: *Maggie* and *George's Mother.*" *The Critic* ns 25 (13 June 1986): 421. A brief note on Crane's Bowery works.

4.112   WALCUTT, CHARLES CHILD. "Stephen Crane: Naturalism and Impressionism." *American Literary Naturalism: A Divided Stream.* 1956. 66–86. Naturalism in Crane, especially *Maggie.* Walcutt, like Pizer (4.92), finds that an inappropriate morality is the problem. In the "landscape of hysteria [which Crane shows us] people [are] victimized by their ideas of moral propriety which are so utterly inapplicable to their lives that they constitute a social insanity."

4.113 WERTHEIM, STANLEY. "The Saga of March 23rd: Garland, Gilder, and Crane." *Stephen Crane Newsletter* 3.2 (1968): 1–3. Details on dating correspondence dealing with the 1893 version of *Maggie*.

4.114 ———. Introduction. *The Merrill Studies in "Maggie" and "George's Mother."* Columbus, OH: Charles Merrill, 1970. iii–viii. A term-paper study guide. Wertheim has selected and reprinted excerpts from some three dozen pieces on *Maggie* and *George's Mother*. (All these articles are abstracted elsewhere in this bibliography.) His introduction makes general observations on critics' views of both books, noting especially Crane's realism and his refusal to romanticize or sentimentalize his materials.

4.115 ———. "Franklin Garland's *Maggie*." *Stephen Crane Newsletter* 2.2 (1976): 1–4. A description of a presentation copy of the 1893 *Maggie* given to Hamlin Garland's brother Franklin, plus interesting details about prices of this rare edition of *Maggie*.

4.116 WESTBROOK, PERRY D. "Four Deterministic Novelists." *Free Will and Determinism in American Literature*. Rutherford, NJ: Fairleigh Dickinson UP, 1979. 136–60. Westbrook's monograph is philosophically unsophisticated and critically superficial. Crane receives two pages (132–34) in a chapter also devoted to London, Dreiser, and Norris. Westbrook's Crane section repeats dated dogmas about determinism in *Maggie* and *Red Badge*.

4.117 WITHAM, W. TASKER. "The Rise of Realism: Stephen Crane." *Panorama of American Literature*. NP: Stephen Daye Press, 1947. 213–16. A short piece on Crane's life and work; *Maggie* mentioned as "selective realism."

Also on *Maggie* see

2.2–2.19	3.284
2.55	3.285
2.64	4.132
2.87	4.144
2.94	4.160
2.186	4.169
2.193	4.178

2.197	6.100
2.210	9.19
3.61	11.24
3.77	11.25
3.205	11.41

GEORGE'S MOTHER

Books

4.118 BOWERS, FREDSON, ed. *Bowery Works: George's Mother. The Works of Stephen Crane*, vol. 1. Ed. Fredson Bowers. Charlottesville: UP of Virginia, 1969. xcviii+178. The now accepted critical edition of Crane's second Bowery work. See 4.21 for Bower's textual introduction and 4.123 for Colvert's general introduction.

4.119 FOLLETT, WILSON, ed. *Major Conflicts: "George's Mother", 'The Blue Hotel' and "Maggie." The Work of Stephen Crane*, vol 10. New York: Knopf, 1926. xiii+218. In Follett's eyes *George's Mother* was the key item in this volume of his Crane edition. See 4.127 for Mencken's introduction to this volume.

Articles and Book Chapters

4.120 BASSAN, MAURICE. "An Early Draft of *George's Mother.*" *American Literature* 36 (1965): 518–22. Bassan discovered, on the back of two manuscript pages from Crane's early "Sullivan County Sketches," several paragraphs of an early version of *George's Mother*. For a full discussion of these draft pages with reference to the published version, see Colvert's introduction to the Virginia edition of *George's Mother* (4.123).

4.121 BOWERS, FREDSON. Textual Introduction [to *George's Mother*]. *Bowery Works. The Works of Stephen Crane*, vol. 1. Ed. Fredson Bowers. Charlottesville: UP of Virginia, 1969. 109–12. A brief account of editions collated in producing this edition plus "a diplomatic reprint" of two handwritten pages of Crane's draft.

4.122 BRENNAN, JOSEPH X. "The Imagery and Art of *George's Mother.*" *College Language Association Journal* 4 (1960): 106–15. An essential article on *George's Mother*. Thesis: The novel's theme is the intense struggle between two religions—"uncompromising Christian fundamentalism" and "an alluring, accommodating modern paganism." Conclusion: Neither George nor his mother can understand the other person's "world."

4.123 COLVERT, JAMES B. Introduction [*George's Mother*]. *Bowery Works. The Works of Stephen Crane*, vol. 1. Ed. Fredson Bowers. Charlottesville: UP of Virginia, 1969. 101–8. A brief essay on the circumstances surrounding Crane's writing of this second Bowery work. Colvert argues that Crane had a sophisticated grasp of literary theory and that *George's Mother* was written to conform to the views of his literary fathers, Howells and Garland, that fiction ought to concern itself with the "typical and the ordinary."

4.124 CURRENT-GARCIA, EUGENE, and WALTON R. PATRICK. *"George's Mother." Realism and Romanticism in Fiction*. Ed. Eugene Current-Garcia and Walton R. Patrick. Chicago: Scott, Foresman, 1962. 392–93. A biographical note on Crane as a naturalist who excelled at honest realism; also a brief summary of *George's Mother*.

4.125 GIAMO, BENEDICT. *On the Bowery: Confronting Homelessness in American Society*. Iowa City: U of Iowa P, 1989. xix, 267. Initially a doctoral dissertation concerned with understanding "American culture and subculture." In book form his new title is trendier and potentially more interesting but the emphasis on homelessness skews the reader's expectations. Still, Giamo's ambitious, complex, and sometimes dense analysis of the ability of mainline culture to enter the lived experience of a subculture is worthy of note.

   The chief value of the study is a skillful and detailed analysis of nineteenth-century literary efforts to enter the world of the Bowery. Giamo find that Riis and Howells preached realism but they were mere tourists in a strange land; more successful were the immersion experiences of Dreiser and Crane. *George's Mother*, "An Experiment in Misery," and "Men in the Story" are examined at length.

4.126 JACKSON, AGNES MORELAND. "Stephen Crane's Imagery of Conflict in *George's Mother*." *Arizona Quarterly* 25 (1969): 313–18. Jackson argues that the central conflict in *George's Mother* is between George's mother and George's brotherhood-of-the-brew confreres. This is an important article.

4.127 MENCKEN, H. L. Introduction. *Major Conflicts: "George's Mother", 'The Blue Hotel' and "Maggie." The Work of Stephen Crane*, vol. 10. Ed. Wilson Follett. New York: Knopf, 1926. ix–xiii. This short essay discusses themes in Crane and contains Mencken's famous contention that he could not sustain a long novel for "he had, so to speak, no literary small talk; he could not manage what the musicians call passage work."

4.128   MURPHY, BRENDA. "A Woman with Weapons: The Victor in Stephen Crane's *George's Mother." Modern Language Studies* 11 (1981): 88–93. Crane's original title for *George's Mother* was *A Woman without Weapons.* Murphy makes the interesting case that the original title was ironic, for Mrs. Kelcey is well armed with her Methodism.

4.129   ORLOV, PAUL A. "Psychology, Style and The Cityscape in Stephen Crane's *George's Mother. CLA Journal* 34.2 (1940): 212–27. Orlov summarizes previous scholarship to show how Crane's second Bowery work "reveals a pointedly qualified portrayal of environmental determinism." Like many others before him Orlov notices the escapism and self-delusion of George and his mother: his based on liquid spirits, hers on the "soothing spirits of religion."

4.130   SIMONEAUX, KATHERINE G. "Color Imagery in Crane's *George's Mother." CLA Journal* 14 (1971): 410–19. Crane's use of color (Simoneaux tabulates 139 instances) underscores his "ironic, fatalistic and deterministic view of life." See also Simoneaux's study of *Maggie* (4.99).

4.131   SMITH, LEVERETT T., JR. "Stephen Crane's Calvinism." *Canadian Review of American Studies* 2 (1971): 13–25. Smith sees in Crane's concern with human actions in a naturalistic universe (the overpowering environment in *George's Mother* and nature's indifference in "The Open Boat") a modified Calvinistic "sense of the total domination of man by the force which governs him." Smith's examination is insightful for the clearly naturalistic works of Crane. That is, while his argument is appropriate for *George's Mother,* it ignores Crane's stress on meaningful action and solidarity in "The Open Boat."

4.132   STRONKS, JAMES B. "A Realist Experiments with Impressionism: Hamlin Garland's 'Chicago Studies.'" *American Literature* 36 (1964): 38–52. Garland shows that Crane's *Maggie* and *George's Mother* influenced Garland's attempts to combine accuracy, individuality, and impressionism in his "Chicago Studies." Compare with Wertheim (11.53).

4.133   WEIMAR, DAVID R. "Landscapes of Hysteria: Stephen Crane." *The City as Metaphor.* New York: Random House, 1966. 52–64. While

Howell's view of the poor was "picturesque," Crane's "impressionistic" picture was realistic, gritty, and honest.

4.134 WEINSTEIN, BERNARD. *"George's Mother* and the Bowery of Experience." *Markham Review* 9 (1980): 45–49. It is too bad this article is so brief. Thesis: *George's Mother* is a more subtle, better crafted book because it followed Crane's own Bowery experiences. That is, *Maggie*'s flaw is too wide a gulf between "unbelievable innocence and surrounding depravity"; with *George's Mother* there is less disparity. Thus George is partially responsible for his own disintegration.

See also on *George's Mother:*

1.1–1.4	4.43
1.10	4.50
1.55	4.51
2.1–2.19	4.59
2.87	4.71
2.193	4.86
2.197	4.111
2.210	4.114
3.132	4.116
4.15	11.41
4.28	

NEW YORK CITY SKETCHES

Books

4.135 FOLLETT, WILSON, ed. *Midnight Sketches and Other Impressions. The Work of Stephen Crane,* vol. 11. Ed. Wilson Follett. New York: Knopf, 1926. xv+313. Follett collected and brought to the attention of the public important pieces of Crane's journalism. See 4.139 for Anderson's introduction.

4.136 FRYCKSTEDT, OLAF W. *Stephen Crane: Uncollected Writings.* Uppsala: Studia Anglistica Upsaliensia, 1963. lxxiii+452. This volume was very important for Crane's scholars, as it reprinted 123 newspaper sketches and little-known tales. See 12.48 for Fryckstedt's introduction.

4.137   STALLMAN, ROBERT W., and E. R. HAGEMANN. *The New York City Sketches of Stephen Crane and Related Pieces.* Ed. Robert W. Stallman and E. R. Hagemann. New York: New York UP, 1966. xix+302. See 4.174 for the editors' introduction. Stallman and Hagemann reprinted a generous selection of Crane's journalistic pieces and sketches at a time when there was intense competition to be the first to discover and print previously unknown Crane works. Stallman's desire to get credit for "related pieces" led him to publish items that were remotely, if at all, connected with New York City. When reviewers pointed this out, he cried "foul" and yet another debate of Stallman versus everybody else was launched. Cady and Stallman had an especially vigorous exchange over this: See Cady's review (*American Literature* 38 [1967]: 570–71), Stallman's rebuttal ("Reply to Reviewer Cady," *American Literature* 40 [1968]: 83–85), and Cady's response ("Mr. Cady's Response [to Mr. Stallman]," *American Literature* 40 [1968]: 85).

Articles and Book Chapters

4.138   AARON, DANIEL. "The Unholy City: A Sketch." *American Letters: Essays in Honor of Louis P. Simpson.* Ed. Gerald Kennedy and Daniel Mark Fogel. Baton Rouge: Louisiana State UP, 1987. 177–90. Several of Crane's city sketches are seen as contributing to the gradual evolution in American letters away from the nature=good and the city=bad premise.

4.139   ANDERSON, SHERWOOD. Introduction. *Midnight Sketches and Other Impressions. The Work of Stephen Crane,* vol. 11. Ed. Wilson Follett. New York: Knopf, 1926. xi–xv. A very brief introduction more to the body of Crane's work than to the New York City sketches here reprinted. Regarding the former, "The thing to do is to have all his books on your shelves. Get him in relation to his times, the drama of the man, of his life. He did a lot. He was an explosion all right. It's about time people began to hear the explosion."

4.140   BASSAN, MAURICE. "Misery and Society: Some New Perspectives on Stephen Crane's Fiction." *Studia Neophilologia* 35 (1963): 104–20. Crane's "Experiment in Misery" put in context of other sociological, environmental, and literary studies of tramps and tramping.

4.141 ———. "The Design of Stephen Crane's Bowery 'Experiment.'" *Studies in Short Fiction* 1 (1964): 129–32. An examination of Crane's "Experiment in Misery" in which Bassan argues that the sketch's circular structure lets the reader appreciate the plight of the powerless poor. That is, Crane was a social crusader who strove to bring his reader "to an act of identification and sympathy."

4.142 ———. "Stephen Crane and 'The Eternal Mystery of Social Condition.'" *Nineteenth-Century Fiction* 19 (1965): 387–94. The companion piece to Crane's description of a night in a Bowery flophouse ("An Experiment in Misery") was his "Experiment in Luxury," which tells of an evening spent at the home of a wealthy friend. The title of the Bassan article comes from Crane's reflections on wealth and poverty. Bassan argues that when Crane's two sketches are considered as a pair the reader is left with a tension generated by "the juxtaposition of reasonable points of view" and that at the end Crane holds that "there is no fixed point of value, no sense of either cosmic or sublunary responsibility or justice."

4.143 BONNER, THOMAS. "Crane's 'An Experiment in Misery.'" *Explicator* 34 (1976): Item 56. A note on Crane's fondness for the word "assassin" and its role in this acclaimed story. Compare with Johnson (4.154).

4.144 BREMNER, ROBERT H. *From the Depths: The Discovery of Poverty in the United States.* New York: New York UP, 1967. 104–7. Bremner speaks (105–6) of "An Experiment in Misery" and *Maggie,* calling Crane's contribution to the discovery of poverty in America his "truthfulness to reality."

4.145 BROOKS, VAN WYCK. *John Sloan: A Painter's Life.* New York: Dutton, 1955. Passing comments (54–57) on how both Sloan and Crane were intrigued with the Bowery.

4.146 CANDELA, JOSEPH L. "The Domestic Orientation of American Novels, 1893–1913." *American Literary Realism* 13 (1980): 1–18. A sketchy survey to the effect that serious late nineteenth-century American novelists were concerned about "family pathologies." *Maggie* and *George's Mother* are treated as anti-alcohol tracts. Candela assumes that all naturalists were also social reformers. The piece contains errors on details; for example, George is described as "a *lifelong* inhabitant of the Bowery."

4.147 COAN, OTIS, W., and RICHARD G. LILLARD. "*Twenty Stories* and *Bowery Tales.*" *America in Fiction.* Stanford: Stanford UP, 1941.

Passim. The monograph presents "an annotated list of novels that interpret aspects of life in the United States." Crane's works are cited in various places and topics; most often his city sketches are cited as good depictions of life in the slums.

4.148   CONRAD, PETER. "Knight Errantry." *The Art of the City: Views and Versions of New York.* New York: Oxford UP, 1984. 44–64. Scattered comments on Crane's New York City sketches and stories; nothing very useful, though.

4.149   FRYCKSTEDT, OLAF W. "Stephen Crane in the Tenderloin." *Studia Neophilologia* 34 (1962): 135–63. Along with Gallagher (4.150), the best account of Crane's wrangle with the New York City police (including Commissioner Theodore Roosevelt) following his attempt to defend a prostitute named Dora Clark.

4.150   GALLAGHER, ROBERT S. "Stephen Crane's Tenderloin Adventure." *New York, New York.* Ed. David G. Lowe. New York: American Heritage, 1968. 128–33. Along with Fryckstedt (4.149), this is the best account of the Dora Clark affair. Gallagher is very even-handed in showing how Crane's notoriety gave plausibility to the police's case. Several good pictures of Crane and New York are included.

4.151   HALL, DEAN. "Stephen Crane's Glittering Possession." *American Notes and Queries* 19 (1981): 147–48. An examination of "An Ominous Baby," especially Tommie's taking a toy fire engine from the rich toddler.

4.152   ITABASHI, YOSHIE. "Stephen Crane and the New York City Sketches: Looking for Humanity." *Tsuda Review* 16 (1971): 11–41. Itabashi's piece is little more than a very general survey of themes; as this journal is very hard to get, readers may want to bear in mind the point of diminishing returns.

4.153   ———. "New York City Sketches—Crane's Creed and Art." *Studies in English Literature* (Tokyo, English number), (1972), 243–58. An ambitious but unfortunately unfocused and unorganized analysis of a half-dozen of Crane's 1892 New York City sketches. Thesis: Crane combated romantic treatment of the city by his realism.

4.154   JOHNSON, CLARENCE O. "Crane's 'Experiment in Misery.'" *Explicator* 35 (1976): 20–21. Johnson offers suggestions concerning Crane's use of the term *assassin* in this famous Bowery sketch. Compare with Bonner (4.143).

4.155 ———. "Stephen Crane and Zola's *Germinal.*" *American Notes & Queries* 16 (1977): 40–43. Johnson argues that Zola's depiction of draft animals in the mines is strikingly similar to Crane's description of the mine mules in "In the Depths of a Coal Mine."

4.156 ———. "Mr. Binks, Read Emerson: Stephen Crane and Emerson's 'Nature.'" *American Literary Realism* 15 (1982): 104–10. Johnson sees in the city–country confrontation in "Mr. Binks' Day Off" Emersonian and transcendentalist influences.

4.157 KATZ, JOSEPH. "Stephen Crane: Muckraker." *Columbia Library Columns* 17 (1968): 2–7. A brief account of Crane's trip (with artist friend C. K. Linson) to Scranton, Pennsylvania, for *McClure's Magazine.* The result of this trip was his celebrated "In the Depths of a Coal Mine."

4.158 ———. "Eroticism in American Literary Realism." *Studies in American Fiction* 5 (1977): 35–50. Though the title gets one's attention there is not much here to titillate. Crane is discussed in passing in connection with "Why Did the Young Clerk Swear?" which manages to sustain the reader's attention by its skillful omissions.

4.159 MARCHAND, ERNEST. *Frank Norris: A Study.* London: H. Milford, 1942. Passim. Scattered comments on similarities between the Norris's and Crane's treatment of slum life.

4.160 MAURICE, ARTHUR BARTLETT. *The New York of the Novelists.* New York: Dodd, Mead, 1917. 100–107. Maurice's ninth chapter treats the Bowery and briefly examines Crane's *Maggie* as a faithful depiction of life in the slums.

4.161 McILVAINE, ROBERT. "A Literary Source for Hurstwood's Last Scene." *Research Studies* 40 (1972): 44–46. Source hunting in reverse: Crane's "The Men in the Storm" is the source of the last scene in Dreiser's *Sister Carrie.*

4.162 MIMS, ELLE PURYEAR. "Stephen Crane's 'A Dark-Brown Dog' is My Favorite Story." *The Golden Book* 12 (Dec. 1930): 56. Mims entered *The Golden Book*'s competition, "My Favorite Story and Why." She won the contest so they printed Crane's story and her brief essay. She points out Crane's "strange, morbid humor" and his ability to involve the reader emotionally even though his story is "casually, almost impersonally" told.

4.163 MOERS, ELLEN. "Teddy Roosevelt: Literary Feller." *Columbia University Forum* 6.3 (1963): 10–16. Though Roosevelt's literary career is the focus, Moers provides information on Crane's friendship and later his feud, after the Dora Clark affair, with Roosevelt.

4.164 ———. *Two Dreisers*. New York: Viking, 1969. Passim. A discussion of the influence of Crane's Bowery sketches, especially "Men in the Storm" and "An Experiment in Misery," upon Dreiser.

4.165 ———. "When New York Made It." *New York Times Book Review* 120 (16 May 1971): 31–32. New York made it in the 1890s and Moers comments on four artists of that period: Crane, Dreiser, painter John Sloan, and ragtime composer James Weldon Johnson.

4.166 MONTEIRO, GEORGE. "Society and Nature in Stephen Crane's 'The Men in the Storm.'" *Prairie Schooner* 45 (1971): 13–17. Monteiro attempts to work out the tensions he sees in Crane's "intellectual commitment to naturalism and his emotional tie to the nineteenth-century Protestantism of his family." He fails, however, to make a clear connection between this effort and nature and society of "The Man in the Storm."

4.167 ———. "John Sloan's 'Cranes.'" *Journal of Modern Literature* 14 (1988): 584–98. A curious, intriguing article. Though Sloan explicitly denied any Crane influence, he had read Crane's works, was an illustrator at the *Philadelphia Press* when it published the newspaper version of *Red Badge,* and illustrated *Great Battles of the World*. The payoff of the article is Monteiro's contention that similar themes and scenes populate the works of Crane and Sloan, a case he makes by reproducing ten of Sloan's drawings paired with extended quotations from Crane stories and interview comments made by Sloan.

4.168 MORRISON, ELTING E. *The Letters of Theodore Roosevelt,* vol. 1. Cambridge, MA: Harvard UP, 1951. 550. Roosevelt and Jacob Riis going slumming with Crane.

4.169 MOTT, FRANK LUTHER. "'The *Arena.*'" *A History of American Magazines, 1885–1905*. 4 vols. Cambridge, MA: Harvard UP, 1957. 4: 401–14. Mott's chapter on the *Arena* gives valuable background on the publishing climate Crane faced. Brief mention is made of Garland's review of *Maggie* in the *Arena* as well as the publication of Crane's sketches "Ominous Baby" and "Men in the Storm" in the May and October 1894 volumes.

4.170 NAGEL, JAMES. "Structure and Theme in Crane's 'An Experiment in Misery.'" *Studies in Short Fiction* 10 (1973): 169–74. A retelling of Crane's story to support Nagel's contention that, in this story at least, Crane was a crusader for social justice.

4.171 OSBORN, NEAL J. "Optograms, George Moore, and Crane's 'The Silver Pageant.'" *American Notes and Queries* 4 (1965): 39–40. Minor details about an early, minor Crane sketch: Crane might have been aware of scientific reports of optograms, "pictures in the eyes."

4.172 PARRY, ALBERT. *Garretts and Pretenders: A History of Bohemianism in America*. New York: Dover, 1933. 89–91 and passim. In his description of the brief time Crane spent with the art students at East Twenty-Third Street, Parry downplays Crane's bohemianism.

4.173 SLOTKIN, ALAN R. "Dialect Manipulation in 'An Experiment in Misery.'" *American Literary Realism* 14 (1981): 273–76. Slotkin belabors the obvious: Crane used dialect manipulation to show how the observer gradually becomes a participant in this noted New York City sketch. Slotkin concludes that Crane was no tourist; for more on this point see Giamo (4.125).

4.174 STALLMAN, ROBERT W., and E. R. HAGEMANN. Introduction. *The New York City Sketches of Stephen Crane and Related Pieces*. Ed. Robert W. Stallman and E. R. Hagemann. New York: New York UP, 1966. ix–xvi. Background details on the Dora Clark affair along with general comments on his New York City sketches. The editors argue that these journalistic stories are a piece with the rest of his works, exhibiting "irony fused with pity."

4.175 ST. JOHN, BRUCE. *John Sloan's New York Scene*. New York: Harper and Row, 1965. xx, 239. Brief mention of Crane; Sloan denies that he was influenced by Crane's (and Dreiser's) slum stories. See also Monteiro (4.167).

4.176 TRACHTENBERG, ALLEN. "Experiments in Another Country: Stephen Crane's City Sketches." *Southern Review* 10 (1974): 265–85. An essential article on Crane's New York City sketches. Thesis: Crane's journalistic pieces take his readers on a tour so they can experience the mystery of the city.

4.177 VANOUSE, DONALD. "Popular Culture in the Writings of Stephen Crane." *Journal of Popular Culture* 10 (1976): 424–30. Vanouse points out Crane's awareness of popular cultural icons, especially evident in his New York City sketches.

4.178 WARSHAVER, GERALD E. "A Window on the City: Towards an Urban Folk Aesthetic." *New York Folklore* 6 (1980): 57–65. Warshaver says, this is a step "toward" an urban folk aesthetic. For now we have to be content with the fact that "viewed from a city 'window,' nature is an epiphenomenon." A fact, according to Warshaver, especially evident in "When a Man Falls, a Crowd Gathers," *Maggie,* and *George's Mother.*"

4.179   WERTHEIM, STANLEY. "Stephen Crane's 'A Detail.'" *Markham Review* 5 (1975): 14–15. A retelling of one of Crane's shorter Bowery sketches.

4.180   WILSON, RUFUS ROCKWELL. *New York in Literature.* Elmira, NY: Primavera, 1947. 102–3, 277–78. The subtitle of this volume is "the story told in the landmarks of town and country." Crane was involved in the story by living at 165 West Twenty-third in New York City (102–3) and being born at 14 Mulberry Place in Newark (277–78). If Wilson's description of these buildings is no better than his grasp of the composition and publication histories of *Maggie* and *Red Badge,* one had better be wary of the "information" in this book.

4.181   YOSHIDA, HEROSHIGE. "A Note on Stephen Crane's Use of Colloquial and Slangy Words and Idioms." *Anglica* 4 (1961): 59–71. Crane used slang for a realistic picture of the Bowery. To be sure, however, Yoshida's unfamiliarity with English makes for some humorous mistakes; see Slotkin (4.173).

See also on Crane's New York City sketches and tales:

1.1–1.4
1.10
2.1–2.19
4.125
5.93
9.22–9.42

5

"The Open Boat"

Overview

Crane's greatest short story has had widespread impact. One measure of this is the frequency with which it appears in textbooks, readers, and literature anthologies. Nearly one fourth of the entries in this section are study/discussion/term paper pieces. (See below for similar textbook attention to "The Blue Hotel" and "The Bride Comes to Yellow Sky.")

Influential scholarly work on "The Open Boat" has focused upon nautical and meteorological research:

Begley 5.7
DAY 5.24
Hagemann 5.41
STALLMAN 5.94

The drowning of Billie and the apparently Darwinian message therein:

AUTREY 5.5
Burns 5.18
Going 5.36
RATH AND SHAW 5.82

The brotherhood of men in an indifferent universe:

Adams 5.2
BENDER 5.10
Buitenhuis 5.17

149

COLVERT 5.23
Gerstenberger 5.34
Lewis 5.56
NAGEL 5.68
SHULMAN 5.90

Book

5.1 FOLLETT, WILSON, ed. *"The Open Boat" and Other Tales. The Work of Stephen Crane,* vol. 12. New York: Knopf, 1927. xxiv+268. Follett reprinted the collection of stories as selected by Crane during his own lifetime. See 5.63 for Michaelson's introduction.

Articles and Book Chapters

5.2 ADAMS, RICHARD P. "Naturalistic Fiction: 'The Open Boat.'" *Tulane Studies in English* 4 (1954): 137–46. Adams struggles to reconcile the impact of human actions in an indifferent universe with his supposition that Crane is a doctrinaire naturalist. He concludes that Crane is an inconsistent naturalist.

5.3 ALTENBERND, LYNN, and LESLIE L. LEWIS. "The Elements of Fiction: Stephen Crane's 'The Open Boat.'" *A Handbook for the Study of Fiction.* London: Collier-Macmillan, 1966. 29–80. After a one-page introduction, "The Open Boat" is reprinted, followed by a general discussion of techniques and themes in Crane's greatest story.

5.4 ARCHIBALD, ELIZABETH. "A Study of the Imagery in Stephen Crane's 'The Open Boat.'" *Exercise Exchange* 2.2 (1955): 3–5. Discussion exercises stressing Crane's skill at engaging the imagination of the reader.

5.5 AUTREY, MAX L. "The Word out of the Sea: A View of Crane's 'The Open Boat.'" *Arizona Quarterly* 30 (1974): 101–10. Autrey fixes on the death of Billie, leading him to see only futility and failure in Crane's "outlook"—he ignores themes of solidarity and brotherhood.

5.6 BARROLL, JOHN, and AUSTIN M. WRIGHT. "The Open Boat." *The Art of the Short Story: An Introductory Anthology.* New York: Allyn and

Bacon, 1969. 95–125. Introductory comments on how Crane organized his story, followed by a reprinting of "The Open Boat."

5.7   BEGLEY, SHARON. "Found: Crane's 'Open Boat.'" *Newsweek* 5 Jan. 1987: 52. Recounts discovery by Elizabeth Friedmann—Crane scholar, skindiver—of the wreck of the *Commodore*. Fascinating confirmation of descriptions from "The Open Boat"; for example, precisely as Crane said, from the wreck sight, "The lighthouse of Mosquito Inlet stuck up above the horizon like the point of a pen."

5.8   BELLEVILLE, BILL. *"Commodore* Wreck: Prototype 'Open Boat.'" *Oceans* 20 (May–June) 1987): 58–59. A recast of the *Newsweek* story of scholar–skindiver Elizabeth Friedman's discovery of the wreck of the *Commodore* twelve miles off Daytona Beach. (Note: there are still sharks in the water in that area.)

5.9   BENDER, BERT. "The Nature and Significance of 'Experience' in 'The Open Boat.'" *Journal of Narrative Technique* 9 (1979): 70–80. A connection of the work of Crane and the American pragmatists—John Dewey is specifically mentioned. Thesis: The only valid approach to knowledge is by way of experience; "The Open Boat" is a study in the differences between the understandings of the captain and the others. The captain knows the situation fully because his past experiences have prepared him for skilled seeing.

5.10 ———. "The Experience of Brotherhood in 'The Open Boat.'" *Sea Brothers: The Tradition of American Sea Fiction from "Moby-Dick" to the Present.* By Bert Bender. Philadelphia: U of Pennsylvania P, 1988. 68–82. Bender's book contains the best recent essay on Crane's short story masterpiece. In his Crane chapter Bender elucidates "The Open Boat" as a "traditional sea journey to knowledge." Crane, he argues, powerfully documented both knowledge about—"no seaman has ever faulted Crane's presentation of nautical reality"—and knowledge by acquaintance—"the *only* valid kind of knowledge is experience." The experiential awareness to which Crane finally brings his readers is religious in scope—contact with ultimate realities of self, the world, and above all, others. "Crane's short sea journey took him exactly this far: from the condition of one 'who had been taught to be cynical of men' to that of a man who had been 'moved' sorrow for another." Or as Crane himself puts it, the distance traveled was from "none of them knew the color of the sky" to the point that the survivors "felt that they could then be interpreters."

5.11 BERRYMAN, JOHN. Commentary [on "The Open Boat"]. *The Arts of Reading.* Ed. Ralph Ross, John Berryman, and Allen Tate. New York:

Crowell, 1960. 279–88. A classroom exercise with study questions guiding students through "the general method of disappointment-of-expectation, which characterizes this story."

5.12   ——. " 'The Open Boat.' " *The Freedom of the Poet.* Ed. John Berryman. New York: Farrar, Straus, 1976. 176–84. An excellent, though sadly too brief, examination of "The Open Boat." A detailed look at the first paragraph followed by the suggestion that the story is made up of three "waves": comradeship (sections 1–3), the ordeal (4–6), and the death of Billie (7).

5.13   BEWLEY, MARIUS. "The Land of Oz: America's Great Good Place." *Masks & Mirrors: Essays in Criticism.* Ed. Marius Bewley. New York: Atheneum, 1970. 255–67. The highly questionable contention that Crane's "The Open Boat" was the model for the hurricane in *The Land of Oz.*

5.14   BOHNER, CHARLES H. "The Open Boat." Instructor's Manual for *Classic Short Fiction.* Englewood Cliffs, NJ: Prentice-Hall, 1986. 39–40. Discussion questions on "The Open Boat."

5.15   BROER, LAWRENCE R. "The Open Boat." Instructor's Manual for *The Art of Fiction.* 4th Ed. R. F. Dietrich and Roger H. Sundell. New York: Holt, Rinehart, 1983. 60–68. A solipsistic, skeptical, sardonic Crane requiring the reader to ignore the final sections of "The Open Boat."

5.16   BROWN, BILL. "Interlude: The Agony of Play in 'The Open Boat.' " *Arizona Quarterly* 45 (1989): 23–46. An elaborate (complete with trendy jargon) discussion of Crane's mixing of game-playing and war metaphors in his works. Or as Brown would have it, "the ludic figuration context," which he finds not only in "The Open Boat" but also in *Red Badge* and *Active Service.* Also included are interesting observations about "the fact that rowing is a *form* of amusement, as well as a *form* of suvival" as the key to "The Open Boat"; Crane's early piece about shipwreck, "Wreck of the New Era"; and his father's condemnation of play in *Popular Amusements.*

5.17   BUITENHUIS, PETER. "The Essentials of Life: 'The Open Boat' as Existentialist Fiction." *Modern Fiction Studies* 5 (1959): 243–50. Thesis: Crane is at least as compelling as Camus in his treatment of the themes of initiation, an indifferent universe, and "the subtle brotherhood of men." A landmark essay. Reprinted in Buitenhuis, *Five American Moderns* (Toronto: Roger Ascham, 1968).

5.18   BURNS, LANDON C. "On 'The Open Boat.'" *Studies in Short Fiction* 3 (1966): 455–57. A note seeing Crane in Darwinism wondering why Billie, the strongest and best equipped swimmer, drowns.

5.19   CARLSON, RALPH S. "Stephen Crane." *Critical Survey of Short Fiction.* 7 vols. Ed. Frank N. Magil. Englewood Cliffs, NJ: Salem Press, 1981. Vol. 3: 1216–21. Brief biography followed by a discussion of the shock endings of Crane's episodic stories. Carlson's treatment of "The Open Boat" is very good and would be helpful as a class handout. His treatment of other stories tails off badly, however.

5.20   CASSILL, R. V. "The Open Boat." *Norton Anthology of Short Fiction: Instructor's Handbook.* New York: Norton, 1977. 54–55. Study guide and discussion questions.

5.21   CHAMETZKY, JULES. "Realism, Cultural Politics, and Language as Mediation in Mark Twain and Others." *Prospects* 8 (1983): 183–95. An elaborate and pretentious analysis that contends that language constitutes reality for experiences. Thesis: In a threatening world we have to learn to read experiences as Twain speaks of reading the river. This leads Chametzky to make brief parallel comments about reading the ocean in "The Open Boat."

5.22   COLLAMORE, H. B. "Some Notes on Modern First Editions: Stephen Crane, 'The Open Boat'—N.Y. 1898." *Colophon* 3 (1938): 354–58. Of interest to book collectors; information on two bindings of the same first edition.

5.23   COLVERT, JAMES B. "Style and Meaning in Stephen Crane's 'The Open Boat.'" *Texas Studies in English* 37 (1958): 34–45. Early critics, believing Crane was a naturalist, had difficulty dealing with his outlook in "The Open Boat." Colvert suggests that attention to Crane's style and point of view lead to a consistent philosophy based on Crane's perceptions of the irreconcilable contradictions in reality and the limitations of human consciousness. A valuable and persuasive article.

5.24   DAY, CYRUS. "Stephen Crane and the Ten-foot Dinghy." *Boston University Studies in English* 3 (1957): 193–213. Exhaustive nautical (maps and charts included) and meteorological research comparing the facts during "The Open Boat" ordeal with Crane's "fictional" retelling. Day's conclusion is that "the physical hardships endured by Crane and his companions in the ten-foot dinghy have been grossly exaggerated." See Hagemann (5.41) and Stallman (5.94) for similar nautical details.

5.25 DEMARR, MARY JEAN. "The Cook and the Shark: A Reading of 'The Open Boat.'" *Indiana English Journal* 6 (1971): 21–28. A minor article in a minor journal. The cook is a symbol of unrealistic attitudes and the shark stands for the loneliness that brings an awareness of the importance of brotherhood.

5.26 DENDINGER, LLOYD N. "Stephen Crane's Inverted Use of Key Images of 'The Rime of the Ancient Mariner.'" *Studies in Short Fiction* 5 (1968): 192–94. A very short note asserting an elaborate thesis. Crane uses a gull, the wind tower, and a shark to foreshadow interpreters; Coleridge uses an albatross, a lighthouse, and watersnakes to symbolize answers.

5.27 DIECKMANN, EDWARD A., JR. "The Hemingway Hypnosis." *Mark Twain Journal* 11 (1962): 3–4, 16. Dieckmann complains that adoration for Hemingway has duped students into thinking the opposite of the truth. The correct description is that Hemingway wrote like Crane. He quotes a long section of "The Open Boat" and then comments, "Here, in the terse yet unliterary tone, the repetitions, the muted tension, are all the flatness and cadence and 'realism' of the famous 'Hemingway style.'"

5.28 DITSKY, JOHN. "The Music in 'The Open Boat.'" *North Dakota Quarterly* 56 (1988): 119–30. An implausible and tedious article: "The Open Boat" can be read as an opera. The value of Ditsky's contribution can be guessed by the tone of his introductory caveat: "For purposes of this essay, I will respect the intelligences of my readers not only by assuming familiarity with Crane's text, but also by not indulging in the application to it of a highly technical, cookiejargon meant to wrench 'The Open Boat' into a posture never intended by its author."

5.29 DOLCH, MARTIN. "Stephen Crane and 'The Open Boat.'" *Insight I: Analyses of American Literature*. Ed. John V. Hagopian and Martin Dolch. Frankfurt: Hirschgraben-Verlag, 1962. 35–41. A classroom exercise from a textbook, designed to show how "The Open Boat" is a masterpiece of American impressionism.

5.30 DOW, EDDY. "Cigars, Matches and Men in 'The Open Boat.'" RE: *Artes Liberales* 2 (1975): 47–49. A piece on the numbers Dow finds in "The Open Boat": eight cigars (four are wet and four are dry) and three dry matches. See Muhlenstein (5.67) for a better treatment of the same topic.

5.31 FREDERICK, JOHN T. "The Fifth Man in 'The Open Boat.'" *CEA Critic* 30.8 (1968): 1, 12–14. A tedious retelling of Crane's story as "an intense paradigm of the human situation as a whole." Be wary of any commentator who has Crane and the others in the open boat for "fifty hours"—it was bad enough without adding nearly another day at sea!

5.32 FRUS, PHILLIS. "Two Tales 'Intended to Be after the Fact': 'Stephen Crane's Own Story' and 'The Open Boat.'" *Literary Nonfiction: Theory, Criticism, Pedagogy.* Ed. Chris Anderson. Carbondale: Southern Illinois UP, 1989. 125–51. Frus argues that there is no great difference between fiction and journalism—"both discourses are equally constituting structures"; both are interpretations of event. Crane's fictional recasting, "The Open Boat," is compared with his newspaper dispatch "Stephen Crane's Own Story."

5.33 FULLER, MARY ELBIN. "The Subtle Metaphor." *English Journal* 57 (1968): 708–9. A mininote: The subtle metaphor in "The Open Boat" is Crane's comparison of a wave to a wild mountain cat.

5.34 GERSTENBERGER, DONNA. "'The Open Boat': Additional Perspective." *Modern Fiction Studies* 17 (1971): 557–61. Gerstenberger argues for an existentialist Crane: "The Open Boat" portrays the human situation. Though we seek a just and meaningful world, we find an indifferent universe.

5.35 GERSTENBERGER, DONNA, and FREDERIC GARBER. "The Open Boat." *Microcosm: An Anthology of the Short Story.* San Francisco: Chandler, 1969. A reprinting of "The Open Boat" with comments for study and classroom discussion.

5.36 GOING, WILLIAM T. "William Higgins and Crane's 'The Open Boat': A Note about Fact and Fiction." *Papers on English Language and Literature* 1 (1965): 79–82. Going argues that the drowning of Billie, the oiler, is the key to "The Open Boat" for "an understanding of the indifference of Nature that comes to the men through the comradeship of suffering, through the meaningless confusion of death."

5.37 GORDON, CAROLINE. "Stephen Crane." *Accent* 9 (1949): 153–57. A few glib observations on Crane's techniques (in "The Open Boat") for making the reader sense the events, and a comparison of the power of Crane's prose with a flat, unsuccessful passage in Stendahl.

5.38 GORDON, CAROLINE, and ALLEN TATE. "The Open Boat." *The Houses of Fiction.* 2nd ed. New York: Scribner's, 1960. 168. "The Open Boat" reprinted with a commentary stressing Crane's breakthrough style.

5.39 GUERIN, WILFRED L. "The Open Boat." Instructor's Manual for *Mandala: Literature for Critical Analysis.* New York: Harper and Row, 1966. 8–11. Study, discussion, and term paper suggestions for "The Open Boat."

5.40 GULLASON, THOMAS A. "The New Criticism and Older Ones: Another Ride in 'The Open Boat.'" *CEA Critic* 31.9 (1969): 8. Gullason argues that "where new critics have 'discovered' new approaches to Crane's art, [these] were clearly and succinctly presented many years before by older critics."

5.41 HAGEMANN, E. R. "'Sadder Than the End': Another Look at "The Open Boat.'" *Stephen Crane in Transition.* Ed. Joseph Katz. De Kalb: Northern Illinois UP, 1972. 66–85. A painstaking retelling of the events of "The Open Boat," strong on nautical details like the pieces by Day (5.24) and Stallman (5.94).

5.42 HEINES, DONALD E. "The Open Boat." *Times Four: The Short Story in Depth.* Englewood Cliffs, NJ: Prentice-Hall, 1968. 168. A reprinting, with study questions, of "The Open Boat."

5.43 HIGGINSON, WILLIAM J. "For Stephen Crane: The Sea beyond the Breakers." *William Carlos Williams, Stephen Crane, Philip Freneau.* Ed. W. John Bauer. Trenton: New Jersey Historical Commission, 1989. 113–15. Free verse reflections on Crane and "The Open Boat."

5.44 HOLLANDER, ROBERT, and SIDNEY E. LIND. "The Open Boat." *The Art of the Story.* New York: American, 1968. "The Open Boat" reprinted with study questions.

5.45 HUCK, WILBUR, and WILLIAM SHANAHAN. "The Open Boat." *The Modern Short Story.* New York: American, 1968. "The Open Boat" reprinted with a brief introduction and study questions.

5.46 HUBBARD, ELBERT. "Stevie Crane." *Selected Writings of Elbert Hubbard.* Ed. Elbert Hubbard, Jr. New York: William H. Wise, Roycroft Press, 1922. vol. 5, 140–43. A eulogy for Crane. Hubbard has difficulty steering away from himself but eventually he manages to get to Crane's life and works. Of the "The Open Boat," he writes, it is the "sternest, creepiest bit of realism ever penned."

5.47 IHEAKARAM, PAUL O. "John Pepper Clark and Stephen Crane: An Investigation of Source and Influence." *Research in African Literature* 13 (1982): 53–59. An interesting sample of the putative influence of Crane: Nigerian native Clark's short play *The Raft* is traced to "The

Open Boat." In each there are four men in a boat; in each, the best swimmer drowns.

5.48 JACKSON, DAVID H. "Textual Questions Raised by Crane's 'Soldier of the Legion.'" *American Literature* 55 (1983): 77–80. Jackson argues that the four lines of verse that have a central thematic importance for "The Open Boat" were lines Crane remembered. Therefore Bowers was in error when he substituted the "corrected" version of Caroline Norton's "Bingen on the Rhine."

5.49 JAFFE, ADRIAN H., and VIRGIL SCOTT. "The Open Boat." Instructor's Manual for *Studies in Short Fiction*. New York: Holt, Rinehart, 1968. 78–83. Ambitious comments, study questions, and term paper topics for "The Open Boat."

5.50 KAPLAN, MILTON A. "Style *Is* Content." *English Journal* 57 (1968): 1330–34. Crane's abrupt and disjointed style is the source of the power of "The Open Boat."

5.51 KATZ, JOSEPH. "Stephen Crane and Irving Bacheller's Gold." *Stephen Crane Newsletter* 5.1 (1970): 4. Katz suggests that although Bacheller gave Crane $700, only $200 was lost at sea; Crane had deposited the rest in a bank without telling Bacheller or anyone else.

5.52 KENT, THOMAS L. "The Problem of Knowledge in 'The Open Boat' and 'The Blue Hotel.'" *American Literary Realism* 14 (1981): 262–68. Kent argues for a nihilistic Crane on the basis of his contention that the protagonists in these two stories cannot know the forces and situations they must deal with. For example, Kent concludes in "The Blue Hotel" that no one "understands the conspiratorial and essentially tragic nature of existence."

5.53 KENNEDY, X. J. "Stephen Crane's 'The Open Boat.'" *Literature: An Introduction to Fiction, Poetry, and Drama*. 3rd ed. Boston: Little, Brown, 1983. 143–44. Kennedy reprints "The Open Boat" along with discussion questions and term-paper topics.

5.54 KISSANE, LEEDICE. "Interpretation through Language: A Study of the Metaphors in Stephen Crane's 'The Open Boat.'" *Rendezvous* 1 (1966): 18–22. A title this long ought to convey the thesis of the article, and it does. Unfortunately, Kissane cannot shake the old school belief that Crane is a deterministic naturalist and so she struggles to deal with metaphors that betoken choice and autonomy. In the end she resorts to the claim that Crane's "inadvertent choice of figures" undercut his "deterministic beliefs."

5.55   LaPoint, Charles. "The Day That Crane Was Shipwrecked."
        Daytona Beach News Journal 22 April 1962. A layman's attempt to sort
        out the facts of the *Commodore* disaster; see Day (5.24), Hagemann
        (5.41), and Stallman (5.94) for more reliable discussions. Stallman
        reports (in his *Stephen Crane: A Critical Bibliography* 14.3: 262) that
        La Point recast an article that Odell Hathaway submitted to *News
        Journal* after he had interviewed (in 1961 and 1962) several people
        who were eyewitnesses to the events at Daytona Beach.

5.56   Lewis, R. W. B. "Albert Camus: The Compassionate Mind." *The
        Picaresque Saint: Representative Figures in Contemporary Fiction.* Phila-
        delphia: Lippincott, 1958. 57–108. An important article on Camus's
        sense of an indifferent universe citing Crane's "The Open Boat" with a
        "double discovery, first, of the remote indifference of the universal
        power ('she was indifferent, flatly indifferent') and of the absurdity of
        life ('the whole affair was absurd'); second, of the one irreducible value
        remaining—'the subtle brotherhood of men . . . established on the
        seas."

5.57   Lytle, Andrew. "'The Open Boat': A Pagan Tale." *The Hero with
        the Private Parts.* Baton Rouge: Louisiana State UP, 1966. 60–75. A
        wordy and redundant, often clumsy, retelling of Crane's great short
        story.

5.58   Marcus, Mordecai. "The Three-Fold View of Nature in 'The
        Open Boat.'" *Philological Quarterly* 41 (1962): 511–15. A brief but
        convincing case is made that Crane's view of nature in "The Open
        Boat" progresses from "malevolently hostile" to "thoughtlessly hos-
        tile" to "wholly indifferent." Compare with Nagel (5.68).

5.59   Matlaw, Myron, and Leonard Lief. "The Open Boat." *Story and
        Critic.* New York: Harper and Row, 1963. "The Open Boat" reprinted
        with a commentary.

5.60   Meredith, Robert, and John D. Fitzgerald. "The Concealed
        Narrator." *The Professional Story Writer and His Art.* New York:
        Crowell, 1963. 104–11. A preachy treatment of Crane's use of a
        "concealed narrator" in "The Open Boat."

5.61   Metzger, Charles R. "Realistic Devices in Stephen Crane's 'The
        Open Boat.'" *Midwest Quarterly* 4 (1962): 47–54. A discussion of
        obvious techniques in "The Open Boat": irony, spare presentation of
        facts, and an omniscient narrator.

5.62   Meyers, Robert. "Crane's 'The Open Boat.'" *Explicator* 21 (1963):
        Item 60. Meyers finds in "The Open Boat" an inversion of religious

motifs and rituals amounting to a "mockery of traditional Christianity."

5.63   MICHELSON, CHARLES. Introduction. *"The Open Boat" and Other Tales. The Work of Stephen Crane,* vol. 12. Ed. Wilson Follett. New York: Knopf, 1927. ix–xxiv. Michelson was a fellow reporter with Crane in Cuba. This introduction is rich in insights into Crane's personality and the ways imagination and experience made their way into his best tales.

5.64   MOLLE, CHARLES A. "The Ironical Triumph of Stephen Crane's 'The Open Boat.'" *Wittenberg Review* 1 (1990): 105–15. Molle assumes that Crane is an atheist, yet he sees in "The Open Boat" positive moral messages of solidarity, compassion, and success. Though Molle's reading stops far short of optimism, he notes that three of four survive and, for him, this qualified success is the significant point of the story.

5.65   MONTEIRO, GEORGE. "The Logic beneath 'The Open Boat.'" *Georgia Review* 26 (1972): 326–35. "The Open Boat" explores man *in extremis:* When ordinary efforts and normal expectations are faulty what happens to our sense of human efficacy and human knowledge? Perhaps, suggests Monteiro, our ordinary, everyday life is seen as illusory.

5.66   ———. "Text and Picture in 'The Open Boat.'" *Journal of Modern Literature* 11 (1984): 307–11. Comments to the effect that in his writing Crane relied on his experience, visual clues, and literary reminders. Also, Monteiro sees "The Open Boat" as a religious symbol of pilgrims, with the boat as the church.

5.67   MUHLESTEIN, DANIEL K. "Crane's 'The Open Boat.'" *Explicator* 45 (1978): 42–43. A tidy examination of the numbers in the story: eight cigars—eight men in the original boat, four good cigars—four men in the open boat, three matches—three survivors. See also Dow (5.30).

5.68   NAGEL, JAMES. "The Narrative Method in 'The Open Boat.'" *Revue des Langues Vivantes* 39 (1973): 409–17. One of the best examinations of "The Open Boat." Thesis: Crane's attention to perspective shifts underscores the human's limited accessibility to data and ultimately to reality. Nagel traces shifting attitudes toward nature (hostility, thoughtlessness, and indifference) and toward humans (self-centeredness, isolation, solidarity). On the former, compare with Marcus (5.58).

5.69   _____. "Impressionism in 'The Open Boat' and 'A Man and Some Others.'" *Research Studies* 43 (1975): 27–37. Nagel argues that Crane's basic motif is a depiction of episodic and fragmentary impressions; hence, Crane is more of an impressionist than a naturalist.

5.70   NAPIER, JAMES. "Indifference of Nature in Crane and Camus." *CEA Critic* 28 (1966): 11–12. A minicomparison of Crane's "flatly indifferent" universe with Camus's view that the universe offers only "benign indifference."

5.71   _____. "Land Imagery in 'The Open Boat.'" *CEA Critic* 29.7 (1967): 15. Conjectures about the wealth of land imagery in a sea story. See also Stallman (5.95).

5.72   OSBORNE, WILLIAM. "Form and Value in Four Short Stories: Some Critical Approaches." *Interpretations* 1 (1968): 22–27. A sketchy, shallow pedagogical treatment to the effect that the sea is the central character of Crane's story. The other stories considered are by Steinbeck, Faulkner, and London.

5.73   OWEN, GUY, JR. "Crane's 'The Open Boat' and Conrad's 'Youth.'" *Modern Language Notes* 73 (1958): 100–102. Thesis: Conrad read Crane's story, and with that reminder of his own experience in an open boat, he wrote "The Youth."

5.74   [PAPERTEXTS]. "The Open Boat." *Papertexts, Intermediate Series.* New York: Simon & Schuster, 1968. "The Open Boat" plus questions, printed in pamphlet form.

5.75   PARKS, EDD WINFIELD. "Crane's 'The Open Boat.'" *Nineteenth-Century Fiction* 8 (1977): 77. A two-paragraph note insisting that the power of Crane's "The Open Boat" is most strongly felt when his descriptions are taken in their literal, not their figurative, sense.

5.76   PEDEN, WILLIAM HARWOOD. "The Open Boat." *Twenty-Nine Stories.* 2nd ed. Boston: Houghton Mifflin, 1967. "The Open Boat" reprinted with study questions.

5.77   PIACENTINO, EDWARD J. "Kindred Spirits: The Correspondent and the Dying Soldier in Crane's 'The Open Boat.'" *Markham Review* 12 (1983): 64–67. Comments to the effect that Crane's impending death is psychologically parallel to the fate of the dying soldier in the poem "Bingen on the Rhine," which the correspondent remembers.

5.78 PROFITT, EDWARD. "The Open Boat." Teacher's Manual for *Reading and Writing about Short Fiction*. San Diego: Harcourt Brace, 1988. "The Open Boat" reprinted with study questions.

5.79 RANDEL, WILLIAM. "The Cook in 'The Open Boat.'" *American Literature* 34 (1962): 405–11. Randel identifies the cook as Charles Montgomery and adds more details about the ill-fated *Commodore's* voyage.

5.80 ———. "Stephen Crane's Jacksonville." *South Atlantic Quarterly* 62 (1963): 268–74. Details on what Jacksonville was like when Crane waited to ship out to Cuba on the *Commodore*.

5.81 ———. "From Slate to Emerald Green: More Light on Crane's Jacksonville Visit." *Nineteenth-Century Fiction* 19 (1965): 357–68. More details, mostly from local newspapers, on Jacksonville, where Crane waited to go filibustering in Cuba.

5.82 RATH, SURA P., and MARY NEFF SHAW. "The Dialogic Narrative of 'The Open Boat.'" *College Literature* 18.2 (1991): 94–106. One of the best recent essays on "The Open Boat." The authors discuss Crane's difficult task of being both storyteller and experiencer. "In 'The Open Boat' the 'plurality of consciousness, mirrors the narrator's divided consciousness, the two parts representing the two Cranes— the correspondent who records the facts and the author who seeks poetic justice—and setting up a 'polyphony' between his two voices as the actor and the spectator." The authors reject naturalistic and ironic interpretations of the story and conclude that at the end "the men can indeed be interpreters of the sea."

5.83 REED, KENNETH T. "'The Open Boat'" and Dante's *Inferno:* Some Undiscovered Analogs." *Stephen Crane Newsletter* 4.4 (1970): 1–3. A bit farfetched, but analogs can always be found between any two pieces of literature.

5.84 ROHRBERGER, MARY. "The Open Boat." Instructor's Manual for *Story to Anti-story*. Boston: Houghton Mifflin, 1979. 13–14. Discussion questions for "The Open Boat."

5.85 ROSS, DANFORTH. *The American Short Story*. Minneapolis: U of Minnesota P, 1961. Ross pamphlet surveys the American short story; Crane's "The Blue Hotel" and "The Open Boat" are briefly (32–34) examined.

5.86 RUDE, DONALD W. "Joseph Conrad, Stephen Crane and W. L. Courtney's Review of *The Nigger of the 'Narcissus.'*" *English Literature in Transition* 21 (1978): 188–97. Courtney was the reviewer who claimed that Conrad patterned *The Nigger* after "The Open Boat." Rude discusses this allegation and reprints Conrad's letters to Courtney and to Crane on the matter. To the critic Conrad was polite and civil, but he wrote to Crane, "Have you seen the Daily Tele. article by that ass Courtney?"

5.87   SCHIRMER, GREGORY A. "Becoming Interpreters: The Importance of Tone in Crane's 'The Open Boat.'" *American Literary Realism* 15 (1982): 221–31. A technical examination of the syntax embedded in Crane's story, arguing that Crane employed three distinct tones: neutral (indifferent world), terror (danger), and caring (brotherhood).

5.88   SCOTT, VIRGIL, and DAVID MADDEN. "The Open Boat." Instructor's Manual for *Studies in Short Fiction*. 4th ed. New York: Holt, Rinehart, 1976. 78–81. Teaching tips for "The Open Boat."

5.89   SHEIDLEY, WILLIAM E., and ANN CHARTERS. "The Open Boat." Instructor's Manual for *The Short Story and Its Writer: An Introduction to Short Fiction*. New York: St. Martin's, 1983. 48–52. A summary of "The Open Boat" plus study exercises.

5.90   SHULMAN, ROBERT. "Community, Perception, and the Development of Stephen Crane: From *The Red Badge* to 'The Open Boat.'" *American Literature* 50 (1978): 441–60. A thoughtful and insightful essay exploring Crane's evolution on the development of brotherhood in the face of an indifferent nature and the tensions of danger and stress. From this perspective "The Open Boat" expresses Crane's mature as well as most optimistic stance.

5.91   SIRLIN, RHODA. "The Open Boat." Instructor's Manual for *The Borzoi Book of Short Fiction*. New York: Knopf, 1983. 25–26. Routine summary comments and discussion topics.

5.92   SKERRETT, JOSEPH T., JR. "Changing Seats in the Open Boat: Alternative Attitudes in Two Stories by Stephen Crane." *Studies in the Humanities* 4 (1982): 22–27. "The Open Boat" is compared with "Flanagan and His Short Filibustering Adventure" to show that Crane's "normal" attitude was cynicism and so the optimism and brotherhood themes in "The Open Boat" were temporary aberrations. Skerrett's thesis is provocative but it lacks convincing evidence and argumentation.

5.93   SPOFFORD, WILLIAM K. "Crane's 'The Open Boat': Fact or Fiction." *American Literary Realism* 12 (1979): 316–21. Spofford argues that the sinking of the *Commodore* merely presented Crane with the opportunity to express, in "The Open Boat," his longstanding adherence to the indifference of nature and the necessity of brotherhood. Spofford argues his case with illustrations from his poetry and "In the Depths of a Coal Mine."

5.94 STALLMAN, ROBERT W. "Journalist Crane in That Dinghy." *Bulletin of the New York Public Library* 72 (1968): 261–77. Compare with Day (5.24) and Hagemann (5.41); Stallman's considerable resources are marshaled to sort out all the factual details of the sinking of the *Commodore* and the open boat ordeal that followed—complete with drawings and charts.

5.95 ———. "The Land–Sea Irony in 'The Open Boat.'" *CEA Critic* 30 (1968): 15. Stallman rises to defend himself against plagiarism. He insists that Napier's (5.71) contention that Crane used land images to illustrate the perils of the sea was first made by him in his 1952 article "Stephen Crane: A Revaluation" (2.186). Following Stallman's brief note Napier replies in a one-paragraph touché. "The similarity of my observations to Professor Stallman's is indisputable": still, he argues that he takes the point further to stress his notice of Crane's anticipation of the "absurd."

5.96 STALLMAN, ROBERT W., and R. E. WATTERS. "Newspaper Reports of the Wreck of the *Commodore*." *The Creative Reader: An Anthology of Fiction, Drama, Poetry*. Ed. Robert W. Stallman and R. E. Watters. New York: Ronald, 1962. 232–41. An interesting collection of headline stories on the open boat ordeal.

5.97 STAPPENBECK, HERB. "Crane's 'The Open Boat.'" *Explicator* 34 (1976): Item 41. Comments on the Norton poem that the correspondent recalls. "The correspondent (as child) was to the soldier as nature is to the correspondent (as adult), or as the universe is to every man. Nature's indifference to the correspondent is comparable to his earlier indifference to the dying soldier." Indifference in either case requires solidarity.

5.98 STEPHENSON, EDWARD R. "The 'Subtle Brotherhood' of Crane and Hemingway." *Hemingway Review* 1 (1980): 42–52. A fairly good retelling of "The Open Boat" but the stretched references to *The Old Man and the Sea* are unimpressive.

5.99 STEWART, RANDALL. "The Amoralists." *American Literature & Christian Doctrine*. Baton Rouge: Louisiana State UP, 1958. 108–13. Crane (and Norris) are half-naturalists who see humans partially responsible in an indifferent world. "The Open Boat" is given a few paragraphs.

5.100   STONE, EDWARD. "Crane's 'Soldier of the Legion.'" *American Literature* 30 (1958): 242–44. Stone locates the poem by Caroline Norton, the source of "Soldier of the Legion," and discusses its role in "The Open Boat."

5.101   TIMKO, MICHAEL, and CLINTON OLIVER. "The Open Boat." *38 Short Stories An Introductory Anthology*. New York: Knopf, 1968. "The Open Boat" reprinted with study questions.

5.102   TRIMMER, JOSEPH F., and C. WADE JENNINGS. "The Open Boat." *Fictions*. 2nd ed. New York: Harcourt Brace, 1989. "The Open Boat" reprinted with study questions.

5.103   VIDAN, IVO. "Forms of Fortuity in the Short Fiction of Stephen Crane." *Studia Romanica et Anglica Zagrabiensia* 38 (1974): 17–48. A plodding and unconvincing treatment of many of Crane's shorter works, stressing "The Blue Hotel" and "The Open Boat." Thesis: Crane transcends naturalism but he falls short of freedom and moral responsibility.

5.104   WAGER, WILLIS. "Twain to James." *American Literature: A World View*. New York: New York UP, 1968. 168–70. In a survey chapter on modern American literature the influence of "The Open Boat" is described. Wager finds that influence to have been Crane's realism, his attack on moral smugness, and his depiction of an indifferent world.

5.105   WALHOUT, CLARENCE. "Ives, Crane, Marin, and 'The Mind Behind the Maker.'" *Christian Scholar Review* 16 (1987): 355–73. "This essay adopts what I would characterize *loosely* as a structuralist methodology" in order to find "deep rather than surface" patterns. As near as one can tell, Walhout discovers in "The Open Boat" that the deep pattern in Crane amounts to the unremarkable claim that art does not mirror reality but is "an exploration of possible *visions* of reality." Perhaps a "strict" structuralist methodology would have been more enlightening.

5.106   WEST, RAY B., and ROBERT W. STALLMAN. "Analysis [:'The Open Boat']. *The Art of Modern Fiction*. New York: Reinhart, 1949. 53–58. An analysis for the beginner: Nature is indifferent to human effort but one's fellows are not. "The Open Boat" is a realistic initiation story.

5.107 WHITE, M. W. "The Crane–Hemingway Code: A Revaluation." *Ball State University Forum* 10 (1969): 15–20. General comments on bravery and manhood as ideals in Crane and Hemingway. "The Open Boat" is given attention. See Young (11.54) for more on the Crane–Hemingway connection.

5.108 ZHANG, HEZHEN. "Nature in Works of Mark Twain and Stephen Crane." *Foreign Literature Studies* (China) 36.2 (June 1987): 24–27. The abstract (in English) indicates that the article contains comments on indifferent nature in "The Open Boat"; unfortunately, the article itself is in Chinese. Note: The same situation applies to a citation (in English) in the MLA computer data base regarding "Early Naturalist Literature in the United States." *Foreign Literature Studies* 26.4 (1984): 36–46, 58.

For more on "The Open Boat" see:

1.1–1.4	2.215
1.10	3.54
1.38	3.81
2.1–2.19	3.132
2.32	4.78
2.35	4.131
2.64	6.19
2.67	6.51
2.80	6.92
2.86	9.97
2.87	11.8
2.181	11.12
2.186	11.39
2.193	12.10
2.197	12.32
2.210	

6

Western Tales

Overview

Crane's western and Mexican trip (during the winter and spring of 1895, bankrolled by Irving Bacheller) changed his outlook (see DEAMER 6.11–6.13) and inspired some of his best short fiction, especially "The Blue Hotel" and "The Bride Comes to Yellow Sky"; each of these is given a special subsection. KATZ'S essay (6.3) about Crane's western trip is essential; Cather's often-quoted "interview" with Crane (at Lincoln, Nebraska) *is not,* as her biographer, Woodress (6.30), has established. The articles by Paredes (6.23) and Robinson (6.25) on Crane's depiction of Mexicans are important. BERGON (6.5), Johnson (6.18), Mayer (6.21), and ROBERTSON (6.24) have examined a number of Crane's lesser-known western tales.

"THE BLUE HOTEL." Several interesting pieces on fixing responsibility and/or blame for the death of the Swede have been written. The following culprits have been indicted:

No one:

Cox 6.39
GLECKNER 6.46
Grenberg 6.50

The Swede himself:

McFARLAND 6.69
Monteiro 6.72

Scully and the others:

Gibson 6.45
Johnsen 6.55
Law 6.65
Satterwhite 6.85
WESTBROOK 6.100

Also of note are articles on the playscript (6.32) and the film versions (6.60) of "The Blue Hotel."

"THE BRIDE COMES TO YELLOW SKY." This story is Crane's most playfully ironic, parodic, and humorous story. Several commentators have noted this:

Ferguson 6.117
Marovitz 6.129
TIBBITS 6.141

Other interesting pieces have been written on "Bride" as an elegy over the passing of the Old West:

Barnes 6.107
Bernard 6.108
OVERTON 6.132
VORPAHL 6.142

See also Agee's movie script (6.105) as well as comments on his film version by French (6.119) and Fultz (6.120).

WESTERN TALES AND REPORTS

Books

6.1 BERGON, FRANK, ed. *The Western Writings of Stephen Crane.* New York: NAL, 1979. 230. Bergon's volume was intended to bring the full range of Crane's western and Mexican stories to a general readership. See 6.5 for his introduction.

6.2 BOWERS, FREDSON, ed. *Tales of Adventure. The Works of Stephen Crane,* vol. 5. Charlottesville, UP of Virginia, 1970. cxcv+242. Bowers's critical edition reprints Crane's western tales along with "The Open Boat." See 6.6 for Bowers's textual introduction and 6.19 for Levenson's general introduction.

6.3   KATZ, JOSEPH. *Stephen Crane in the West and Mexico.* Kent, OH: Kent
       State UP, 1970. xxv+109. Katz collected and edited the stories and
       newspaper dispatches Crane composed on his trip to the West and
       Mexico. His introduction (ix–xxv) is the best source for information
       on that trip; a reproduction of C. K. Linson's cartoon, "Mr. S. Crane
       starts WEST on a journalistic tare," is a nice bonus.

Book Chapters and Articles

6.4   BENNETT, MILDRED R. *The World of Willa Cather.* New York: Dodd,
       Mead, 1951. Cather's unreliable account of meeting Crane in Lincoln
       during the spring of 1895 (see Woodress 6.30) is considerably and
       fancifully embellished by Bennett (205–8). (Bennett's book was
       reissued by the University of Nebraska Press in 1961.)

6.5   BERGON, FRANK. Introduction. *The Western Writings of Stephen
       Crane.* New York: NAL, 1979. 1–27. Bergon's essay provides basic
       information about Crane's western excursions and his western tales.
       Bergon's thesis is that Crane was a western writer before the modern
       genre was invented; his gift was an ability to combine realism with the
       myth of the West. Several stories, notably "One Dash—Horses,"
       "The Bride Comes to Yellow Sky," and "The Five White Mice," are
       given special attention.

6.6   BOWERS, FREDSON. Textual Introduction. *Tales of Adventure. The
       Works of Stephen Crane,* vol. 5. Ed. Fredson Bowers. Charlottesville:
       UP of Virginia, 1970. cxxxiii–cxcv. Most of these tales were collected
       by Crane for publication in *The Open Boat* (1898). However, earlier
       versions of many stories were syndicated in newspapers and/or
       appeared in magazines. Bowers explains variations among the texts
       and how he arrived at a definitive text for each story.

6.7   BROWN, E. K. *Willa Cather: A Critical Biography.* New York: Knopf,
       1953. Another biographer uncritically retells (74–76) Cather's ver-
       sion of her meeting Crane in Lincoln during the spring of 1895; see
       Woodress (6.30) for the flaws in Cather's account.

6.8   CADY, EDWIN H. "Stephen Crane and the Strenuous Life." *English
       Literary History* 28 (1981): 376–82. Crane's basic trope was "the
       game." Crane adopted Roosevelt's neo-romanticism as "he com-
       manded the cosmic gambler's stoic outlook: despising the petty, safe
       and comfortable; prizing the chance-taking, the enterprising, the
       seeking, aggressive and tough."

6.9   CATHER, WILLA. "When I Knew Stephen Crane." *Prairie Schooner* 23
        (1949): 231–36. Originally written under the pen name of Henry
        Nicklemann (*Library* 23 June 1900). Cather writes of her meeting
        Crane in Lincoln where she worked her way through college at the
        State Journal. This eyewitness report is widely quoted but Cather's
        biographer, James Woodress (see 6.30), is leery of its reliability.

6.10   COLLINS, MICHAEL J. "Realism and Romance in the Western Stories
        of Stephen Crane." *Under the Sun: Myth and Realism in Western
        American Literature*. Ed. Barbara Meldrum. Troy, NY: Whiteson,
        1985. 139–48. A simplistic, shallow, and sophomoric survey of
        Crane's western writings. Thesis: Crane plays off external (romantic)
        simplicity against internal (realistic) complexity. For example, in
        "Blue Hotel" Crane contrasts the artificiality of the Palace Hotel with
        the reality of the saloon.

6.11   DEAMER, ROBERT GLEN. "Stephen Crane and the Western Myth."
        Western American Literature 7 (1972): 111–23. A careful and compel-
        ling case is made that "the West profoundly changed Crane's outlook
        on life by teaching him to believe in man's potential for courage" and
        further, that "his writings show that he did have an intense awareness
        of the American myth of the West and that his essential attitude
        toward "The Passing of the West" was not parodic, not satiric—but
        serious, sympathetic, and even tragic." An essential article on Crane
        and the West. Deamer's comments are important not only for an
        understanding of the frequently examined "The Bride Comes to
        Yellow Sky" and "The Blue Hotel," but for an adequate appreciation
        of Crane's "minor" western tales and newspaper reports. For more on
        Deamer's contention see his review of Bergon's *Stephen Crane's
        Artistry* (*Western American Literature* 12 [1977]: 335–37).

6.12   ———. "Remarks on the Western Stance Of Stephen Crane." *Western
        American Literature* 15 (1980): 123–44. In the West Crane was not a
        tourist but he experienced and was influenced by the real West. As a
        result, these "rough and elemental encounters" colored not only his
        western stories but much of his later fiction.

6.13   ———. "Stephen Crane's 'Code' and Its Western Connections." *The
        Importance of Place in the American Literature of Hawthorne, Thoreau,
        Crane, Adams, and Faulkner*. Lewiston, NY: Edwin Mellen, 1990.
        139–52. An extension of Deamer's earlier articles on Crane and the
        West (6.11; 6.12). Thesis: Crane's westering experiences changed him
        from an environmental defeatist to a believer in the possibility of
        solidarity and limited success in combating indifference in an appar-
        ently meaningless universe. Crane's code of heroism is explained and

then briefly traced in several of Crane's middle and later tales such as "Death and the Child," "A Man and Some Others," and *The Monster*.

6.14   DEAN, JAMES L. "The Wests of Howells and Crane." *American Literary Realism* 10 (1977): 254–66. Both Howells and Crane sought an "anti-romantic" West; in addition, as a setting for danger and action, Crane sought wildness and challenge. Dean argues that Crane's use of humor to understate the place of violence effectively undercuts the mythical Old West.

6.15   GROSS, DAVID S. "The Western Stories of Stephen Crane." *Journal of American Culture* 11.4 (1988): 15–21. A sketchy examination of Crane's Western stories. None is treated in any sort of depth; "Blue Hotel" is dispatched in four paragraphs.

6.16   GUNN, DREWERY WAYNE. "Fact, Fantasy, Fiction." *American and British Writers in Mexico, 1556–1973*. Austin: U of Texas P, 1979. 35–52. A portion of the chapter (45–49) comments on Crane's travel notes on Mexico and his three Mexican stories: "Five White Mice," "The Wise Men," and "One Dash—Horses." Gunn observes, "The first American writer of real talent to be attracted by the fictional possibilities of Mexican life was Stephen Crane."

6.17   HALLADAY, JEAN R. "Stallman's *Turned* vs. Crane's *Trun*." *American Notes and Queries* 13 (1975): 105. A dispute about a Stallman "correction" of Crane's letter to "Deadeye Dick." The dispute is moot now, as this letter (#741 in *Correspondence of Stephen Crane* 13.3) is one of the letters Wertheim and Sorrentino judge a fabrication by Beer.

6.18   JOHNSON, GLEN M. "Stephen Crane's 'One Dash—Horses': A Model of 'Realistic' Irony." *Modern Fiction Studies* 23 (1977): 571–87. Johnson sees in this western tale by Crane "the ironic conflict of perspectives on situations and actions," which he argues is the key to the humanistic realism of Crane finest works.

6.19   LEVENSON, J. C. "Introduction." *Tales of Adventure. The Works of Stephen Crane*, vol. 5. Ed. Fredson Bowers. Charlottesville: UP of Virginia, 1970. xv–cxxxii. Beyond a leisurely paced (and exhaustive) analysis of the business and publishing history of every story in this volume, Levenson examines thematic elements of each story. Of interest are his observations concerning Crane's stress upon the multiplicity of nature and the fragility and limitations of the human ordering of reality. Important discussions of Crane's best western tales and "The Open Boat" are included.

6.20   LEWIS, ANTHONY. "Teaching the Western Stories of Stephen Crane."
       American Renaissance and the American West. Ed. Christopher Durer.
       Laramie: U of Wyoming P, 1982. 97–103. Superficial and predictable
       (also out of date—Lewis was apparently not aware of the Virginia
       critical edition let alone Bergon's *Western Writings of Stephen Crane*).
       Lewis sees West versus East and the transition from barbarism as the
       central themes in the only two stories he takes up: "The Blue Hotel"
       and "The Bride Comes to Yellow Sky."

6.21   MAYER, CHARLES W. "Two Kids in the House of Chance: Crane's
       'The Five White Mice.'" *Research Studies* 44 (1976): 52–57. Mayer
       uses this Mexican story to argue that Crane's worldview was not one
       of "unqualified fatality."

6.22   MONTEIRO, GEORGE. "Stephen Crane's 'Yellow Sky' Sequel." *Arizo-
       na Quarterly* 30 (1974): 119–26. A tedious retelling of "Moonlight
       in the Snow." Note, this story is a "sequel" to "The Bride Comes to
       Yellow Sky" only in the sense that Jack Potter, now "sheriff of the
       county," has as a deputy Scratchy Wilson, "once a no less famous
       desperado."

6.23   PAREDES, RAYMUND A. "Stephen Crane and the Mexican." *Western
       American Literature* 6 (1971): 31–38. Perhaps the best treatment of
       Crane's western-Mexican tales; still, Paredes sees abundant racism in
       Crane. While his contention is justified, he fails to see the moderating
       influence of Crane's irony in some of his depictions of Mexicans. See
       also Robinson (6.25).

6.24   ROBERTSON, JAMIE. "Stephen Crane, Eastern Outsider in the West
       and Mexico." *Western American Literature* 13 (1978): 243–56. A
       thoughtful and important analysis of Crane's western stories. Thesis:
       Crane, a tourist in the West, sees through the western myth as he "uses
       it to show that the courageous confrontation of the unknown . . . can
       lead to an insight into what he believes is the chief characteristic of any
       person's individual development: a humble awareness of one's own
       insignificance. On Crane and the myth of the West, see Deamer (6.11,
       6.12).

6.25   ROBINSON, CECIL. "Mexican Traits—A Later Look." *Mexico and the
       Hispanic Southwest in American Literature.* Tucson: U of Arizona P,
       1977. 164–209. A general treatment of Mexicans in several of Crane's
       tales and newspaper dispatches. While he notes Crane's praise of
       ancient Mexican civilization, Robinson (like Paredes, 6.23) finds
       racism and bias in Crane's depiction of Mexicans.

6.26   SHIVELY, JAMES R. "The Campus Years." *Writings from Willa
       Cather's Campus Years.* Lincoln: U of Nebraska P, 1950. 11–27.

Standard details of Cather's impressions of Crane at his Lincoln stopover midway through his western trip.

6.27   SLOTE, BERNICE. "Stephen Crane and Willa Cather." *Serif* 6.4 (1969): 3–15. Midway through his western trip for the Bacheller syndicate, while Crane waited in Lincoln, Nebraska, for money to be wired to him at the offices of the *State Journal,* he met Willa Cather. Slote shows that Cather's "vivid and essentially true" and famous article "When I Knew Stephen Crane" has many fictionalized elements and has to be used with caution. See also Woodress (6.30).

6.28   _____. "Stephen Crane in Nebraska." *Prairie Schooner* 43 (1969): 192–99. Slote sorts out the facts of Crane's trip including the severe drought and the awful winter he described in "Nebraska's Bitter Fight for Life." Slote's essay, along with Katz's Introduction to *Stephen Crane in the West and Mexico* (6.3), is essential background for Crane's western trip.

6.29   WIMBERLY, LOWRY CHARLES. "How A Dull Western City Takes on Class." *American Mercury* 33 (1934): 364–68. Notes that Crane visited Lincoln, Nebraska, on his 1895 western trip.

6.30   WOODRESS, JAMES. *Willa Cather: Her Life and Work.* New York: Pegasus, 1970. 68–69. Woodress explains the writing of Cather's account of meeting Crane in the offices of the Nebraska *Journal* in 1895. She met Crane in the dead of winter, yet when she wrote her account (see Cather 6.9), she referred to the hot wind of late spring. "The rest of her account seems equally untrustworthy, either as Cather autobiography or as Crane biography."

6.31   WRIGHT, AUSTIN McG. "People and Places." *The American Short Story in the Twenties.* Chicago: U of Chicago P, 1961. 25–31 and passim. Crane is selected to illustrate certain short story techniques, especially his use of geographical details in his western tales and in his descriptions of New York City.

For other items on Crane's western writing see:

1.1–1.4
1.10
2.1–2.19
5.69

(Note: "The Blue Hotel" and "The Bride Comes to Yellow Sky" are treated separately below.)

"THE BLUE HOTEL"

6.32   ALBERTS, FRANK. "*The Blue Hotel:* A Play in Three Acts Based on the Story by Stephen Crane." *Theater* 2 (1960): 27–42. Albert's adaptation is more faithful than Jan Kadar's film; still, there are some changes—the Swede is shot. Agee also wrote a television script of "The Blue Hotel"; see Fultz (6.43). For more on Kadar's version see Keenan (6.60), Petrakis (6.80), and Skaggs (6.86).

6.33   ASKEW, MELVIN. "Psychoanalysis and Literary Criticism." *Psychoanalytic Review* 51 (1964): 211–18. Though psychoanalytic literary criticism is often wrongheaded and simplistic, Askew argues that it can be illuminating. In three paragraphs he shows how "The Blue Hotel" can be unified by seeing the Swede as a "paranoiac [who] himself arranges, manipulates, and finally forces the circumstances which accomplish his own destruction."

6.34   BEARDS, RICHARD D. "Stereotyping in Modern American Fiction: Some Solitary Swedish Madmen." *Moderna Sprak* 63 (1969): 329–37. Four modern fictional stereotypes of Swedish madmen are considered, including the "shaky and quick-eyed Swede" in "The Blue Hotel." Beard's piece is valuable, as it shows how the Swede can be viewed sympathetically.

6.35   BOHNER, CHARLES H. "The Blue Hotel." Instructor's Manual for *Classic Short Fiction*. Englewood Cliffs, NJ: Prentice-Hall, 1986. 36–37. "The Blue Hotel" reprinted along with study and discussion questions.

6.36   BRIDGMAN, RICHARD. *The Colloquial Style in America*. New York: Oxford UP, 1966. 137–40. Comments on Crane's use of slang in "The Blue Hotel" with special attention to Scully's mix of Irish brogue and western twang.

6.37   CASSILL, R. V. "The Blue Hotel." *Norton Anthology of Short Fiction Instructor's Handbook*. New York: Norton, 1977. 56–57. Study guide and discussion questions for "The Blue Hotel."

6.38   CATE, HOLLIS. "Seeing and Not Seeing in 'The Blue Hotel.'" *College Literature* 9 (1982): 150–52. A modest and insightful analysis of more than two dozen "ocular" references in "Blue Hotel." An especially good treatment of the Swede's eyes fixed on the legend of the cash register in death.

6.39   COX, JAMES TRAMMELL. "Stephen Crane as Symbolic Naturalist: An Analysis of the 'Blue Hotel.'" *Modern Fiction Studies* 3 (1957): 147–58. Crane is a strict determinist; the chain of events having been set, no one is responsible for the Swede's death. As part of this strained reading, Cox stretches to find religious symbols at every turn. Cox's piece is, however, useful for its treatment of Crane's color images.

6.40   DAVIDSON, RICHARD ALLEN. "Crane's 'Blue Hotel' Revisited: The Illusion of Fate." *Modern Fiction Studies* 15 (1970): 537–39. A short but valuable article: Crane saw moral grayness rather than a black and white universe. "The Blue Hotel" skillfully depicts "the illusion of fate" in a world in which human actions are limited but not determined.

6.41   DILLINGHAM, WILLIAM B. "'The Blue Hotel' and The Gentle Reader." *Studies in Short Fiction* 1 (1964): 224–26. A short, helpful, stimulating piece. Thesis: The reader of "The Blue Hotel" is left "with a feeling not unlike that of a man who has approvingly witnessed from afar a lynching and then has thought it all over." Crane is able to bring this off, suggests Dillingham, because the Swede is a basically honest, though unattractive figure.

6.42   ELLIAS, JAMES. "The Game of High-Five in 'The Blue Hotel.'" *American Literature* 49 (1977): 440–42. A note showing that the card game (according to Hoyle) was "an American off-shoot of All Fours" and explaining how the game is played.

6.43   FULTZ, JAMES R. "Heartbreak at the Blue Hotel: James Agee's Scenario of Stephen Crane's Story." *Midwest Quarterly* 21 (1978): 423–34. An examination of Agee's television script of "The Blue Hotel." Conclusion: Agee's Blue Hotel is not Crane's "The Blue Hotel" for he casts the Swede as a hero who is "up against ignorance and prejudice that fully match his own." Also see Alberts (6.32).

6.44   GARDNER, JOHN, and LENNIS DUNLAP. "Stephen Crane: 'The Blue Hotel.'" *The Forms of Fiction*. Ed. John Gardner and Lennis Dunlap. New York: Random House, 1962. 329–57. A classroom exercise book. "The Blue Hotel" is reprinted, followed by ten discussion questions.

6.45 GIBSON, DONALD B. "'The Blue Hotel' and the Ideal of Human Courage." *Texas Studies in Language and Literature* 6 (1964): 388–97. An early middle-of-the-road piece: just because *Maggie* was deterministic does not mean all Crane's works are naturalistic. Gibson sees the possibility of solidarity and brotherhood despite the tragic end of "The Blue Hotel."

6.46 GLECKNER, ROBERT F. "Stephen Crane and the Wonder of Man's Conceit." *Modern Fiction Studies* 5 (1959): 271–81. A pessimistic, quasi-deterministic reading of "The Blue Hotel." Thesis: Whenever men exert their wills and attempt to control their lives tragedy results. Scully's attempt at control in the hotel leads to a fight, and when the Swede tries to control the situation in the saloon he is killed.

6.47 GLORFELD, LOUIS E., ROBERT N. BROADUS, and TOM E. KAKONIS. "The Blue Hotel." *The Short Story: Ideas and Background.* Columbus, OH: Charles Merrill, 1967. "The Blue Hotel" reprinted along with study and discussion questions.

6.48 GREBSTEIN, SHELDON NORMAN. "Hemingway's Dark and Bloody Capital." *The Thirties: Fiction, Poetry, Drama.* Ed. Warren French. Deland, FL: Everett Edwards, 1967. 21–30. Grebstein sees parallels in "The Blue Hotel" and Hemingway's "The Capital of the World": In both, the protagonist is "a victim of excessive courage and illusion, or delusion, and likewise the victim of a knife thrust."

6.49 GREET, T. Y., CHARLES E. EDGE, and JOHN M. MUNRO. "'The Blue Hotel.'" *The Worlds of Fiction: Stories in Context.* Boston: Houghton Mifflin, 1964. 136–65. The editors reprint "The Blue Hotel" and then add several pages (161–65) of notes for beginning readers.

6.50 GRENBERG, BRUCE L. "Metaphysics of Despair: Stephen Crane's 'The Blue Hotel.'" *Modern Fiction Studies* 14 (1968): 203–13. As the title indicates, a nihilistic reading of "The Blue Hotel": "Crane's irony reveals the complex fate of man to be that only the foolish survive and only the dead are wise."

6.51 GRIFFITH, CLARK. "Stephen Crane and the Ironic Last Word." *Philological Quarterly* 47 (1968): 83–91. Griffith argues that the ironic ending in many of Crane's works (he cites *Red Badge*, "The Blue Hotel," and "The Open Boat") is meant to declare the "human ignorance [and] the helplessness of man in a naturalistic universe."

6.52 HEINES, DONALD E. "The Blue Hotel." *Times Four: The Short Story in Depth.* Englewood Cliffs, NJ: Prentice-Hall, 1968. "The Blue Hotel" reprinted along with study and discussion questions.

6.53   HEMINGWAY, ERNEST. *The Green Hills of Africa.* New York: Scribner's, 1935. 22. The source of Hemingway's famous quote, "The good writers are Henry James, Stephen Crane, and Mark Twain. That's not the order they're good in. There is no order for good writers. . . . Crane wrote two fine stories, 'The Open Boat' and 'The Blue Hotel.' The last is best."

6.54   HOUGH, ROBERT L. "Crane on Herons." *Notes and Queries* 9 (1962): 108–9. Crane states in "The Blue Hotel," "The Palace Hotel at Fort Romper was painted a light blue, a shade that is on the legs of a kind of heron . . ." Hough points out an error: Only immature herons have blue legs, so it is the *age,* not the *kind* of heron that is at issue. See also Peterson (6.78).

6.55   JOHNSEN, WILLIAM A. "Rene Girard and the Boundaries of Modern Literature." *Boundary 2: A Journal of Post-Modern Literature* 9 (1981): 271–93. A modernist, deconstructionist analysis of "The Blue Hotel." Heavy-duty jargon is used to examine the Swede's ritualistic expulsion and scapegoat mechanisms he suffers in the hotel and at the saloon.

6.56   JOHNSON, WILLOUGHBY, and WILLIAM C. HAMLIN. "'The Blue Hotel': Comment." *The Short Story.* New York: American, 1966. 15–41. Johnson and Hamlin reprint "The Blue Hotel" and offer brief comments insisting that it is deterministic from beginning to end.

6.57   KATZ, JOSEPH. "An Early Draft of 'The Blue Hotel.'" *Stephen Crane Newsletter* 3.1 (1968): 1–2. Katz found on the back of Cora Crane's manuscript "Peter the Great" a fragment of an early draft of "The Blue Hotel." In this version Scully is named Renigan.

6.58   ———. Introduction. *Stephen Crane: "The Blue Hotel."* Columbus, OH: Charles Merrill, 1969. 1–4. This volume is a term-paper guide to "The Blue Hotel." Katz's introduction makes brief remarks on Crane's western trip, "The Blue Hotel," and some thirty essays Katz has brought together. (All these essays are treated elsewhere in this bibliography.)

6.59   KAZIN, ALFRED. "On Stephen Crane and 'The Blue Hotel.'" *The American Short Story.* Ed. Calvin Skaggs. New York: Dell, 1977. 77–81. A sketch of Crane's life; Kazin argues that each of us sees the world from a particular slant, and he applies this contention to the skewed perceptions of the Swede and Scully.

6.60 KEENAN, RICHARD. "The Sense of the Ending: Jan Kadar's Distortion of Stephen Crane's 'The Blue Hotel.'" *Literature/Film Quarterly* 16 (1988): 265–68. Kadar's film of "The Blue Hotel" is very faithful to Crane's story until he inexplicably changes the ending: The Swede is knifed in the Blue Hotel. Keenan argues that Kadar's version reduces Crane's great story to that of "an offensive boor who is given his fatal comeuppance." See Petrakis (6.80).

6.61 KIMBALL, SUE L. "Circles and Squares: The Designs of Stephen Crane's 'The Blue Hotel.'" *Studies in Short Fiction* 17 (1980): 425–30. A refreshing and interesting essay. In Crane's great western tale there is lots of talk of squares and circles; Kimball sorts much of it out. For instance, the square is the arena for contests, both cards and fist fights; the circle is, among other things, the tight clique the Swede cannot break into.

6.62 KINNAMON, JON M. "Henry James, the Bartender in Stephen Crane's 'The Blue Hotel.'" *Arizona Quarterly* 30 (1974): 160–63. Kinnamon proposes that because the bartender is named Henry and since his reactions are "predictably Jamesian," he refuses to "seize control of the situation; his behavior reflects meekness and passivism," and given his antipathy to violence, there can be no doubt that Crane intended us to conclude the bartender was the Old Master. Still, doubt remains.

6.63 KLEIN, MARCUS, and ROBERT PACK. "'The Blue Hotel.'" *Short Stories: Classic, Modern, Contemporary.* Boston: Little, Brown, 1967. 246. A very abbreviated biographical sketch followed by a reprint of "The Blue Hotel."

6.64 KLOTZ, MARVIN. "Stephen Crane: Tragedian or Comedian, 'The Blue Hotel.'" *University of Kansas City Review* 27 (1961): 170–74. Klotz argues that "The Blue Hotel," published at the height of the naturalism-realism controversy, is "a deliberate burlesque of literary naturalism."

6.65 LAW, RICHARD A. "The Morality Motif and Imagery of Diabolism in 'The Blue Hotel.'" *Wisconsin English Journal* 13 (1970): 11–15. Law sees in "The Blue Hotel" a reverse morality play with Scully as the devil.

6.66 LEVIN, GERALD. "'The Blue Hotel': Suggestions for Study." *The Short Story: An Inductive Approach.* New York: Harcourt, Brace, 1967. 378–80. Levin reprints "The Blue Hotel" and then offers study questions, the best of which deal with environmental determinism in the tale and the theme of collaboration.

6.67 LYNSKEY, WINIFRED. "Partial Analysis: ['The Blue Hotel']." *Reading Modern Fiction.* 3rd ed. New York: Scribner's, 1952. 173–75. If you want discussion questions and term paper suggestions for "The Blue Hotel," look here first.

6.68 MACLEAN, HUGH N. "The Two Worlds of 'The Blue Hotel.'" *Modern Fiction Studies* 5 (1959): 260–70. Maclean argues that "The Blue Hotel" explores both the world of freedom (the hotel) and the world of determinism (the saloon) and that though success is improbable, humans must struggle to assert their wills.

6.69 McFARLAND, RONALD E. "The Hospitality Code in Crane's 'The Blue Hotel.'" *Studies in Short Fiction* 18 (1981): 447–51. An insightful and useful examination of "The Blue Hotel" in light of the hospitality code in the *Odyssey* and folk literature in general: The Swede breaks the code and thereby causes his own destruction.

6.70 MENCKEN, H. L. "['The Blue Hotel']." *Smart Set* 40 (1913): 159. Passing comments on "The Blue Hotel" as a Greek tragedy.

6.71 MILLER, JEROME, and BERNICE SLOTE. "Stephen Crane's 'The Blue Hotel.'" Instructor's Manual for *The Dimensions of the Short Story: A Critical Anthology.* 2nd ed. New York: Harper and Row, 1981. 10. Discussion questions on "The Blue Hotel."

6.72 MONTEIRO, GEORGE. "Crane's Coxcomb." *Modern Fiction Studies* 31 (1985): 295–305. Diffuse reflections on "The Blue Hotel" to the effect that this story is "the chronicle of a loner moving toward self-destruction."

6.73 MURPHY, BRENDA. "'The Blue Hotel': A Source in *Roughing It.*" *Studies in Short Fiction* 20 (1983): 39–44. An unconvincing effort to link Crane's story with Twain's book.

6.74 NARVESON, ROBERT. "Conceit in 'The Blue Hotel.'" *Prairie Schooner* 43 (1969): 187–91. Narveson retells the story, proposing that not only the Swede but virtually all the characters in "The Blue Hotel" act with extravagance and conceit.

6.75 NEGLIA, ERMINIO G. "Fictional Death in Stephen Crane's 'The Blue Hotel' and Jorge Luis Borges' 'El Sur.'" *Chasqui: Revista de Latinamericana* 10.2–3 (1981): 20–25. Neglia proposes influence on Borges by Crane, and shows parallels in Crane's story and the Argentinian writer's story: Both are stories of men choosing their own deaths.

6.76 PEDEN, WILLIAM H. "The Blue Hotel." *Twenty-Nine Stories.* 2nd ed. Boston: Houghton Mifflin, 1967. "The Blue Hotel" reprinted along with study and discussion questions.

6.77 PEIRCE, J. F. "Stephen Crane's Use of Figurative Language in 'The Blue Hotel.'" *South Central Bulletin* 34 (1974): 160–64. Peirce is critical of the lack of development in Crane's story but he argues that "because of his imaginative use of figurative language, the faults of 'The Blue Hotel' seem unimportant."

6.78 PETERSON, CLELL, T. "Replies: Crane on Herons." *American Notes and Queries* 10 (1963): 29. Hough (6.54) was wrong about the color of the legs of herons; in the correct light even adult herons have the sort of blue legs Crane had in mind.

6.79 PETITE, JOSEPH. "Expressionism and Stephen Crane's 'The Blue Hotel.'" *Journal of Evolutionary Psychology* 10.3–4 (1989): 322–27. A minor piece in a minor journal. Thesis: We can "more clearly understand the Swede if we interpret him expressionalistically, as symbolizing the irrational in man, loosing a social storm in the hotel."

6.80 PETRAKIS, HARRY MARK. "Scene from 'The Blue Hotel.'" *The American Short Story.* Ed. Calvin Skaggs. New York: Dell, 1977. 65–69. A reprinting of the climactic last scene of Petrakis's screenplay of "The Blue Hotel." This is the scene that Petrakis substantially altered—the Swede is knifed in the Palace Hotel, not the saloon. See Keenan (6.60) for more on this changed ending.

6.81 PILGRIM, TIM A. "Repetition as a Nihilistic Device in Stephen Crane's 'The Blue Hotel.'" *Studies in Short Fiction* 11 (1974): 125–29. Thesis: "Crane is not only trying to project the universal possibility of nonacceptance. He is pointing up the complexity of conditions which surround *failure* when it manifests itself in social alienation." Pilgrim holds that Crane does all of this by his techniques of repetition.

6.82 PROUDFIT, CHARLES L. "Parataxic Distortion and Group Process in Stephen Crane's 'The Blue Hotel.'" *University of Hartford Studies in Literature* 15 (1983): 47–54. An overblown and underwhelming thesis: Parataxic distortion (as explained by American psychologist Harry Stack Sullivan), that inadequate adolescent development causes anxiety and "thinking in stereotypes," is the source of the Swede's difficulties.

6.83   REES, ROBERT A., and BARRY MENIKOFF. "The Blue Hotel." *The Short Story: An Introductory Anthology.* Boston: Little, Brown, 1969. 118–45. "The Blue Hotel" reprinted along with study and discussion questions.

6.84   ROOKE, CONSTANCE. "Another Visitor to 'The Blue Hotel.'" *South Dakota Review* 14 (1977): 50–56. "The Blue Hotel" is examined as a study of insiders and outsiders; Rooke wonders why Crane "makes it easy to dislike this Swede—suspiciously easy."

6.85   SATTERWHITE, JOSEPH N. "Stephen Crane's "The Blue Hotel": The Failure of Understanding." *Modern Fiction Studies* 2 (1956): 238–41. Satterwhite proposes that because Scully and the others fail to understand the Swede they are the real cause of his death, a thesis that fails to address the Swede's paranoia and misconceptions.

6.86   SKAGGS, CALVIN. "Interview with Jan Kadar." *The American Short Story.* Ed. Calvin Skaggs, New York: Dell, 1977. 70–76. Kadar, director of the movie version of "The Blue Hotel," explains that he changed the ending (Swede is knifed in the Palace Hotel) so all the card players could see their "silent conspiracy"; also explains how he cast Scully as a well-meaning host. On Skaggs's changing of the ending see Keenan (6.60) and Petrakis (6.80).

6.87   STARR, ALVIN. "The Concept of Fear in the Works of Stephen Crane and Richard Wright." *Studies in Black Literature* 6 (1975): 6–10. Starr compares Wright's treatment of fear with Weiss's (3.247) psychoanalytic examination of the same in "The Blue Hotel."

6.88   ———. "A 'Blue Hotel' for a 'Big Black Good Man.'" *American Notes & Queries* 21 (1982): 19–21. Starr sees similarities between "The Blue Hotel" and Richard Wright's story.

6.89   STONE, EDWARD. "Stephen Crane." *A Certain Morbidness: A View of American Literature.* Carbondale: Southern Illinois UP, 1969. 53–69. Stone discusses "The Blue Hotel" as a study in hysteria, morbid mania, and the death wish of the Swede. His study is all black and white: Either the patrons of the hotel are responsible for the Swede's fate or he was doomed. Partial responsibility on both sides is never considered.

6.90   SUTTON, WALTER. "Pity and Fear in 'The Blue Hotel.'" *American Quarterly* 4 (1952): 73–78. A short, illuminating discussion of courage in "The Blue Hotel." The Swede had courage but the wrong kind—his was blind because he was driven wild by fear.

6.91 TAYLOR, JOHN CHESLEY. "The Blue Hotel." *The Short Story: Fiction in Transition.* New York: Scribner's, 1969. "The Blue Hotel" is reprinted along with study and discussion questions.

6.92 THORP, WILLARD. "The Persistence of Naturalism in the Novel." *American Writing in the Twentieth Century.* Cambridge, MA: Harvard UP, 1960. 143–95. Though he denies the influence of Zola, he finds Crane an exemplar of naturalism in his "clinical studies of particular passions," especially fear, in "The Blue Hotel" as well as in "The Open Boat" and *Red Badge.*

6.93 TIMKO, MICHAEL. "The Blue Hotel." Instructor's Manual for *Twenty-Nine Short Stories: An Introductory Anthology.* New York: Knopf, 1975. 36–37. "The Blue Hotel" is reprinted along with study and discussion questions.

6.94 TRIMMER, JOSEPH F., and C. WADE JENNINGS. "The Blue Hotel." *Fictions.* 2nd ed. San Diego: Harcourt Brace, 1989. "The Blue Hotel" reprinted along with study and discussion questions.

6.95 VANDERBEETS, RICHARD. "Character as Structure: Ironic Parallel and Transformation in 'The Blue Hotel.'" *Studies in Short Fiction* 5 (1968): 294–95. An examination of parallels between the patrons of the saloon and the guests at the Palace Hotel.

6.96 WARD, J. A. "'The Blue Hotel' and 'The Killers.'" *CEA Critic* 21 (1959): 1, 7–8. Hemingway's story, like Crane's, dramatizes "the impersonality and inevitability of evil in the world."

6.97 WEINIG, SISTER MARY ANTHONY. "Heroic Convention in 'The Blue Hotel.'" *Stephen Crane Newsletter* 2.3 (1968): 6–7. Classical, mostly Homeric, allusions in "The Blue Hotel."

6.98 WELKER, ROBERT L., and HERSHEL GOWER. "Stephen Crane's 'The Blue Hotel.'" *The Sense of Fiction.* Englewood Cliffs, NJ: Prentice-Hall, 1966. 70–96. A study guide. "The Blue Hotel" is reprinted, followed by (92–96) comments on the story's structure and several discussion questions.

6.99 WEST, RAY B., ed. Introduction. *American Short Stories.* New York: Crowell, 1959. 1–15. In the short section on Crane (7–9) West calls Crane the initiator of the modern American short story and explains how Crane's selective "vision refined certain aspects until they took on an added, transcendent significance." He reprints "The Blue Hotel" as an illustration of both his theses.

6.100   WESTBROOK, MAX. "Stephen Crane's Social Ethic." *American Quarterly* 14 (1962): 587–96. Westbrook tests his hypothesis that Crane believed humans were responsible; hence he endorsed ethical imperatives. Accordingly, Westbrook argues that "Maggie is not censured for allowing Pete to seduce her, since her motive (with realistic qualifications) is love," and conversely, Crane indicts the five in "The Blue Hotel" who fail to respond to a fellow human in need.

6.101   WOLFORD, CHESTER L. "The Eagle and the Crow: High Tragedy and Epic in 'The Blue Hotel.'" *Prairie Schooner* 51 (1977): 260–74. Wolford retells the story, stressing classical, Homeric elements of "epic and tragedy" in the story. Particular stress is laid on the Swede as a tragic hero.

6.102   WOLTER, JURGEN. "Drinking, Gambling, Fighting, Paying: Structure and Determinism in 'The Blue Hotel.'" *American Literary Realism* 12 (1979): 285–98. An insightful observation that the characters are determined by a cycle of drinking, gambling, fighting, and paying; a pattern repeated three times.

6.103   WYCHERLEY, H. ALAN. "Crane's 'The Blue Hotel': How Many Collaborators?" *American Notes & Queries* 4 (1966): 88. Crane mentions that five were involved in the Swede's death (the Easterner, the Cowboy, Scully, Johnnie, the Gambler). Wycherley correctly points out there were six, adding the Bartender.

See also on "The Blue Hotel":

1.1–1.4	4.66
1.10	4.78
2.1–2.19	5.52
2.35	5.85
2.64	5.103
2.84	6.10
2.186	6.15
2.193	6.20
3.54	8.19

"THE BRIDE COMES TO YELLOW SKY"

6.104   ABCARIAN, RICHARD, and MARVIN KLOTZ. "The Bride Comes to Yellow Sky." Instructor's Manual for *Literature: The Human Experi-*

ence. 2nd ed. New York: St. Martin's, 1982. 6–7. Study and discussion tips on "The Bride Comes to Yellow Sky."

6.105 AGEE, JAMES. "The Bride Comes to Yellow Sky." *Counterpoint in Literature.* Ed. Robert C. Pooley, et al. Glenville, IL: Scott Foresman, 1967. 305–26. A film adapted from Crane's story. Agee's script is a faithful retelling expanded with several scenes in the Weary Gentleman Saloon plus several townspeople's experiences with Scratchy Wilson. Originally published by Huntington Hartford in 1958.

6.106 ARP, THOMAS. "Stephen Crane's 'The Bride Comes to Yellow Sky.'" Instructor's Manual for *Story and Structure.* 6th ed. New York: Harcourt Brace, 1983. 53–55. A competent study guide stressing humor and irony in Crane's story.

6.107 BARNES, ROBERT. "Crane's 'The Bride Comes to Yellow Sky'" *Explicator* 16 (1958): Item 39. The East (bride) conquers the West (Sheriff Potter) and the funnel-shaped tracks that Scratchy makes are the West's hourglass—the Old West's time has run out.

6.108 BERNARD, KENNETH. "'The Bride Comes to Yellow Sky': History as Elegy." *English Record* 17 (1967): 17–20. A minor piece: "Bride" is neither humor nor parody but an elegy on the passing of the Old West.

6.109 BLOOM, EDWARD A. "Critical Commentary on 'The Bride Comes to Yellow Sky.'" *The Order of Fiction: An Introduction.* New York: Odyssey, 1964. 100–104. Classroom exercises. Bloom's ponderous treatment of myth and symbol appears to miss the lightness and humor in Crane's story.

6.110 BOHNER, CHARLES H. "The Bride Comes to Yellow Sky." Instructor's Manual for *Classic Short Fiction.* Englewood Cliffs, NJ: Prentice-Hall, 1986. 37–38 "The Bride Comes to Yellow Sky" is reprinted with study and discussion questions.

6.111 BONAZZA, ROY. "The Bride Comes to Yellow Sky." *Studies in Fiction.* 3rd ed. enlarged. New York: Harper and Row, 1982. "The Bride Comes to Yellow Sky" is reprinted with study and discussion questions.

6.112 BROOKS, CLEANTH, and ROBERT PENN WARREN. "The Bride Comes to Yellow Sky: Interpretation." *The Scope of Fiction.* New York: Appleton-Century-Crofts, 1960. 147. The editors follow up their reprinting of "The Bride Comes to Yellow Sky" with study and term-paper questions stressing the structure of Crane's story.

6.113   BURNS, SHANNON, and JAMES A. LEVERNIER. "Androgyny in Stephen Crane's 'The Bride Comes to Yellow Sky.' " *Research Studies* 45 (1977): 236–43. The authors' obvious thesis—with the coming of civilization to the Old West the old male–female stereotypes are being compromised into "terms of shared human identity"—is spiced up with a Freudian interpretation of Scratchy's shooting his guns into the air.

6.114   COOK, ROBERT G. "Stephen Crane's 'The Bride Comes to Yellow Sky.' " *Modern Fiction Studies* 2 (1965): 368–69. The figure of the funnel-shaped tracks Scratchy makes in the sand "is the perfect visual summation for a story in which the converging elements are brought together inconclusively."

6.115   CURRENT-GARCIA, EUGENE, and WALTON R. PATRICK. "Stephen Crane." *American Short Stories: 1820 to the Present.* Chicago: Scott, Foresman, 1964. 319–20. Standard introductory piece, followed by a reprinting of "A Mystery of Heroism" and "The Bride Comes to Yellow Sky."

6.116   FENSON, HARRY, and HILDRETH KRITZER. "The Bride Comes to Yellow Sky." *Reading, Understanding, and Writing about Stories.* New York: Free Press, 1966. 227–238. "The Bride Comes to Yellow Sky" is reprinted with study and discussion questions.

6.117   FERGUSON, S. C. "Crane's 'The Bride Comes to Yellow Sky.' " *Explicator* 21 (1963): Item 59. A note to the effect that "Bride" is a "charming spoof" of dime novels. The moral of the story: Potter assumes adult responsibilities and Scratchy stays a child.

6.118   FOLSOM, JAMES K. " 'The Sea of Grass.' " *The American Western Novel.* New Haven, CT: College and University, 1966. 60–98. Crane treated in passing. "The Bride Comes to Yellow Sky" is a fictional rendering of the Turner thesis of the passing of the frontier.

6.119   FRENCH, WARREN. "Face to Face: Film Confronts Story." *English Symposium Papers* 4 (1974): 43–74. French discusses a filmmaker's difficulty in "externalizing" the consciousness of characters; the second half of his article is a detailed examination of the changes James Agee's script (6.105) made to portray the inner thoughts of Potter, Scratchy, and the unnamed bride. See also Fultz (6.120).

6.120 FULTZ, JAMES R. "High Jinks at Yellow Sky: James Agee and Stephen Crane." *Literature/Film Quarterly* 11 (1983): 46–55. An interesting and very detailed examination of the changes Agee (6.105) made in the movie script for "The Bride Comes to Yellow Sky." Fultz is most critical of Agee's expansion of Crane's four scenes into the fifteen in his forty-five-minute movie version of the story. See also French (6.119).

6.121 GERLACH, JOHN. "The Bride Comes to Yellow Sky." *Toward the End: Closure and Structure in the American Short Story.* Tuscaloosa: U of Alabama P, 1985. A comment on the ending of "The Bride Comes to Yellow Sky."

6.122 HALL, JAMES B. "The Bride Comes to Yellow Sky." Teacher's Manual for *The Realm of Fiction: 61 Short Stories.* New York: McGraw-Hill, 1965. "The Bride Comes to Yellow Sky" is reprinted with study and discussion questions.

6.123 HEINES, DONALD. "The Bride Comes to Yellow Sky." *Times Four: The Short Story in Depth.* Englewood Cliffs, NJ: Prentice-Hall, 1968. 168. "The Bride Comes to Yellow Sky" is reprinted with study and discussion questions.

6.124 HUFFMAN, GRANT, ed. *Six Scripts for Three Media: Television, Movies, Theater.* Toronto: McClelland and Stewart, 1964. 177–243. Huffman's brief Introduction and Questions introduce and then follow a reprinting of Crane's short story (181–95) as well as Agee's film script (197–240) of "The Bride Comes to Yellow Sky." Pitched at high-school readers.

6.125 ISAACS, NEIL D. "Yojimbo Comes to Yellow Sky." *Kyushu American Literature* 10 (1967): 81–86. A comparison between the samurai movie *Yojimbo* and *The Bride Comes to Yellow Sky:* In both the older order crumbles before an advancing "civilization."

6.126 KANE, THOMAS S., and LEONARD J. PETERS. *Short Story and the Reader: Discovering Narrative Techniques.* New York: Oxford UP, 1975. 52–53. The subtitle of the book describes the authors' comments on "The Bride Comes to Yellow Sky"; special attention is given to the characters' names, clothing, and physical appearance.

6.127 LID, R. W. "The Bride Comes to Yellow Sky." Instructor's Manual for *The Short Story: Classic and Contemporary.* New York: Lippincott, 1966. 158–71. A reprinting plus discussion questions for "The Bride Comes to Yellow Sky."

6.128   MACKENZIE, AENEAS, dir. *Face to Face*. New York: Threesquare
        Productions, 1952. The film adaptation of "The Bride Comes to
        Yellow Sky" released by R.K.O. Radio Pictures.

6.129   MAROVITZ, SANFORD E. "Scratchy the Demon in 'The Bride Comes
        to Yellow Sky.'" *Tennessee Studies in Literature* 16 (1971): 137–40.
        Marovitz works hard to manufacture a demonic Crane, thereby
        making Scratchy into Lucifer.

6.130   MATLAW, MYRON, and LEONARD LIEF. "The Bride Comes to
        Yellow Sky." *Story and Critic*. New York: Harper and Row, 1963.
        223–37. "The Bride Comes to Yellow Sky" is reprinted with a
        commentary.

6.131   MONTEIRO, GEORGE. "Stephen Crane's 'The Bride Comes to Yellow
        Sky.'" *Approaches to the Short Story*. Ed. Neil Isaacs and Louis Leiter.
        San Francisco: Chandler, 1963. 221–38. A lengthy analysis of "The
        Bride" that sees all characters as victims or victors depending on code
        and environment. Reprinted in Instructor's Manual for *The Art of
        Fiction*, 4th ed., Ed. R. F. Dietrich and Roger H. Sundell (New York:
        Holt, 1983): 121–32.

6.132   OVERTON, JAMES P. "The 'Game' in 'The Bride Comes to Yellow
        Sky.'" *Xavier University Studies* 4 (1965): 3–11. A helpful and
        insightful look at the games in "Bride": No one will play Scratchy
        Wilson's game, and the other "games" supported by the Old West's
        social customs collapse with Potter's marriage. The result is the New
        West where Scratchy is a dinosaur.

6.133   [PAPERTEXTS]. "The Bride Comes to Yellow Sky." *Papertexts,* Inter-
        mediate Series. New York: Simon and Schuster, 1968. "The Bride
        Comes to Yellow Sky" and discussion questions, printed in a pam-
        phlet.

6.134   PERRINE, LAWRENCE, and THOMAS R. ARP. "The Bride Comes to
        Yellow Sky." Instructor's Manual for *Story and Structure*. 7th ed. San
        Diego: Harcourt Brace, 1988. "The Bride Comes to Yellow Sky" is
        reprinted with study and discussion questions.

6.135   PETRY, ALICE HALL. "Crane's 'The Bride Comes to Yellow Sky.'"
        Explicator 42 (1983): 45–47. A useful note on the names in "The
        Bride Comes to Yellow Sky," which Petry finds "ideally suited to the
        revelation of [Crane's] characters' personalities and situations, to the
        development of the story's theme, and to the setting of tone."

6.136   REHDER, JESSE. "The Bride Comes to Yellow Sky." *The Short Story at
        Work: An Anthology*. New York: Odyssey, 1963. 191–203. Discussion

questions for "The Bride Comes to Yellow Sky," plus a brief commentary.

6.137 SCHORER, MARK. " 'The Bride Comes to Yellow Sky.' " *The Story: A Critical Anthology*. New York: Prentice-Hall, 1950. 21–35. Reprints "Bride" along with discussion questions, and comments on how "the form that Crane has developed engenders a certain amount of suspense."

6.138 SHEIDLEY, WILLIAM E., and ANN CHARTERS. Instructor's Manual for *The Short Story and Its Writer: An Introduction to Short Fiction*. New York: St. Martin's, 1983. 52–54. A summary of "The Bride Comes to Yellow Sky" plus study exercises.

6.139 SMITH, ELLIOT, and WANDA A. SMITH. "Stephen Crane's 'The Bride Comes to Yellow Sky.' " Instructor's Manual for *Access to Literature: Understanding Fiction, Drama and Poetry*. New York: St. Martin's, 1981. 13–14. Discussion and term-paper questions on "The Bride Comes to Yellow Sky."

6.140 TATE, J. O. "The Force of Example: Flannery O'Connor and Stephen Crane." *Flannery O'Connor Bulletin* 11 (1982): 10–24. An examination of "the teasing matter of influence": The uppity porter in O'Connor's *Wise Blood* and in "The Bride Comes to Yellow Sky," and the wafer image in "A Temple of the Holy Ghost" and in *Red Badge*.

6.141 TIBBETTS, A. M. "Stephen Crane's 'The Bride Comes to Yellow Sky.' " *English Journal* 54 (1965): 314–16. As "The Bride Comes to Yellow Sky" is a playful story, Crane's sense of humor is the main point here.

6.142 VORPAHL, BEN MERCHANT. "Murder by the Minute: Old and New in 'The Bride Comes to Yellow Sky.' " *Nineteenth-Century Fiction* 26 (1971): 196–218. Thesis: The story is about death, and Scratchy's "funnel-shaped tracks" represent an hourglass of the old mythic West running out of time. Also to be found in Vorpal's article is the interesting note that Crane's setting is Amarillo, which is the Spanish word for yellow.

6.143 WELTY, EUDORA. "The Reading and Writing of Short Stories." *Atlantic Monthly* 183 (Feb.–Mar. 1949): 54–58, 46–49. Among several short stories, Welty singles out "The Bride Comes to Yellow Sky" for comment. She calls attention to Crane's skill at describing situations and his ability to maintain suspense. Reprinted in her *Short Stories,* New York: Harcourt, Brace, 1949. 19–23.

6.144 WEST, RAY B. "The Use of Action in 'The Bride Comes to Yellow Sky.'" *Reading the Short Story.* New York: Crowell, 1968. 17–23. In an introductory essay, West retells the story, stressing that "action is the dominant element . . . the characters are negligible."

For more on "The Bride Comes to Yellow Sky" see:

1.1–1.4
1.10
2.1–2.19
2.32
2.35
2.84
2.193
3.54
6.20
11.18

7
Poetry

Overview

Legends about why and how Crane wrote his poetry abound. Crane, so the story goes, had some of Emily Dickinson's verses read to him (see Cunliffe, 7.20) at a luncheon with William Dean Howells. Crane almost immediately began to produce verses by a magical process of simply drawing off the lines, which stood in rows in his head (see Garland, 1.97–1.98). Consult COLVERT (7.18) for reliable information on how and when Crane wrote his "lines" and BOWERS (7.16) for a textual discussion of his poetry.

For scholarly work on Crane's poetry, three volumes are essential: Hoffman's outstanding monograph (7.6) plus the Virginia critical edition (7.2) and Crosland's concordance (7.3) keyed to it. Though there have not been many articles or full chapters on Crane's poetry, the following deserve mention:

Blair 7.13
Cox 7.19
Dickason 7.24
Dooley 2.5
Katz 7.46
LOWELL 7.58
MILLER 7.65
Nelson 7.69
WESTBROOK 7.95

Books

7.1   BARON, HERMAN. *A Concordance to the Poems of Stephen Crane.* Ed.
Joseph Katz. Boston: G. K. Hall, 1974. xv+311. Concordance, word
counts, plus frequency lists keyed to Katz, 1966 edition of Crane's
poetry, *The Poems of Stephen Crane.* See 7.53 for Katz's introduction.

7.2   BOWERS, FREDSON, ed. *Poems and Literary Remains. The Works of
Stephen Crane,* vol. 10. Charlottsville: UP of Virginia, 1975.
xxix+383. The standard edition of Crane's poems. See 7.16 for
Bowers's textual introduction and 7.18 for Colvert's general introduction.

7.3   CROSLAND, ANDREW T., compiler. *A Concordance to the Complete
Poetry of Stephen Crane.* xx+189. Detroit: Gale Research, 1975.
Computer-generated word counts plus frequency lists; keyed to the
Bowers, Virginia edition.

7.4   FOLLETT, WILSON, ed. *"The Black Riders" and Other Lines. The Work
of Stephen Crane,* vol. 6. New York: Knopf, 1926. xxix+155. The first
collection of Crane's poems. See 7.58 for Lowell's introductory
comments.

7.5   ———, ed. *The Collected Poems of Stephen Crane.* New York: Knopf,
1930. 132. A separate reissue of Crane's poems, reprinting the Knopf
edition (7.4) plus three posthumously published poems.

7.6   HOFFMAN, DANIEL G. *The Poetry of Stephen Crane.* New York:
Columbia UP, 1957. 304. Hoffman's book was the first full-length
treatment of Crane's poetry. His study was so comprehensive and
convincing that there has been no other detailed examination since.
Hoffman's extensive biographical treatment and his investigation of
the impact of Crane's ancestors' religious treatises pave the way for a
Freudian interpretation of Crane's "lines" amplified by Hoffman's
forays into Crane's prose for evidence and further confirmation.
    In the more than thirty years since its issue Crane scholars have
taken exception to minor points but the book remains *the* standard
work on Crane's poetry. A fourth printing and Columbia Paperback
edition were issued by Columbia in 1971. For a representative, very
positive review see Kenneth Rexroth, "Is Anybody Out There?"
Saturday Review 41 (5 July 1958): 19, 30.

7.7   KATZ, JOSEPH, ed. *The Poems of Stephen Crane: A Critical Edition.*
New York: Cooper Square, 1966. xix+258. A critical edition of
Crane's poems several years before the now-accepted Virginia critical

edition of Crane's poetry. Katz's textual and general introduction is annotated below (see 7.46). Note: This volume was reissued in paperback without the textual apparatus as *The Complete Poems of Stephen Crane* (Ithaca, NY: Cornell UP, 1972).

Articles and Book Chapters

7.8   ALLEN, GAY WILSON, WALTER B. RIDEOUT, and JAMES K. ROBIN-SON. "Stephen Crane." *American Poetry.* New York: Harper and Row, 1965. 639–59, 1087–89. A generous reprinting of Crane's poems: 26 from *The Black Riders,* nine from *War Is Kind* plus four others, along with brief biographical and bibliographical notes.

7.9   BARRY, JOHN D. "A Note on Stephen Crane." *Bookman* 13 (1901): 148. Barry briefly attempts to set the record straight about his involvement with Crane's newspaper apprenticeship and his support of *The Black Riders and Other Lines.* Barry read some of Crane's poems to a Manhattan literary group—the Uncut Leaves Society. Here he argues that Crane was "directly inspired by Miss Dickinson."

7.10   BASKETT, SAM S., and THEODORE STANDNESS. "Stephen Crane." *The American Identity: A College Reader.* Boston: D. C. Heath, 1962. 301–5. Brief comments on Crane followed by a reprinting of short selections from *War Is Kind* and a short segment from *Red Badge.*

7.11   BASSAN, MAURICE. "A Bibliographical Study of Stephen Crane's Poem, 'In the Night.'" *Papers of the Bibliographical Society of America* 58 (1964): 173–79. An early attempt to provide a definitive text of one of Crane's poems.

7.12   BASYE, ROBERT C. "Color Imagery in Stephen Crane's Poetry." *American Literary Realism* 13 (1980): 122–31. As others have noted with reference to *Red Badge* and "The Open Boat," color is crucial to Crane's message. Basye shows that attention to Crane's use of color gives important insights into his poetry.

7.13   BLAIR, JOHN. "The Posture of the Bohemian in the Poetry of Stephen Crane." *American Literature* 61 (1989): 215–29. Blair proposes a sharp break between Crane's earlier poems (which he sees as severely critical of religion) and the later ones (which adopt "the appearance of rebellion while still adhering to a core of beliefs which were entirely conventional"). Blair accounts for this shift in terms of Crane's bohemianism. A good analysis of theological themes in Crane.

7.14   BLUM, MORGAN. "Berryman as Biographer, Stephen Crane as Poet."
        Poetry 78 (1951): 298–307. An essay on Berryman's *Stephen Crane*
        (1.2) that complains of Berryman's lack of documentation and
        criticizes his overbrief treatment of Crane's poetry.

7.15   BOGAN, LOUISE. "The Forerunners." *Achievement in American Poe-
        try*. Chicago: Regnery, 1951. 1–13. Crane's poetry is credited with
        beginning the modern era of American poetry; also remarks on his
        impressionism and the presence of "adolescent irony" in his verses.

7.16   BOWERS, FREDSON. "The Text: History and Analysis [The Poems and
        Literary Remains]." *Poems and Literary Remains. The Works of Stephen
        Crane*, vol. 10. Ed. Fredson Bowers. Charlottesville: UP of Virginia,
        1975. 189–239, 283–304. Textual information on Crane's poems
        (many appearing in *The Bookman* and *The Philistine*) as well as the
        avant-garde layout of *The Black Riders and Other Lines*. (Note: Bowers
        concludes his critical edition with errata and addenda to the first nine
        volumes of this historic University of Virginia textual effort.)

7.17   BROGUNIER, JOSEPH E. "The Two Cranes and 'Blind Baggage.'"
        Hart Crane Newsletter 2 (1978): 33–35. An observation that both
        Hart Crane and Stephen Crane used the phrase "blind baggage" in
        their poetry.

7.18   COLVERT, JAMES B. Introduction. *Poems and Literary Remains. The
        Works of Stephen Crane*, vol. 10. Ed. Fredson Bowers. Charlottesville:
        UP of Virginia, 1975. xvii–xxix. A general account of Crane's output
        of "pills" or "lines" as he refered to his poetry. Colvert proposes that
        his poems are "gnomic utterances" that employ many of the same
        images as his best prose. Also useful are Colvert's comments on the
        tender and the bullying gods in Crane's verses and his oscillation
        between an indifferent and a malevolent universe.

7.19   COX, JAMES M. *"The Pilgrim's Progress* as Source of Stephen Crane's
        The Black Riders." *American Literature* 28 (1957): 478–87. An
        interesting, convincing case is made that Crane's poetry is the "full
        echo" of Bunyan's *Pilgrim's Progress*. In both Crane and Bunyan, Cox
        sees a pattern of "revelation, interrogation and interpretation" used to
        stage "miniature dramas."

7.20   CUNLIFFE, MARCUS. "Realism in American Prose." *The Literature of
        the United States*. Baltimore: Penguin, 1959. 213–19. Crane is treated
        quickly; his poetry more than his prose gets Cunliffe's notice.
        "Howells told Crane about the recently published poems of Emily
        Dickinson, and Crane produced some of his own, jerky, individual,
        full of unexpected images and epithets."

7.21 DAMERON, J. LASLEY. "Symbolism in the Poetry of Poe and Stephen Crane." *Emerson Society Quarterly* 60 (Fall 1970): 22–28. Unconvincing assertion that Poe influenced Crane. This claim is "supported" by observations that both used symbolism to set forth physical scenes and that both had an interest in the grotesque and the bizarre.

7.22 DAMON, S. FOSTER. *Amy Lowell: A Chronicle with Extracts from Her Correspondence.* Boston: Houghton Mifflin, 1935. 175–77, 651–52. Interesting details on the Lowell–Follett negotiations concerning her writing the introduction for the poetry volume (VI) of *The Works of Stephen Crane.* Follett asked if "he should respect Crane's rather modernistic lack of capitals in his verse". She replied, "There is no possible doubt on the matter of having Crane's poems set up as he wrote them in manuscript." Lowell goes on to discuss Crane's impact on nonstandard printings in the poetry of "H. D." and e. e. cummings.

7.23 DASKAM, JOSEPHINE DODGE. "The Distinction of Our Poetry." *Atlantic* 87 (1901): 696–705. A general essay on American poets, Emerson on down. Crane is mentioned as having been impressed by Whitman. Daskam opines that since Whitman is bad enough, Crane need not be treated.

7.24 DICKASON, DAVID H. "Stephen Crane and *The Philistine.*" *American Literature* 15 (1943): 279–87. Elbert Hubbard, head of the Society of the Philistines, was an enthusiastic supporter of Crane, arranging a testimonial dinner in his honor in Buffalo in 1895. More important, he was especially keen on Crane's icon-smashing poetry, which he sought to popularize. Dickason makes remarks on the two dozen Crane poems published in *The Philistine.* See White (1.222) for more on this topic.

7.25 FORD, FORD MADOX. "Literary Causeries." *Chicago Tribune* (Paris) 4–10 (Mar.–Apr. 1924): 3–11. These appear to be an irregular series of articles containing Ford's comments on the current literary scene. The only information I have on them is in Stallman's *Stephen Crane: Critical Bibliography* (14.3: 313). On the *Black Riders* Ford is quoted as commenting that Crane "had all the hard exactness of language of a French writer but managed nevertheless to get into his *vers libre* a great deal conversational fluidity."

7.26 FRYCKSTEDT, OLAF W. "Crane's *Black Riders:* A Discussion of Dates." *Studia Neophilologia* 34 (1962): 282–93. The title is self-explanatory.

7.27   GILLIS, EVERETT, A. "A Glance at Stephen Crane's Poetry." *Prairie
        Schooner* 28 (1954): 73–79. This is a brief glance. Gillis sees most of
        Crane's poetry as the product of an eccentric adolescent noticing
        hypocrisy as he bids for attention.

7.28   GOMOLL, ROBERT E. "Stephen Crane Had a Beef with the World
        Too!" *English Journal* 73 (1974): 80. My guess is that the editors of
        English Journal needed a half-page of text and so they printed this
        inane comment. Gomoll enlightens us with the observation that the
        Wendy's hamburger commercial " 'Where's the beef?' also takes on a
        similiar context in asking [as Crane did in his poetry] where is
        God?"

7.29   GREGORY, HORACE. "Stephen Crane's Poems." *New Republic* 63 (25
        June 1930): 159–60. A review essay on *The Collected Poems of Stephen
        Crane* (7.5). Nice comments on Crane's economy of words, his
        "profound concern about the exact nature of human fear," and his
        being an active spectator of life. Several poems are then cited as proof
        of these contentions.

7.30   GREGORY, HORACE, and MARYA ZATURENSKA. "A Note on Ste-
        phen Crane." *History of American Poetry, 1900–1940.* New York:
        Harcourt, Brace, 1942. 133–37. An assessment of Crane's poetry:
        Though the authors find in his poems "epigrammatic sharpness,
        experimentation and a brilliant, precocious gesture of revolt," they
        still find his poems shocking. In the end, they beg off, saying history
        will make a final evaluation.

7.31   GRIFFITH, BENJAMIN W. "Robinson Jeffers' 'The Blood Sire' and
        Stephen Crane's 'War is Kind.' " *Notes on Contemporary Literature* 3
        (1973): 14–15. Crane's putative influence on Jeffers.

7.32   GULLASON, THOMAS A. "Tennyson's Influence on Stephen Crane."
        Notes and Queries ns 5 (1958): 164–65. Tennyson's influence was
        negative: "War Is Kind" is "the complete antithesis of 'The Charge of
        the Light Brigade' " which is also satirized in the Whilomville tale
        "Making an Orator."

7.33   HAGEMANN, E. R. "Stephen Crane in the Pages of *Life* (1896–1901):
        A Checklist." *Stephen Crane Newsletter* 3.3 (1969): 1, 3–5. Hage-
        mann has prepared a list of articles, reviews, and, of most interest,
        parodies of Crane's poetry (and prose) in this turn-of-the-century
        humor magazine.

7.34   HALLADAY, JEAN R. "A Misdated Crane Poem." *American Notes and
        Queries* 12 (1974): 83–84. Stallman's *Stephen Crane* (1.10) misdates

and misidentifies "One came from the skies . . . ," one of the poems Crane had to remove from the *Black Rider* volume. See the Virginia critical edition of Crane poems for full discussion of this poem.

7.35 HARTER, PENNY. "Stephen Crane—1980." *William Carlos Williams, Stephen Crane, Philip Freneau: Papers Celebrating New Jersey's Literary Heritage.* W. John Bauer, ed., Trenton: New Jersey Historical Commission, 1989. 107–9. A poem about Crane and his poetry.

7.36 HASLEY, LOUIS. "On Reading Verses by Stephen Crane." *Prairie Schooner* 41 (1967): 409. A poem about Crane's poems.

7.37 HOFFMAN, FREDERICK J. "The War and the Postwar Temper." *The Twenties: American Writing in the Postwar Decade.* New York: Free Press, 1962. 75–76. Crane's treatment of war (*War Is Kind* is especially emphasized) is found to anticipate themes and details in the twenties generation of American writers.

7.38 HOWELLS, WILLIAM DEAN. "Editor's Easy Chair." *Harper's Magazine* 131 (Sept. 1915): 634. Passing comments on *The Black Riders* to the effect that Crane's verses are "shredded prose."

7.39 HUBBARD, ELBERT. "As to the Man, Stephen Crane." *Roycroft Quarterly* 1 (1896): 16–26. A reprinting of part of the program for the testimonial dinner given in Crane's honor by Hubbard and the Philistine Society in Buffalo on 19 December 1895. Hubbard concentrates on Crane's poetry, "the 'lines' in *The Black Riders* seem to me very wonderful; charged with meaning like a storage battery." See *The Critical Heritage,* 2.17: #23 for a reprinting of Hubbard's remarks.

7.40 _____. [Editor's Note on Stephen Crane]. *Philistine* 6.3 (Feb. 1898): 1. Hubbard writes, "Arrangements have been made with Stephen Crane (there is only one) to supply 'Lines' for the back [cover] of every *Philistine* for a decade. Stevie has sent me enuff of the choice stuff to last several lifetimes."

7.41 _____. [Editorial note]. *Fra* 6 (July 1910): xxv. Hubbard comments on Crane's poem, "What? You define me God with these trinkets?" and prints the second stanza of the fourth poem in *War Is Kind* (#72 in Volume 10, Virginia critical edition): "A little ink more or less."

7.42 HUNTER, IRENE, ed. *American Mystical Verse: An Anthology.* New York: Appleton, 1925. 133–34. Hunter reprints "In the Night," (#86 in Volume 10 of the Virginia critical edition).

7.43 ITABASHI, YOSHIE. "The Modern Pilgrimage of *The Black Riders:* An Interpretation." *Tsuda Review* 12 (1967): 1–41. A detailed exegetical exposition of *The Black Riders.* Itabashi treats Crane's first book of poems as if it were a long expository essay that examines religion in the post-Darwinian era.

7.44 JOHNSON, CLARENCE O. "Crane's 'I Was in the Darkness.'" *Explicator* 34 (1975): Item 6. Johnson explicates the obvious: Crane's poetry, particularly this poem, is best understood as a rejection of his parents' religion.

7.45 KATZ, JOSEPH. "Cora Crane and the Poetry of Stephen Crane." *Papers of the Bibliographical Society of America* 58 (1964): 469–76. Cora transcribed some of Crane's poems. Noting this, Katz gives a thorough list of her mortal (and venial) sins of omission and commission (such matters as stanza breaks, line breaks, and the like). Despite all of this Katz concludes that "Cora's copies are fairly dependable transcriptions."

7.46 ———. Introduction. *The Poems of Stephen Crane: A Critical Edition.* New York: Cooper Square, 1966. xvii–li. Katz's lengthy essay provides biographical and publishing details on Crane's books of poetry. In a section on themes Katz stresses Crane's explorations of the absurdity of life and his depictions of love crushed by sham. The critical reception afforded Crane's "lines" is also treated.

7.47 ———. "'The Blue Battalions' and the Uses of Experience." *Studia Neophilologia* 38 (1966): 107–16. A close examination of the holograph of this middle poem of Crane, which, Katz suggests, "offers a unique glimpse into Crane's workshop."

7.48 ———. "A 'New' Stephen Crane Poem: An Evaluation." *Notes and Queries* 13 (1966): 346–49. Katz objects to Richard Peck's contention ("A 'New' Stephen Crane Poem," *Notes and Queries* 12 [1965]: 64–66) that "A Prologue" belongs in the canon of Crane's poetry. Apparently Katz was persuasive. "A Prologue" appears in the Virginia edition in vol. 8, *Tales, Sketches and Reports.* On this point see also Peck (7.71).

7.49 ———. "Stephen Crane and 'Holland.'" *Stephen Crane Newsletter* 1.4 (1967): 2. "Holland" (Elisha Jay Edwards) wrote a newspaper story about Barry reading Crane's poems before the Uncut Leaves Society.

7.50 ———. "Whitman, Crane, and the Odious Comparison." *Notes and Queries* 14 (1967): 66–67. Katz reprints and makes brief remarks on an early review of *The Black Rider* that alleges Whitman's influence on Crane's poetry.

7.51   _____. "The 'Preceptor' and Another Poet: Thomas Wentworth Higginson and Stephen Crane." *Serif* 5 (1968): 17–21. A biographical sketch of a literary critic for the *Nation* and his opinion of Crane's poetry.

7.52   _____. "Stephen Crane in *The Fly Leaf.*" *Stephen Crane Newsletter* 4.3 (1970): 3–4. Crane got caught in the middle of a squabble between Elbert Hubbard and Walter Harte, so while Hubbard published his poetry, Harte ridiculed it.

7.53   _____. Introduction. *A Concordance of the Poems of Stephen Crane.* Ed. Joseph Katz. Boston: G. K. Hall, 1974. xiii–xv. Katz's brief introduction stresses the modernity of Crane's poetry. Note: This concordance (by Herman Baron) is keyed to Katz's *The Poems of Stephen Crane* (7.7); more useful because it is keyed to the Virginia edition is Crosland's *A Concordance to the Complete Poetry of Stephen Crane* (7.3).

7.54   KAY, ULYSSES. *Stephen Crane Set for Mixed Chorus and Thirteen Players.* New York: Dutchess Music, 1972. 54. Several of Crane's poems from *The Black Riders* and *War Is Kind* have been set to music.

7.55   KINDILIEN, CARLIN T. *American Poetry in the Eighteen Nineties.* Providence, RI: Brown UP, 1956. Passim. Crane's poetry is given a very sympathetic reading by Kindilien. Most attention and space (155–67) are given to *The Black Riders:* The wrong in the world is not due to "sinful man" but to a careless God.

7.56   _____. "Stephen Crane and the 'Savage Philosophy' of Olive Schreiner." *Boston University Studies in English* 3 (1957): 97–107. Kindilien pursues Hamlin Garland's suggestion (in *Roadside Meetings*, 1.99) that the inspiration for *War Is Kind* was allegories in the works of Schreiner. Kindilien's source is possible but so too are a half-dozen others.

7.57   KREYMBORG, ALFRED. "The Respectable Democracy." *Our Singing Strength: An Outline of American Poetry, 1630–1930.* New York: Coward-McCann, 1929. 231–52. Crane's poetry is quickly dismissed, as it lacks the intensity of *Red Badge* and his better short stories.

7.58   LOWELL, AMY. Introduction. *"The Black Riders" and Other Lines.*
       The Work of Stephen Crane, vol. 6. Ed. Wilson Follett. New York:
       Knopf, 1926. ix–xxix. Longer than the other introductions in the
       Knopf edition, Lowell's essay is a valuable examination of Crane's
       poetry, especially his treatment of religious themes.

7.59   LUCCOCK, HALFORD E. "War Literature." *Contemporary American
       Literature and Religion.* Chicago: Willett, Clark, 1934. 190–91.
       Luccock uses "Do not weep, maiden, for war is kind" to introduce a
       discussion of the sort of cynicism that was prevalent from the end of
       the Civil War until the turn of the century.

7.60   LUDEKE, HENRY. "Stephen Crane's Poetry." *The 'Democracy of Henry
       Adams' and Other Essays.* Bern: Verlag A. Francke, 1950. 111–22.
       Very general and sketchy; Ludeke examines Crane's poetry to deter-
       mine whether he was a philosophical atheist or not. Ludeke cannot
       decide.

7.61   MARCUS, MORDECAI. "Structure and Irony in Stephen Crane's 'War
       is Kind.'" *College Language Association Journal* 9 (1966): 274–78.
       Marcus sees in this poem support for the contention that Crane's
       outlook changed from that of a "despairing determinist [to that of] an
       affirming humanist."

7.62   MCCORMICK, EDGAR L. "Thomas Wentworth Higginson, Poetry
       Critic for the *Nation,* 1877–1903." *Serif* 2 (1965): 15–20. Crane's
       poetry did not appeal to Higginson: Though it was original, it (and
       Crane) lacked discipline.

7.63   MCDONALD, GERALD D. Introduction. *Poems of Stephen Crane.* Ed.
       Gerald D. McDonald. New York: Crowell, 1964. vii–xvi. A flashback
       to the sixties: Crane as James Dean and selection of Crane poems that
       speak to "the youth of today. . . . He was an angry young man, in
       rebellion against easy respectability and the genteel tradition."

7.64   MILLER, EVELYN E. "A Trilogy of Irony." *English Journal* 59 (1970):
       59–62. Crane's *War Is Kind* along with Hemingway's short story
       "Old Man at the Bridge" and Robert Sherwood's drama *Idiots's
       Delight* uses irony to achieve powerful treatments of war.

7.65   MILLER, RUTH. "Regions of Snow: The Poetic Style of Stephen
       Crane." *Bulletin of the New York Public Library* 72 (1968): 328–49.
       An essential essay on appreciating Crane's poetry. Miller explicates
       Crane's use of dramatic conflicts, encounters, objects, and colors in his
       poetic search for truth and his attempts to capture the nature of God.

7.66   MONROE, HARIETT. "Stephen Crane." *Poetry* 14 (1919): 148–52. An early estimate of Crane's poetry: He was better with prose because his poetry was sentimental and he had a tendency to orate.

7.67   MONTEIRO, GEORGE. "Crane's 'A Man Adrift on a Small Spar'" *Explicator* 32 (1973): Item 14. Monteiro argues that the "a doomed assassin's cap" phrase in this most famous of Crane uncollected poems refers to a hood that covered the condemned man at his execution.

7.68   MOORE, JANE M. "Fear in the Poetry of Stephen Crane." *Indiana English Journal* 7 (1973): 53–60. Moore finds in Crane's poetry three kinds of fear: of a revengeful God, of primitive spirits, and of an indifferent God.

7.69   NELSON, HARLAND S. "Stephen Crane's Achievement as a Poet." *Texas Studies in Language and Literature* 4 (1963): 564–82. Nelson disagrees with Hoffman (*The Poetry of Stephen Crane,* 7.3) that Crane's most complex poetry is most like modern poetry and therefore is his best. Nelson argues that those poems that are simplest and most consonant with Crane's positive view of human life are his finest. Several specific poems are examined.

7.70   O'DONNELL, THOMAS F. "A Note on the Reception of Crane's *The Black Riders.*" *American Literature* 24 (1952): 233–35. O'Donnell shows that, contrary to the popular view that *The Black Riders* was panned by the critics, several top-quality magazines published favorable reviews.

7.71   PECK, RICHARD E. "A "New" Stephen Crane Poem." *Notes and Queries* 12 (1965): 64–65. Peck argues that "A Prologue," which appeared in Hubbard's *Roycroft Quarterly* along with other items concerned with the testimonial dinner he gave for Crane ought to be counted as a Crane poem. The Virginia editors disagree—"A Prologue" appears in "Tales and Sketches" in volume 8. See also Katz (7.48).

7.72   ———. "Stephen Crane and Baudelaire: A Direct Link." *American Literature* 37 (1965): 202–4. Peck argues that there is direct influence of Charles Baudelaire's "The Buffoon and the Venus" on some of Crane's *Black Rider* poems.

7.73   PULOS, C. E. "The New Critics and the Language of Poetry." *University of Nebraska Studies* 19 (1958): 10–13. Crane is mentioned as a breakthrough figure.

7.74   QUARTERMAIN, PETER. "Stephen Crane." *American Poets, 1880–1945. Dictionary of Literary Biography,* vol 54. Detroit: Gale Research, 1987. 48–57. A general sketch, quoting standard sources and using early reviews. Quartermain concludes that Crane's poetry is startling but "generally unsatisfactory." Reproductions of several handwritten drafts are included.

7.75   SANDBURG, CARL. "Letters to Dead Imagists . . . Stevie Crane." *Chicago Poems.* New York: Holt, 1916. 176. A verse tribute to Crane, *The Black Riders* and *War Is Kind.*

7.76   ———. *The Letters of Carl Sandburg.* Ed. Herbert Mitgang. New York: Harcourt, Brace 1968. 92. A 1915 letter from Sandburg to Harriet Monroe (founder of *Poetry* magazine) stating, "I am finding the quickest way to convince them that free verse is worth while is to show them that Stevie Crane and other crack newspapermen did some terribly serious work in libertarian rhythms."

7.77   SHAY, FELIX. *Elbert Hubbard of East Aurora.* New York: William H. Wise, 1926. 553. Shay edited (with Hubbard) *The Philistine* and *The Fra.* Shay briefly describes Crane's visit to East Aurora and comments that Crane's poetry is best suited for epitaphs.

7.78   SHIMA, HIDEO. "Nature Love, and Solitude in Stephen Crane's Poems." *Collected Essays by Members of the Faculty* (Kyorita, Japan) 13 (1969): 82–102. According to the English summary this is a competent general essay on general themes in Crane's poetry but the article itself is in Japanese so I cannot confirm that assessment.

7.79   SINCLAIR, UPTON, ed. *The Cry for Justice: An Anthology of the Literature of Social Protest.* San Francisco: Upton Sinclair, 1925. Long titles often need even longer subtitles: In this case, "The Writing of Philosophers, Poets, Novelists, Social Reformers, and Others Who Have Voiced the Struggle against Social Injustice: Selected from Twenty-Five Languages Covering a Period of Five Thousand Years." Given that range Crane did well. A section from "Death and the Child" and "Have You Ever Made a Just Man?" were selected by Sinclair.

7.80   STALLMAN, ROBERT W. "'A Soldier Young in Years.'" *Fine Arts Magazine,* np. 1964. Reproduces the holograph of Crane's poem in an undergraduate journal published at the University of Connecticut.

7.81   SUTTON, WALTER. "The Modernity of Stephen Crane's Poetry: A Centennial Tribute." *Courier* 7 (1971): 3–7. Sutton sees modern thematics in Crane's poetry: a sense of the void and a meaningless universe that encourages irony but does not justify cynicism.

7.82 TANSELLE, G. THOMAS. "Addenda to Stallman's *Crane:* Thomas Wood Stevens." *Papers of the Bibliographical Society of America* 70 (1976): 416–19. Tanselle adds to Stallman's list of contemporary reviews and other reactions to Crane's poetry.

7.83 TAYLOR, JOHN CHESLEY. "In Search of Light: Three Poems for Stephen Crane." *Stephen Crane: An Appreciation.* Ed. Christopher Farlekas. Port Jervis, NY: Colonial School and Camp, 1962. 8–9. For his part of the memorial celebration for Crane, Taylor explicates themes from some of Crane's better-known *Black Rider* poems.

7.84 UNTERMEYER, LOUIS. "Stephen Crane." *Makers of the Modern World.* New York: Simon and Schuster, 1955. 444–49. A typical sketch of Crane and his works; memorable only for the comment that his poems present arguments that are usually "clenched."

7.85 VANOUSE, DONALD. "Hobby-Horses, Horseplay and Stephen Crane's *Black Riders.*" *Courier* 13.3 (1976): 28–31. Vanouse comments on the illustrations that accompanied Crane's poems on the cover of the *Roycroft Quarterly* arguing that the black riders on polka dot hobbyhorses "epitomize [both] the mock and respect in the Roycrofter response to Crane's works." For the full story on Crane, Hubbard, and the Roycrofters see White (1.222).

7.86 ———. "Women in the Writings of Stephen Crane: Madonnas of the Decadence." *Southern Humanities Review* 12 (1978): 141–48. Crane's personal and professional fascination with fallen women is especially evident, Vanouse argues, in his poetry.

7.87 ———. "Schoberlin's Annotated Copy of *War Is Kind.*" *Courier* 21 (1986): 89–102. Vanouse interprets the annotations in Crane's copy of *War Is Kind.* His view is that either Crane or Cora made marginal comments linking the "Intrigue" poems to Nellie Crouse.

7.88 WAGGONER, HYATT H. "Stephen Crane." *American Poets from the Puritans to the Present.* Boston: Houghton Mifflin, 1968. 240–49. An excellent general essay on Crane's poetry stressing that "argument" is primary for Crane and poetic considerations are very secondary. "The line division seems dictated primarily by the movement of the thought, so much indeed that if the poem were printed as prose it would probably not be suspected that it was intended as stripped-down verse." Further, Waggoner argues that the subject matter for

Crane's poetic argumentation is philosophical. More precisely Crane's themes are theological—the problem of evil and man's relationships to a supreme being. See Dooley (2.5) on this point.

7.89   WAGNER, LINDA W. "Berryman: From the Beginning." *American Modern: Essays in Fiction and Poetry*. Port Washington, NY: Kennikat Press, 1980. 158–64. Berryman's immersion in Crane to write his book (*Stephen Crane,* 1.2) had a lasting influence on his own poetry. For anyone interested in more on the transfer of his Crane study to Berryman's poetry, see J. D. McClatchy, "John Berryman: The Impediments to Salvation." *Modern Poetry Studies* 4 (1975): 246–77.

7.90   WALTON, EDA LOU. "Stephen Crane, A Poet in Parables." *New York Times Book Review* 14 Sept. 1930, 4.2. Crane's poetry reflects biblical influences, especially parables as a motif.

7.91   WEATHERFORD, RICHARD M. "Stephen Crane in *The Lotus* and *Chips.*" *Stephen Crane Newsletter* 4.3 (1970): 2–3. Weatherford tracked down comments, reviews, and, of special interest, parodies of his poetry in these two late nineteenth-century satiric magazines.

7.92   ———. "A Manuscript of 'Black Riders Came from the Sea.'" *Stephen Crane Newsletter* 4.4 (1970): 3–4. Comments and a facsimile reproduction of Crane's beautiful handwriting.

7.93   WEGELIN, CHRISTOF. "Crane's 'Man Said to the Universe.'" *Explicator* 20 (1961): Item 9. Crane's "inveterate humanism."

7.94   WEST, JERRY, LARRY KRUPKA, and ERIC LUNDE. "Three Poems + Three Professors = Third Culture?" *University College Review* 23 (1977): 13–23. A freshman-level discussion by three nonliterary specialists; *Black Riders* (#33), "Many workmen . . ." is the focus.

7.95   WESTBROOK, MAX. "Stephen Crane's Poetry: Perspective and Arrogance." *Bucknell Review* 11 (1963): 24–34. An indispensable article on Crane's poetry. Thesis: A proper appreciation of Crane's "lines" requires that we notice two voices: the voice of perspective with messages of humanism and modesty (the New Testament God) and the voice of arrogance with messages of dogma and certitude (the Old Testament God).

7.96   WILLIAMS, OSCAR. Introduction. *A Little Treasury of American Poetry*. New York: Scribner's, 1948. xv–xxxvi. A general essay on American poetry grouping Crane with Dickinson and Whitman. In the volume itself, ten of Crane's poems are reprinted (273–277).

7.97 WILSON, EDMUND. "Poetry of the War." *Patriotic Gore: Studies in the Literature of the American Civil War.* New York: Oxford UP, 1962. 500–501 and passim. Though of course Wilson mentions *Red Badge,* interestingly, his most sustained comments are devoted to "the two volumes of extremely unconventional verse [*War Is Kind* and *Black Riders* with] their nihilistic fables and their laconic irony."

On Crane poetry see also:

1.1–1.4	2.94
1.10	2.100
1.34	2.172
1.97	2.174
1.195	2.178
2.2–2.6	5.92
2.8	9.14
2.9	11.13
2.13–2.17	

8

Tales of Whilomville

Overview

Crane's Whilomville tales are a mixed bag. Levenson's introduction (8.38) is the best general essay on them. Though placed with the other tales, *The Monster* is a novel (while the rest are short stories) that contains a serious and substantial examination of prejudice, mores, morality, and heroism. The following analyses of *The Monster* are important:

Church 8.4
DOOLEY 2.5
Gullason 8.8
MAYER 8.14
Mitchell 8.15
Morace 8.17
Warner 8.26
WERTHEIM 8.27
Westbrook 8.28

The other Whilomville tales are light, humorous short stories. Except for two articles by Monteiro (8.41 and 8.42) they have received little critical attention.

Books

8.1   BOWERS, FREDSON, ed. *Tales of Whilomville. The Works of Stephen Crane,* vol. 7. Ed. Fredson Bowers. Charlottesville: UP of Virginia,

1969. xl+277. Bowers's critical editions of *The Monster* and other Whilomville tales. See 8.31 for an annotation on three separate textual introductions by Bowers as well as Levenson's general introduction in 8.38.

8.2   FOLLETT, WILSON, ed. *Whilomville Stories. The Work of Stephen Crane,* vol 5. Ed. Wilson Follett. New York: Knopf, 1926. xiii+207. Follett's collection of Crane's tales of small town life. See 8.43 for the introduction by Phelps.

THE MONSTER

8.3   ANDERSON, MARGARET. "A Note on 'John Twelve' in Stephen Crane's *The Monster.*" *American Notes and Queries* 14 (1976): 23–24. Religious symbolism in *The Monster:* The grocer, John Twelve, is a reference to John 12:9–11, which contains Lazarus's being brought back from the tomb.

8.4   CHURCH, JOSEPH. "The Black Man's Part in Crane's *Monster.*" *American Imago* 45 (1989): 375–88. A Freudian, Oedipal interpretation of *The Monster* that contends that Crane was, after all, racially unenlightened. Church believes that in "his interest in the problem of masculine individualism" Crane was conducting an argument against America's decadence.

8.5   COOLEY, JOHN. "'The Monster'—Stephen Crane's 'Invisible Man.'" *Markham Review* 5 (1975): 10–14. Cooley's anachronistic thesis imports twentieth-century racial sensitivity to condemn harshly late nineteenth-century sensibilities. He concludes that *The Monster* is "a significant failure" and that Crane's "artistic maladroitness or loss of nerve" is due to a "sadly limited racial consciousness."

8.6   _____. "The Savages: Stephen Crane." *Savages and Naturals: Black Portraits by White Writers in Modern American Literature.* Newark: U of Delaware P, 1982. 38–49. A slightly expanded treatment of the thesis and conclusion Cooley offered in 1975 (8.5). Crane is one of eight writers treated. Cooley's analysis of *The Monster* holds that while the first half contains a good examination of Henry Johnson's heroism, when Crane turns his attention to Dr. Trescott in the second half, Johnson and the other blacks are reduced to stereotypes.

8.7   FOSTER, MALCOLM. "The Black Crepe Veil: The Significance of Stephen Crane's *The Monster.*" *International Fiction Review* 3 (1976):

87–91. A strained and unconvincing thesis depicting Trescott as a villain—a "weak-willed and compromising meliorist"—who makes false and empty promises to Johnson and who caves in to his wife's wishes.

8.8   GULLASON, THOMAS A. "The Symbolic Unity of 'The Monster.'" *Modern Language Notes* 75 (1960): 663–68. Gullason argues that seen as a classic tragedy, with the townspeople serving as a Greek chorus, *The Monster* amounts to an indictment of Whilomville. While this interpretation can be sustained, Gullason overdoes, seeing Alex Williams's request for more money to board Henry Johnson as "monstrous hypocrisy."

8.9   HAFLEY, JAMES. "'The Monster' and the Art of Stephen Crane." *Accent* 19 (1959): 159–65. Hafley uses the motif of "face saving" to examine appearance and reality, including tensions between the individual morality of Trescott and the "social" ethic of the citizens of Whilomville.

8.10 HARTER, PENNY. "For The Monster." *William Carlos Williams, Stephen Crane, Philip Freneau: Papers Celebrating New Jersey's Literary Heritage*. Ed. W. John Bauer. Trenton: New Jersey Historical Commission, 1989. 111–12. A poem on *The Monster*.

8.11 HILFER, ANTHONY CHANNELL. "From Eggleston to Frederic." *The Revolt from the Village, 1915–1930*. Chapel Hill: U of North Carolina P, 1969. 35–63. Hilfer examines various attacks by American novelists on "the mellow serenity [of] the myth of the small town." Crane's *The Monster* is briefly discussed as a study in the courage and decency of Dr. Trescott in the face of a town that had become "the monster."

8.12 KAHN, SY. "Stephen Crane and the Giant Voice of the Night: An Explication of 'The Monster.'" *Essays in Modern American Literature*. Ed. Richard Langford. DeLand, FL: Stetson UP, 1963. 35–45. A beginner's explication: a routine outline of Crane's life and career and the usual examination of *The Monster* as a critique of norms of respectability. Kahn sees Trescott as an autobiographical sketch of Crane: each was "at war with the misjudging mob, with philistines and with ruthless conventions." Reprinted in *Stetson Studies in the Humanities* 1 (1963): 35–45.

8.13 LOCKE, ALAIN. "The Negro in America." *New World Writing*. New York: NAL, 1952. 18–33. Brief mention (28) of Crane's treatment of blacks in *The Monster*.

8.14 MAYER, CHARLES W. "Social Forms VS. Human Brotherhood in Crane's *The Monster." Ball State University Forum* 14.3 (1973): 29–37. A competent, helpful examination of *The Monster* arguing that human brotherhood is arrived at by learning that men are dependent on one another and that we must resist "comfortable roles and forms" in order to understand our mutual dependence.

8.15 MITCHELL, LEE CLARK. "Face, Race and Disfiguration in Stephen Crane's *The Monster." Critical Inquiry* 17 (1990): 174–92. Mitchell offers helpful and challenging discussions of defacement, disfiguration, and race in *The Monster.* "The question posed by *The Monster* is rather more pointed than simply: What does it mean to be black? It might instead take the form: What does it mean to be defaced, deformed or otherwise disfigured?" Mitchell argues that, as a black, Johnson "has always been slightly faceless and voiceless," so Crane's novella, in effect, explores (in the extreme) depersonalization and racism in late nineteenth-century American society.

8.16 MODLIN, CHARLES E., and JOHN R. BYERS, JR. "Stephen Crane's 'The Monster' as Christian Allegory." *Markham Review* 3 (1973): 110–13. Thesis: Crane's *The Monster* is a retelling of the Gospel according to John. So far so good, but their religious reading gets the better of the authors: "Thus 'The Monster' becomes not only Crane's commentary on the state of Christendom but also his assessment of the lost condition of man."

8.17 MORACE, ROBERT A. "Games, Play, and Entertainments in Stephen Crane's 'The Monster.' " *Studies in American Fiction* 9 (1981): 65–81. Morace gives composition and publication details about *The Monster* and then turns to a detailed and fruitful examination of the many sorts of intertwining games played in Whilomville by Trescott and the townspeople, both white and black.

8.18 NETTELS, ELSA. " 'Amy Foster' and Stephen Crane's 'The Monster.' " *Conradiana* 15 (1983): 181–90. Both stories deal with "the effect upon people of a small town in the presence of an outcast."

8.19 OSBORN, NEAL. "Crane's *The Monster* and 'The Blue Hotel.' " *Explicator* 23 (1964): Item 10. Wordplay (mostly with characters' names) in these Crane stories.

8.20 PETRY, ALICE HALL. "Stephen Crane's Elephant Man." *Journal of Modern Literature* 10 (1983): 346–52. Source-hunting: Crane's *The Monster* is linked to the elephant man, Merrick, who lived in England in the 1890s.

8.21 PIZER, DONALD. "Stephen Crane's 'The Monster' and Tolstoy's *What to Do?: A Neglected Allusion.*" *Studies in Short Fiction* 20 (1983): 127–29. Pizer traces the comment by Dr. Trescott, "What am I to do for him," to the title of Tolstoy's polemic on Christian duties.

8.22 SPOFFORD, WILLIAM K. "CRANE'S *The Monster.*" *Explicator* 36 (1977): 5–7. Spofford disputes Solomon's contention (in 2.15) that Crane wants his readers to think Judge Hagenthorpe is right in believing that Trescott's saving Henry was a "questionable charity." Spofford's case turns on the word "oratory," which Crane used to describe the judge's speech; whenever Crane uses this word (Spofford has located more than fifty-five instances) it connotes insincerity and fraudulent speech.

8.23 STARKE, CATHERINE JUANITA. "Alter-Ego Symbols." *Black Portraiture in American Fiction.* New York: Basic Books, 1971. 155–66. Starke argues that in *The Monster* Crane indicts Whilomville, with Henry Johnson serving as a sounding board for criticisms of small-town life.

8.24 TENENBAUM, RUTH BETSY. "The Artful Monstrosity of Crane's *The Monster.*" *Studies in Short Fiction* 14 (1977): 403–5. Crane shows Whilomville's cruelty by his use of animal images and his depiction of men as machines.

8.25 WAGENKNECHT, EDWARD. "Stephen Crane, Harbinger." *Cavalcade of the American Novel.* New York: Holt, Rinehart, 1952. 212–16. A broad survey; of special note is Wagenknecht's interest in *The Monster,* noting Trescott's "unwise gratitude" and Henry's "presence in the little town to test the decency and humanity of its inhabitants."

8.26 WARNER, MICHAEL. "Value, Agency and Stephen Crane's 'The Monster.'" *Nineteenth-Century Fiction* 40 (1985): 76–93. A complex examination of morality and heroism in *The Monster.* While thought-provoking, terminological static and Warner's confusion over the relationship of intentions and consequences in an ethical act muddy the waters.

8.27 WERTHEIM, STANLEY. "Stephen Crane's *The Monster* as Fiction and Film." *William Carlos Williams, Stephen Crane, Philip Freneau: Papers Celebrating New Jersey's Literary Heritage.* W. John Bauer, ed., Trenton: New Jersey Historical Commission, 1989. 97–105. An important article on *The Monster.* Wertheim argues that the film version *Face of Fire* (with Louis Garfinkle as screenwriter and Albert Bond as director) correctly focuses upon "the destruction of a man by prejudice"—not racial prejudice as Church (8.4), Cooley (8.5), Mayer (8.14), and others have proposed, but a destruction caused by "the inability of society to transcend convention." Thus Wertheim claims: "The basic theme of *The Monster,* which is also central to *Face of Fire,* has only the most tangential relationship to the question of race. It is rather the futility of any attempt to reconcile ethical values and social norms in the moral facelessness of the Whilomvilles of this country, and the idyllic setting of the American small town."

8.28   WESTBROOK, MAX. "Whilomville: The Coherence of Radical Language." *Stephen Crane in Transition: Centenary Review.* Ed. Joseph Katz. De Kalb: Southern Illinois UP, 1972. 86–105. An interesting discussion of *The Monster* emphasizing Trescott's "consistent moral courage." Other Whilomville tales are examined in light of honesty of will in a world that is even richer than the experience of observers and the observed.

8.29   WYATT, EDITH. "Stephen Crane." *New Republic* 4 (11 Sept. 1915): 148–50. A brief but perceptive essay, notable also for its early date. Wyatt seeks a readership beyond *Red Badge,* calling attention to *The Monster* and both *War Is Kind* and *Black Riders.* Reprinted in *Great Companions* (New York: Appleton, 1917): 31–40.

See also on *The Monster:*

1.1–1.4	3.54
1.10	4.59
1.20	6.13
1.86	8.33
2.1–2.19	8.34
2.35	8.36
2.83	10.5
2.193	10.20
2.215	10.100

OTHER TALES

8.30   BEFFEL, JOHN N. "The Fauntleroy Plague." *Bookman* 65 (March 1927): 135–141. Beffel states that Crane once gave two boys money to get their Fauntleroy haircuts trimmed. If Beffel is to be believed, "The Angel Child" is based on Crane's "generosity," for he goes on to report that while the two boys' mothers wept hysterically, one of the fathers "sent Crane an anonymous box of cigars with a card inscribed, 'From a grateful public.' "

8.31   BOWERS, FREDSON. Textual Introduction[s]. *Tales of Whilomville. The Works of Stephen Crane,* vol. 7. Ed. Fredson Bowers. Charlottesville: UP of Virginia, 1969. 3–6, 75–79, 103–26. Bowers discusses separately the texts of *The Monster* and "His New Mittens" before he takes up, as a group, the textual problems involved in the rest of the Whilomville Tales.

8.32   BROWN, ELLEN A. "Stephen Crane's *Whilomville Stories:* A Backward Glance." *Markham Review* 3 (1972): 105–9. A broad-stroke exagge-rated reading of these stories: a dark, Darwinian tooth-and-nail depiction of the savage power struggles of children that ignores Crane's humor and irony.

8.33   BROWN, ELLEN A., and PATRICIA HERNLUND. "The Source for the Title of Stephen Crane's *Whilomville Stories." American Literature* 50 (1978): 116–18. Whilom means "once upon a time" and it comes from a Peck ancestor's (relatives on his mother's side) talk of a "Whilom drum corps."

8.34   FICKEN, CARL. "Jimmie Trescott's Age." *Stephen Crane Newsletter* 5.1 (1970): 2–3. The answers: about four in *The Monster* and about eight in the other Whilomville stories.

8.35   HERRON, IMA. *The Small Town in American Literature.* Durham, NC: Duke UP, 1939. Passim. Heron's large book surveys all. Crane is treated in three pages (184–86): The *Whilomville Tales* are "sympa-thetic and realistic studies of child life" and *The Monster* is a study in "provincial stupidity."

8.36   ITABASHI, YOSHIE. "A Landscape of Complexity: A Study of *Whilomville Stories." Tsuda Review* 15 (Nov. 1970): 37–70. Lengthy study of general themes in Crane's *Whilomville Stories.*

8.37   KAZIN, ALFRED. "A Procession of Children." *The American Scholar* 33 (1964): 171–83. Kazin criticizes Crane's *Whilomville Tales* as romantic and uneventful.

8.38   LEVENSON, J. C. "Introduction." *Tales of Whilomville. The Works of Stephen Crane,* vol. 7. Ed. Fredson Bowers. Charlottesville: UP of Virginia, 1969. ix–lx. Levenson describes Crane's emotional center of

Port Jervis as the inspiration of these tales of growing up in a small town. He argues that Crane's unique realism is not a "direct rendering of an observed object" but a faithful vicarious experience of another's world. Whilomville as Crane presents it is at once so well ordered that a haircut is a disaster in "The Angel Child" and in *The Monster* the loci of exclusion and alienation brought on by an "imprudent commitment and its consequences."

8.39   LOGAN, ANNIE R. M. [Review of *Whilomville Tales*]. *Nation* 72 (1901): 182. Logan misses the humor and irony in Crane's tales and accuses him of destroying the innocence of children. Reprinted in Weatherford's *A Critical Heritage* 2.17: #122)

8.40   MARTIN, JOHN C. "Childhood in Stephen Crane's *Maggie,* 'The Monster,' and *Whilomville Stories.*" *Midwestern University Quarterly* 2 (1967): 40–46. Martin manages to miss Crane's ironic exaggerations so he too concludes that, for Crane, children are vicious, malicious, and cruel.

8.41   MONTEIRO, GEORGE. "Whilomville as Judah: Crane's 'Little Pilgrimage.'" *Renascence* 19 (1967): 184–89. Monteiro attempts to get a better reception for one of the Whilomville tales, "A Little Pilgrim."

8.42   ———. "With Proper Words (Or without Them) the Soldier Dies: Stephen Crane's 'Making an Orator.'" *Cithera* 9 (1970): 64–72. A full-scale analysis of one of Crane's lesser Whilomville tales, which concerns the childhood agony of memorizing Tennyson's "The Charge of the Light Brigade."

8.43   PHELPS, WILLIAM LYON. "Introduction. *Whilomville Stories. The Work of Stephen Crane,* vol 5. Ed. Wilson Follett. New York: Knopf, 1926. ix–xiii. A brief essay stressing Crane's ability to a capture the world of children.

8.44   SOJKA, GREGORY S. "Stephen Crane's 'A Young Pilgrim': Whilomville's Young Martyr." *Notes on Modern American Literature* 3 (1977): Item 3. A brief, overserious note contending that Crane's Whilomville stories, first to last, deal with "young Jimmie Trescott, the little pilgrim, who is victimized by adult Whilomville dishonesty." Sojka has managed, as have several others, to miss Crane's ironic, light tone.

8.45   WOOLLCOTT, ALEXANDER. "Stephen Crane's 'Whilomville Stories.'" *Saturday Review* 16 (1937): 14. Celebrates Crane's *Whilomville*

Tales as a tool to evoke nostalgia. He notes that when Crane's tales were first published they were framed with cartoons so readers would be sure to catch Crane's irony. Reprinted as "An Afterword on 'Whilomville Tales' " in *Woollcott's Second Reader*, New York: Viking, 1937, 965–67.

9

Journalism, Tales, and Reports

Overview

Items annotated in this section span nearly the whole of Crane's writing career from his first Asbury Park newspaper dispatches to his Graeco-Turkish War reports. Several subcategories have been used.

ASBURY PARK SKETCHES. The importance of Crane's early journalism, Elconin (9.1), Gullason (9.2), and LaFrance (9.3) have convincingly argued, is that the ironic style and outlook characteristic of the best of Crane's mature works are obvious in his very early pieces. Schellhorn (9.6) and WILSON (9.8) have examined an early sketch, "The Pace of Youth."

SULLIVAN COUNTY SKETCHES. The books and introductions by Schoberlin (9.9 and 9.17) and Stallman (9.10 and 9.19) are important. COLVERT'S ARTICLE (9.14) is the best short examination of these early sketches.

OTHER JOURNALISM. Vol. 8 of the Virginia edition, *Tales, Sketches and Reports* (9.22) is a massive catchall of more than 1,200 pages. Levenson's introduction (9.23) and his notes to this volume are indispensable. Crane's newspaper apprenticeship did much to shape his personality, style, and outlook; see:

Gullason 9.27
KWIAT 9.33–9.35
Weinstein 9.41

THE LITTLE REGIMENT. Vol. 9 of the Virginia edition, *Reports of War* (9.44), is the important item here; COLVERT's Introduction (9.51) is excellent. Nearly all the articles on individual stories are well done; see especially:

NAGEL 9.57
Solomon 9.60
Witherington 9.62

SPANISH-AMERICAN WAR TALES AND REPORTS. Several accounts of Crane as a war correspondent, written by his newspaper colleagues, are noteworthy; see Richard Harding Davis, (9.71), Robert Davis (9.74), MARSHALL (9.86), and Paine (9.97). Freidel (9.78) was not one of Crane's fellow correspondents but his book on the Spanish-American war is the best on the topic and his treatment of Crane is informative. GULLASON's article (9.79), *Wounds in the Rain,* is an excellent general treatment of these war writings by Crane. "The Clan of No-Name" deserves the analysis it gets from NAGEL (9.93) and OSBORN (9.95).

GRAECO-TURKISH WAR REPORTS AND TALES. Not much beyond Bowers's Textual Introduction (9.107) and Colvert's General Introduction (9.108) to the Virginia edition, vol. 9, *Reports of War* (9.44), is important here.

ASBURY PARK TALES

9.1   ELCONIN, VICTOR A. "Stephen Crane at Asbury Park." *American Literature* 20 (1948): 275–89. Elconin argues that the style and themes present in Crane's early Asbury Park newspaper articles stayed with him throughout his life. Elconin's case is solid and convincing; Crane was early and late a social nonconformist. Several Asbury Park sketches are cited for their obvious sardonic attitude toward conventions, their flippant cynicism, and their iconoclastic tone.

9.2   GULLASON, THOMAS A. " 'Four Men in a Cave': A Critical Appraisal." *Readers and Writers.* 1 (Apr.–May 1967): 30–31. Gullason devotes considerable space to an analysis of Crane's first professional appearance (in the New York *Tribune,* 3 July 1892). "Four Men in a Cave" is, he argues "a youthfully slick, theatrical, and superficial anecdote." Still, Gullason sees in this early piece signs of Crane's mature works, especially his "ironic view of man and the universe."

9.3   LaFRANCE, MARSTON. "The Ironic Parallel in Stephen Crane's 1892 Newspaper Correspondence." *Studies in Short Fiction* 6 (1968): 101–3. A brief note to the effect that even Crane's earliest newspaper pieces were ironic in tone.

9.4   PIZER, DONALD. "Crane Reports Garland on Howells." *Modern Language Notes* 70 (1955): 37–39. A reprinting with brief comment of an early Crane newspaper report, "Howells Discussed at Avon-by-the-Sea."

9.5 PROFITT, EDWARD. "The Snake." *Reading and Writing about Short Fiction*. San Diego: Harcourt Brace, 1988. "The Snake" is reprinted along with study and discussion questions.

9.6 SCHELLHORN, G. C. "Stephen Crane's 'The Pace of Youth.'" *Arizona Quarterly* 25 (1969): 334–42. A very sympathetic and illuminating analysis of the most noteworthy of Crane's Asbury park stories. Schellhorn stresses the humor that is very evident in this story.

9.7 WERTHEIM, STANLEY. "Stephen Crane's 'Battalion Notes.'" *Resources for American Literature Study* 6 (1976): 79–80. Notes a Crane contribution to the Claverack *Vidette*.

9.8 WILSON, CHRISTOPHER P. "The Pace of Youth: Stephen Crane's Rhetoric of Amusement." *Journal of American Culture* 6 (1983): 31–38. An interesting essay on Crane's Asbury Park pieces that focuses on fun, carnival rides, and resort pleasures. "The Pace of Youth" is examined at some length with regard to Crane's celebration of amusement and play as a rebellion against his parents' dead seriousness and stress on work.

See also:

1.1–1.4
1.10
1.214
2.1–2.19
12.99

SULLIVAN COUNTY TALES

Books

9.9 SCHOBERLIN, MELVIN, ed. *The Sullivan County Sketches of Stephen Crane*. Syracuse, NY: Syracuse UP, 1949. vii+85. Schoberlin's collecting and editing these Crane sketches was a significant contribution to early Crane scholarship; see 9.17 for his general introduction.

9.10   STALLMAN, ROBERT W., ed. *Stephen Crane: "Sullivan County Tales and Sketches."* Ames: Iowa State UP, 1968. xii+151. Stallman reprints seventeen Sullivan County tales and two fables, most of which had appeared in the New York *Tribune* in 1892; see 9.19 for his introduction.

Articles and Book Chapters

9.11   "Delta U's in the News." *Delta Upsilon Quarterly* October 1930. Notes the discovery of Crane's *Sullivan County Tale,* "The Cry of Huckleberry Pudding."

9.12   ARNOLD, HANS. "Stephen Crane's 'Wyoming Valley Tales': Their Source and Their Place in the Author's War Fiction." *Jahrbuch für Amerikastudien* 4 (1959): 161–69. Contrary to Ahnebrink (2.1), Crane's war motifs had as their source his family's history, not Tolstoy or Zola.

9.13   COAD, ORAL S. "Jersey Gothic." *Proceedings of the New Jersey Historical Society* 84 (1966): 89–112. An essay on the contributions of New Jersey citizens to ghost and gothic tales. Crane is cited for "The Ghostly Spink of Metedeconk" and "The Tale of the Black Dog."

9.14   COLVERT, JAMES B. "Stephen Crane's Magic Mountain." *Stephen Crane: A Collection of Critical Essays.* Ed. Maurice Bassan. Englewood Cliffs, NJ: Prentice-Hall, 1967. 95–105. "Most of the stories in Crane's earliest work, *Sullivan County Sketches, . . .* show its hero in conflict with various natural presences." In "The Mesmeric Mountain," after the little man gains the summit he loses his illusions and finds his way. Colvert then argues that this magic mountain theme obviously relates to *Red Badge* as well as to theological remarks in several *Black Rider* poems.

9.15   KATZ, JOSEPH. "Solving Stephen Crane's Pike County Puzzle." *American Literature* 55 (1983): 171–82. Katz examines the "Pike County Puzzle," the parody of the small-town newspaper that Crane composed as a souvenir of an 1894 camping trip. Katz holds that this camping trip came at a pivotal moment in his career when he experienced the clash of small-town wholesomeness and the evil of big-city slums.

9.16   MAYFIELD, JOHN S. "Stephen Crane's Bugs." *Courier* 4 (1963): 22–31. A treatment of the particulars of Crane's spoof "Great Bugs of

Onondaga" published in the New York *Tribune* while he was its stringer at Syracuse University.

9.17 SCHOBERLIN, MELVIN. Introduction. *The Sullivan County Sketches of Stephen Crane.* Syracuse, NY: Syracuse UP, 1949. 1–20. Schoberlin's introduction covers Crane's themes, especially "the egotism of the little man"; also biographical details surrounding Crane's writing of these tales, including the real-life identity of the central characters: the little man, the pudgy man, the tall man, and the quiet man.

9.18 STALLMAN, ROBERT W. "Stephen Crane and Cooper's Uncas." *American Literature* 39 (1967): 392–96. Crane's Sullivan County tale, "The Last of the Mohicans," as a put-down of Cooper's famous book.

9.19 ———. Introduction. *Stephen Crane: "Sullivan County Tales and Sketches."* Ed. Robert W. Stallman. Ames: Iowa State UP, 1968. 3–24. After Stallman gets through extolling his detective skill in finding these sketches, he offers general background information. More substantial are his observations that the painterly style of these sketches is also found in *Maggie* and *Red Badge,* which were written at almost the same time.

9.20 THIFFAULT, GEORGE F. "Stephen Crane: U Conn Author Sheds New Light on Great Writer." *Hartford Courant* 17 May 1964. An account of Robert Stallman's interviews with three of Crane's boyhood friends. These interviews, Stallman reports, were conducted while "dining with them at the home of David Balch near the Hartwood Club and the Stephen Crane Pond."

9.21 WARSHAVER, GERALD E. "Bushwacked by Reality: The Significance of Stephen Crane's Interest in Rural Folklore." *Journal of the Folklore Institute* 19 (1981): 1–15. After some predictable (and ingratiating) comments about the importance of folklore, Warshaver retells a half-dozen Sullivan County tales for folklorists.

See also on Crane's Sullivan County tales:

1.1–1.4
1.6
1.7
1.10
1.55
1.114

OTHER EARLY JOURNALISM

Book

9.22   BOWERS, FREDSON, ed. *Tales, Sketches, and Reports. The Works of Stephen Crane*, vol. 8. Ed. Fredson Bowers. Charlottesville: UP of Virginia, 1973. xli+1183. A massive volume containing nearly 150 tales, sketches, and news reports plus some three-dozen more "Possible Attributions." See 9.23 for a description of Bowers's indispensable introductory remarks and notes and 9.24 for the annotation on Cady's general introduction.

Articles and Book Chapters

9.23   BOWERS, FREDSON. "The Text: History and Analysis and Appendices." *Tales, Sketches, and Reports. The Works of Stephen Crane*, vol. 8. Ed. Fredson Bowers. Charlottesville: UP of Virginia, 1973. 769–1174. The textual comment, notes, and appendixes in this volume are absolutely essential for anyone who wants to study how Crane the journalist became Crane the storyteller and novelist. Bowers has assembled all the necessary publications information, even tracking down all the newspaper printings of syndicated items. An outstanding scholarly resource.

9.24   CADY, EDWIN H. Introduction. *Tales, Sketches and Reports. The Works of Stephen Crane*, vol. 8. Ed. Fredson Bowers. Charlottesville: UP of Virginia, 1973. xxi–xli. Perhaps Cady was overwhelmed by the task of commenting on 180 pieces. He begins, "There is nothing of Stephen Crane's finest artistic quality in this volume," though he explains that these pieces offer "an opportunity to watch young Crane in his workshop," and he repeats his contention (from his Twayne volume *Stephen Crane*, 1962, rev. ed. 1980, 2.4) that Crane can be best understood as a preacher's kid. Still, Cady's premise is troublesome, for this volume contains outstanding gems, for instance, early pieces —"The Snake," "A Dark-Brown Dog"; middle sketches—"An Experiment in Misery," "Men in the Storm," "In the Depths of a Coal

Mine"; and late works—"London Impressions" and "The Scotch Express."

9.25   CHURCHILL, ALLEN. "The Favored Ones: Stephen Crane and Richard Harding Davis." *Park Row*. New York: Rinehart, 1958. 194–213. An interesting general study of the days of Yellow Journalism. Churchill's scattered comments on Crane frequently contain factual errors (Crane did not travel to Alaska); also, apparently Churchill's research on Crane did not go beyond Beer's *Stephen Crane* (1.1).

9.26   DAVIS, CHARLES BELMONT, ed. *Adventures and Letters of Richard Harding Davis*. New York: Scribner's, 1917. Passim. Crane is mentioned in passing in three letters Davis wrote to his family; also described is Crane's attendance at a fancy luncheon in England.

9.27   GULLASON, THOMAS A. "Stephen Crane's Private War on Yellow Journalism." *Huntington Library Quarterly* 22 (1959): 201–8. Gullason studies a number of Crane's war dispatches concluding that "in his own work, Crane tried to attain his ideal of honest reporting."

9.28   _____. "The 'Lost' Newspaper Writings of Stephen Crane." *Courier* 21 (1986): 57–87. Gullason examines several newspaper articles that Melvin Schoberlin attributes to Crane. He agrees that several are by Crane and relegates the rest to possible Crane attributions.

9.29   _____. "A Stephen Crane Find: Nine Newspaper Sketches." *Southern Humanities Review* 2 (1968): 1–37. Good information on Crane's early newspaper days, his love of the outdoors (which Gullason relates to his Sullivan County sketches), and his interest in American literature and history. He also argues (not as convincingly) that his mature works exhibit the themes, styles, and techniques of these early newspaper pieces.

9.30   HONCE, CHARLES. "Legends of Stephen Crane." *The Public Papers of a Bibliomaniac*. Mount Vernon, VA: Golden Eagle, 1942. 114–25. Honce comments on Crane's actual burial place in Evergreen Cemetery, Hillside, New Jersey, and he retells (using Johnson's account, (1.136) the story of Steve's and Townley's dismissal over "Parades and Entertainment"—Crane's newspaper account of the parade of the Junior Order of United American Mechanics, 20 August 1892. Also of note in this rare book (only 100 copies were printed) are two drawings of Crane: Crane is depicted Beardsley-style with long smoking jacket and fancy slippers (iv) and in a stark woodcut (114).

9.31   KATZ, JOSEPH. "Crane's Interview with William Dean Howells." *Stephen Crane Newsletter* 4.4 (1970): 7–9. Katz reproduces Crane's editing of a newspaper proof sheet.

9.32   ———. "Stephen Crane: Metropolitan Correspondent." *Kentucky Review* 4.3 (1983): 39–51. Katz reprints several newspaper stories he discovered, and recounts details of Crane's run-in with Theodore Roosevelt and the New York City police following the Dora Clark affair in September 1896.

9.33   KWIAT, JOSEPH J. "The Newspaper Experience: Crane, Norris, and Dreiser." *Nineteenth-Century Fiction* 8 (1953): 99–117. Kwiat examines how the newspaper apprenticeships of these three American naturalists affected their art. In Crane's case Kwiat argues that newspapers gave Crane "a vital subject matter" and he surveys several of his New York City sketches to show this.

9.34   ———. "Stephen Crane and Frank Norris: The Magazine and the 'Revolt' in American Literature in the 1890's." *Western Humanities Review* 30 (1976): 309–22. Kwiat explores the impact of magazines on both authors as well as how magazines changed in the 1890s, in part because of the influence of Crane and Norris. He argues that "Crane's magazine assignments made him acutely aware of social injustices," and thereafter the "little magazines" gave him the forum to make his case.

9.35   ———. "Stephen Crane, Literary-Reporter: Commonplace Experience and Artistic Transcendence." *Journal of Modern Literature* 8 (1980): 129–38. Kwiat's title is new, the rest is not; it is a verbatim reprinting of his 1953 piece (9.33).

9.36   MARMELLI, RONALD S. "Stephen Crane." *Biographical Dictionary of American Journalism*. Ed. Joseph P. McKerns. New York: Greenwood, 1989. 143–44. A standard chapter in a reference book: a sketch of his life and his work in newspapers. Marmelli decries that "his journalistic work has generally been underappreciated and underrated."

9.37   O'CONNOR, RICHARD. *The Scandalous Mr. Bennett.* Garden City, NY: Doubleday, 1962. 90–91. Crane's days as a reporter for the New York *Herald* are mentioned in passing.

9.38   PAUL, ANGUS. "Rising Interest in Analysis of American Nonfiction is Exemplified by Work on Agee, Crane, Parkman and Others." *Chronicle of Higher Education* 34 (13 Jan. 1988): A4, A5, A10. A report on a PMLA annual meeting symposium on journalistic writings of Crane, among others.

9.39 STALLMAN, ROBERT W., and E. R. HAGEMANN. Introduction. *The War Dispatches of Stephen Crane.* Ed. Robert W. Stallman and E. R. Hagemann. New York: New York UP, 1964. 1–11. A biographical sketch of Crane's activities in covering the Graeco-Turkish and Spanish-American Wars. See 12.14 for the annotation on the book.

9.40 WATSON, ELMO SCOTT. "The Syndicate Enters the Metropolitan Field." *A History of Newspaper Syndicates in the United States, 1865–1935.* Chicago: Privately printed, 1936. 42–59. Watson discusses pioneer syndicates with brief comments on S. S. McClure and Irving Bacheller—who arranged the serial publication of *Red Badge* in the newspapers.

9.41 WEINSTEIN, BERNARD. "Stephen Crane, Journalist." *Stephen Crane in Transition: Centenary Essays.* Ed. Joseph Katz. De Kalb: Northern Illinois UP, 1972. 3–24. Sound and reliable examination of Crane's journalistic apprenticeship; the article's critical comments on motifs in Crane's newspaper pieces are less informative.

9.42 WELLS, LESTER G. "The Iron Monster, the Crackling Insects of Onondaga County, and Stephen Crane." *Courier* 3 (1963): 1–7. Wells tells the story of Crane's spoof "Great Bugs in Onondaga" written when he was a stringer for the New York *Tribune* during his short stay at Syracuse. The story is also reprinted. See also Chase (12.41).

See also on Crane's New York City sketches and tales:

1.1–1.4
1.6
1.7
1.10
2.1–2.19
4.135–4.181

THE LITTLE REGIMENT AND OTHER WAR TALES

Books

9.43 BOWERS, FREDSON, ed. *Tales of War. The Works of Stephen Crane,* vol. 6. Ed. Fredson Bowers. Charlottesville: UP of Virginia, 1970.

cxci+401. A reprinting of Crane's tales of the Civil War, the Spanish-American War, and his Spitzenberg stories. See 9.49 for Bowers's textual introduction and 9.51 for Colvert's general introduction.

9.44   ———. *Reports of War. The Works of Stephen Crane,* vol. 9. Charlottesville: UP of Virginia, 1971. xxix+678. This volume collects Crane's war dispatches. See 9.107 for Bowers's textual introduction and 9.108 for Colvert's general introduction.

9.45   FOLLETT, WILSON, ed. *Tales of Two Wars. The Work of Stephen Crane,* vol. 2. Ed. Wilson Follett. New York: Knopf, 1925. xxiv+259. Follett collects most of Crane's best war tales. See 9.74 for the introduction by Robert H. Davis.

9.46   ———. *"Wounds in the Rain" and Other Impressions of War. The Work of Stephen Crane,* vol. 9. New York: Knopf, 1926. xiv+258. Follett reprints Crane's own collection of his war stories, *Wounds in the Rain,* along with other selected stories. See 9.70 for Cather's introduction to this volume.

9.47   STALLMAN, ROBERT W., and E. R. HAGEMANN, eds. *The War Dispatches of Stephen Crane.* New York: New York UP, 1964. A collection of Crane's war dispatches. See 9.39 for the editors' introduction.

Book Chapters and Articles

9.48   BARROWS, HERBERT. "The Little Regiment." *An Introduction to Literature: Reading the Short Story.* Boston: Houghton Mifflin, 1959. "The Little Regiment" is reprinted along with study questions.

9.49   BOWERS, FREDSON. Textual Introduction. *Tales of War. The Works of Stephen Crane,* vol. 6. Ed. Fredson Bowers. Charlottesville: UP of Virginia, 1970. xxxvii–cxci. Many of these tales were printed in *The Little Regiment* (1896), but others appeared in various magazines and newspapers, some as late as 1900. Bowers sorts out all the textual problems and explains his choice of copy texts.

9.50   BROOKS, CLEANTH, et al. "'An Episode of War.'" *An Approach to Literature.* New York: Appleton-Century-Crofts, 1941. 45–46. "An Episode of War" is reprinted, followed by a half-dozen study-discussion questions. Up to and including the 1964 fourth edition, the same material is repeated.

9.51   COLVERT, JAMES B. Introduction. *Tales of War. The Works of Stephen Crane,* vol. 6. Ed. Bowers Fredson. Charlottesville: UP of Virginia, 1970. ix–xxxvi. Colvert considers two themes: Crane's struggles to recapture the brilliance of *Red Badge* and, a closely related matter, his efforts to reconcile the accuracy of his imagination of combat with an experiential realism grounded in first-hand observations of war.

9.52   GARGANO, JAMES W. "Crane's 'A Mystery of Heroism': A Possible Source." *Modern Language Notes* 74 (1959): 22–23. Gargano suggests 2 Samuel 23:13–17, which describes three men breaking through the enemy lines to draw water from a well as the source for Fred Collins's reckless dash through no-man's-land to get a bucket of water.

9.53   HEINES, DONALD. "An Episode of War." *Times Four: The Short Story in Depth.* Englewood Cliffs, NJ: Prentice-Hall, 1968. 168. "An Episode of War" is reprinted along with discussion questions.

9.54   IVES, C. B. " 'The Little Regiment' of Stephen Crane at the Battle of Fredericksburg." *Midwest Quarterly* 8 (1967): 247–60. Ives "proves" that "The Little Regiment" closely follows the actual events of the battle of Fredericksburg. Not of much interest beyond this historical point.

9.55   MAY, CHARLES E. "The Unique Effect of the Short Story: A Reconstruction and an Example." *Studies in Short Fiction* 13 (1976): 289–79. Thesis: The unique effect of the short story is that its shortness "compels it to deal with a different mode of reality and knowledge than the novel." As an example, May then examines Crane's "An Episode in War" wherein, he argues, the reader confronts the precariousness of the human situation.

9.56   MAYER, CHARLES W. "Stephen Crane and the Realistic Tradition: 'Three Miraculous Soldiers.' " *Arizona Quarterly* 30 (1974): 127–34. Mayer argues that Crane's central motif is an "exploration of the discrepancies between illusion and reality" and he uses the various perspectives in "Three Miraculous Soldiers" to make his case.

9.57   NAGEL, JAMES. "Stephen Crane's Stories of War: A Study of Art and Theme." *North Dakota Quarterly* 43 (1975): 5–19. An insightful examination of the war stories Crane wrote after *Red Badge*. Nagel argues that the tales focus on regiments instead of individuals and the voice of the narrator is more objective. The best tales in *The Little Regiment* and *Wounds in the Rain* are looked at; especially noteworthy are Nagel's analyses of "A Mystery of Heroism," "An Episode of War," "The Clan of No-Name," and "The Upturned Face."

9.58   PATRICK, WALTON R. "Poetic Style in the Contemporary Short Story." *College Composition and Communication* 18 (1967): 77–84. Crane's "A Mystery of Heroism" is singled out as an example of the technique of "metaphorical dilation of language . . . to pack the utmost meaning into [a] restricted space."

9.59   PROFITT, EDWARD. "An Episode of War." *Reading and Writing about Short Fiction.* San Diego: Harcourt Brace, 1988. "An Episode of War" is reprinted along with study and discussion questions.

9.60   SOLOMON, ERIC. "A Gloss on *The Red Badge of Courage.*" *Modern Language Notes* 75 (1960): 111–13. Solomon observes that old Henry Fleming in "The Veteran" has "learned honesty and self-abnegation."

9.61   ———. "Stephen Crane's War Stories." *Texas Studies in Language and Literature* 3 (1961): 67–80. Solomon studies Crane's war stories from "A Mystery to Heroism" through middle tales such as "Death and the Child" to one of his last, "The Upturned Face," to document that "Crane's attitude toward war as a subject for fiction was steadily refined throughout his writing career."

9.62   WITHERINGTON, PAUL. "Stephen Crane's 'A Mystery of Heroism': Some Redefinitions." *English Journal* 58 (1969): 210–4, 218. An interesting contrast of Fred Collins's run to courage with Fleming's run from courage. Criticizes Solomon's (9.61) failure to see any moral message in "A Mystery of Heroism."

See also on Crane's war tales and reports:

1.1–1.4
1.10
2.1–2.19
2.35
2.91
3.64
3.153
6.13
11.40

SPANISH-AMERICAN WAR TALES AND REPORTS

9.63 [Review of *Wounds in the Rain*]. *Critic* 38 (1901): 88. Unlike *Red Badge,* which was the product of Crane's imagination, the stories in *Wounds in the Rain* are "work of the story teller." The reviewer does not say which source produces better fiction. Reprinted in Weatherford's *The Critical Heritage* 2.17: #127.

9.64 AZOY, A. C. M. *Charge! The Story of the Battle of San Juan Hill.* New York: Longmans, Green, 1961. 145–46. Azoy relates the story of Crane's "coolness under fire," standing on top of the trench, attracting fire from the enemy sharpshooters.

9.65 BOWERS, FREDSON. "Notes on Editing 'The Revenge of the *Adolphus*': A Combined, Selective Text." *The Author's Intention: An Exhibition for the Center for Editions for American Authors at the Folger Shakespear Library, Washington D.C.* Ed. Matthew J. Bruccoli. Columbia: U of South Carolina P, 1972. 37–41. An interesting account of a typescript and its carbon. Commander J. C. Collwell USN read Crane's typescript and suggested numerous corrections having to do with Crane's "mistakes in naval terminology and procedures." Crane recalled the typescript and revised it before it was published in London by *Strand Magazine;* the uncorrected carbon was the copy used in the American *Collier's Weekly* version of the same story. Later a third, partially corrected version was published as part of *Wounds in the Rain.* Bowers explains how he and his helpers sorted all of this out.

9.66 BOYD, THOMAS. "Semper Fidelis." *Bookman* 60 (1924): 409–12. Factual confirmation of Crane's account of the bravery of the signal-man John Quick in "Marines Signaling under Fire at Guantanamo."

9.67 BRUCCOLI, MATTHEW J. "'The Wonders of Ponce': Crane's First Puerto Rican Dispatch." *Stephen Crane Newsletter* 4.1 (1969): 1–3. Brief comments and a reprinting of this newspaper dispatch.

9.68 BULLARD, FREDERIC L. "Reporting the Spanish-American War." *Famous War Correspondents.* New York: Beekman, 1974. 409–24. A general discussion of Yellow Journalism's stake in the Spanish-American War. Several comments by Richard Harding Davis and other correspondents about Crane's coolness under fire.

9.69 CARNES, CECIL. "Underfire and Mopping Up." *Jimmy Hare, News Photographer.* New York: Macmillan, 1940. 60–75; 76–80. Lively account of fellow correspondents (and a photographer) of Crane as journalist in the Spanish-American War.

9.70　CATHER, WILLA. Introduction. *"Wounds in the Rain" and Other Impressions of War. The Work of Stephen Crane,* vol. 9. Ed. Wilson Follett. New York: Knopf, 1926. ix–xiv. Cather examines Crane's techniques of collecting impressions and his uncanny ability to seize just enough detail. Very little is said about the particular stories contained in the Knopf volume. Reprinted in Cather's *On Writing* (New York: Knopf, 1949), 67–74.

9.71　DAVIS, RICHARD HARDING. "Our War Correspondents in Cuba and Puerto Rico." *Harper's New Monthly Magazine* 98 (May 1899): 938–48. This is the standard source for Crane's fellow war correspondents' opinion of him. Davis tells of his "foolhearty bravery," his coolness under fire, and his bout with yellow fever. Interesting photographs of Crane and eight other reporters.

9.72　———. "How Stephen Crane Took Juana Dias." *In Many Wars by Many Correspondents*. Ed. George Lynch and Frederic Palmer. Tokyo: Tokyo Printing, 1904. 43–45. Tells the story of Crane's arriving before the troops so he was the one to accept the surrender of a small provincial village.

9.73　———. "The Passing of San Juan Hill," *Notes of a War Correspondent.* New York: Scribner's, 1914. 113–34. Often-told tale of the taking of San Juan Hill: Crane "wore a long India rubber rain-coat and was smoking a pipe. He appeared as cool as though he were looking down from a box at a theater."

9.74　DAVIS, ROBERT H. Introduction *Tales of Two Wars. The Work of Stephen Crane,* vol. 2. Ed. Wilson Follett. New York: Knopf, 1925. ix–xxiv. Little on the stories in this volume, yet this is perhaps the best of the introductions commissioned for the Follett edition. Lovely, melancholy, highly personal reminiscences of Crane.

9.75　DILLINGHAM, WILLIAM B. *Frank Norris: Instinct and Art.* Lincoln: U of Nebraska P, 1969. Passim. This is a biography of Norris. Crane is mentioned in passing along with a few details on Crane writing war dispatches in Cuba and information on Norris's parodies of *Red Badge* and *Black Riders*.

9.76　DOWNEY, FAIRFAX. *Richard Harding Davis and His Day.* New York: Scribner's, 1933. 160–61 and passim. Standard accounts of Crane's walking above the trenches and drawing fire plus Davis's alleged gallant defense of Crane against the gossips who alleged that he was dying "from disgraceful diseases."

9.77 FLEMING, THOMAS. "The Press at War." *This Week Magazine: Milwaukee Journal* 2 June 1968. Crane's reports on the Battle of San Juan briefly mentioned.

9.78 FREIDEL, FRANK. *The Splendid Little War.* New York: Bramhall House, 1958. Passim. A valuable resource on the Spanish-American War. Crane is a prominent figure in this lively narrative; there are hundreds of interesting pictures [though the man identified as Crane on page 66 is not he], drawings, and maps. In addition, several of Crane's dispatches are quoted at length.

9.79 GULLASON, THOMAS A. "The Significance of 'Wounds in the Rain.' " *Modern Fiction Studies* 5 (1959): 235–42. Gullason argues that a change in style—from the "brilliant impressionistic writing" of *Red Badge* to "transcriptions of reality" in *Wounds in the Rain*—was caused by his observation as opposed to his imagination of war.

9.80 HARRIS, KENNETH F. "Rough Rider O'Neill." *Chicago Record's War Stories.* Chicago: Chicago Record, 1898. 131–33. Harris's dispatch is a routine account of the Roughriders in Cuba. Of special value, however, is a detailed drawing, "A Typical Spanish Block House in Cuba," which is very helpful in following the battle described in Crane's "Clan of No-Name."

9.81 HOHENBERG, JOHN. *Foreign Correspondence: The Great Reporters and Their Times.* New York: Columbia UP, 1964. 137 and passim. Hohenberg tells of Crane's news reports from Cuba, especially how he embarrassed the *World* by telling the truth about the 71st New York Regiment at San Juan Hill. Crane's report that the New York Regiment had gotten in the way of the Rough Riders was accurate; nevertheless, this fact did not set well with readers of the New York paper.

9.82 HUNEKER, JAMES GIBBONS. "Stephen Crane." *Americans in the Arts: Critiques by James Gibbons Huneker.* Ed. Arnold T. Schwab. New York: AMS, 1985. 329–31. A reprinting of a brief parody of one of Crane's Spanish-American War dispatches.

9.83 JAKES, JOHN. "Stephen Crane in Greece and Cuba." *Great War Correspondents.* New York: Putnams's, 1967. 35–51. A superficial and somewhat factually erroneous chapter on Crane. For instance, Jakes writes that unlike Richard Harding Davis, Crane was a "perpetually unsuccessful reporter."

9.84 KATZ, JOSEPH. "The Reception of *Wounds in the Rain.*" *Stephen Crane Newsletter* 4.2 (1969): 9–10. It sold well, four editions in one year.

9.85 LANGFORD, GERALD. *The Richard Harding Davis Years.* New York: Holt, 1961. Passim. Scattered references to Crane in a book devoted to Davis.

9.86 MARSHALL, EDWARD. "A Wounded Correspondent's Recollections of Guasimas." *Scribner's Magazine* 24.3 (1898): 273–76. Marshall covered the Roughriders in Cuba along with Crane. After he was paralyzed by a bullet, Marshall recounts how Crane and Richard Harding Davis carried him to a field hospital. Like Crane, Marshall tried to capture the sound of rifles and artillery.

9.87 MASON, GREGORY. *Remember the Maine.* New York: Holt, 1939. Passim. Scattered comments on Crane as a war correspondent.

9.88 MCINTOSH, BURR. *The Little I Saw of Cuba.* London: F. Tennyson Neely, 1899. Passim. A fellow news correspondent's memoirs of the Rough Riders' campaign: Crane is briefly discussed several times; interesting pictures of Crane as well as of "That Balloon," which gave away the position of General Shafter's troops, described in "Stephen Crane's Vivid Story of the Battle of San Juan."

9.89 MICHELSON, CHARLES. *The Ghost Talks.* New York: Putnam's, 1944. 89. xi, 161. A fellow reporter mentions his trip to Cuba with "quite a crew of Hearst people, including Stephen Crane."

9.90 MILTON, JOYCE. *The Yellow Kids: Foreign Correspondents in the Heyday of Yellow Journalism.* New York: Harper and Row, 1989. Mainly a biography of Sylvester Scovel, with much on Richard Harding Davis and some material of other war correspondents. The Crane sections rely heavily on Stallman's *Stephen Crane* (1.10) and Gilkes's *Cora Crane* (10.20). There are several interesting, previously unpublished letters referring to Crane by fellow correspondents and their wives.

9.91 MONTEIRO, GEORGE. "Stephen Crane and John Hay: Two Notes." *Stephen Crane Newsletter* 4.4 (1970): 5–6. Hay attended the Philistine dinner; later as Secretary of State he was contacted to help locate Crane in Havana during September and October 1898.

9.92 ———. "Ralph Paine and 'The Memory of Stephen Crane.'" *Stephen Crane Newsletter* 2.1 (1976): 6–7. Details about a fellow news correspondent in Cuba and Ralph Paine's dedicating his *Roads of Adventure* to the memory of Crane.

9.93 NAGEL, JAMES. "Stephen Crane's 'The Clan of No-Name.'" *Kyushu American Literature* 14 (1972): 34–42. Mostly a retelling of Crane's tale stressing the theme that "idealized human conduct (in war or courtship) is a distortion of reality which leads to disillusionment, destruction and death."

9.94 NORRIS, FRANK. "Newsgathering at Key West." *Letters of Frank Norris.* ed. Franklin Walker. San Francisco: Book Club of California, 1956. 9–18. Norris describes Crane (and Richard Harding Davis) as fellow news correspondents aboard *Three Friends.* Norris tells of Crane holding a beer bottle between his heels as he composed a dispatch.

9.95 OSBORN, NEAL J. "The Riddle in 'The Clan': A Key to Crane's Major Fiction." *Bulletin of the New York Public Library* 69 (1965): 247–58. Osborn argues that Crane's story "The Clan of No-Name" covers the same ground as *Red Badge* — the catalysts of brotherhood are fear and danger.

9.96 OSBORN, SCOTT C. "The 'Rivalry-Chivalry' of Richard Harding Davis and Stephen Crane." *American Literature* 28 (1956): 50–61. Davis respected Crane as a writer and a war correspondent though he deplored his moral lapses and his bohemianism.

9.97 PAINE, RALPH D. "A Castaway of the *Commodore;* My Friend the Sugar Boiler." *Roads of Adventure.* Boston: Houghton Mifflin, 1922. 154–71; 239–62. Valuable and detailed memoirs by a Crane friend and fellow journalist. Records Crane under fire and his reaction to combat. Paine relates that he overheard Crane and Captain Edward Murphy, commander of the lost filibustering steamer *Commodore,* discussing the shipwreck and the subsequent "Open Boat" ordeal. The second chapter is "The Lone Charge of William B. Perkins" told as Paine (he was Perkins) remembered it. Several good photographs of Crane are included.

9.98 SEITZ, DON C. *Joseph Pulitzer: His Life and Letters.* New York: Simon and Schuster, 1924. 241–42 and passim. An inaccurate and biased account of Crane's newspaper dispatches from Cuba. For instance, he harshly criticizes Crane for a story written by Sylvester Scovel, not Crane.

9.99   ———. "Stephen Crane: War Correspondent." *Bookman* 72 (1933): 137–40. Seitz was the business manager of Hearst's *The World,* which sent Crane to Cuba. Instead of providing detail and insight about hiring Crane and his work as a correspondent, Seitz is content to quote snippets of some of Crane's well-known dispatches.

9.100   SORRENTINO, PAUL. "A Reminiscence of Stephen Crane." *Courier* (Syracuse University) 19 (1984): 111–14. Sorrentino reprints a brief reminiscence by Samuel Riggs who saw Crane recuperating at Old Port Comfort and made comments about Crane as a good newspaper correspondent.

9.101   WILLIAMS, AMES W. "Stephen Crane: War Correspondent." *New Colophon* 1 (1948): 113–23. An essay on Crane's war correspondent days (in Cuba and Greece) including a list of his Spanish-American War dispatches appearing in the New York *World* and the New York *Journal.*

9.102   WILLIAMS, BEN AMES. "The Santiago Campaign by Stephen Crane." *Amateurs at War.* Boston: Houghton Mifflin, 1943. 291–323. Crane is the victim of Williams's sloppiness. Crane's "War Memories" is reprinted as "Well, Begawd, We Done It" (296–323) after a short introductory note that informs readers of this anthology of war stories that "Crane in '98 was still in his *thirties.*"

9.103   WINKLER, JOHN K. *W. R. Hearst: An American Phenomenon.* New York: Simon and Schuster, 1928. Brief comments on Crane (67–69) including a quotation from Beer's specious letter *(Correspondence of Stephen Crane* 13.3: #763) to the effect that "nobody understands the popular mind as well as Oscar Hammerstein, unless it's Willie Hearst."

9.104   WINTERICH, JOHN T. "Made in Japan." *Saturday Review of Literature* 9 (29 January 1933): 406. Brief mention of the reprinting of Richard Harding Davis's article "How Stephen Crane Took Juana Dias."

GRAECO-TURKISH WAR TALES AND REPORTS

9.105   ANDERSON, HAROLD MacDONALD. "The War Correspondent." *Bookman* 19 (March 1904): 24–41. Crane's photograph and a brief account (39) of him as a war correspondent claiming that he was so disorganized that a manager had to take care of all the details, leaving Crane to do just the writing.

9.106 BOWERS, FREDSON. "Notes on Editing 'Death and the Child.'" *The Author's Intention: An Exhibition for the Center for Editions for American Authors at the Folger Shakespeare Library, Washington D.C.* Ed. Matthew J. Bruccoli. Columbia: U of South Carolina P, 1972. 28–33. Bowers's editorial task on this important story of the Graeco-Turkish War was complicated by the existence of four independent texts; "technically . . . any one of these four texts is equal in authority." Bowers discovered, however, that the usual source for this story, the Heinemann collection, *The Open Boat,* is "the most corrupt text of all." He argues that his "established" text "comes within a perhaps 98 percent perfection in reprinting what must have been the form and details of the lost manuscript."

9.107 ———. "The Text: History and Analysis." *Reports of War. The Works of Stephen Crane,* vol. 9. (See 9.44). Ed. Fredson Bowers. Charlottesville: UP of Virginia, 1971. 409–62. Bowers provides his usual complete and thorough account of the texts available to him and why he chose the copy texts he did.

9.108 COLVERT, JAMES B. Introduction. *Reports of War. The Works of Stephen Crane,* vol. 9. (See 9.44). Ed. Fredson Bowers. Charlottesville: UP of Virginia, 1971. xix–xxix. This volume collects Crane's war dispatches. Colvert argues that Cuba and Greece "added little of radical importance to his resources" for he was not a professional reporter but "an artist." Colvert then discusses general artistic themes rather than the individual pieces (87) contained in this volume.

9.109 GEISMAR, MAXWELL. "Stephen Crane: Halfway House." *Rebels and Ancestors: The American Novel, 1890–1915.* Boston: Houghton Mifflin, 1953. 69–136. A generally unsympathetic psychoanalytic account of Crane as a rebellious adolescent. Geismar makes brief comment on Crane's major works and important short stories. His examination of "Death and the Child" is especially good.

9.110 GILKES, LILLIAN. "Stephen and Cora Crane: Some Corrections, and a 'Millionaire' Named Sharefe." *American Literature* 41 (1969): 270–77. More on the route the Cranes took to "the little 'bathtub war' in Greece." The corrections are aimed at Stallman (9.112 and 9.113); see also Gilkes (10.68) and Friedman (10.26).

9.111 HAGEMANN, E. R. "'Correspondents Three' in the Graeco-Turkish War: Some Parodies." *American Literature* 30 (1958): 339–44.

Hagemann discovered three parodies (by Charles Loomis, published in the *Critic)* that mock Crane, Richard Harding Davis, and Rudyard Kipling.

9.112   STALLMAN, ROBERT W. "Was Crane's Sketch of the Fleet Off Crete a Journalistic Hoax?: A Reply to Miss Gilkes." *Studies in Short Fiction* 2 (1964): 72–76. More of the Stallman–Gilkes feud; his sarcasm and spleen-venting are much in evidence. See also Friedman (10.26).

9.113   _____. "How Stephen Crane Got to Crete." *American Literature* 44 (1972): 308–13. More on the Stallman–Gilkes dispute about a travel detail. Apparently Stallman was eager to air his side in this prestigious journal for his customary barbs are moderated. Still, he calls her theory "utter conjecture." See also Friedman (10.26).

10

Potboilers, England, Cora, and Last Works

Overview

Annotations in this section cover books and articles on Crane's early, middle, and late potboilers and the Cranes in England.

THE THIRD VIOLET. Gilkes (10.6) and Levenson (10.10) struggle to say good things about Crane's weak attempt at a novel of manners. ANDREWS (10.3) says good things too, and he says them much more quickly.

ACTIVE SERVICE. The articles by GULLASON (10.17) and Levinson (10.18) are significant.

CORA CRANE. Gilkes's biography (10.20) of Crane's "wife" is essential; the second half of Gilkes's volume describing Crane's money and health problems is heartrending. Also her comments on *The Monster* are insightful. For more on Cora see the articles by Beer (10.22), KAZIN (10.32), and Osborne (10.34).

ENGLAND. Both books on the Cranes in England, by Milne (10.38) and Solomon (10.39), are useful; so too are discussions of life at Brede Place by Mrs. Joseph Conrad (10.44) and Ford (10.53 and 10.57). GULLASON (10.70) has the best short account of why Crane went to England; Liebling's *New Yorker* article (10.80) speculates that without his health and money problems Crane could have regained his *Red Badge* writing level. Stronks (10.96) has the best information on Crane's finances at the end.

LAST WORKS. Only "The Upturned Face" has been examined in detail; see CHRISTOPHERSEN (10.109), Dillingham (10.110), and Witherington (10.115).

THE O'RUDDY. This work, begun by Crane and finished by Robert Barr, is forgettable. However, speculation by O'Donnell (10.136) and then the discovery of the manuscript, see Bowers (10.125) and Levenson (10.133), has made for an interesting exchange about who wrote which chapters.

THE THIRD VIOLET

Books

10.1   BOWERS, FREDSON, ed. *The Third Violet [and Active Service]. The Works of Stephen Crane,* vol. 3. Charlottesville: UP of Virginia, 1976. xxii+492. The critical edition of Crane's try at a Howellsian novel. See 10.4 for Bowers's textual introduction and 10.10 for Levenson's general introduction.

10.2   FOLLETT, WILSON, ed. *The Work of Stephen Crane,* vol. 3: *["The Monster" and] "The Third Violet."* New York: Knopf, 1926. xxii+231. Follett was either fond of this work of Crane or he could find no one else to write an introduction for the text he had prepared. See 10.5 for his introduction.

Articles and Book Chapters

10.3   ANDREWS, WILLIAM L. "Art and Success: Another Look at Stephen Crane's *The Third Violet." Wascana Review* 13 (1978): 71–82. A heroic attempt to see value in Crane's unsuccessful effort at a love story. Thesis: Crane turned to romanticism to escape being typecast as a war novelist. Andrews concludes, *"The Third Violet* stands as a significant and suggestive work in the Crane canon, a potboiler perhaps, but one drawn from the fires of an authentic and fundamentally serious creative forge."

10.4   BOWERS, FREDSON. "The Text: History and Analysis *[The Third Violet]." The Third Violet; Active Service. The Works of Stephen Crane,* vol. 3. Ed. Fredson Bowers. Charlottesville: UP of Virginia, 1976. 331–45. Bowers describes the time of composition and textual problems with the book, the syndicated newspaper version, and several early editions.

10.5   FOLLETT, WILSON. Introduction. *The Work of Stephen Crane,* vol. 3: *"The Monster" and "The Third Violet."* New York: Knopf, 1926.

ix–xxii. Follett sets up a nice framework that enables him to find something useful in *The Third Violet:* it is one of Crane's weakest because it is derived from his experiences; on the contrary, *The Monster* is one of his best due to its source, his imagination. He also finds interesting parallels between the lady gossips in *The Third Violet* and Martha Goodwin in *The Monster.*

10.6 GILKES, LILLIAN. *"The Third Violet, Active Service* and *The O'Ruddy.* Stephen Crane's Potboilers." *Stephen Crane in Transition: Centenary Essays.* Ed. Joseph Katz. De Kalb: Northern Illinois UP, 1972. 106–26. Gilkes makes an appeal for a fresh look at Crane's potboilers. She sees much merit in these books; her opinion is decidedly in the minority.

10.7 GULLASON, THOMAS A. "Stephen Crane: The Novelist at War with Himself." *Stephen Crane's Career: Perspectives and Evaluations.* Ed. Thomas A. Gullason. New York: New York UP, 1972. 395–406. An attempt to see value in *The Third Violet* and *The O'Ruddy.* In these works, at least, Crane was "more than moderately successful as a novelist."

10.8 ITABASHI, YOSHIE. "Comedies of Love: A Study of *The Third Violet* and *Active Service." Tsuda Review* 13 (Nov. 1968): 15–63. An ambitious effort to see value in two of Crane's potboilers.

10.9 KATZ, JOSEPH. "Corwin Knapp Linson on *The Third Violet." Stephen Crane Newsletter* 3.1 (1968): 5. In a note tipped into his copy of *The Third Violet* Linson says Crane told him he (Linson) was Hawker in this book.

10.10 LEVENSON, J. C. Introduction: *The Third Violet. The Third Violet; Active Service. The Works of Stephen Crane,* vol. 3. Ed. Fredson Bowers. Charlottesville: UP of Virginia, 1976. xi–xl. Levenson manages to say many things about Crane's stab at a Howellsian realism in this "novel of manners and sentiment"; still the upshot is that "there is less fever, exhilaration or intensity in *The Third Violet* than in any other of Crane's early works."

10.11 MACSHANE, FRANK. *The Life and Work of Ford Madox Ford.* New York: Horizon, 1965. 238. Ford makes the remarkable claim that among the six *classics* he wished he had at hand (during his visit to New York) was *The Third Violet.* It evidently takes little to be rated a classic by Ford.

See also on *The Third Violet:*

1.1–1.4
1.10
2.1–2.19

ACTIVE SERVICE

Books

10.12   BOWERS, FREDSON, ed.*[The Third Violet]; Active Service. The Works of Stephen Crane,* vol. 3. Charlottesville: UP of Virginia, 1976. lxiii+492. The standard text. See 10.15 for Bowers's textual introduction and 10.18 for Levenson's general introduction.

10.13   FOLLETT, WILSON, ed. *The Work of Stephen Crane,* vol. 3: [*"The Monster"] and "The Third Violet."* New York: Knopf, 1926. xxi+231. Follett's edition of Crane's war adventure. See Follett's introduction (10.5).

Articles and Book Chapters

10.14   "The Beautiful War." *London Times Literary Supplement* 25 Nov. 1960, 758. Compares *Active Service* with Hemingway's *Men without Women* and offers the opinion that Crane was played out at the end. Liebling (10.80) offers the opposite view that had Crane lived longer he would have produced several other top-notch works.

10.15   BOWERS, FREDSON. "The Text: History and Analysis *[Active Service]." The Third Violet; Active Service. The Works of Stephen Crane,* vol. 3. Ed. Fredson Bowers. Charlottesville: UP of Virginia, 1976. 345–86. Bowers describes the typescript of *Active Service,* differences between the American and English versions, and his principles for the choice of copy text.

10.16   FOLLETT, WILSON. Introduction. *The Work of Stephen Crane,* vol. 3: *"The Monster" and "The Third Violet."* New York: Knopf, 1926. ix–xxii. Follett sets up a nice framework that enables him to find something useful in *The Third Violet:* It is one of Crane's weakest because it is derived from his experiences; on the contrary, *The Monster* is one of his best due to its source, his imagination. See also Follett (10.5.).

10.17 GULLASON, THOMAS A. "The Jamesian Motif in Stephen Crane's Last Novels." *The Personalist* 42 (1961): 77–84. Though Crane's *Active Service, The Third Violet* and *The O'Ruddy* are usually passed over as potboilers, Gullason holds that they represent Jamesian elements in his fiction: concern about class stratification and real versus contrived aristocracy. Gilkes (10.6) agrees that these works are significant and of high quality but few other Crane scholars do.

10.18 LEVENSON, J. C. Introduction: *Active Service." The Third Violet; Active Service. The Works of Stephen Crane,* vol. 3. Ed. Fredson Bowers. Charlottesville: UP of Virginia, 1976. lv–lxii. Levenson explains that while in England when Crane was writing some of his very best short works ("The Bride Comes to Yellow Sky" and "The Blue Hotel") he set aside time to work on a big war book. The book is big but not very good, though Levenson finds several things of merit in it.

10.19 VAN DOREN, CARL. Introduction. *Active Service. The Work of Stephen Crane,* vol. 4. Ed. Wilson Follett. New York: Knopf, 1926. ix–xv, 501–7. Though this book was (and is) panned, Van Doren manages to find good things to say about it: "its value lies in its incidental details" and "the book glitters with impressionistic phrases," but even he agrees that the characters are "wooden."

See also on *Active Service:*

1.1–1.4
1.10
1.114
2.1–2.19
2.84
3.190
5.16
10.6
10.7
10.8

CORA CRANE

Book

10.20 GILKES, LILLIAN. *Cora Crane: A Biography of Mrs. Stephen Crane.* Bloomington: Indiana UP, 1960. 416. A full-length biography of

Cora. Gilkes depicts Cora's life as a generally tough go, with a few good years confined to her days in England (both at Ravensbrook and Brede) with Stephen. However, even those good years were marred by Crane's disappearance in Cuba during the last half of 1898 and their truly pathetic financial situation and his health struggles at the end. Cora's part in the writing of some of Crane's later works is described along with critical observations on some of those works. For example, Gilkes finds in *The Monster* that Crane joined two favorite themes, "rescue and the deflation of heroism."

Book Chapters and Articles

10.21   ["Crane and Cora."] *Critic* ns 35 (1901): 198–99. Portraits of the Cranes plus information on Cora's supposed coauthoring some of Crane's last works; see Stallman, *Stephen Crane: A Critical Bibliography*, 14.3:288.

10.22   BEER, THOMAS. "Mrs. Stephen Crane." *The American Mercury* 31 (1934): 289–95. According to Beer, Crane's "wife" was not genteel enough for English society; this opinion is based on many semiderogatory comments, mostly from letters.

10.23   BRUCCOLI, MATTHEW J. "Cora's Mouse." *Papers of the Bibliographical Society of America* 59 (1965): 188–89. An inscription in Kipling's *The Seven Seas* reveals that Cora's pet name for Crane was "mouse."

10.24   CABELL, JAMES BRANCH, and A. J. HANNA. "Cora Comes Back." *The St. John: A Parade of Diversities*. New York: Farrar and Rinehart, 1943. 275–86. Details on Crane and Cora: the dinner after his "Open Boat" ordeal, life at her bordello, Hotel de Dreme, and her building "The Court" after Crane's death upon her return to Jacksonville.

10.25   DOSSETT, GORDON. "A Letter from Grant Richard to Cora Crane." *Studies in the Novel* 10 (1978): 156–57. A minor item of little value dealing with a contract for *Wounds in the Rain*.

10.26   FRIEDMAN, ELIZABETH. "Cora's Travel Notes, 'Dan Emmonds,' and Stephen Crane's Route to the Greek War: A Puzzle Solved." *Studies in Short Fiction* 27 (1990): 264–65. Friedman argues that Cora's travel notes were written during 1892 long before she met Crane. This settles a longstanding Stallman–Gilkes feud; see 9.110, 9.112, and 9.113.

10.27 FRIEDMAN, PEGGY. "Jacksonville's Most Famous Madam." *Jacksonville Magazine* (May–June 1990): 12–20. On Cora's lavish "gaming houses."

10.28 GILKES, LILLIAN. "Frederic, Crane and the Stallman Biography." *Frederic Herald* 3 (1969): 4. More errors in Stallman's *Stephen Crane: A Biography* (1.10). Beyond their feud, this piece is noteworthy for several details on the Crane–Harold Frederic friendship.

10.29 ———. "The Stephen Crane Collection before Its Acquisition by Columbia: A Memoir." *Columbia Library Columns* 22 (1973): 12–22. Chatty stories about an old trunk kept out back of Cora's Whitehouse "Hotel" in Jacksonville, how Cora's girls lived high on the hog, and how Columbia got the materials—mostly pictures and notes on Cora.

10.30 KATZ, JOSEPH. "Not at Columbia: Postcards to Cora Crane." *Columbia Library Columns* 23 (1974): 21–30. A personal chronicle of Katz and Lillian Gilkes (biographer of Cora, *Cora Crane,* (10.20) traveling to Jacksonville to find more Crane memorabilia. Details on Cora's life after Crane died and she returned to the United States are also included.

10.31 ———. "Cora's Box." *Columbia Library Columns* 24 (1975): 3–9. A sentimental and folksy account of the contents of a safety deposit box registered under the name of Cora Taylor, acquired by Columbia University in 1974.

10.32 KAZIN, ALFRED. "Stephen Crane's Scarlet Woman." *Contemporaries.* Boston: Little, Brown, 1962. 60–64. A review essay (originally published in 1960) on Lillian Gilkes's *Cora Crane* (10.20). In addition, Kazin discusses Crane's life in England, especially his friendships with Henry James and Harold Frederic.

10.33 O'DONNELL, THOMAS F. "Hall Cane, R. W. Stallman, and 'The Cate Lyon Fund.'" *The Frederic Herald* 2 (1969): 4. O'Donnell corrects a minor detail about Cora's effort to support Kate Lyon and her three fatherless children on the death of Harold Frederic.

10.34 OSBORN, SCOTT C. "Stephen Crane and Cora: Some Corrections." *American Literature* 26 (1954): 416–18. Minor details on Cora: She was old enough to be his mother and she was a "bi-roxide" blonde.

10.35 STARRETT, VINCENT. "Mrs. Stephen Crane." *Books and Bipeds.* New York: Argus, 1947. 101–2. A note on Cora.

10.36 WERTHEIM, STANLEY. "Cora Crane's Thwarted Romance." *Columbia Library Columns* 36 (1986): 26–37. Cora's dealings with a "controversial American journalist, historian, and political commentator."

10.37   WOOD, WAYNE W. "La Villa." *Jacksonville's Architectural Heritage.* Jacksonville: U of Jacksonville P, 1989. 86–89. In a section on Jacksonville's red light district, Cora's "Hotel de Dreme" and her later establishment, "The Court," are discussed; photographs are included.

See also on Cora:

1.1–1.4
1.10
2.1–2.19
10.38–10.102

ENGLAND

Books

10.38   MILNE, W. GORDON. *Stephen Crane at Brede: An Anglo-American Literary Circle of the 1890's.* Washington, DC: UP of America, 1980. 63. Life at Brede, including Milne's contention that Crane was the kingpin of the circle that included H. G. Wells, Harold Frederic, Joseph Conrad, and Henry James.

10.39   SOLOMON, ERIC. *Stephen Crane in England: A Portrait of the Artist.* Columbus: Ohio State UP, 1964. 136. Solomon sorts out the details of Crane's two-year stay in England, especially the expatriate support group he found there, and examines themes in the best mature works he wrote in England. Solomon states that his purpose is to bring together "all the more important information related to Crane in England"; slightly over 100 pages are not enough for that, but his book is more than just a good start. For more on Crane in England see Delbanco (10.49) and Milne (10.38).

Articles and Book Chapters

10.40   ANDREWS, ALLEN. *The Splendid Pauper.* Philadelphia: Lippincott, 1968. A biography of Morton Frewen, who rented Brede Place to the

Cranes. Interesting details on Cora's setting up the arrangements and a few tidbits on their money troubles.

10.41 AUSTIN, EDMUND. *Brede, the Story of a Sussex Parish.* Rye (Sussex, UK): Adams, 1945. A rare book; so far only the Library of Congress copy shows up on the OCLC terminal. I have not seen this item cited in Stallman's *Stephen Crane: A Critical Bibliography* 14.3:366.

10.42 BAINES, JOCELYN. *Joseph Conrad: A Critical Biography.* New York: McGraw-Hill, 1960. 203–8, 230–33 and passim. Discusses the Conrad–Crane personal and professional relationships.

10.43 BEER, THOMAS. "Stephen Crane." *New York Evening Post Literary Review* 19 July 1924: iv, 910. Beer explains that Crane was paid only half of what Ford Madox Ford claimed in his *Thus to Revisit* (10.53). See also Stronks (10.96) for details on Crane's earnings in England.

10.44 CONRAD, JESSE (MRS. JOSEPH). *Joseph Conrad and His Circle.* New York: Dutton, 1935. 57–59, 72–75. A few details on the Conrads' visits with the Cranes at Ravensbook and Brede Place, noting, among other things, Crane's fondness for dogs and horses.

10.45 CONRAD, JOSEPH. *Joseph Conrad: Life and Letters.* Ed. George Jean-Aubry. Garden City, NY: Doubleday, 1927. 211–12, 234–35. Two important letters on Crane: 5 December 1897 to Edward Garnett, "He is certainly *the* impressionist and his temperament is curiously unique," and his 7 May 1900 report to John Galsworth about seeing Crane on a stretcher at Dover on his way to Badenweiler —Crane died on 5 June.

10.46 ———. *Letters of Joseph Conrad, 1895–1924.* Ed. Edward Garnett. Indianapolis: Bobbs-Merrill, 1928. 291–92 and passim. Several letters mention Crane, and Conrad comments on his preface to Beer's biography (1.1): "The Crane article for Beer is gone. It's just personal gossip, not critical—not even literary. Our first day together and so on."

10.47 ———. *Joseph Conrad: A Personal Record.* Marlboro, VT: Marlboro P, 1988. A reissue of Conrad's reminiscences (London 1912) with sections on the Conrad–Crane friendship, including a vintage Crane vignette. Crane told Conrad he ought to have a dog for his son. When Conrad delayed, Crane stepped in. Conrad comments, "I suspect that he was shocked at my neglect of parental duties. Ultimately it was he who provided the dog."

10.48 CRISLER, JESSE S. "'Christmas Must Be Gay': Stephen Crane's *The Ghost*—A Play by Diverse Hands." *Proof* 3 (1973): 69–120. An exhaustive study of the play Crane and his Christmas houseguests staged at the Brede schoolhouse in 1899. Beyond lengthy commentary, Crisler's text corrects the Stallman version (*Omnibus*, 2.16). Facsimiles of manuscript fragments are also included.

10.49 DELBANCO, NICHOLAS. "Stephen Crane in England." *Group Portrait: Joseph Conrad, Stephen Crane, Ford Madox Ford, Henry James and H. G. Wells*. New York: Morrow, 1982. 39–81. The chapter on Crane in England is neither as informative nor as perceptive as Solomon's short book (10.39) or Milne's study (10.38). Delbanco's most useful comments deal with Crane's early successes and the quality of his later works. Delbanco holds that Crane could have reversed the trend and done more great works had he lived longer. See also on this point Leibling (10.80).

10.50 EDEL, LEON. "A Ghostly Rental." *Henry James: The Master, 1901–1916*. Philadelphia: Lippincott, 1972. 57–68. An elegant chapter on the Henry James–Stephen Crane connection. A bittersweet, touching account of the Cranes at Brede: "For Cora it was a perpetual lark; for Crane it was a continual sad grind."

10.51 EDEL, LEON, and GORDON N. RAY, eds. *Henry James and H. G. Wells*. Urbana: U of Illinois P, 1958. 7, 167. James's letter to Wells on hearing of Crane's terminal condition. "You will have felt, as I have done, the miserable sadness of poor Crane's so precipitated and, somehow, so unnecessary extinction. I was at Brede Place this afternoon—and it looked conscious and cruel," plus other brief comments.

10.52 FINLAYSON, IAIN. "Stephen Crane at Brede." *The Sixth Continent: A Literary History of Romney March*. New York: Atheneum, 1986. 113–35. Lots of comments by other people about Crane at Brede—sad talk of dying and lack of money. Nothing original or striking.

10.53 FORD, FORD MADOX. "Henry James, Stephen Crane and the Mainstream." *Thus to Revisit: Some Reminiscences*. New York: Dutton, 1921. 102–25. Ford's interest is in James, especially his concern and benevolence for Crane. Memorable details about Crane's writing process; "it used to be terrible to see the words, in a tiny writing, slowly filling the immense sheet of white foolscap; falling from the pen which made that passionate pilgrimage, to keep going that immense house, that not so much riotous as uncalculated hospitality." Partly reprinted in *Portraits from Life* (Chicago: Regnery, 1937), which was reissued as *Mightier than the Sword* (London: G. Allen, 1938) and also in *The March of Literature* (New York: Dial, 1938).

10.54   _____. *Joseph Conrad: A Personal Remembrance*. London: Duckworth, 1924. Passim. Scattered comments on the Crane–Conrad friendship.

10.55   _____. *It Was the Nightingale*. Philadelphia: Lippincott, 1933. 18. Ford again describes Crane's "tiny handwriting [on] immense sheets of white paper."

10.56   _____. "Two Americans—II." *New York Evening Post Literary Review* 26 March 1921, 1–2. The two Americans are Crane and Henry James. Hueffer (before he changed his last name to Ford) tells of party life at Brede.

10.57   _____. "Stevie & Co." *New York Herald Tribune Books* 2 Jan. 1927: 1, 6. A roundabout endorsement of the Follett edition of Crane's works (12.5) plus tales of Crane's cowboy antics at Oxted.

10.58   _____. *Return to Yesterday: Reminiscences 1894–1914*. London: Victor Gollancz, 1931. Passim. Standard stories: Conrad's admiration for "The Open Boat," Crane's painfully slow writing pace, and Conrad's visits with the Cranes at Ravensbrook and Brede.

10.59   _____. *Letters of Ford Madox Ford*. Ed. Richard M. Ludwig. Princeton, NJ: Princeton UP, 1965. 300–302. Ludwig includes Ford's 1938 letter to the editor of the *Saturday Review of Literature* wherein Ford stresses Crane's significant influence on "today's Anglo-Saxon literary stream."

10.60   FORTENBERRY, GEORGE E., et al., eds. *The Correspondence of Harold Frederic*. Fort Worth: Texas Christian UP, 1984. Three letters by and to Crane and to Cora (see *The Correspondence of Stephen Crane*, 13.3:#362, 366, 780) and letters from Frederic concerning spending holidays (Thanksgiving and New Year's Day) with the Cranes. Two other matters are worth note: The editors claim that "Frederic located a home for Crane and Cora, and their odd entourage at Ravensbrook, and drew Crane into his Surrey circle," and second, the editors give details about Kate Lyon doing the research and much of the writing for Crane's *Great Battles of the World*.

10.61   FOX, AUSTIN McC. "Stephen Crane and Joseph Conrad." *Serif* 6.4 (1969): 16–20. A brief recounting of the Crane–Conrad friendship.

Regarding their works: Both "thought romanticism is an excessive form of egoism" and both sought out unconventional topics.

10.62   FREWEN, HUGH. *Imogene: An Odyssey.* Sidney, Australia: Australasian Publishing Co., nd [1944]. 99–100. Brief notes on the Cranes at Brede.

10.63   GALEN, NINA. "Stephen Crane as a Source for Conrad's Jim." *Nineteenth-Century Fiction* 38 (1983): 78–96. More on Conrad than Crane; several highly convoluted, psychoanalytic numerological conjectures on Conrad's *Lord Jim* and *Red Badge.*

10.64   GALSWORTHY, JOHN. "Reminiscences of Conrad." *Scribner's Magazine* 77 (January 1925): 3–10. Crane is mentioned in passing as a kindred spirit of Conrad.

10.65   GARLAND, HAMLIN. *My Friendly Contemporaries.* New York: Macmillan, 1932. 499 and passim. Garland retells Conrad's impressions of the Cranes at Brede and he adds a small section on his own part in a Crane memorial service.

10.66   GARNER, STANTON. "Some Notes on Harold Frederic in Ireland." *American Literature* 39 (1967): 60–74. Brief mention of the trip to Ireland Frederic and his "wife," Kate, and Crane and his "wife," Cora, took in September 1897.

10.67   GILKES, LILLIAN. "Stephen Crane and the Harold Frederics." *Serif* 6.4 (1969): 21–48. Though this piece is more on Frederic than Crane it is the most informative examination of the Crane–Frederic friendship.

10.68   ———. "The London Newsletters of Stephen and Cora Crane: A Collaboration." *Studies in American Fiction* 4 (1976): 173–201. Gilkes offers opinions on which "London Newsletters" were by Cora and which by Crane. "We know that he [Crane] quite often took the germ of an idea from Cora's raw material and reworked it." Note: Just in case Stallman is looking she manages to get back to their dispute about how the Cranes got to Greece (see 9.110, 9.112 and 9.113).

10.69   GORDAN, JOHN D. "*The Ghost* at Brede Place." *Bulletin of the New York Public Library* 56 (1952): 591–95. A few details on Crane at Brede. Gordan's Crane is Gatsbyesque as he stresses elaborate parties, including the gala Christmas of 1899 and the staging of the play *The Ghost.*

10.70 GULLASON, THOMAS A. "Stephen Crane as Literary Expatriate." *William Carlos Williams, Stephen Crane, and Philip Freneau: Papers and Poems Celebrating New Jersey's Literary Heritage.* Ed. W. John Bauer. Trenton: New Jersey Historical Commission, 1989. 87–95. Why did Crane become a literary expatriate? Gullason explains what he was running from and what he was running to, but mostly that he was just running. "Crane had far subtler reasons for going to England and to Europe. His journey was not really a defensive action but a basic part of his nature. He had the soul of a restless wanderer who was always on the road." Gullason also briefly discusses "the fabulous creative friendships he found waiting for him in England."

10.71 HARRIMAN, KARL EDWIN. "Last Days of Stephen Crane." *New Hope* 2 (Oct. 1934): 7–9, 19–21. Brief memoirs on visits to Brede along with side trips to see Henry James at Rye.

10.72 HARVEY, DAVID. *Ford Madox Ford, 1873–1939: A Bibliography of Works and Criticism.* Princeton, NJ: Princeton UP, 1962. 204 and passim. Some two-dozen short entries on Ford's criticism on Crane's works and comments on his life.

10.73 HEILBRUN, CAROLYN G. *The Garnett Family.* London: George Allen, 1961. 128–30 and passim. Reprints Garnett's letter to Conrad that initiated the arrangements to have Conrad write the introduction to Beer's *Stephen Crane* (1.1); Garnett also decries America's neglect of Crane in the period between his death and the revival sparked by Beer's book and the Knopf edition, *The Work of Stephen Crane* (12.5).

10.74 HEPBURN, JAMES. *The Author's Empty Purse and the Rise of the Literary Agent.* London: Oxford UP, 1968. 57 and passim. Mention is made of James Pinker as Crane's agent.

10.75 HYDE, H. MONTGOMERY. "Visitors and Visiting." *Henry James at Home.* New York: Farrar, Straus, 1969. On the Crane–James relationship: A section of this chapter (183–88) discusses life at Brede Place, the Christmas play, *The Ghost,* and James's admiration for the young American genius.

10.76 JONES, EDITH R. "Stephen Crane at Brede." *Atlantic Monthly* 194 (1954): 56–61. Romantic memoirs of life at Brede: There was no worry about money and there is no talk of Crane's illness. Still, Jones offers interesting comments about the Frewens—Mrs. Frewen was Lady Randolph Churchill's sister and Winston Churchill's aunt.

10.77 LESLIE, ANITA. "Stephen Crane at Brede." *Mr. Frewen of England.* London: Hutchinson, 1966. 158–62. Standard stories of Crane at

Brede: dinner parties (requiring brandy to bribe the cook) and the staging of *The Ghost.*

10.78 LESLIE, SHANE. "Brede—A Note." *Sussex County Magazine* 5 (1931): 543–44. A brief historical sketch of the Brede manor house the Cranes rented in Sussex, England.

10.79 ———. "Stephen Crane in Sussex." *Stephen Crane, 1871–1971: An Exhibition from the Collection of Matthew J. Bruccoli.* Columbia: U of South Carolina P, 1971. 13–19. Leslie reprints several letters from Cora to Moreton and Clara Frewen, the Cranes's landlords at Brede Place. Cora's extravagance is amply illustrated: She describes "over three hundred very choice roses . . . I had planted against the front of the house" and she discusses planting trees and shrubs for a maze.

10.80 LIEBLING, A. J. "The Dollars Damned Him." *New Yorker* 37 (5 August 1961): 48–60, 63–66, 69–72. Crane was killed by money worries. "Crane was not the victim of self-indulgence or a death wish. . . . He died, unwillingly, of the cause most common among American middle-class males—anxiety about money." In addition, Liebling argues that many of Crane's works were of high quality and he would have again reached *Red Badge* levels had he lived longer. An abridged version of this article was reprinted in *Stephen Crane: A Collection of Critical Essays* (2.2: 18–26). See also Walcutt (11.52).

10.81 LINDBERG-SEYERSTED, BRITA. *Ford Madox Ford and His Relationship to Stephen Crane and Henry James.* Atlantic Highlands, NJ: Humanities P International, 1987. 107. There is only one a short chapter (15–28) on Crane. A few nice bits on life at Brede Place and Ford's impression of Crane as a "blend of Apollo and outdoors-man."

10.82 MACSHANE, FRANK, ed. *Critical Writings of Ford Madox Ford.* Lincoln: U of Nebraska P, 1964. Scattered comments on Crane, mostly in connection with Conrad.

10.83 MCLEAN, DAVID. "Brede Place, Sussex and America." *Sussex County Magazine* 5 (1931): 540–44. Information on life at Brede Place.

10.84 ———. "Brede Place, Sussex and America." *Sussex County Magazine* 5 (1931): 540–44. Interesting details on the Frewens and the manor house they leased to the Cranes. The poster announcing the Christmas play, *The Ghost,* is reproduced.

10.85 O'DONNELL, THOMAS F. Editor's Foreword. *Harold Frederic's Stories of York State.* Syracuse, NY: Syracuse UP, 1966. v–viii. O'Donnell tells of Crane and Frederic meeting and the mutual respect they held for each other's works.

10.86　O'DONNELL, THOMAS F., and HOYT C. FRANCHERE. *Harold Frederic*. New York: Twayne, 1961. Crane is mentioned here and there; his favorable review, "Harold Frederic," is discussed (106).

10.87　PARTINGTON, WILFRED. "The 'Lost Souls' of Stephen Crane and His Sussex Days." *The Bookman's Journal and Print Collector* 8 (1923): 145–47. Details of the Cranes at Brede from a book collector's angle: comments on some dozen alleged lost works of Crane.

10.88　PRESTON, HAYTER. "The Real Stephen Crane." *First Editions and Book Collector* 2 (Sept./Oct. 1924): 75–77. Preston seeks to counter the dissolute Crane stories along with an account of his visit to Rye and Brede Place. Included also is his account of an old neighbor's reminiscences. Crane was "a thin gentleman who rode a lot. . . . he looked delicate . . . he certainly had a great many friends."

10.89　RANDALL, DALE. "Conrad Interviews, No. 3: Thomas B. Sherman." *Conradiana* 2.3 (Spring 1969–1970): 122–27. In response to a question on Crane, Conrad speaks warmly of the impact of *Red Badge*.

10.90　RIDGE, W. PETT. *I Like to Remember*. New York: George H. Doran, 1929. 210–11. A comment about a Rye doctor visiting Crane at Brede and his having two brandies and soda for breakfast.

10.91　SECOR, ROBERT, and DEBRA MODDELMOG. "Conrad and Stephen Crane." *Joseph Conrad and American Writers: A Bibliographical Study of Affinities, Influences and Relations*. Westport, CT: Greenwood, 1985. 45–62. A thorough and reliable listing of Crane–Conrad comments on each other plus an account of the Crane–Conrad relationship as revealed in secondary literature on each author.

10.92　SEYMOUR, MIRANDA. "Imaginative Truths: The Cranes" and "Living Dangerously, The Cranes." *A Ring of Conspirators: Henry James and His Literary Circle, 1895–1915*. By Miranda Seymour. London: Hodder and Stoughton, 1988. 23–44, 199–224. With a focus on James, Seymour's book is sort of a house tour of other writers who lived at (or visited) the literary colony in Sussex. Though lively, her two chapters on Crane mostly recite information from Gilkes (10.20) and *Letters of Stephen Crane* (13.2). The first chapter stresses party life at Brede, especially staging the Christmas play, *The Ghost*; the second treats Crane's last sick and financially desperate days. Of James and the

Cranes Seymour writes, "The new owners of Brede were, in short . . . out of place. . . . Pistol-shooting and rowdy parties were not what Sussex expected to be associated with Brede and Crane's was not the sort of behaviour James cared to see in a fellow American. He resolved to be cordial, but distant."

10.93 SHERIDAN, CLAIRE. *Naked Truth*. London: Harper, 1928. 383. An autobiography of one of the Frewen children (whose parents leased Brede Place to the Cranes); Claire was a painter and sculptor of some note. A few details on life at Brede and Sussex. Also published as *Nuda Veritas*. Sheridan continued her memoirs, including some interesting information on Brede, in *My Crowded Sanctuary* (London: Methuen, 1945) and in *To the Four Winds* (Tonbridge, Kent: Tonbridge Printers, 1957).

10.94 SHERRY, NORMAN. "A Conrad Manuscript." *Times Literary Supplement* 25 June 1970, 691. Sherry describes a recently discovered Conrad manuscript that tells of Conrad meeting Crane when Sidney Pawlings of Heinemann took both of them to lunch in October 1897.

10.95 STAPE J. H. "The Date and Writing of Conrad's 'Stephen Crane: A Note without Dates.'" *Notes and Queries* 33 (1986): 184–85. Deals with Conrad; Conrad wrote the Crane piece in mid 1919.

10.96 STRONKS, JAMES B. "Stephen Crane's English Years: The Legend Corrected." *Papers of the Bibliographical Society of America* 57 (1963): 340–49. The details of the state of Crane's finances in England, including how much he made, per word, for the works he sold during this time.

10.97 THEROUX, ALEX. "Comfort Food." *Lears* 3.12 (Feb. 1991): 82–87. A single-sentence mention (the sort Stallman ferreted out for his *Stephen Crane: A Critical Bibliography,* 14.3): "Henry James was addicted to Cora Crane's (wife of novelist Stephen Crane) doughnuts." A bit overstated, to say the least.

10.98 URSELL, GEOFFREY. "Conrad: Two Misdated Letters." *Notes and Queries* 17 (1970): 36–37. One of Conrad's letters to Crane was written in March though Conrad had dated it "5th Febr. 98."

10.99 WATT, IAN. *Conrad and the Nineteenth Century*. Berkeley: U of California P, 1979. 126–27 and passim. The Conrad-Crane friendship, especially how Crane tried to further Conrad's career.

10.100 WEINTRAUB, STANLEY. "Brede Place." *The London Yankees: Portraits of American Writers and Artists in England, 1894–1914*. New York:

Harcourt Brace, 1979. 144–77. Breezy account of Crane and Cora in England, Cora's possessive loyalty, and Crane's best work during his last days, especially *The Monster.*

10.101 WELLS, H. G. "Edifying Encounters." *Experiment in Autobiography.* New York: Macmillan, 1934. 509–44. A rambling chapter on Wells's acquaintances; a small section (522–25) devoted to memories of the Cranes at Brede Place. Also interesting comments on Crane's style: "an admirable bare prose. . . . He had an intense receptiveness to vivid work; he had an inevitably right instinct for the word in his stories."

10.102 ———. *Boon.* London: George H. Doran, 1915. Passim. Wells decries America's neglect of Crane; for a typical instance of Wells's complaint see Pattee (2.161).

For more on the Cranes in England see:

1.1–1.4
1.10
1.37
1.135
2.1–2.19
10.20
10.22
10.33

LAST WORKS

Articles and Book Chapters

10.103 [Review of *Great Battles of the World*]. *Critic* 38 (1901): 88. The facts constrained him and his art suffered. Reprinted in *The Critical Heritage,* 2.17:#128.

10.104 [Review of *Great Battles of the World*]. *Dial* 30 (1901): 114. Crane's war history is a disappointment. Reprinted in *The Critical Heritage,* 2.17:#129.

10.105 [Review of *Great Battles of the World*]. *Atheneum* 29 June 1901: 819. Except for his chapters on Bunker Hill and the campaign of New

Orleans, Crane's book is disappointing. Reprinted in *The Critical Heritage,* 2.17:#130.

10.106 [Review of *Great Battles of the World*]. *Spectator* 87 (3 Aug. 1901): 158–59. Though "these 'great battles' are unworthy of their author, they are not without merit." Their chief merit is Crane's evenhanded objectivity. Reprinted in *The Critical Heritage,* 2.17:#131.

10.107 [Review of *Great Battles of the World*]. *Graphic* [London] 64 (10 Aug. 1901): 194. Crane "has not given us enough for our money." Reprinted in *The Critical Heritage,* 2.17:#132.

10.108 [Review of *Last Works*]. *Graphic* [London] 65 (5 Apr. 1902): 476. Crane's posthumous book is slight but it is of good quality; "one and all possess that curious vivid quality which first brought the work of this writer to note." Reprinted in *The Critical Heritage,* 2.17:#133.

10.109 CHRISTOPHERSEN, BILL. "Stephen Crane's 'The Upturned Face' as Expressionist Fiction." *Arizona Quarterly* 38 (1982): 147–61. There are only a handful of articles on this very late minimasterpiece by Crane. Christophersen's discussion is one of the most sustained. Beyond expected comments on expressionism, he argues that "The Upturned Face" is a statement of existentialism; humans have to manufacture meanings despite lack of information and ambiguity: "We know nothing of the war being described—neither when, where, nor why it is being fought—and next to nothing of the characters involved, especially the dead man."

10.110 DILLINGHAM, WILLIAM B. "Crane's One-Act Farce: 'The Upturned Face.' " *Research Studies* 35 (1967): 324–30. Crane's "reputation as a literary craftsman rests largely on his skill in incongruities." To wit: "The Upturned Face" is both a horror story and a one-act farce. This last gem of Crane deserves better.

10.111 HOFFMAN, DANIEL G. "Stephen Crane's Last Novel." *Bulletin of the New York Public Library* 64 (1960): 337–43. Hoffman reprints and make comments on Crane's sketch of a historical novel "on the fortunes of his own New Jersey forbearers during the American Revolution" less than a year before his death.

10.112 KATZ, JOSEPH. "*Great Battles of the World:* Manuscripts and Method." *Stephen Crane Newsletter* 3.2 (1968): 5–7. From holograph fragments it is clear that Crane wrote only bridge paragraphs stringing together material Kate Frederic had researched.

10.113 MORRIS, HARRISON S. Note. *Great Battles of the World*. Philadelphia: Lippincott, 1901. 3.4. Morris's Note is a four-paragraph introductory promotion piece.

10.114 SHORT, RAYMOND W., and RICHARD B. SEWALL. "'The Upturned Face' by Stephen Crane." *Short Stories for Study*. New York: Holt, 1941. 134–38, 591–92. A reprinting of "The Upturned Face" along with brief comments on Crane's interest in "human emotions under conditions of stress."

10.115 WITHERINGTON, PAUL. "Public and Private Order in Stephen Crane's 'The Upturned Face.'" *Markham Review* 6 (1977): 70–71. Thesis: In crises, military roles self destruct and idiosyncratic beliefs take over—an interesting assertion lacking convincing argumentation.

THE O'RUDDY

Books

10.116 BOWERS, FREDSON, ed. *The O'Ruddy. The Works of Stephen Crane*, vol. 4. Charlottesville: UP of Virginia, 1971. lxxiv+362. Bowers sorted out the Crane portion and the parts written by Robert Barr. See 10.125 for Bowers's account of the dual authorship of *The O'Ruddy* and 10.133 for Levenson's general introduction.

10.117 FOLLETT, WILSON, ed. *The O'Ruddy. The Work of Stephen Crane*, vols. 7 & 8. New York: Knopf, 1926. xv+193, 176. Follett devoted two volumes to his reissue of *The O'Ruddy*; see 10.123 for Beer's introduction to this last effort of Crane.

Articles and Book Chapters

10.118 [Review of *The O'Ruddy*]. *Book News* 22 (Dec. 1903): 428. "*The O'Ruddy* is a brilliantly witty, essentially Irish tale." Reprinted in *The Critical Heritage*, 2.17:#134.

10.119 [Review of *The O'Ruddy*]. *Academy* 67 (6 Aug. 1904): 99. The book is delightful, "written with just the right amount of wit and humor." Reprinted in *The Critical Heritage*, 2.17:#136.

10.120 [Review of *The O'Ruddy*]. *Saturday Review* 97 (6 Aug. 1904): 177. An Irish swashbuckler; the reviewer worries about "the respective shares of the two authors." Reprinted in *The Critical Heritage*, 2:17:#136.

10.121 [Review of *The O'Ruddy*]. *Atheneum* 13 Aug. 1904, 200. An animated masterpiece! Reprinted in *The Critical Heritage*, 2.17:#138.

10.122 BARR, ROBERT. "Stephen Crane's Last Story." *New York Herald* 21 June 1900, 10. A letter concerning Crane's last days and his problems in completing *The O'Ruddy*.

10.123 BEER, THOMAS. Introduction. *The O'Ruddy*. *The Work of Stephen Crane*, vols. 7 & 8. Ed. Wilson Follett. New York: Knopf, 1926. ix–xv. A brief essay on Crane's life and work and even briefer comments on Crane's failure to handle an Irish swashbuckling romance.

10.124 BOHNENBERGER, CARL. "Stephen Crane and Robert Barr." *Saturday Review of Literature* 10 (16 Dec. 1933): 352. A letter to the effect that Robert Barr had serious reservations about finishing *The O'Ruddy*.

10.125 BOWERS, FREDSON. "The Text: History and Analysis." *The O'Ruddy*. *The Works of Stephen Crane*, vol. 4. Ed. Fredson Bowers. Charlottesville: UP of Virginia, 1971. 271–98. Crane wrote chapters 1–25 and using Crane's outlines, Robert Barr wrote the rest. By the time Bowers and his crew went to work on *The O'Ruddy* the manuscript had turned up. Before then it is not clear whether Crane had written twenty-four or twenty-five chapters. (Hence O'Donnell's computer analysis concluding that Crane wrote chapters 1–24 was off by one chapter; see 10.136). Bowers describes the Crane–Barr dual authorship along with other copy text problems.

10.126 ———. "Stephen Crane's *The O'Ruddy*: Editorial Process." *The Author's Intention: An Exhibition for the Center for Editions for American Authors at the Folger Shakespeare Library, Washington, D.C.* Ed. Matthew J. Bruccoli. Columbia: U of South Carolina P, 1972. 17–24. Bowers describes the research and procedures used to produce the critical text of *The O'Ruddy;* more generally, this article gives a step-by-step account of the exacting and painstaking process required to win the CEAA seal of approval.

10.127 ———. "Notes on Editing *The O'Ruddy.*" *The Author's Intention: An Exhibition for the Center for Editions for American Authors at the Folger Shakespeare Library, Washington, D.C.* Ed. Matthew J. Bruccoli.

Columbia: U of South Carolina P, 1972. 10–16. Bowers describes the partial holograph manuscript and other materials used to produce the Virginia edition of *The O'Ruddy*. He also gives details of the bowdlerized syndicated magazine version that appeared in *The Idler* and he explains how the CEAA-approved edition "restores the purity and truth of Crane's text, sometimes in far-reaching literary ways, and offers to the critic an authentic and perceptibly different version of the novel from that which has previously been available in corrupt and distorted versions." See also 10.128.

10.128 BRADSHAW, JAMES STANFORD. "Completing Crane's *O'Ruddy:* A New Note." *American Notes and Queries* 3 (1990): 174–78. What is new here is Bradshaw's reprinting a long excerpt from Barr's monthly *The Idler* wherein he tells his side of the story of his involvement with finishing *The O'Ruddy*. Incidentally, from October 1903 to July 1904 *The Idler* published an abbreviated, serialized version of the joint Crane–Barr novel. See also 10.127.

10.129 BRUCCOLI, MATTHEW J. "Robert Barr's Proofs of *The O'Ruddy*." *Stephen Crane Newsletter* 4.3 (1970): 8–9. Brief comments on Barr's proofs; the initial page of chapter 26 is reproduced.

10.130 GILKES, LILLIAN, and JOAN H. BAUM. "Stephen Crane's Last Novels: *The O'Ruddy*." *Columbia Library Columns* 6 (1957): 41–48. Gilkes and Baum lay out the difficulties Cora had getting someone to finish Crane's last work. Robert Barr refused, Kipling refused, Cora tried her hand, and A. E. W. Mason worked on it for a while. Two years later it was back to Barr, who eventually finished it.

10.131 KATZ, JOSEPH. "Crane's Chapter Headings for *The O'Ruddy*." *Stephen Crane Newsletter* 4.3 (1970): 1. Katz gives a facsimile of Crane's holograph, which gives headings for chapters 1–4.

10.132 LEED, JACOB, and ROBERT HEMENWAY. "Use of the Computer in Some Recent Studies of Literary Style." *Serif* 2.2 (1965): 16–20. Describes how a computer analysis of style can be used to establish authorship. O'Donnell's (10.136) study of *The O'Ruddy* is cited as an example.

10.133 LEVENSON, J. C. Introduction. *The O'Ruddy. The Works of Stephen Crane*, vol. 4. Ed. Fredson Bowers. Charlottesville: UP of Virginia, 1969. xiii–lxxiv. How could anyone write sixty-plus pages on this potboiler? Levenson did it by lengthy discussions of other Crane books and stories, his health problems, his debts, his hassles with his British agent, Pinker, and difficulties in getting Robert Barr to finish the book. Yes, there are some observations on themes and motifs in *The O'Ruddy,* too.

10.134 MONTEIRO, GEORGE. "Stephen Crane, *Public Opinion:* An Annotated Checklist, an Unrecorded Parody, and a Review of *The O'Ruddy." Stephen Crane Newsletter* 5.1 (1970): 5–8. Important, Monteiro argues, for gauging Crane's contemporaneous reputation.

10.135 _____. "Stephen Crane: A New Appreciation by Edward Garnett." *American Literature* 50 (1978): 465–71. Monteiro reprints a notice by Garnett, Crane's most astute and appreciative English critic. The notice in question deals with *The O'Ruddy,* which Garnett labels "the misfire of a man of genius," though he takes the opportunity to celebrate Crane's best works.

10.136 O'DONNELL, BERNARD. "Stephen Crane's *The O'Ruddy:* A Problem in Authorship Discrimination." *The Computer and Literary Style.* Ed. Jacob Leed. Kent, OH: Kent State UP, 1966. 107–15. O'Donnell "proved" by computer analysis, what has long been debated: Crane wrote chapters 1–24, 25 is a transitional chapter, and the rest were by Robert Barr. By the time Bowers did the critical edition of *The O'Ruddy* the manuscript had turned up. O'Donnell missed it by one—Crane wrote chapters 1–25. For those interested in more on computer investigations of style, see O'Donnell's *An Analysis of Prose Styles to Determine Authorship,* Paris: Mouton, 1970, and Leed and Hemenway (10.132).

10.137 PAYNE, WILLIAM MORTON. [Review of *The O'Ruddy.*] *Dial* 36 (16 Feb. 1904): 121. Payne loved the book: "The book is a singularly racy one, and may be read with unflagging interest." Reprinted in *A Critical Heritage* (2.17:#135).

On *The O'Ruddy* also see:

1.1–1.4	10.6
1.10	10.7
2.1–2.4	
2.8	
2.9	
2.13–2.16	

11
Style

Overview

Crane's brilliant style has attracted numerous brief (and quotable) comments; see especially:

Beer 11.7
Ford 11.14
GARNETT 11.17
HONIG 11.23
Norris 11.41
STARETT 11.48

Of more value and importance are several insightful examinations of how Crane was able to surprise, astonish, persuade, and delight his readers; see:

COLVERT 11.10
Guetti 11.20
Hough 11.24
KWIAT 11.34 and 11.35
MILNE 11.38
Nagel 11.40
Overland 11.43
Rogers 11.46

Incidentally, the best and most detailed examinations of Crane's style and writing technique are to be found in the books by Halliburton (2.9) and Nagel (2.14).

Articles and Book Chapters

II.1   "Kinds of Courage and Realism." *London Times Literary Supplement* 9 July 1964: 588. A review essay on *Stephen Crane: Uncollected Writings*. Ed. Olov W. Fryckstedt (12.6). Many insightful general comments including this wonderful synopsis of Crane's approach and style: "Crane studies appearances with a realistic eye in the search for those occasions when a disturbance in the ordinary allows a glimpse of the extraordinary lying in wait."

II.2   "The Last of Stephen Crane." *Literary Digest* 21 (1900): 647. Brief review comments on Crane's technique of stringing together a bundle of short sentences before he hits his reader with "the horror of some homely comparison."

II.3   "The New Art of Descriptive Fiction." *Literary Digest* 20 (1900): 182. Crane is at the forefront of the new style marked by "brevity and crisp, vivid outline."

II.4   [Review of Thomas Beer's *Stephen Crane*]. *Times Literary Supplement* 4 Sept. 1924: 537. Compliments Beer, especially his grasp of Crane's style; Crane is called both an impressionist and "a realist who obtained his effects by his use of adjectives and adverbs."

II.5   "Stephen Crane as the American Pioneer of the Free Verse Army." *Current Opinion* 62 (Mar. 1917): 202–3. Mostly a reprinting of an article by Dounce; see 11.12.

II.6   BATES, H. E. "American Writers after Poe: Crane." *The Modern Short Story: A Critical Survey.* Boston: The Writer, 1941. 65–71. Crane is very briefly treated in part of a chapter. Though several of his stories are mentioned, more valuable are Bates's comments on Crane's impressionistic style and his stress upon "casual, episodic moments."

II.7   BEER, THOMAS. "Stephen, Henry and the Hat." *Vanity Fair* 18 (1922): 63, 88. Sprightly comments about Crane's "staccato, nervous prose" and a description of a lost, unpublished Crane story, "The Hat," which allegedly anticipates both *Maggie* and *George's Mother.*

II.8   BRENNAN, JOSEPH X. "Stephen Crane and the Limits of Irony." *Criticism* 11 (1969): 183–200. "The whole range of Crane's fiction offers examples of a constant opposition between the involved, self-deluded character and the detached ironic narrator." Hence "The Open Boat" is not an isolated instance but typical of Crane's style and technique; to this end, several other Crane items are examined.

II.9 BROOKS, VAN WYCK. "A Reviewer's Notebook." *Freeman* 4 (18 Jan. 1922): 455. Brooks's essay on Crane and the nineties is a classic. He explains that "Crane was a minor artist, without doubt: a writer of prose who dies before he is thirty can scarcely be anything else." Still, Crane's impact has been legendary and it is his style to which Brooks gives credit—a style that is ever selective. "Crane was a preternaturally sensitive man . . . acting upon such an acute sensibility these trifling situations assume for the moment a prodigious importance."

II.10 COLVERT, JAMES B. "Stephen Crane: Style as Invention." *Stephen Crane in Transition: Centenary Essays*. Ed. Joseph Katz. De Kalb: Northern Illinois UP, 1972. 127–52. One of the most insightful and convincing analyses of Crane's style. Thesis: Realism assumes that there is a reality and humans can know it; Crane, to the contrary, was led by experience to complexity and qualification regarding reality's problematic character. Instead of stating this philosophical conclusion, however, Crane reveals it indirectly through his style.

II.11 ———. "Stephen Crane's Literary Origins and Tolstoy's *Sebastapol*." *Comparative Literature Studies* 15 (1977): 66–82. Though there were ample American sources for Crane's subject matter and "plots" (see Cunliffe, 4.23 for more on this), Crane's stylistic devices came from Tolstoy (not Zola). Colvert examines the Crane–Tolstoy connection with regard to figurative and exclusive selection of details, "the observing mind and the drama of experience."

II.12 DOUNCE, HARRY ESTY. "Stephen Crane as a Craftsman." *New York Evening Sun* 8 Jan. 1917: 14. Though Crane's poetry anticipated the free verse army, his more significant contribution was his impressionistic prose. For example, though "The Open Boat" has little plot it is a classic and a masterpiece due to the "systematic exaggeration" of Crane's style.

II.13 FOERSTER, NORMAN, et al. "Literary Naturalism; Stephen Crane." *Poetry and Prose*. Boston: Houghton Mifflin, 1970. 829–31; 1022–23. The first is a general essay describing Crane as the most artistic American naturalist. The second emphasizes "his unusual style," which the authors find throughout Crane's works. Further, they cite his skill at depicting the psychology of actors and actions under stress and his flair for color images. Crane selections reprinted in this anthology are "The Experience of Misery," "The Upturned Face," "The Open Boat," and seven poems from *War Is Kind* and *The Black Riders*.

II.14   FORD, FORD MADOX. "Techniques." *Southern Review* 1 (1935): 20–35. Crane's style is treated briefly: his strategy of "nervous meticulousness [which] excises and excises."

II.15   ———. *Critical Writings of Ford Madox Ford*. Ed. Frank MacShane. Lincoln: U of Nebraska P, 1964. 66 and passim. Observations on Crane's terse style.

II.16   GARNETT, DAVID, ed. *The Letters of T. E. Lawrence*. New York: Doubleday, 1939. 777–79. Letters to Garnett stating how impressed he is with Crane's style: "a man of astonishment—one who surprised and shocked, by turns of incident and vivid phrases."

II.17   GARNETT, EDWARD. "Mr. Stephen Crane: An Appreciation." *Academy* 55 (17 Dec. 1898): 483–84. A classic of Crane criticism. Garnett stresses Crane's technique of impressionism and his emphasis on episodes and surfaces: "a few oaths, a genius for slang, an exquisite and unique faculty of exposing an individual scene by an odd simile, a power of interpreting a face or an action, a keen realizing of the primitive emotions." Reprinted in Weatherford, *A Critical Heritage* (2.17: #91).

II.18   GRABO, CARL H. *The Art of the Short Story*. New York: Scribner's, 1913. Passim. Grabo briefly discusses Crane (161–63) and finds in several of Crane's stories, notably "The Bride Comes to Yellow Sky," the same impressionism he finds in *Red Badge*. He likens Crane's style to a poster (not a portrait or a photograph) because he selects details that have no intrinsic importance.

II.19   GRANT, DOUGLAS. "Stephen Crane: Kinds of Courage and Realism." *Purpose and Place: Essays on American Writers*. New York: St. Martin's, 1965. 136–41. An interesting, short general essay on Crane's impressionistic style, stressing his "describing not for description's sake but for the sake of the truth that lies in appearances" and his realism, which is not Zola's but instead "the realism of the Salvation Army."

II.20   GUETTI, JAMES. "Mixed Motives." *Word-Music: The Aesthetic Aspect of Narrative Fiction*. New Brunswick: Rutgers UP, 1980. 108–69. An interesting analysis of Crane's style (123–39). Crane's attention to a "progressive sequence of perceived images" is compared with techniques used by Conrad and Hemingway. Also includes an examination of Crane's staccato, brittle, and telegraphic "aural rhetoric."

11.21 GUINN, DOROTHY MARGARET. "The Making of a Masterpiece: Stephen Crane's *The Red Badge of Courage.*" *Computers and the Humanities* 14 (1980): 231–39. If nothing else this piece shows the extent of the Crane industry. Guinn turns to a computer analysis of *Red Badge* to demonstrate that "Crane's revisions show him seeking a more concrete, more precise, more complete expression of his ideas. In the process, he often increases coherence, emphasis, and syntactic variety beyond that of his draft." Improvements anyone would welcome! More helpful are Guinn's observations that Crane's revisions were expansive, rather than contractive.

11.22 HERZBERG, MAX J. "New and Old Data on Stephen Crane." *Torch* 4 (1931): 36–38. A brief, early examination of the style and themes in Crane that Herzberg argues were a clear anticipation of modern fiction.

11.23 HONIG, DONALD. "Introduction." *Stephen Crane's 'An Illusion in Red and White' and Ten Other Stories.* Ed. Donald Honig. New York: Avon, 1962. 7–13. An obscure book (Stallman calls it "a drug-store paperback," *Stephen Crane: A Critical Bibliography,* 14.3: 470) reprinting several of Crane's early Sullivan County sketches. Honig explains that his intent is to get a readership beyond *Red Badge* and Crane's better-known short stories. The volume's introduction is a hidden gem. Though Honig's biographical sketch contains the common error that Crane died at 29, his grasp of Crane's themes and techniques is worthy of note: "He was an observer of significant detail. . . . All this is expressed in Crane's slim, spearlike sentences. With images and metaphors as startling as they are abrupt, he paints his picture."

11.24 HOUGH, ROBERT L. "Crane and Goethe: A Forgotten Relationship." *Nineteenth-Century Fiction* 17 (1962): 135–48. Hough pursues the comment by a classmate and fraternity brother, Frank Noxon (see 1.175) that Crane had been very impressed with Goethe's views on the impact of color on ideas and emotions. Hough tracks down specifics from Eastlake's *Goethe's Theory of Color* (1840) and relates them to passages in *Red Badge, Maggie,* and other of Crane's works.

11.25 HOWARD, LEON, LOUIS B. WRIGHT, and CARL BODE, eds. "The Rebels of the Nineties." *American Heritage: An Anthology and Interpretive Survey of Our Literature,* vol. 2. Boston: Heath, 1955. 458–60. The editors find Crane the most talented of the rebels of the nineties. Moreover, he was secure enough of his grasp of Bowery conditions that he could make his social protest points without preaching. Better yet, he made his case using dialect and humor. The first chapter of *Maggie* is reprinted as proof of their estimate of Crane.

11.26   HUBBARD, ELBERT. "Heart to Heart Talks." *Philistine* 11.4 (1900): 123–28. Hubbard states that American critics drove Crane to England, compares him with Frederic Chopin, and comments that "the seemingly careless style of Crane is really lapidaric." Webster says the word means volcanic, tending to petrify. I'm still not sure if I agree but it is a striking adjective.

11.27   JOHNSON, BRUCE. "Conrad's Impressionism and Watt's 'Delayed Decoding.'" *Conrad Revisited: Essays for the Eighties.* Tuscaloosa: U of Alabama Press, 1985. 51–70. A careful account of what impressionism meant to Conrad, including the claim that though Conrad called Crane an impressionist, he had in mind an impressionism different from his own. This is because Conrad's comments on Crane refer "largely [to Crane's] taste for striking metaphors."

11.28   KAMHOLTZ, JONATHAN. "Literature and Photograph: The Captioned Vision vs. the Firm, Mechanical Impression." *Centennial Review* 24 (1980): 385–402. Kamholtz sees in Crane's style affinities with the approaches of Julio Cortazar (*Blow Up*) and James Agee (*Let Us Now Praise Famous Men*): All three artists present uncaptioned pictures and unlabeled images.

11.29   KARL, FREDERICK R. "Joseph Conrad's Literary Theory." *Criticism* 2 (1960): 217–335. Karl discusses Conrad's view of Crane as "a seer who saw the significant on the surface of things." Conrad's analysis of Crane's style is also briefly discussed.

11.30   KARLEN, ARNO. "Farewell the Plumed Troop . . ." *Nation* 199 (10 Aug. 1964): 54–55. A negative review essay on the issue of *The War Dispatches of Stephen Crane,* edited by Robert Stallman (9.47). Stallman's volume aside, the value of this essay is its early notice of the clash between Crane's explosive style and the deterministic ideology of naturalism.

11.31   ———. "The Craft of Stephen Crane." *Georgia Review* 28 (1974): 470–84. Karlen asserts that Crane's works lack craft; he sees instead mostly "inflated diction." The upshot for Karlen is a nihilistic, pessimistic Crane; for example, in the several works wherein Crane talked of nature's indifference, he actually depicted "cosmic abandonment."

11.32 KATZ, JOSEPH. "John William De Forest on Stephen Crane." *Stephen Crane Newsletter* 4.1 (1969): 6. Interview comments by De Forest on the "short, sharp, jerky" style of *Red Badge*.

11.33 KIRSCHKE, JAMES J. "The Accuracy of Impressionism." *American Scholar* 42 (1973): 702–6. Kirschke, reviewing the reissue of Ford Madox Ford's *Return to Yesterday* (10.53), retells anecdotes concerning the expatriate colony at Sussex: Henry James "always referred" to Crane as " 'my young compatriot of a genius' " and Ford described Crane deliberately writing "hovering 'over his foolscap sheets using a pen as a white moth uses its proboscis.' "

11.34 KWIAT, JOSEPH J. "Stephen Crane and Painting." *American Quarterly* 4 (1952): 331–38. An early and influential examination of the impact of painting on Crane's impressionistic style.

11.35 ———. "Stephen Crane's Literary Theory: 'An Effort Born of Pain.' " *Amerikastudien* 24 (1979): 152–56. A short article contending that Crane's literary creed demanded of him precise and engaged observation. Based mostly on Crane letters, Kwiat holds that Crane tried to "recreate as honestly as possible those personal experiences which constitute the artist's materials."

11.36 MANKIEWICZ, HERMAN J. "The Literary Craft of Stephen Crane." *New York Times Book Review* 10 January 1926: 7. An essay on the issue of the Follett edition of Crane (12.5): not men, or even war but "the business of words concerned Crane."

11.37 MARTIN, HAROLD C. "The Development of Style in Nineteenth-Century American Fiction." *Styles in Prose Fiction*. Ed. Harold C. Martin. New York: Columbia UP, 1959. 114–41. A technical syntactical analysis of the evolution of romanticism in Cooper ("leisurely decorum and graciousness") to realism in Crane ("terse, stark concentration"). An abstract of Martin's article appeared in *English Institute Essays* (New York, 1958): 133.

11.38 MILNE, W. GORDON. "Stephen Crane: Pioneer in Technique." *Die Neueren Sprachen* 8 (1959): 297–303. Among the very best and most helpful examinations of Crane's stylistic and technical virtues: his pictorial impressionism, the cult of the simple, and his use of vivid verbs and "homespun and energetic words."

11.39 MUNSON, GORHAM B. "Prose for Fiction: Stephen Crane." *Style and Form in American Prose*. New York: Doubleday, 1929. 159–70. A preachy, pedantic treatment of Crane's style that apparently assumes that students cannot read: "The Open Boat" is outlined in grade-school fashion.

11.40 NAGEL, JAMES. "Stephen Crane and the Narrative Methods of Impressionism." *Studies in the Novel* 10 (1978): 76–85. Another of Nagel's insightful examinations of Crane's impressionistic style: Crane gives his readers "direct sensory experience without expository intrusion." *Red Badge* and "Three Miraculous Soldiers" are examined in some detail.

11.41 NORRIS, FRANK. "Stephen Crane's Stories of Life in the Slums: *Maggie* and *George's Mother.*" *Wave* 15 (4 July 1896). Great comments on Crane's style: "The picture he makes is not a single carefully composed painting, serious, finished, scrupulously studied, but rather scores and scores of tiny flashlight photographs." Note: The easiest access to this piece is in *The Literary Criticism of Frank Norris.* Ed. Donald Pizer (Austin: U of Texas P, 1964): 164–66.

11.42 ———. *The Literary Criticism of Frank Norris.* Ed. Donald Pizer. Austin: U of Texas P, 1964. 159–74. Though Norris disliked reviewing and found it nearly impossible to bracket his own literary dispositions, his reviews of *Maggie* and *George's Mother* and his parody of *Red Badge* are important. In the former (the reviews), his grasp of Crane's style is sure: "The charm of his style lies chiefly in his habit and aptitude for making phrases—short, terse epigrams struck off in the heat of composition, sparks merely, that cast a momentary gleam of light upon whole phases of life," and in the latter (the parody), he outdistances Crane with unusual color words.

11.43 OVERLAND, ORM. "The Impressionism of Stephen Crane: A Study in Style and Technique." *Americana Norvegica* 1 (1966): 239–85. A detailed and fruitful examination of the characteristics of Crane's impressionistic style. Compares favorably with Nagel's book-length study of impressionism in Crane (2.14).

11.44 PATTEE, FRED LEWIS. "The Journalization of the Short Story." *The Development of the American Short Story.* New York: Harper and Brothers, 1923. 341–43. In the barely three pages Crane merits, his style wins Pattee's praise: "The style is stacatto, short of sentence, compressed like a night letter, stripped bare of all but essentials," but a lack of plot receives his censure.

11.45 PEROSA, SERGIO. "Naturalism and Impressionism in Stephen Crane's Fiction." *Stephen Crane: A Collection of Critical Essays.* Ed. Maurice Bassan. Englewood Cliffs, NJ: Prentice-Hall, 1967. 80–94. An important essay: Crane nimbly straddled two significant literary trends—

impressionism and naturalism. Perosa explains the characteristics of each style with reference to *Red Badge* and *Maggie.*

11.46 ROGERS, RODNEY O. "Stephen Crane and Impressionism." *Nineteenth-Century Fiction* 24 (1969): 292–304. An important and insightful examination of Crane's style and its relationship to his view of reality: "Impressionism is a realistic style of description precisely because reality is ephemeral, evanescent, constantly shifting its meaning and hence continually defying precise definition."

11.47 SLOTKIN, ALAN R. "'Bungstarter,' 'Mightish Well,' and Cultural Confusion." *American Speech* 54 (1979): 69–71. Humorous comments on cultural misunderstandings of dialect in Yoshida's (2.220) examination of Crane's use of slang.

11.48 STARRETT, VINCENT. "Stephen Crane: An Estimate." *Sewanee Review* 28 (1920): 405–13. A good examination of Crane's "unphotographic" episodic style, his unconventional use of adjectives, and his instinct for the commonplace. Republished in *Men, Women and Boats, by Stephen Crane* (New York: Boni and Liveright, 1921), 9–20 and in *Buried Caesars* (Chicago: Covici-McGee, 1923), 73–86, there entitled "Stephen Crane: A Wonderful Boy."

11.49 ———. Introduction. *Stephen Crane: A Bibliography.* Ed. Ames Williams and Vincent Starrett. Glendale, CA: John Valentine, 1948. 7–12. An excellent short sketch on Crane, his themes and his style, "highstrung impressionism" and "grim flippancy."

11.50 STEGNER, WALLACE. "Stephen Crane: The First of the Moderns." *Stephen Crane: An Appreciation.* Ed. Chris Farlekas. Port Jervis, NY: Colonial School and Camp, 1962. 3–4. Stegner briefly discusses the influence of Crane's intense style and his "picture-making eye" on modern prose, especially short stories.

11.51 SUNDQUIST, ERIC J. "The Country of the Blue." *American Realism: New Essays.* Baltimore: Johns Hopkins UP, 1982. 3–24. Sundquist introduces a book of essays on realism. His piece discusses the social and intellectual climate of the 1890s, concluding with brief comments about Crane's "experiments in technique."

11.52 WALCUTT, CHARLES CHILD. "Sherwood Anderson: Impressionism and the Buried Life." *Sewanee Review* 60 (1952): 28–47. Crane is briefly discussed at the beginning of the piece. His impressionism and his ability to get inside people are, for Walcutt, indications that had he lived another twenty-five years he would have attained "the quality of Sherwood Anderson's exquisite insight." Liebling agrees; see 10.80.

11.53   WERTHEIM, STANLEY. "Crane and Garland: The Education of an
        Impressionist." *North Dakota Quarterly* 35 (1967): 23–28. Wertheim
        argues that for a time Garland "had actually functioned as Crane's
        literary mentor" in the sense that Garland's theories (not his practice)
        were responsible for Crane's impressionism. Compare with Stronks
        (1.205).

11.54   YOUNG, PHILIP. *Ernest Hemingway: A Reconsideration.* University
        Park: Penn State UP, 1966. 191–96 and passim. Biographical and
        stylistic similarities between Crane and Hemingway. Reprinted in
        Bassan's *Stephen Crane: A Collection of Critical Essays* (2.2): 52–56.
        Young's book was first published as *Ernest Hemingway* (New York:
        Rinehart, 1952).

See also for comments on Crane's style:

1.1–1.4	2.135
1.7	2.151
1.8	2.170
1.10	2.191
1.35	2.207
1.90	3.14
1.91	3.89
1.181	3.97
1.224	3.119
2.3–2.7	3.188
2.9	3.258
2.14	3.295
2.40	3.296
2.50–2.52	4.91
2.60–2.62	5.37
2.67	5.50
2.69	5.61
2.72	9.79
2.78	10.101
2.80	12.57
2.115	12.62
2.134	12.64

12

Collections, Manuscripts, Rare Books, and First Editions

Overview

The milestone editions of Crane have been by Follett, published by Knopf, 1925–1927 (12.5), and by Bowers, published by University Press of Virginia, 1969–1976 (12.2). Several other collection of Crane's works are also described in this section.

Also included here are several dozen articles that announced the discovery of new, previously unknown Crane pieces. The excitement, competition, and jealousy that characterized some Crane scholarship from 1950 to 1975 are much in evidence in these articles.

The Crane manuscript collection of the University Libraries at Columbia (12.1 and 12.26), the George Arents collection of Syracuse University (12.45 and 12.85), and the C. Waller Barrett collection of the University of Virginia (12.3 and 12.24) are invaluable resources.

Of interest, too, from a book collector's point of view, are articles on Crane's status in the rare book and print market; see:

[on *Maggie*] 12.22
BRUCCOLI 12.36
Joan Crane 12.43
Gordon 12.52–12.54
Johnson 12.68–12.70
STARRETT 12.127
Winterich 12.137

265

Books

12.1   BAUM, JOAN H., compiler. *Stephen Crane (1871–1990): An Exhibition of His Writings Held in the Columbia University Libraries September 17–November 30, 1956.* New York: Columbia UP, 1956. 61. Baum arranged the materials and wrote short descriptive comments used at the exhibition. This catalog contains a list of the Crane holographs, rare first editions, and other materials that were displayed. This volume also includes a short essay on Crane by Lewis Leary (see 12.81) and a brief bibliographical appendix. Announcing this exhibit were "Stephen Crane Exhibit," *Columbia Library Columns* 6 (Nov. 1956): 44 and [Stephen Crane and New York City], *New York Times Book* 12 (Sept. 1930): 59; "Who's Who in the *Golden Book*," *Golden Book* 12 (Dec. 1930): 4–5; and "Notes on Rare Books," *New York Times Book Review* 9 March 1930.

12.2   BOWERS, FREDSON, ed. *The Work of Stephen Crane.* 10 vols. Charlottesville: UP of Virginia. 1969–1976. Bowers and his team of tireless editors produced a critical edition of "every known piece of his creative work and journalism, but excluding his letters and memoranda." Each of these volumes contains a general introduction by a noted Crane scholar along with a detailed textual introduction and notes by Bowers. All of these introductions have been discussed in an appropriate section of this bibliography. Some of Bowers's critical editions, especially his *Maggie* and *Red Badge* editions, generated considerable controversy, threatening at times to become a Crane subindustry; annotations for each of these polemical articles can be found elsewhere in this bibliography.

12.3   CAHOON, HERBERT. *A Brief Account of the Clifton Waller Barrett Library.* Charlottesville: UP of Virginia, 1960. A booklet describing the magnificent Barrett collection in the Alderman Library of the University of Virginia. Though the Barrett collection is legendary, the crown jewel is its Crane section: "The Stephen Crane collection, among the largest group of his notebooks, scrapbooks and letters ever brought together, proudly displays the manuscript of *The Red Badge of Courage,* with a discarded version of the novel on the verso of the pages on which the final version was written."

12.4   COLVERT, JAMES B. *Great Short Works of Stephen Crane.* New York: Harper and Row, 1965, xv+368. This volume reprints *Red Badge, Maggie,* and *The Monster* plus eight of his best-known short stories. Colvert's Introduction (vii–xv) explains how Crane's basic beliefs— reality's ambivalent, ambiguous, and elusive nature plus humans' remarkable ability to be victimized by conceit and pride—provide focuses for Crane's main works. Another version of this volume (with the same title) was also issued by Harper and Row (also in 1965), and in this second version Colvert's remarks appear in an abbreviated "Afterword" and "Biography."

12.5   FOLLETT, WILSON, ed. *The Work of Stephen Crane.* 12 vols. New York: Knopf, 1925–27, reprinted in six volumes by Russell and Russell (New York) in 1963. Though Follett's edition did not contain all of Crane's writings, and some of the reprinted texts were not scrupulously accurate, these twelve volume were the impetus for the first Crane revival. Follett commissioned distinguished writers and scholars to prepare short introductions to each of the volumes. Annotations on each of these introductions can be found in the appropriate section of this bibliography.

12.6   FRYCKSTEDT, OLOV W. *Stephen Crane: Uncollected Writings.* Uppsala: Studia Anglistica Upsaliensis, 1963. lxvii+452. This volume was very important for Crane scholars because it reprinted 123 newspaper sketches and little-known tales. See 12.48 for Fryckstedt's introduction and also 4.136 for information on the newspaper sketches reprinted here.

12.7   GREINER, DONALD J., and ELLEN B. GREINER, eds. *The Notebooks of Stephen Crane.* Charlottesville: Bibliographical Society of the University of Virginia, 1969. 76. A Stephen Crane notebook has been known to exist since 1936—the Greiners' volume reprints the notebook in its entirety. Among other sketches, the notebook contains complete drafts of "Art Student's League Building" and "Matinee Girls." Their introduction (v–xxi) explains that though Stallman published some of this material in 1956 in *Bulletin of the New York Public Library* (see 12.113 and 12.115), there are three reasons to have the whole notebook reproduced: Stallman's reprintings were not accurate; the whole notebook, especially brief paragraphs and even incomplete sentence fragments give a sense of Crane's compositional process; and finally, these notebook fragments give more evidence that impressionism indeed captures Crane's literary creed.

12.8   GULLASON, THOMAS A., ed. *The Complete Short Stories and Sketches of Stephen Crane.* Garden City, NY: Doubleday, 1963. 790. Not quite as advertised, but most of Crane's short stories and sketches are to be found here. See 12.56 for Gullason's preface and introduction.

12.9   ———. *The Complete Novels of Stephen Crane.* New York: Doubleday and Co., 1967. xvi+821. Gullason's volume contains *Maggie* (1896 edition with 1893 variants published in an appendix), *Red Badge of Courage* (both the shortened newspaper version and the regular 1895 Appleton edition), *George's Mother, The Third Violet, Active Service,* and *The O'Ruddy* (he considers *The Monster* a short story). See 12.57 for Gullason's Introduction.

12.10   KATZ, JOSEPH. *The Portable Stephen Crane.* New York: Viking, 1969. xxv+550. This volume contains most of Crane's important works, though Katz's introduction and notes (vii–xii) concentrate on *Red Badge,* "The Open Boat," and *The Monster.* More generally, Katz explores Crane's "code of experience" and his mistrust of the outlooks of previous generations.

12.11   LEVENSON, J. C., ed. *Stephen Crane, Prose and Poetry: Maggie, A Girl of the Streets, The Red Badge of Courage, Stories, Sketches and Journalism. Poetry.* New York: Library of America, 1984. ix+1379. A reprinting of the best of Crane from the Virginia edition (with two notable exceptions, Levenson used the 1893 *Maggie* and the 1895 Appleton *The Red Badge of Courage*). Except for a half-dozen shorter minor pieces (perhaps "The Snake," "A Lovely Jag in a Crowded Car," "Three Miraculous Soldiers," and "Making an Orator" should have been included), everything of value is here. His "Chronology; Note on the Texts; Notes" (1353–71) provide the normal apparatuses for reprinted texts.

12.12   STALLMAN, ROBERT W., ed. *Stephen Crane: Stories and Tales.* New York: Vantage, 1955. xxxii+350. A shortened paperback version of *Stephen Crane: An Omnibus,* leaving out *Red Badge of Courage;* poems, letters, and related introductory matters. See 3.215 for information on Stallman's Introduction.

12.13   ———. , ed. *The Stephen Crane Reader.* Glenview, IL: Scott, Foresman, 1972. xii+604. A useful collection of Crane including *Red Badge* plus five new manuscript pages, the 1893 *Maggie, George's Mother* plus representative early, middle, and late short stories and poems. The introduction and notes (very detailed, 537–575) reprint (sometimes in shortened and recast form) Stallman's previously published criticism. A sorted checklist of Crane comments is also included (576–604).

12.14   STALLMAN, ROBERT W., and E. R. HAGEMANN, eds. *The War Dispatches of Stephen Crane.* Ames: Iowa State UP, 1964. xv+343. Stallman and Hagemann reprint nearly four dozen of Crane's journalistic articles on the Graeco-Turkish and Spanish-American Wars. Their historical annotations are helpful (see 9.39).

12.15 WEST, HERBERT FALKNER. *A Stephen Crane Collection.* Hanover, NH: Dartmouth College Library, 1948. 31. A catalog of the George Matthew Adams collection at Dartmouth.

Articles and Book Chapters

12.16 [A Presentation Copy of *Maggie*]. *Modern Library in First Editions.* New York: Scribner's, 1938. 53. A report on yet another presentation copy of the 1893 *Maggie.*

12.17 "Book Sales and Rare Books." *New York Evening Post Literary Review* 24 Jan. 1925. A report on the sale of Crane letters and Crane first editions.

12.18 [*Maggie*]. *Book Prices Current* 46 (Nov. 1931): 228. The news that a presentation copy of the 1893 *Maggie* brought $230.

12.19 *Maggie, a Girl of the Streets. Anderson Galleries, Catalog # 4174.* New York: American Art Association, 1935. Items 71 and 72. An auction description of nearly a dozen copies of the 1893 *Maggie* to be sold 24–25 April 1935.

12.20 "Presidential Parade: A Newstory by Stephen Crane." *Library* (Public Library, Newark) 5.1 (1932): 3. Reprints an early Asbury Park sketch, "On the New Jersey Coast."

12.21 "Rare Books, Autographs and Prints." *Publisher's Weekly* 100 (12 Nov. 1921): 168. The state of things for Crane manuscripts and rare books in 1921 along with a notice of the Newark Free Library's memorial to Crane.

12.22 "The Rarest Book in Modern American Literature [Crane's Presentation Copy of *Maggie* from the Estate of Dr. Lucius Button]." *Anderson's Gallery Catalog, Sale 3827* 11–12 Mar. 1930, Item 76. In 1930 the family of Dr. Lucius Button put up for auction perhaps the most valuable 1893 *Maggie,* the presentation copy that contained Crane's comment that "it tries to show that environment is a tremendous thing in the world and frequently shapes lives regardless." (See *Correspondence* 13.3: #21 for the full inscription.) Stallman reports that the volume brought $3,700. In his *Stephen Crane: A Critical Bibliography* (14.3: 329–330) Stallman gives other sources of information on the prices of Crane first editions: George Matthew Adams, "I Buy a Rare Book," *News,* 25 September 1930; "Rare Book by Stephen Crane," *Delta Upsilon Quarterly,* October 1930; "When Genius Markets Its Wares: Stephen Crane," *Golden Book* 12 (Sept. 1930): 59; "Who's Who in the *Golden Book*" 12 (Dec. 1930): 4–5; and "Notes on Rare Books," *New York Times Book Review* 9 March 1930.

12.23   ANDREWS, WILLIAM L. "A New Stephen Crane Fable." *American Literature* 47 (1975): 113–14. Scholars were aware of several Crane fables printed in *Truth;* Andrews discovered another fable, "How the Ocean Was Formed," printed earlier in *Puck.*

12.24   BARRETT, C. WALLER. *The American Writer in England: An Exhibition Arranged in Honor of the Sesquicentenial of the University of Virginia.* Charlottesville: UP of Virginia, 1969. xxxii–xxxiii and 110–114. A description of the C. Waller Barrett Crane collection at Virginia.

12.25   BASSAN, MAURICE. "Our Stephen Crane." *Mad River Review* 1 (1964): 85–90. Review essay on three recent collections of Crane works: Gullason (12.8), Fryckstedt (12.6), and Stallman-Hagemann (12.14).

12.26   BAUGHMAN, ROLAND. *Manuscript Collection in the Columbia University Libraries.* New York: Columbia UP, 1959. Columbia's Crane collection (among others) is described. (All of these holdings have now been microfilmed; these microfilms can be obtained by writing to the Columbia library.)

12.27   BOWERS, FREDSON. "Crane's *Red Badge of Courage* and Other 'Advance Copies.'" *Studies in Bibliography* 22 (1969): 273–77. Explains Appleton's practice of sending advance copies of its books to English publishers for copyright purposes.

12.28   ———. "The Text of the Virginia Edition." *Bowery Works. The Works of Stephen Crane,* vol. 1. Ed. Fredson Bowers. Charlottesville: UP of Virginia, 1969. xi–xxix. Describes the scope of the Virginia edition, "intended to contain every known piece of his creative work and journalism, but excluding his letters and memoranda," and explains the principles on which Bowers's editing has been based.

12.29   ———. "The New Look in Editing." *South Atlantic Bulletin* 35 (1970): 3–10. A defense of the definitive edition industry; details about his editing of "Death and the Child" and "The Revenge of the *Adolphus.*"

12.30   ———. "Multiple Authority: New Problems and Concepts of Copy-Text." *The Library* 27 (1972): 81–115. Ambitious explanation of modern text editing; complete details about the editing of several Crane tales—later summarized in several notes in the Virginia critical edition.

12.31   _____. "Remarks on Eclectic Texts." *Proof* 5 (1975): 31–76. A defense of Bowers's preference for eclectic texts. With regard to Crane, for the Virginia edition of *Maggie* Bowers produced a synthesis of the 1893 and 1896 versions. Crane scholars have generally shied away from the Virginia edition of *Maggie,* preferring to use either the 1893 or the 1896 versions.

12.32   _____. "Recovering the Author's Intentions." *Pages* 1 (1976): 218–27. A caveat emptor about using paperback edition classics for classroom use. Specific examples from selected editions of *Red Badge* and "The Open Boat" are discussed.

12.33   _____. "Mixed Texts and Multiple Authority." *Text: Transactions of the Society for Textual Scholarship.* 3 (1978): 63–90. Bowers uses examples from several of Crane's minor pieces to explain principles for deciding upon a copy text when several texts compete for authority. (Examples from Shakespeare and William James are also discussed.)

12.34   BRUCCOLI, MATTHEW J. "An Unrecorded Parody of Stephen Crane." *Stephen Crane Newsletter* 4.4 (1970): 7. Add it to the list on pages 151–152 of Stallman's *Stephen Crane: A Critical Bibliography* (14.3).

12.35   _____. "Stephen Crane, 1871–1971: An Exhibition from the Collection of Matthew J. Bruccoli." *Bibliographical Series of the University of South Carolina* 6 (1971): 1–19. A catalog for the exhibition (77 first editions, several letters and cards) from Bruccoli's collection of Craneana.

12.36   _____. "Stephen Crane as a Collector's Item." *Stephen Crane in Transition: Centenary Essays.* Ed. Joseph Katz. 1977. 153–73. Bruccoli is a book collector; he here presents information on the numbers and prices of rare Crane items.

12.37   BRUCCOLI, MATTHEW, and JOSEPH KATZ. "A Colonial Edition of *Great Battles of the World.*" *Stephen Crane Newsletter* 1.2 (1966): 3–4. An important discovery for assessing the impact of Crane beyond England and America.

12.38   _____. "The Heinemann *War Is Kind.*" *Stephen Crane Newsletter* 1.4 (1967): 6. The apparent discovery of one of the "six copies of the original edition [that] were prepared with Heinemann title-pages for copyright purposes."

12.39 _____. "Scholarship and Mere Artifacts: The British and Empire Publications of Stephen Crane." *Studies in Bibliography* 22 (1969): 277–87. Useful discussion of "the realities of Crane's literary position in England and the British Empire." Seeks to dispel the myth of "a Gatsbyesque" Crane in England.

12.40 BUTTERFIELD, ROGER. *First Books by American Authors.* New York: Seven Gables Bookshop, 1965. 25–26. A rare book catalogue, listing and offering an 1893 *Maggie* for $1,000.

12.41 CASE, RICHARD G. " 'Great Bugs of Onondaga' Invented by Crane: Famed Writing Style Gives Him Away." *Syracuse Standard* 26 May (1963). A follow-up newspaper piece on the March 1963 publication by Lester G. Wells of Crane's spoof in the Syracuse University *Courier* (see 9.42).

12.42 CHEW, SAMUEL C. "The House of Appleton." *Fruit among the Leaves: An Anniversary Anthology.* Ed. Samuel C. Chew. New York: Appleton-Century-Crofts, 1950. 3–66. History of the publishing house with comments about Hamlin Garland bringing Crane to Appleton and publishing *Red Badge* and subsequent titles.

12.43 CRANE, JOAN ST. C. "Rare or Seldom-Seen Dust Jackets of American First Editions: VII—*The Red Badge of Courage.*" *Serif* 9.1 (1972): 31–32. Book collector information; detailed description of six Crane first editions.

12.44 EICHELBERGER, CLAYTON. "Stephen Crane's 'Grand Opera for the People': A Bibliographic Identification and a Correction." *Papers of the Bibliographical Society of America* 65 (1971): 70–72. For the bibliophiles, a big deal is made about the text of a minor Crane western sketch; an issue rendered moot by the Virginia edition.

12.45 FABIAN, R. CRAIG. "Stephen Crane Collection, Report for 1948." *Syracuse University Alumni News* 10 and 11 (1948–49): 11 and 11. A description of the items George Arents contributed to the Syracuse Crane collection.

12.46 FINE, LEWIS H., ed. "Two Unpublished Plays of Stephen Crane." *Resources for American Literary Study* 1 (1971): 200–16. Fine describes Crane's acquaintance with the theater and his interest in plays and offers the texts of Crane's unfinished script for *The Fire Tribe and the Pale-Face* and an untitled play set in a French tavern.

12.47 ———. *"The Fire Tribe and the Pale-Face:* An Unfinished and Unpublished Play by Stephen Crane." *Markham Review* 3 (1972): 37–38. An overblown note on a play Crane never finished or published. Fine argues that Crane was a crusader who hated war's destruction and the unjust treatment of American Indians.

12.48 FRYCKSTEDT, OLAF W. "Introduction." *Stephen Crane: Uncollected Writings.* Uppsala: Studia Anglistica Upsaliensia, 1963. xvii–lxvii. Fryckstedt's introduction is strong on factual information and chronology; weaker on style, substance, and themes to be found in the reprinted writings. See 12.6 and 4.136.

12.49 GARNER, STANTON. "Stephen Crane's 'The Predecessor': Unwritten Play, Unwritten Novel." *American Literary Realism* 13 (1980): 97–100. After the Virginia edition of Crane's works, only tertiary recovery was left. Garner's piece describes an unwritten, unpublished plan (in fact, little more than an idea) entertained by Crane.

12.50 GILKES, LILLIAN. "A New Stephen Crane Item." *Studies in American Fiction* 5 (1977): 255–57. Gilkes argues that a four-paragraph newspaper piece attributed to Harold Frederic belongs with Crane's London newsletters.

12.51 ———. "Stephen Crane's 'Dan Emmonds': A Pig in a Storm." *Studies in Short Fiction* 2 (1964): 66–71. Gilkes sorts out the facts about a sketch that Crane planned to write but that never appeared. See Virginia edition (X: 112–117) for the manuscript fragment that remains.

12.52 GORDAN, JOHN D. "Novels in Manuscript, An Exhibition from the Berg Collection: *The Red Badge of Courage.*" *Bulletin of the New York Public Library* 69 (1965): 317–29, 396–413. For the book and manuscript collector, with details on a discarded page of the first draft of *Red Badge.*

12.53 ———. "Novels in Manuscript: An Exhibition from the Berg Collection, *The Red Badge of Courage* by Stephen Crane." *Bulletin of the New York Public Library* 29 (1965): 403–4. Gordon describes one page of the discarded manuscript of *Red Badge* that the New York Public Library holds.

12.54 ———. "Stephen Crane." *An Anniversary Exhibition: The Henry W. and Albert A. Berg Collection.* New York: New York Public Library, 1965. 48. The *Maggie* owned by the New York Public Library.

12.55 GULLASON, THOMAS A. "Additions to the Canon of Stephen Crane." *Nineteenth-Century Fiction* 12 (1957): 157–60. Gullason comments on and reprints portions of two newspaper sketches: "The Gratitude of the Nation" and "Harvard University against the Carlisle Indians."

12.56 ―――. Preface and Introduction. *The Complete Short Stories and Sketches of Stephen Crane.* Garden City, NY: Doubleday, 1963, 1–14, 18–45. Gullason's preface and introduction contain a very brief checklist sort of treatment of themes and motifs to be found in the stories and sketches that follow. Gullason's best comments are on Crane's early satires and burlesques, his middle short stories, and his last efforts. (See 12.8.)

12.57 ―――. Introduction. *The Complete Novels of Stephen Crane.* New York: Doubleday, 1967. 3–97. Gullason's introduction provides a detailed and informative discussion of Crane's life, including the impact of the writings of his ancestors and his parents, which Gullason sees in Crane's ambivalence toward religion and in his ironic, mock-heroic view of life. Gullason also makes general observations on Crane's style and techniques as well as helpful comments on each of the six novels he reprints. (See 12.9.)

12.58 ―――. "Stephen Crane and the *Arena:* Three 'Lost' Reviews." *Papers of the Bibliographical Society of America* 65 (1971): 297–99. Three favorable reviews that Crane himself recorded; all three notice social concern in his works.

12.59 ―――. "Stephen Crane: Onward and Upward." *CEA Critic* 34 (1972): 30–31. Gullason offers comments on the Crane industry, both textual and critical.

12.60 ―――. "Stephen Crane's 'The Wreck of the *New Era*': The First Known Printing." *American Literary Realism* 11 (1977): 295–96. Gullason reports the discovery of an earlier-known printing of a minor sketch that he says anticipates themes in "The Open Boat."

12.61 HOFFMAN, DANIEL G. "The Unwritten Life of Stephen Crane." *Columbia Library Columns* 2 (1953): 12–16. An announcement that Columbia University had acquired Cora Crane's treasure trove and details about some of the most important items.

12.62 ―――. "Stephen Crane's New Jersey Ghosts." *Proceedings of the New Jersey Historical Society* 71 (1953): 239–53. A reprinting of two newly recovered sketches. Hoffman comments that these early pieces contain the hallmarks of his mature work: odd adjective–noun combinations and the depiction of an indifferent universe.

12.63 _____. "Crane's Decoration Day Article and *The Red Badge of Courage.*" *Nineteenth-Century Fiction* 14 (1959): 78–80. Hoffman argues that "The Gratitude of a Nation" "is erroneously attributed to Crane." Apparently most Crane scholars disagreed, including the editors of the Virginia edition, for the article appears in vol. 8 (587–590).

12.64 _____. "Stephen Crane's First Story." *Bulletin of the New York Public Library* 64 (1960): 273–78. At the age of 14 Crane wrote "Uncle Jake and the Bell-Handle." Hoffman points out that the "abrupt images and startling use of metaphor" characteristic of Crane's best work are clearly present in this juvenile piece.

12.65 HOFFMAN, HESTER R. "Stephen Crane." *The Reader's Adviser.* 10th ed. New York: Bowker, 1964. 1083–84. Hoffman lists the books by and about Crane in print in 1964.

12.66 HONCE, CHARLES. "Stephen Crane's *Maggie*": A Sherlock Holmes Birthday. Mount Vernon, VA: Golden Eagle, 1938. 104–8. Prices on various 1893 *Maggies* including the report that "an inscribed copy of the 1893 edition of *Maggie* fetched at an Anderson Gallery auction in 1930 one of the highest prices ever paid for a book of an American author: $3,700."

12.67 _____. "Crane, Stephen (1971–1900). 'The Famine of Hearts.'" *Papers of the Bibliographical Society of America* 35 (1941): 297. Honce describes a printing of "In the Tenderloin" in an obscure 1899 New York magazine.

12.68 JOHNSON, MERLE. "My Adventures with Stephen Crane." *Bookseller and Print Dealers Weekly* 2.63 (8 Dec. 1927): 6. Reports of an upsurge of interest in Crane books with the publication of Beer's *Stephen Crane* (1.1).

12.69 _____. "*Red Badge of Courage* and *War Is Kind.*" *High Spots in American Literature.* New York: Jenkins, 1929. 25–26. Rare-book-seller descriptions of *Red Badge* and *War Is Kind.*

12.70 _____. "Crane, Stephen." *American First Editions.* New York, 1929. 54–55. A listing of Crane first editions.

12.71 JONES, JOSEPH, et al. "Crane, Stephen." *American Literary Manuscripts*. Austin: U of Texas P, 1960. 88–89. A list of libraries holding Crane manuscripts (and letters).

12.72 KATZ, JOSEPH. "Toward a Descriptive Bibliography of Stephen Crane: *The Black Riders.*" *Papers of the Bibliographical Society of America* 59 (1965): 150–57. The sort of thing one would expect to find in PBSA: "a definitive treatment of the format and transmission of the important first volume of verse by Stephen Crane."

12.73 ———. "The Unmistakable Stephen Crane." *Antioch Review* 25 (1965): 337–41. Katz surveys recent editions of Crane works, finds them all unsatisfactory, and looks forward to the Virginia critical edition and the time when, Katz hopes, Crane will be unmistakable not for his fin de siècle blasphemy but for his literary art.

12.74 ———. "The Wondrous Painting Cow of Old K. C." *Kansas City Star* 31 Dec. 1967: Section D. 1. Katz reprints Crane's sketch "Art in Kansas City."

12.75 ———. "An Early Draft of 'Death and the Child.'" *Stephen Crane Newsletter* 3.3 (1969): 1–2. A manuscript fragment of "Death and the Child" appeared on the back of Cora Crane's manuscript for "Peter the Great."

12.76 ———. "An Early Draft of 'Moonlight in the Snow.'" *Stephen Crane Newsletter* 3.4 (1969): 1–2. Katz transcribes the three-paragraph fragment.

12.77 ———. "Two Uncollected Articles." *Prairie Schooner* 44 (1969): 287–96. Katz reprints "Filibustering" and "The War Correspondents: Stephen Crane Talks of American and English Examples."

12.78 ———. "*The Lanthorn Book:* A Census (Parts I and II)." *Stephen Crane Newsletter* 4.3, 4.4 (1970): 10–12, 10. Katz has located thirteen copies of a special volume in which members of the Lanthorn Club contributed pieces and autographed the limited printing (125 copies). Crane's contribution was a Western tale, "The Wise Men."

12.79 KATZ, JOSEPH, and MATTHEW J. BRUCCOLI. "Toward A Descriptive Bibliography of Stephen Crane: 'Spanish-American War Songs.'" *Papers of the Bibliographical Society of America* 61 (1967): 267–69. The bibliographical details on the book in which Crane's poem "The Blue Battalions" first appeared in 1898.

12.80   KYLES, GILLIAN G. M. "Stephen Crane and 'Corporal O'Connor's Story.'" *Studies in Bibliography* 27 (1974): 294–95. Kyles offers an opinion about some unpublished Crane notes in the Columbia University Library collection. "Advanced" textual scholars will be interested in this piece.

12.81   LEARY, LEWIS. Foreword. *Stephen Crane: An Exhibition.* New York: Columbia UP, 1956. 3–10. Brief remarks on Crane's life and work in conjunction with an exhibition of his writings at Columbia in 1956. Leary sees Crane "driven by demons of desperation, despair and doubt."

12.82   ———. "Stephen Crane: 1871–1900." *Columbia Library Columns* 6 (1956): 44–45. Leary announces the upcoming exhibition of Crane's writings, including a display of Linson's oil painting of Crane now hanging in the Alderman Library of the University of Virginia.

12.83   LINDER, LYLE D. "'The Ideal and the Real' and 'Brer Washington's Consolation': Two Little Known Stories by Stephen Crane?" *American Literary Realism* 11 (1978): 1–33. Linder transcribes two unpublished drafts of stories attributed to Crane. It is not clear to Linder whether these are Crane's stories that Cora typed or ones of which she was the primary author. Neither story appears in the Virginia edition, so the latter must have been judged the case.

12.84   LINNEMAN, WILLIAM R. "Stephen Crane's Contributions to *Truth.*" *American Literature* 31 (1959): 196–97. The first discovery of Crane's stories "A Night at the Millionaires' Club" and "Why Did the Young Clerk Swear?"

12.85   LYON, EDWARD. "The Stephen Crane Collection at Syracuse University." *Courier* 21 (1986): 135–46. Lyon describes the George Arents Stephen Crane "research collection" at Syracuse.

12.86   MAYFIELD, JOHN S. "Stephen Crane's Curious Conflagration." *American Book Collector* 7.4 (1956): 6–8. Mayfield describes Ames W. Williams's reprinting of Crane's "The Fire" as a Christmas present for book collectors.

12.87   ———. "Stephen Crane's Copy of *Maggie.*" *Courier* 3 (December 1963): 11–13. Mayfield describes a rare 1893 *Maggie* made more dear by two Crane signatures; this volume sold for $3,700 in 1930.

12.88   MILLER, LEON. "Crane, Stephen." *American First Editions: Their Points and Prices.* New York: Norwood Editions, 1975. 28. In 1975

Crane first editions ranged from $500 for *Maggie* (1893) and *Red Badge* to $8 for *Third Violet.*

12.89 MONTEIRO, GEORGE. "Brazilian Translations of Stephen Crane's Fiction." *Stephen Crane Newsletter* 4.2 (1969): 7–8. Monteiro lists seven Portuguese translations in Brazil between 1945 and 1967.

12.90 ———. "'Grand Opera for the People': An Unrecorded Stephen Crane Printing." *Papers of the Bibliographical Society of America* 63 (1969): 29–30. Monteiro discovered another source for another minor Crane western sketch.

12.91 ———. "Stephen Crane's Dan Emmonds: A Case Reargued." *Serif* 6 (1969): 32–36. Monteiro argues that there was another Crane novel, *Dan Emmonds;* it is now lost and the sketch "Dan Emmonds" is "a redaction of the basic materials of the lost novel." Few Crane scholars agree with his first claim.

12.92 ———. "Two Notes on Stephen Crane." *Papers of the Bibliographical Society of America* 74 (1980): 71–73. Monteiro discovered two early notices on Crane.

12.93 ———. "Crane's 'Lines': A Last Note on the *Bookman.*" *Prairie Schooner* 47 (1973): 268. A record of appearances of a manuscript fragment; an article for Crane sleuths.

12.94 ———. "Heinemann's 'Colonial Edition' of Stephen Crane's *Bowery Tales.*" *Papers of the Bibliographical Society of America* 71 (1977): 221. Another one for the text detectives—the full-blown description of a recently located colonial edition of one of Crane's works.

12.95 ———. "Addenda to Stallman and Hagemann: Parodies of Stephen Crane's Work." *Papers of the Bibliographical Society of America* 74 (1980): 402–3. Self explanatory.

12.96 ———. "Notes on Stephen Crane's 'Dan Emmonds.'" *American Literary Realism* 18 (1985): 120–32. A very large commotion over a very minor Crane piece. For the Crane superspecialist.

12.97 ———. "Stephen Crane, Dramatist." *American Literary Realism* 19.1 (1986): 42–51. The story of Crane's love–hate courtship of the theater. Monteiro uses "The Fire-Tribe and the Pale-Face," which he labels an "impressive fragment," to reconstruct a Crane dramatic tale.

12.98 MONTEIRO, GEORGE, and PHILLIP EPPARD. "Addenda to Bowers and Stallman: Unrecorded Contemporary Appearances of Stephen Crane's Work." *Papers of the Bibliography Society of America* 74 (1980): 73–75. More newspaper appearances of Crane's tales and stories.

12.99 MORACE, ROBERT A. "Stephen Crane's 'The Merry-Go-Round': An Earlier Version of 'The Pace of Youth.'" *Studies in the Novel* 10 (1978): 146–53. Textual niceties on an earlier version of one of Crane's best Asbury Park sketches.

12.100 NORDLOH, DAVID J. "On Crane Now Edited: The University of Virginia Edition of *The Works of Stephen Crane.*" *Studies in the Novel* 10 (1978): 103–19. An early, highly critical review—"all the texts are battered by the intrusion of editorial uniformity." By 1991, a small minority strongly agreed with Nordloh's opinion of Bowers's procedures; a few more are mildly critical but most applaud the Virginia edition and its procedures.

12.101 PIZER, DONALD. "On the Editing of Modern American Texts." *Bulletin of the New York Public Library* 75 (1971): 147–53. A short, clear statement of the principles of copy-text editing according to the theory of W. W. Greg, an American copyediting theorist, and why they are "unresponsive to the distinctive qualities of modern American texts." Pizer then argues that Bowers's Virginia edition of Crane is faulty. For more detail on this last point see Pizer's review of the Virginia edition of *Maggie* and *George's Mother* and *Whilomville Tales* in *Modern Philology* 68 (1970): 212–14. For those interested in pursuing the "copy text" debate, especially counterarguments to Pizer, see Norman S. Grabo, "Pizer vs. Copy Text," *Bulletin of the New York Public Library* 75 (1971): 147–53 and Hershel Parker, "In Defense of 'Copy-Text Editing,'" *Bulletin of the New York Public Library* 75 (1971): 337–44.

12.102 PRATT, LYNDON UPSON. "An Addition to the Canon of Stephen Crane." *Research Studies of the State College of Washington* 7 (1939): 55–58. Reprints an early college article by Crane, "Henry M. Stanley," from *Vidette*, the student publication of Claverack College and the Hudson River Institute.

12.103 RANDALL, DAVID A. "Stephen Crane." *Dukedom Large Enough: Reminscences of a Rare Book Dealer, 1929–1956*. New York: Random House, 1962. 22–29. War stories from a veteran of the book collecting game. Facts and figures on the rise and fall of prices for the 1893 *Maggie*.

12.104 REID, B. L. *The Man from New York: John Quinn and His Friends*. New York: Oxford UP, 1968. 124–25. Tells of Conrad giving Quinn the manuscript of "Five White Mice," "which had been given him in friendship during Crane's last days in England."

12.105 SLOTE, BERNICE. "Stephen Crane: 'Waiting for Spring.'" *Prairie Schooner* 38 (1964): 15–26. Reprints what is now known as "Nebraska's Bitter Fight for Life," as it appeared in the *Nebraska State Journal,* 24 February 1895.

12.106 ———. "San Antonio: A Newly Discovered Stephen Crane Article." *Prairie Schooner* 43 (1969): 176–83. A reprinting with a brief two-paragraph introduction of one of Crane's western trip dispatches titled "Stephen Crane in Texas" in vol. 8 of the Virginia edition.

12.107 ———, ed. "Stephen Crane: A Portfolio." *Prairie Schooner* 43 (1969): 175–204. Slote reprints Crane's western newspaper sketches "Patriot Shrine in Texas" and "Apache Crossing." This issue also contains three articles on Crane by Slote, Carmichael, and Narveson described elsewhere in this bibliography.

12.108 ———. "Stephen Crane in the Nebraska *State Journal,* 1894–1896." *Stephen Crane Newsletter* 3.4 (1969): 4–5. Slote lists the twenty Crane items appearing in the Nebraska paper.

12.109 ———. "Crane's 'Line': A Manuscript Facsimile." *Prairie Schooner* 46 (1972): 95. Comments on the cover of *Prairie Schooner,* "a facsimile of a manuscript version of the Stephen Crane poem usually known as 'War is Kind.'"

12.110 SORRENTINO, PAUL. "Stephen Crane's Manuscript of 'This Majestic Lie." *Studies in Bibliography* 36 (1983): 221–29. After the Virginia edition prepared its text of "This Majestic Lie" Sorrentino discovered Crane's holograph manuscript of the story. Sorrentino lists substantive and accidental variants to correct the Virginia edition and to allow Crane scholars to examine Crane's writing practices.

12.111 ———. "Stephen Crane's Sale of 'An Episode of War' to *The Youth Companion.*" *Studies in Bibliography* 37 (1984): 243–48. Sorrentino explains the sale of "An Episode of War" to *The Youth Companion,* which did not publish it, but sold it to *The Gentlewoman,* which did. Some twenty years later *The Youth Companion* also printed the story; Sorrentino compares the two texts, listing substantive variants.

12.112 ———. "Newly Discovered Writings of Mary Helen Peck Crane and Agnes Elizabeth Crane." *Courier* 21 (1986): 103–35. Sorrentino describes and analyzes the materials on Crane's mother and sister in the Melvin Schoberlin collection (see Colvert, 1.68, and Lyon, 12.85, for details) recently acquired by Syracuse University. Interesting comment about the relation of Crane's irony to his sister and her writings.

12.113 STALLMAN, ROBERT W. "Stephen Crane: Some New Stories (Part I)." *Bulletin of the New York Public Library* 60 (1956): 455–62. Stallman notes the first appearance of "The Art Students' League," "Matinee Girls," "Election Night: New York 1894," and "Literary Notes."

12.114 ———. " 'The Wreck of the *New Era.*' " *Fine Arts Magazine* (28 April 1956). Stallman's reprints from the holograph manuscript a heretofore unpublished sketch by Crane.

12.115 ———. "Stephen Crane: Some New Stories (Part II)." *Bulletin of the New York Public Library* 60 (1956): 477–86. Reproduces for the first time "The Raft Story" and "Diamonds and Diamonds."

12.116 ———. "Stephen Crane: Some New Stories (Part III)." *Bulletin of the New York Public Library* 61 (1957): 36–46. Reproduces "Across the Covered Pit" and "A Foreign Policy, in Three Glimpses," and adds comments on other unpublished Crane items.

12.117 ———. "[Crane's Cardtable Cover]." *Fine Art Magazine* [University of Connecticut] 3.1 (Apr. 1958): 64. A facsimile reproduction of a cardtable cover Crane doodled on—the original is part of the Barrett Crane collection of the Alderman Library of the University of Virginia.

12.118 ———. "A Note on the Texts of *Maggie* and *The Red Badge of Courage.*" *The Red Badge of Courage and Other Stories.* Ed. V. S. Pritchett. London: Oxford UP, 1960. 206–24. Comments on the 1893 and 1896 *Maggies* and the excised sections of *Red Badge.*

12.119 ———. " 'A Small Black and White and Tan Hound.' " *Fine Arts Magazine* (University of Connecticut) 6 (1961): Front and back cover. Stallman reproduced Crane's holograph of this story as a cover for *Fine Arts Magazine.*

12.120 ———. "New Short Fiction by Stephen Crane: Part 1, *Dan Emmonds.*" *Studies in Short Fiction* 1 (1963): 1–7. Stallman comments and reprints Crane's unpublished draft of a satiric sketch of 2,300 words.

12.121 ———. "New Short Fiction by Stephen Crane: Part 2." *Studies in Short Fiction* 1 (1963): 147–52. Stallman comments on and reprints two Crane "grotesqueries," "Art in Kansas City" and "In the Country of Rhymers and Writers."

12.122   ———. "Stephen Crane as Dramatist." *Bulletin of the New York Public Library* 67 (1963): 495–511. Stallman argues that "from the start [Crane] hankered to achieve also a name for himself as dramatist" and he observes that much of his fiction has "dialogue readily convertible to the stage." Following these brief remarks Stallman reprints "Drama in Cuba" (published as "Spanish American War Play" in vol. 10 of the Virginia edition, 139–158).

12.123   ———. "Stephen Crane: Some New Sketches." *Bulletin of the New York Public Library* 71 (1967): 554–62. Stallman reproduces three Mexican sketches from the holograph manuscript. These sketches were never printed, though Stallman's reason for this seems far-fetched: "In these three new Crane sketches of the City of Mexico Crane is bitingly critical of American capitalists, and that probably would have prevented the Bacheller and Johnson Syndicate from publishing them."

12.124   ———. "Note on 'Apache Crossing.'" *Prairie Schooner* 43 (1969): 186. A three-paragraph account of the untitled holograph printed for the first time in *Prairie Schooner*.

12.125   STAM, DAVID H. "Preface: A Special Stephen Crane Issue." *Courier* 21 (1986): 3. Stam notes that the acquisition of the Melvin H. Schoberlin collection by the George Arents Research Library of Syracuse University is the reason for the special Stephen Crane issue of the *Courier*. See Colvert 1.68.

12.126   STARRETT, VINCENT. "Note." *"Men, Women and Boats" by Stephen Crane*. Ed. Vincent Starrett. Chicago: Boni & Liveright, 1921. np. A one-page explanation of the sources of the Crane stories Starrett has selected for reprinting.

12.127   ———. "On Collecting Stephen Crane." *Stephen Crane: A Bibliography*. Philadelphia: Centaur Book Shop, 1923. 5–11. Starrett explains that "collecting Stephen Crane is a labor of love" and he tells how he came by some of the rarer volumes. This essay was reprinted in Stallman's *Stephen Crane: A Critical Bibliography*, 14.3: xxxi–xxxvi.

12.128   STOLPER, B. J. R. "Unpublished Crane Material." *Saturday Review of Literature* 10 (30 Dec. 1933): 380. A letter to the editor stating that all sorts of Crane material is bubbling to the surface.

12.129 TANSELLE, G. THOMAS. "The New Editions of Hawthorne and Crane." *Book Collector* 23 (1974): 214–24. A general discussion of the work and principles of the Center for Editions of American Authors and comments on the status of the Crane edition at Virginia. Tanselle defends Bowers's eclectic text of *Maggie* as a definitive edition, not "the definitive text."

12.130 _____. "The Editorial Problem of Final Authorial Intention." *Studies in Bibliography* 29 (1976): 167–211. An extremely lengthy general report on the critical text industry; passing references to "The Pace of Youth" and *Maggie*.

12.131 VAN DOREN, MARK. "The Work of Stephen Crane." *The Private Reader: Selected Articles and Reviews*. New York: Holt, 1946. 156–59. Review of the Follett edition of Crane; Van Doren remarks on Crane's "peculiar intensity," which allows him to be a cool "communicator of terror."

12.132 WELLS, LESTER G. "Stephen Crane—Syracusan Extraordinary." *Syracuse University Alumni News* 27 (Oct. 1946): 14–15. An update on the Crane collection at Syracuse and a call for donations, especially of rare first editions.

12.133 WEST, HERBERT FAULKNER. "Foreword." *A Stephen Crane Collection*. Hanover, NH: Dartmouth College Library, 1948. ix–xiii. Cheerleader comments on Crane and his works: He was "one of the most honest and discerning writers of our literature."

12.134 WILLIAMS, AMES W. "A Stephen Crane Collection." *Antiquarian Bookman* 1 (1948): 717–18. Detailed descriptions of rare first editions of *Maggie* (1893 version) and *Red Badge* at Dartmouth.

12.135 _____. "On Collecting the Writings of Stephen Crane: A Recollection." *Courier* 2.4 (1962): 1–11. Breezy memoirs of a noted Crane collector who with Starrett compiled the first scholarly bibliography of Crane. Despite all of that, Williams slips in his comments on "The Blue Hotel": "A stupid and neurotic Swede manages to provoke a quarrel and get himself murdered in a dismal frontier hotel painted a hideous blue." The Swede was murdered in the hotel in Kadar's film version—maybe Williams was confused by that version. See Keenan (6.60) for Kadar's film version.

12.136 _____. "Stephen Crane's Bugs." *Courier* 3.3 (1963): 22–31. Details about Crane's spoof, "Great Bugs in Onondaga," published in the New York *Tribune* 1 June 1891. Williams shows that the likely source for Crane's tall tale was an article in the Syracuse *Sunday Herald* 24 May 1891, "Caterpillars Delay Trains."

12.137 WINTERICH, JOHN T. *A Primer of Book-Collecting*. New York: Greenberg, 1935. Passim. Comments on Crane's market in the book collector game; prices for *Maggie* in the mid twenties went from $115 to $3,700. Note: A later edition of the book (1966) reproduces Crane's inscription in Garland's copy of the 1893 *Maggie*.

12.138 ———. "Romantic Stories of Books: *The Red Badge of Courage*." *Publishers' Weekly* 118 (1933): 1303–07. Tales of rare editions of *Maggie* and *Red Badge* and a few comments on Crane's struggles before the Bacheller syndication of *Red Badge*. This essay is reprinted as *"The Red Badge of Courage"* in Winterich's *Twenty-Three Books and the Stories behind Them* (Philadelphia: Lippincott, 1939): 121–31.

Also on texts and textual controversies see:

3.260–3.296
5.22
9.9
9.10
10.87

13

Letters

Overview

Crane's letters have been sought for the insights they give into his life and personality. Cady's and Wells's publication of Crane's love letters to Nellie Crouse (13.1) were very illuminating. A half-dozen years later the letters collected by Stallman and Gilkes (13.2) became a standard resource for Crane scholars. Both these volumes have been supplanted by the indispensable volumes edited by Wertheim and Sorrentino (13.3).

The remaining annotations in this section are mostly confined to articles that have reprinted and/or made comments on individual letters by, about, or to Crane. All of Crane's biographers, and in this case his correspondence editors, have found him elusive and his personality ambiguous. Beyond frustrations expressed by his correspondence editors (see 13.9, 13.32, and 13.37), the comments by Mitgang (13.23) and Tuttleton (13.34) are interesting.

Books

13.1   CADY, EDWIN H., and LESTER G. WELLS, eds. *Stephen Crane's Love Letters to Nellie Crouse.* Syracuse, NY: Syracuse UP, 1954. xii+87. A first-time printing of seven letters of Crane to Nellie Crouse along with "six other letters, new materials on Crane at Syracuse University and a number of unusual photographs." See 13.5 for the editors' introduction.

13.2   STALLMAN, ROBERT W., and LILLIAN GILKES. *Stephen Crane: Letters.* Ed. Robert W. Stallman and Lillian Gilkes. New York: New

York UP, 1960. xxx+366. This volume was a landmark in Crane scholarship. Though it has now been supplanted by Wertheim and Sorrentino's *The Correspondence of Stephen Crane,* the observations of Stallman and Gilkes are still worth notice. Another reason to hold on to this volume is that many letters to and about Crane reprinted here do not appear in *Correspondence.* See 13.32 for the editors' introduction. Note: Hereafter in this chapter I will refer to this volume as *Letters.*

13.3   WERTHEIM, STANLEY, and PAUL SORRENTINO, eds. *The Correspondence of Stephen Crane.* 2 vols. New York: Columbia UP, 1988. xx+722. An absolutely essential tool for any research on Crane's life and works. Wertheim and Sorrentino have painstakingly sorted out the dates, places, and persons with whom Crane corresponded. Seven hundred ninety-one letters are included—nearly 400 not collected by Stallman and Gilkes, including some 170 by Crane and more than 20 by Cora. Beer's letters (727–791), they convincingly argue, were fabricated, and as such are relegated to an appendix.

Accompanying the letters themselves are the editors' careful and precise notes. There is more, in particular nine valuable essays introducing various stages of Crane's life along with a very detailed and complete chronology. See 13.37 for the editors' introduction. Note: Hereafter in this chapter this volume will be cited as *Correspondence.*

Articles and Book Chapters

13.4   "Letters of a Shortstop." *This Month at Goodspeed* 9 (1937): 10–14. A description of eight letters of Crane to Copeland and Day (publishers of *The Black Riders*). Goodspeed offered these letters plus a copy of a review for $350. Clifton Waller Barrett bought them and subsequently donated them to the University of Virginia.

13.5   AYERS, ROBERT W. "W. D. Howells and Stephen Crane: Some Unpublished Letters." *American Literature* 28 (1957): 459–77. Though these letters are now accessible in *Correspondence,* Ayers's article remains valuable for its discussion of the Howells–Crane relationship.

13.6   BIRSS, JOHN HOWARD. "Stephen Crane: Letter and Biographical Note." *Notes and Queries* 165 (7 Oct. 1933): 243. An announcement that a collection of Crane letters is being planned.

13.7   ———. "A Letter of Stephen Crane." *Notes and Queries* 166 (7 April 1934): 240–41. The first mention of Crane's letter to Copeland and Day about proposed cuts in *Black Riders;* see *Correspondence,* #44.

13.8   BOHNENBERGER, CARL, and NORMAN MITCHELL HILL, eds. "The Letters of Joseph Conrad to Stephen and Cora Crane." *Bookman* 69 (May–June 1929): 225–35, 367–74. Helps fill in the picture of Crane in England; details of Conrad's help to get money for Crane to go to Cuba to cover the Spanish-American War.

13.9   CADY, EDWIN H., and LESTER G. WELLS. Introduction. *Stephen Crane's Love Letters to Nellie Crouse.* Syracuse, NY: Syracuse UP, 1954. 17–23. An important introduction to an important book on Crane. Cady and Wells briefly relate the facts about Nellie Crouse, how the letters became part of the George Arents Library of Syracuse (an Appendix [75–87] describes the Crane holdings at Syracuse), and how these letters reveal "the ideal of the gentleman as it stood in Crane's time." Cady argues that ending the Crane–Crouse affair fueled Crane's "disillusionment with conventionalities [which] made the ironies of *Maggie,* 'The Monster,' *The Red Badge of Courage* and 'The Open Boat,' to say nothing of the poems and the other tales, possible."

13.10   CADY, ELIZABETH W. "Stephen Crane to Miss Daisy D. Hill: The Letter Recovered." *Stephen Crane Newsletter* 4.2 (1969): 1–4. The letter is reprinted in *Correspondence,* #210. In addition, Ms. Cady makes Cadyesque comments on Crane as a Christian gentleman.

13.11   CONRAD, JOSEPH. *Joseph Conrad on Stephen Crane.* Ed. Vincent Starrett and Edwin B. Hill. Ysleta, TX: Edwin B. Hill, 1932. 1–4. A single undated letter (written about 1920) by Conrad to Peter T. Sommerville, editor of *The Englishman,* commenting on how difficult it is to sustain interest in Crane since his death. Only thirty-one copies of this "book" were printed.

13.12   DRAKE, JAMES F. "A Stephen Crane Letter." *Colophon* 1.4 (1930): np. A facsimile of a letter Crane wrote at Hartwood during the winter of 1896 to the editor of the *Critic;* see *Correspondence,* #206.

13.13   FOX, AUSTIN M. "New Crane Letter Links Him to Hubbard, WNY." *Buffalo Evening News* 20 Dec. 1969. Fox reprints Crane's 29 October 1897 letter to Hubbard; see *Correspondence,* #333.

13.14   GULLASON, THOMAS A. "The Letters of Stephen Crane: Additions and Corrections." *American Literature* 41 (1969): 104–6. Gullason adds to and corrects Stallman and Gilkes, *Stephen Crane: Letters.* The added letter appears in *Correspondence,* #325; Gullason's corrections are mostly quibbles. However, of note is a letter from Joseph Conrad to Edith Crane, daughter of Edmund B. Crane, containing a touching testimonial: "We here had the greatest affection for Stephen and understood his fine character. For he was fine. A straight-thinking straight-acting man without guile. I will say nothing here of his great gifts." Conrad also notes, "I am happy to know that Mrs. Crane approves of my preface" (to Beer's *Stephen Crane,* 1.1).

13.15 HALLADAY, JEAN R. "A Note Regarding Crane Biography." *American Notes and Queries* 16 (1978): 87–88. A suggestion dealing with an obscure reference in one of Crane's letters. Wertheim and Sorrentino accept Halladay's suggestion; see *Correspondence,* #2.

13.16 HICKS, GRANVILLE. "A Life of Desperate Resolution." *Saturday Review* 6 (1960): 14. A carping review of *Letters.* Hicks complains that most of the important letters were previously published but then he acknowledges: "It is a good thing that this book has been published." He changed his mind, it appears, because these letters support his pet view of Crane as a bitter, despairing artist.

13.17 HOUGH, ROBERT L. "New Material on Stephen Crane." *Prairie Schooner* 34 (1960): 175–76. A brief essay review on *Letters* to the effect that Crane remains an elusive and complex figure.

13.18 HUNTER, DARD. "Elbert Hubbard and 'A Message to Garcia'" *New Colophon* 1.1 (Jan. 1948): 33. Crane's letter to Hubbard about the famous message; see *Correspondence,* #511.

13.19 JOLINE, ADRIAN. [A Stephen Crane Letter]. *Meditations of an Autograph Collector.* New York: Harper, 1902. 14. First appearance of Crane's 6 February 1896 letter about his photograph; see *Correspondence,* #201.

13.20 KATZ, JOSEPH. "Stephen Crane, 'Samuel Carlton' and a Recovered Letter." *Nineteenth-Century Fiction* 23 (1968): 220–25. Detective work regarding an alias Crane used in connection with a letter to his brother William. This letter (*Correspondence,* #285) was to serve as his will in case he got killed in Cuba.

13.21 MADIGAN, THOMAS F. [Stephen Crane to Miss Daisy D. Hill]. *Autograph Album* 1 (Oct. 1933): 35. The first appearance of Crane's 2 March 1896 letter to Miss Daisy D. Hill; see *Correspondence,* #210.

13.22 MANGIONE, JERRY G. "Stephen Crane's Unpublished Letters." *Syracuse University Chapbook* 2 (1930): 8–10. An account of Crane's letters to Nellie Crouse—no excerpts were permitted before the full texts were released in *Stephen Crane's Love Letters to Nellie Crouse* (13.1).

13.23 MITGANG, HERBERT. "Stephen Crane's Shifting Image." *New York Times Biographical Service* 18 (Dec. 1987): 1355–56. An interview with Stanley Wertheim just before the issue of *Correspondence* suggesting that an elusive, complex, and ambiguous Crane emerges from the new letters (from Crane and Cora) soon to be available to Crane scholars.

13.24 MONTEIRO, GEORGE. "Cora Crane to John Hay: A New Letter on Stephen Crane's Havana Disappearance." *Stephen Crane Newsletter* 1.3 (1976): 2–3. Details of Cora's attempts to locate Crane, who disappeared in Havana September–October 1898.

13.25 ———. "Stephen Crane and the *Atlantic Monthly.*" *American Notes and Queries* 16 (1978): 70–72. Monteiro reprints two letters to Crane from Walter Page, editor of the *Atlantic Monthly*.

13.26 PARKER, HERSHEL. "The Dates of Stephen Crane's Letters to Amy Leslie." *Papers of the Bibliographical Society of America* 75 (1981): 82–86. Parker proposes another set of dates for Crane's letters to Amy Leslie. The matter has been put to rest in *Correspondence;* see #287, 288, 291, 292, and 329.

13.27 SCHWAB, ARNOLD T. *James Gibbon Huneker.* Stanford: Stanford UP, 1963. Schwab tells several stories about Crane and critic Huneker based on a letter contained in Beer's biography; see *Correspondence,* #759. This is a letter that Wertheim and Sorrentino consider bogus.

13.28 SIMMEN, EDWARD. "Stephen Crane and the Aziola Club of Galveston: A New Stephen Crane Letter." *Journal of Modern Literature* 7 (1979): 169–72. A great deal is made of a very minor letter (*Correspondence,* #92) regarding an invitation to join a businessman's club in San Antonio.

13.29 SORRENTINO, PAUL, and STANLEY WERTHEIM. "New Stephen Crane Letters in the Schoberlin Collection." *Courier* 21 (1986): 35–55. Details on the sixty-two letters by Crane, thirty-nine by Cora, and five book and album inscriptions. All of this is also presented in *Correspondence*.

13.30 STALLMAN, ROBERT W. "Letters of Stephen Crane." *New York Times Book Review* 27 Apr. 1952, 18. Stallman announces that he (and

Lillian Gilkes) are preparing an edition of Crane and he requests information on unpublished Crane letters. A similar announcement and request was placed in the *London Times Literary Supplement* 8 August 1952, 517.

13.31   ———. "Stephen Crane's Letters to Ripley Hitchcock." *Bulletin of the New York Public Library* 60 (1965): 318–32. The first publication of twenty-three important letters, especially the ones dealing with Crane's revision of *Maggie*. Though these letters are now well known, Stallman's picture of Crane as a tough negotiator—"he had a hardboiled bargaining drive uncommon among artists"—is very relevant to debate about the Binder-Parker version of *Red Badge*. See, for example, Colvert's picture of the Crane–Hitchcock relationship (3.273).

13.32   STALLMAN, ROBERT W., and LILLIAN GILKES. Introduction. *Stephen Crane: Letters*. Ed. Robert W. Stallman and Lillian Gilkes. New York: New York UP, 1960. vii–xv. After a brief history on their efforts to collect Crane's letters, the Stallman-Gilkes preface sets out several themes: the many sides of Crane's contradictory nature, contrasts between what a literary work means to its author and to its readers, and Crane's love–hate reaction to his *Red Badge* fame.

13.33   STRONKS, JAMES B. "A Truer Crane." *Commonweal* 71 (1960): 578–79. A brief, matter-of-fact review of *Letters*.

13.34   TUTTLETON, JAMES W. "'A Runaway Dog like Me': Stephen Crane in His Letters." *New Criterion* 6.10 (June 1988): 49–58. A review essay on *Correspondence* endorsing the Wertheim-Sorrentino view (13.3) of a devious Crane.

13.35   WEATHERFORD, RICHARD M. "A New Stephen Crane Letter." *American Literature* 48 (1976): 79–81. A Crane letter to his brother Will; for a reprint see *Correspondence, #315*.

13.36   WERTHEIM, STANLEY. "H. G. Wells to Cora Crane: Some Letters and Corrections." *Resources for American Literature Studies* 19 (1979): 207–12. On the Crane-Wells friendship at Brede; interesting letters.

13.37   WERTHEIM, STANLEY, and PAUL SORRENTINO. Introduction. *The Correspondence of Stephen Crane*. 2 vols. New York: Columbia UP, 1988. 1–13. Wertheim and Sorrentino comment on Crane's elusiveness and argue that a full examination of his letters best reveals him.

What results, they argue, is a demythologized Crane exhibiting an "occasional tendency toward duplicity" and a "contradictory character."

13.38   WHITE, WILLIAM. "A Stephen Crane Letter." *Times Literary Supplement* 3108 (22 Sept. 1961): 636. A letter from Crane to his brother William, missed in *Letters*, but included in *Correspondence*, #479.

See also for mention of letters:

1.5	10.46
1.36	10.51
1.72	10.59
1.120	10.60
1.127	10.73
1.190	10.79
10.45	10.98

14
Bibliography

Overview

Six bibliographical books on Crane are annotated below. Early volumes stressed the listing of Crane's first published writings (plus locating first editions) and identifying unsigned pieces, see:

Herzberg 14.1
Starrett 14.4
Starrett-Williams 14.6

Later bibliographies have emphasized secondary literature on Crane. Stallman's massive volume (14.3) did both tasks.

Numerous checklists of varying length and detail have been described; especially valuable were those in Hudspeth's *Thoth* (14.12) and Katz's *Stephen Crane Newsletter* (14.13). The peaks and valleys in Crane scholarship are ably described in

Cazemajou 14.8
Katz 14.14
LaFrance 14.15

Finally, nearly sixty short bibliographical entries are described in the final pages of this section.

Books

14.1   HERZBERG, MAX. *Stephen Crane and the Stephen Crane Association.* Newark, NJ: Newark Public Library, 1926. A pamphlet containing a short bibliography and remarks on the Stephen Crane society.

14.2   KATZ, JOSEPH. *The Merrill Checklist of Stephen Crane.* Columbus, OH: Merrill, 1969. 41. Merrill checklists "are intended to provide students with the tools that will give them access to the most meaningful published resources for the study of an author." Though Katz's checklist is selective and dated it is still a useful starting point for Crane beginners.

14.3   STALLMAN, ROBERT W. *Stephen Crane: A Critical Bibliography.* Stallman. Ames: Iowa State UP, 1972. xx+642. An exhaustive, careful, and complete listing of Crane's works, manuscripts, letters, and secondary literature from 1896 to mid-1970. Stallman's massive volume was marred by his inability to keep his personal feuds and vendettas at bay. In his concern to be sure *he* was acknowledged as a pioneer in several critical disputes as well as the discoverer of unpublished Crane works, Stallman's defensive and, at times, peevish comments led his readers to suspect the objectivity and value of his annotations. Still, his doggedness and his energy at tracking down everything relating to Crane were incredible. Also of note is his preface (ix–xviii), which surveys all previous bibliographies, sketches the history of the Crane revival—taking ample credit for his part— and explains what he means by a "critical" bibliography.

14.4   STARRETT, VINCENT, compiler. *Stephen Crane: A Bibliography.* Philadelphia: Centaur Book Shop, 1923. 47. The first bibliography of Crane; first editions are described (13–40) and selected critical notices are listed (41–46).

14.5   STOLPER, B. J. R., and MAX J. HERZBERG, compilers. *Stephen Crane: A List of His Writings and Articles about Him.* Newark, NJ: Public Library of Newark, 1930. 30. A brief unannotated bibliography–a short checklist really. The introduction (5–7) to this book is "Stephen Crane and His Reputation," by Max Herzberg, identified as "President, Stephen Crane Society." Herzberg briefly surveys the extent of interest in Crane.

14.6   WILLIAMS, AMES W., and VINCENT STARRETT, compilers. *Stephen Crane: A Bibliography.* Glendale, CA: John Valentine, 1948. xi, 161. An expansion of Starrett's 1923 bibliography (14.4). Once again the emphasis is on locating and describing first editions. Also, it is the first effort to track down Crane's contributions in books and magazines, his letters, contemporary reviews, and a short list of secondary critical essays.

Major Chapters and Special Articles

14.7   BEEBE, MAURICE, and THOMAS A. GULLASON. "Criticism of Stephen Crane." *Modern Fiction Studies* 5 (1959): 282–91. The article's subtitle is accurate: "A Selected Checlist with an Index to Studies of Separate Works."

14.8   CAZEMAJOU, JEAN. "Crane Criticism Today (1948–1970)." *Stephen Crane: A Critical Biography.* Ed. Robert Stallman. Ames: Iowa State UP, 1972. xxi–xxx. A sound summary of nearly twenty-five years of Crane scholarship—international scholars included.

14.9   DENNIS, SCOTT A. "Stephen Crane Bibliography." *Thoth* 11.3 (1971): 33–34. *Thoth's* annual update of Crane scholarship.

14.10   GULLASON, THOMAS A. "Select Bibliography: Stephen Crane and His Novels." *The Complete Works of Stephen Crane.* New York: Doubleday, 1967. 810–21. A useful selection of Crane scholarship.

14.11   ———. "Select Bibliography: Stephen Crane and His Writings. *Stephen Crane's Career: Perspectives and Evaluation.* New York: New York UP, 1972. 496–532. Likewise, a useful selection of Crane scholarship.

14.12   HUDSPETH, ROBERT, et al. "A Bibliography of Stephen Crane Scholarship: 1893–1969." *Thoth* 11, Special Supplement (1970): 1–38. English department graduate students at Syracuse University began publishing a Crane checklist in *Thoth* in 1963. In 1970 Hudspeth prepared a cumulative revision of those checklists. The result was an invaluable addition to Crane bibliography; updates from 1971 to 1975 are listed elsewhere.

14.13   KATZ, JOSEPH. "Quarterly Checklist of Stephen Crane Scholarship." *Stephen Crane Newsletter* 1–5 (1966–1970). In each of four issues each year, Katz published a checklist of Crane scholarship. Volume 1.1 had nearly fifty entries; most issues had at least two dozen. The last issue had only seven and included the announcement that the Crane bibliography project had been handed over to *Thoth*.

14.14 ———. "Afterword: Resources for the Study of Stephen Crane." *Stephen Crane in Transition: Centenary Essays.* Ed. Joseph Katz. De Kalb: Northern Illinois UP, 1972. 205–31. Katz surveys the state of Crane scholarship in 1972. Still valuable are his discussions of the libraries with Crane holdings and his history of Wilson Follett's *The Work of Stephen Crane* (12.5) and the difficulties that Bowers and the Virginia critical edition had to confront.

14.15 LAFRANCE, MARSTON. "Stephen Crane Scholarship Today and Tomorrow." *American Literary Realism* 7 (1974): 125–36. An interesting survey of the ups and downs of Crane scholarship with comments arranged according to three peak periods: 1896–1900, 1921–1950, and 1950 to the present. LaFrance concludes, "Crane criticism seems just to have outgrown the innocence of naturalistic and Freudian speculation, the bumptiousness of symbolic absurdity, and to be finally settled down to serious work."

14.16 PIZER, DONALD. "Stephen Crane." *Fifteen American Authors before 1900: Bibliographical Essays on Research and Criticism.* Ed. Robert A. Rees and Earl N. Harbert. Madison: U of Wisconsin P, 1971. 97–137. A critical and judicious survey of all the main currents of Crane scholarship. A valuable essay with fairly detailed comments on what Pizer sees as the most significant studies–his sense was very discerning. Pizer has twice updated his essay: an article in *Studies in the Novel* in 1978 (14.15) and an expanded version in the 1984 reissue of *Fifteen American Authors since 1900,* the same publications information as in the 1971 volume. In the 1984 expanded version Pizer's "Stephen Crane" bibliography runs from pages 128 to 184.

14.17 ———. "Stephen Crane: A Review of the Scholarship and Criticism since 1969." *Studies in the Novel* 10 (1978): 120–45. Pizer comments on items omitted in his 1971 bibliography (see 14.16) and new scholarship since then.

14.18 WERTHEIM, STANLEY. "Stephen Crane." *Hawthorne, Melville, Stephen Crane.* Ed. Theodore Gross and Stanley Wertheim. New York: Free Press, 1971. 201–301. Though Wertheim's bibliography is highly selective (105 items with another 50 cited in passing), it is reliable, evenhanded, and helpful. Annotations are lengthy and incisive. There are bonuses too: Wertheim's introductory remarks give a good history of the Crane revival, his chronology is useful, and the ambiguities in Crane's personality are made clear.

Articles

14.19   "Stephen Crane." *Biography Index.* New York: Wilson. Vols. 1–45. 1946–1991. Checklist of biographical articles on Crane.

14.20   "Stephen Crane." *Essays and General Literature Index.* New York: Wilson. 1–12 (1900–1990). Checklist of monographs on Crane.

14.21   "Stephen Crane." *Readers' Guide to Periodical Literature.* New York: Wilson. Vols. 1–50. 1900–1990. Guide to popular periodicals.

14.22   "Stephen Crane." *International Index to Periodicals.* New York: Wilson. Vols. 1–18. 1907–1965. Checklist of articles in popular magazines and large newspapers.

14.23   "Stephen Crane." *MLA International Bibliography.* New York: Modern Language Association of America. 1921–1989. Crane entries identified and sorted by major works.

14.24   "Stephen Crane." *Social Sciences and Humanities Index.* New York: Wilson. Vols. 19–27. 1956–1974. Checklist of selected scholarly serials.

14.25   "Stephen Crane." *Annual Bibliography of English Language and Literature.* Ed. Michael Smith, et al. Vols. 37–61. Leeds, UK: Modern Humanities Research Association, 1962–1986. Crane entries identified and sorted by major works.

14.26   "Stephen Crane." *Humanities Index.* Vols. 1–18.2. New York: Wilson, 1971–1991. Crane entries noted.

14.27   "Stephen Crane." *Bibliographic Index.* New York: Wilson. Vols. 1–31.2. 1974–1991. Checklist of bibliographical articles on Crane.

14.28   BESTERMAN, THEODORE. "Stephen Crane." *A World Bibliography of Bibliographies.* Lausanne, Switzerland: Societas Bibliographica, 1965. 1516. Besterman lists the five partial bibliographies that existed before Stallman's *Stephen Crane: A Critical Bibliography* (14.3).

14.29   BLANCK, JACOB, compiler. *Merle Johnson's American First Editions.* 4th ed. New York: Bowker, 1942. 128–30. An early bibliography of and about Crane.

14.30   ———. "Stephen Crane." *Bibliography of American Literature.* Vol. 2. New Haven, CT: Yale UP, 1957. 329–38. A listing of Crane first editions with information about bindings and other details for book collectors.

14.31   BUDD, LOUIS J. "Howells and Crane." *American Literary Scholarship, An Annual/1963.* Ed. James Woodress. Durham, NC: Duke UP, 1965. 112–17. The annual roundup of secondary literature on Crane.

14.32   _____. "Stephen Crane." *American Literary Scholarship, An Annual/ 1964.* Ed. James Woodress. Durham, NC: Duke UP, 1966. 117–19. Second installment of Budd's comments on Crane scholarship. Budd's remark, "The only mark of academic prestige now lacking for Crane is a newsletter," was used by Katz in the first issue of *The Stephen Crane Newsletter.*

14.33   _____. "Stephen Crane." *American Literary Scholarship, An Annual/ 1965.* Ed. James Woodress. Durham, NC: Duke UP, 1967. 137–40. A yearly installment commenting on Crane scholarship; with reference to *Red Badge,* Budd notes "Crane's most famous narrative is still getting almost overwhelmingly solemn scrutiny."

14.34   _____. "Stephen Crane." *American Literary Scholarship, An Annual/ 1966.* Ed. James Woodress. Durham, NC: Duke UP, 1968. 124–27. Survey of yearly scholarship on Crane.

14.35   COPPA, JOSEPH. "Stephen Crane Bibliography." *Thoth* 13.3 (1973): 45–46. Third annual update of Hudspeth's *Thoth* Crane bibliography.

14.36   EICHELBERGER, CLAYTON L., compiler. "Stephen Crane." *A Guide to Critical Reviews of United States Fiction, 1879–1910,* vol. 1. Metuchen, NJ: Scarecrow Press, 1971. 81–82. A very select list of contemporary reviews.

14.37   _____. "Stephen Crane." *A Guide to Critical Reviews of United States Fiction, 1879–1910,* vol. 2. Metuchen, NJ: Scarecrow Press, 1974. 69–71. Another select list of contemporary reviews of Crane's works.

14.38   ENGLE, JAMES D. "Stephen Crane Bibliography." *Thoth* 15 (1975): 27–28. Fifth annual update of the Hudspeth *Thoth* Crane bibliography.

14.39   FENSTER, VALMAI KIRKHAM. "Stephen Crane." *Guide to American Literature.* Littleton, CO: Libraries Unlimited, 1983. 97–99. Brief, informed comments on texts, criticism, biographies, and bibliographies.

14.40 FERRARA, MARK, and GORDON DOSSETT. "A Sheaf of Contemporary American Reviews of Stephen Crane." *Studies in the Novel* 10 (1978): 168–82. A useful sample of contemporary reception to Crane.

14.41 FERSTEL, JOHN W. "Stephen Crane Bibliography." *Thoth* 12.3 (1972): 39–40. The second annual update of Hudspeth's *Thoth* Crane bibliography.

14.42 FRENCH, WARREN. "The Ironic Vision of Stephen Crane." *American Literary Scholarship, An Annual/1974.* Ed. James Woodress. Durham, NC: Duke UP, 1974. 217–20. French reports that there were no new books in 1974 but several very good articles appeared.

14.43 ———. "The Ironic Vision of Stephen Crane." *American Literary Scholarship, An Annual/1975.* Ed. James Woodress. Durham, NC: Duke UP, 1977. 256–59. An annual review.

14.44 ———. "The Ironic Vision of Stephen Crane." *American Literary Scholarship, An Annual/1976.* Ed. J. Albert Robbins. Durham, NC: Duke UP, 1978. 218–21. "This year's scattering of speculations and complaints is generally thin and retrogressive."

14.45 GERSTENBERGER, DONNA, and GEORGE HENDRICK. "Stephen Crane." *The American Novel, 1789–1959: A Checklist of Twentieth-Century Criticism.* Denver: Allan Swallow, 1961. 49–53. A checklist of major criticisms keyed to individual novels of Crane.

14.46 ———. "Stephen Crane." *The American Novel: A Checklist of Twentieth-Century Criticism on Novels Written Since 1789.* volume II, *Criticism Written 1960–1968.* Chicago: Swallow, 1970. 58–64. A checklist of most of the major criticisms keyed to individual novels of Crane.

14.47 GRIFFITH, O. L., compiler. "American First Editions: Stephen Crane." *Publisher's Weekly* 102 (1922): 813. For the book collector, a listing of Crane first editions.

14.48 HENDRICK, GEORGE. "Fin-de-Siècle America: Stephen Crane and the 1890s." *American Literary Scholarship, An Annual/1982.* Ed. J. Albert Robbins. Durham, NC: Duke UP, 1984. 217–18. This year, reports Hendrick, there was not much to celebrate with regard to Crane scholarship.

14.49 HOLMAN, C. HUGH. "Stephen Crane." *The American Novel through Henry James*. New York: Appleton-Century-Crofts, 1966. 423–25. A highly selective "Golden Tree" bibliography totaling 61 items.

14.50 INGE, M. THOMAS. "Stephen Crane." *American Literary Scholarship, An Annual/1970*. Ed. J. Albert Robbins. Durham, NC: Duke UP, 1972. 198–201. More backbiting is obvious to Inge in his annual canvass of Crane scholarship.

14.51 ———. "Stephen Crane." *American Literary Scholarship, An Annual/1971*. Ed. J. Albert Robbins. Durham, NC: Duke UP, 1973. 183–86. Usual review noting especially the "exhaustively thorough and impeccably precise" work of the Virginia edition.

14.52 ———. "Stephen Crane." *American Literary Scholarship, An Annual/1972*. Ed. J. Albert Robbins. Durham, NC: Duke UP, 1974. 200–203. A good year—Holton's *Cylinder of Vision* (2.10) and Katz's *Stephen Crane in Transition: Centenary Essays* (2.11).

14.53 ———. "Stephen Crane." *American Literary Scholarship, An Annual/1973*. Ed. James Woodress. Durham, NC: Duke UP, 1975. 220–21. The big event of the year was the issue of the facsimile edition of Crane's manuscript of *Red Badge,* Fredson Bowers, ed. (3.261)

14.54 JONES, CLAUDE E. "Stephen Crane: A Bibliography of His Short Essays and Stories." *Bulletin of Bibliography* 15.8 and 15.9 (1935): 149–150, 170. One of the earliest bibliographies, notable in its "effort to trace the original appearance of the short prose works."

14.55 KATZ, JOSEPH. "Stephen Crane: 'Bibliographed.'" *Proof* 3 (1973): 455–60. A savage review essay on Stallman's *Stephen Crane: A Critical Bibliography* (14.3). Though Stallman's bibliography was widely criticized, Katz minces no words, calling it "an academic novel . . . a striking burlesque of bibliography and a sharp parody of Crane scholarship."

14.56 KIRBY, DAVID K. "Stephen Crane." *American Fiction since 1900: A Guide to Informational Sources*. Detroit: Gale Research, 1975. 81–91. Another highly selective checklist of Crane's works, editions, and representative secondary criticism.

14.57 LEARY, LEWIS. "Stephen Crane." *Articles on American Literature, 1990–1950*. Durham, NC: Duke UP, 1954. 61–63. Checklist of articles on Crane. Supplements published (same publication information): *Articles on American Literature, 1950–1967* (1970): 88–97, and *Articles on American Literature,* 1968–1975 (1979): 95–104.

14.58   MAY, CANDICE. "Stephen Crane Bibliography." *Thoth* 14 (1974): 53–55. Fourth annual update of Hudspeth's Crane bibliography in *Thoth.*

14.59   NORDLOH, DAVID J. "Fin-de-Siècle America: Stephen Crane and the 1890s." *American Literary Scholarship, An Annual/1983.* Ed. Warren French. Durham, NC: Duke UP, 1985. 229–31. Nordloh remarks that Wolford's *The Anger of Stephen Crane* (2.19) was the only book-length effort of 1983.

14.60   ———. "Fin-de-Siècle America: Stephen Crane and the 1890s." *American Literary Scholarship, An Annual/1984.* Ed. J. Albert Robbins. Durham, NC: Duke UP, 1986. 233–35. Colvert's biography *Stephen Crane* for the Harcourt album series is the good news in 1984.

14.61   ———. "Crane, Chopin, and the 1890s." *American Literary Scholarship, An Annual/1985.* Ed. J. Albert Robbins. Durham, NC: Duke UP, 1987. 224–25. A very slim year—three articles.

14.62   ———. "Crane, Norris and Bierce." *American Literary Scholarship, An Annual/1987.* Ed. James Woodress. Durham, NC: Duke UP, 1989. 214–16. Three essay anthologies on Crane appeared in 1987.

14.63   ———. "Fin-de-Siècle: Crane, Norris, Bierce, Chopin and Adams." *American Literary Scholarship, An Annual/1988.* Ed. J. Albert Robbins. Durham, NC: Duke UP, 1990. 220–21. *The Correspondence of Stephen Crane,* Wertheim and Sorrentino (13.3), was the news in 1988.

14.64   PETRY, ALICE HALL. "Crane, Norris, and Fin-de-siècle Writers." *American Literary Scholarship, An Annual/1989.* Ed. David J. Nordloh. Durham, NC: Duke UP, 1991. 219–221. "Crane scholarship in 1989 was uneven, with the old critical problems generating few convincing new insights."

14.65   RIDGELY, JOSEPH V. "Stephen Crane." *American Literary Scholarship, An Annual/1967.* Ed. James Woodress. Durham, NC: Duke UP, 1969. 145–47. An annual review of Crane scholarship noting among other things, "The piecemeal, often competitive, reprinting of Crane's lesser items continues to be a topic for scholarly acrimony"; Stallman was the center of the nasty exchanges.

14.66 ———. "Stephen Crane." *American Literary Scholarship, An Annual/1968.* Ed. J. Albert Robbins. Durham, NC: Duke UP, 1970. 152–55. Annual review with the customary comment that "partisanship and acrimony" continue to mar studies of Stephen Crane." The catalyst is, as usual, Stallman—who responded with a two-page diatribe in his *Stephen Crane: A Critical Bibliography* (14.3: 608–10).

14.67 ———. "Stephen Crane." *American Literary Scholarship, An Annual/1969.* Ed. J. Albert Robbins. Durham, NC: Duke UP, 1971. 175–78. The big news in the year's roundup is the release of the first two volumes of the Virginia edition.

14.68 RUDE, DONALD W. "Some Additions to the Bibliographies of Joseph Conrad, Stephen Crane, Ford Madox Ford and George Gissing." *Papers of the Bibliographical Society of America* 75 (1981): 347–49. Rude located two reviews of *The Open Boat and Other Stories* not cited in Stallman's *Stephen Crane: A Critical Bibliography* (14.3): St. Paul *Pioneer Press* 22 May 1898: 23, and *The Daily Inter-Ocean* (Chicago), 7 May 1898: 10.

14.69 STARRETT, VINCENT. "Stephen Crane: Notes Biographical and Bibliographical." *Colophon* 2 (1931): Part 7. An attempt to keep the Crane revival rolling after the Knopf edition of *The Work of Stephen Crane* (12.5) and Beer's *Stephen Crane* (1.1). A great picture of Crane on horseback; several rare first edition book covers are also reproduced.

14.70 TALLACK, DOUGLAS. "American Short Fiction: A Bibliographical Essay." *American Studies International* 23.3 (1985): 3–59. Crane gets his fair share of this long bibliographical essay; Tallack's suggestions for general readers are sound.

14.71 TANSELLE, G. THOMAS. "The Descriptive Bibliography of American Authors." *Studies in Bibliography* 21 (1968): 1–24. Tanselle decries the sorry state of bibliographies of American authors; with regard to Crane he opines that the Williams-Starrett (1948) bibliography is "above the level of the average."

14.72 VANDERBILT, KERMIT. "Fin-de-Siècle America: Stephen Crane and the 1890s." *American Literary Scholarship, An Annual/1979.* Ed. James Woodress. Durham, NC: Duke UP, 1981. 216–18. Binder's *Red Badge* (3.260) was the hot topic in 1981.

14.73 ———. "Fin-de-Siècle America: Stephen Crane and the 1890s." *American Literary Scholarship, An Annual/1980.* Ed. J. Albert Robbins. Durham, NC: Duke UP, 1982. 239–41. Nagel's *Stephen Crane and Literary Impressionism* (2.14) was "the year's new book."

14.74 ———. "Fin-de-Siècle America: Stephen Crane and the 1890s." *American Literary Scholarship, An Annual/1981.* Ed. James Woodress. Durham, NC: Duke UP, 1983. 219–21. "The annual season of Crane studies may be described as a slight sprinkle with no thunder."

14.75 WALKER, WARREN S. "Stephen Crane." *Twentieth-Century Short Story Explication: Interpretation 1900–1975, of Short Fiction since 1800.* 3rd ed. Hamden, CT: Shoe String, 1977. 147–60. Articles on select Crane short stories.

14.76 WEIXLMANN, JOE. "Stephen Crane." *American Short-Fiction Criticism and Scholarship, 1959–1977: A Checklist.* Chicago: Swallow, 1982. 118–34. A select list of articles, nicely sorted by Crane stories. A short bibliography of bibliographies is included.

14.77 WOODRESS, JAMES. "Crane, Norris and the Fin-de-Siècle." *American Literary Scholarship, An Annual/1986.* Ed. David J. Nordloh. Durham, NC: Duke UP, 1988. 220–23. The special issue of *Courier* devoted to Crane was the main accomplishment of the year.

14.78 WORTHAM, THOMAS. "Fin-de-Siècle America: Stephen Crane and the 1890s." *American Literary Scholarship, An Annual/1977.* Ed. James Woodress. Durham, NC: Duke UP, 1979. 236–39. An average year with the best work done on Crane's western stories.

14.79 ———. "Fin-de-Siècle America: Stephen Crane and the 1890s." *American Literary Scholarship, An Annual/1978.* Ed. J. Albert Robbins. Durham, NC: Duke UP, 1980. 220–24. Several exchanges on the Binder-Parker version of *Red Badge* heated up scholarship on Crane for the year.

Appendix 1

BIBLIOGRAPHICAL INDEXES SEARCHED

American Literary Scholarship: (1963 to 1989)

Annual Bibliography of English Language and Literature: 1 (1930) to 61 (1986)

Bibliographic Index: 1 (1974) to 31 (1991)

Biography Index: 1 (1946) to 46 (1991)

Essays and General Literature Index: 1 (1900) to 12 (1990)

Humanities Index: 1 (1974) to 18 (1991)

International Index to Periodicals: 1 (1907–1915) to 18 (1964–65)

MLA International Bibliography: 1921 to 1989

MLA Wilson Database: 1 January 1981 to 30 September 1991

Readers Guide to Periodical Literature: 1 (1900–1904) to 50 (1990)

Social Sciences and Humanities Index: 1 (1906–1915) to 27 (1973–74)

JOURNALS SURVEYED

American Literary Realism, 1870–1910

American Literature

AN&Q—American Notes and Queries

American Quarterly

American Studies
American Trancendental Quarterly
Amerika Studien
Ball State University Forum:
Canadian Review of American Studies
Centennial Review
College Literature
CLA Journal
English Language and Literature
ELH — English Literary History
English Language Notes
Essays in Literature
Explicator
Georgia Review
Huntington Library Quarterly
Journal of American Studies
Journal of Modern Literature
Modern Fiction Studies
Modern Language Studies
Mosaic
Nineteenth-Century Literature
Notes and Queries
Papers on Language and Literature
PMLA — Publications of the Modern Language Association of America
Prospects
Resources for American Literary Study
South Atlantic Quarterly
Southern Literary Journal
Southern Review
Studies in American Fiction
Studies in Short Fiction
Studies in the Novel
Texas Studies in Literature and Language
Western American Literature

Appendix 2

ADDITIONS TO ROBERT STALLMAN'S LIST OF CONTEMPORARY REVIEWS OF WORKS BY STEPHEN CRANE

The Red Badge of Courage

[Crane's *Red Badge of Courage*], unsigned. Philadelphia Press (13 Oct. 1895): 30. Reprinted by Richard M. Weatherford in *Stephen Crane: The Critical Heritage* (2.17), #26. Hereafter cited as WEATHERFORD.

Comment [on *Red Badge*], Robert Bridges. *Life* 27 (5 Mar. 1896): 176–77. See WEATHERFORD, #42.

George's Mother

[Crane's *George's Mother*], unsigned. *New York Times* (21 June 1896): 27. See WEATHERFORD, #59.

[Crane's *George's Mother*], unsigned. San Francisco *Argonaut* 38 (22 June 1896): 9. See WEATHERFORD, #60.

The Little Regiment

[Crane's *The Little Regiment*], unsigned. *New York Times* (31 Oct. 1896): 4. See WEATHERFORD, #68.

The Third Violet

"Crane's Superficial Romance," unsigned. *New York Times* (22 May 1897): 5. See WEATHERFORD, #76.

"On Crane's Improving Style," unsigned. *Munsey's Magazine* 17 (Aug. 1897): 788. See WEATHERFORD, #82.

The Open Boat and Other Tales of Adventure

"Current Literature," unsigned. Chicago *Daily Inter-Ocean* (7 May 1898): 10.

"New Books," unsigned. St. Paul *Pioneer Press* (22 May 1898): 23.

Active Service

[Crane's *Active Service*], unsigned. *New York Times* (18 Nov. 1899): 772. See WEATHERFORD, #98.

[Crane's *Active Service*], unsigned. San Francisco *Argonaut* 45 (20 Nov. 1899): 8. See WEATHERFORD, #99.

"Crane's New Maturity," unsigned. *Literary News* 20 (Nov. 1899): 325–26. See WEATHERFORD, #100.

[Crane's *Active Service*], unsigned. *Bookman* 10 (Jan. 1900): 501. See WEATHERFORD, #105.

The Monster and Other Stories

[Crane's *The Monster*], Robert Bridges. *Life* 32 (1 Sept. 1898): 166. See WEATHERFORD, #108.

Whilomville Stories

[Crane's *Whilomville Stories*], unsigned. *Literary News* 21 (Sept. 1900): 273. See WEATHERFORD, #107.

Wounds in the Rain

[Crane's *Wounds in the Rain*], unsigned. *New York Times* (10 Nov. 1900): 766–67. See WEATHERFORD, #124.

Great Battles of the World

[Crane's *Great Battles of the World*], unsigned. *Spectator* 87 (3 Aug. 1901): 158–59. See WEATHERFORD, #131.

[Crane's *Great Battles of the World*], unsigned. London *Graphic* 64 (10 Aug. 1901): 194. See WEATHERFORD, #132.

Last Words

[Crane's *Last Words*], unsigned. London *Graphic* 64 (5 Apr. 1902): 476. See WEATHERFORD, #133.

The O'Ruddy

[Crane's *The O'Ruddy*], unsigned. *Academy* 67 (6 Aug. 1904): 99. See
 WEATHERFORD, #136.

Index